Crusades
Volume 3, 2004

Crusades

Edited by
Benjamin Z. Kedar and Jonathan S.C. Riley-Smith
with Helen J. Nicholson and Michael Evans

Crusades is published annually for the Society for the Study of the Crusades and the Latin East by Ashgate. A statement of the aims of the Society and details of membership can be found following the Bulletin at the end of the volume.

Manuscripts should be sent to either of the Editors in accordance with the guidelines for submission of papers on p. 263.

Subscriptions: Crusades (ISSN 1476–5276) is published annually in July.

Subscriptions are available on an annual basis and are fixed, until after volume 3 (2004), at £65, and £20 for members of the Society. Prices include postage by surface mail. All orders and enquiries should be addressed to: Subscription Department, Ashgate Publishing Ltd, Gower House, Croft Road, Aldershot, Hants GU11 3HR, U.K.; tel.: +44 (0)1252 331551; fax: +44 (0) 1252 344405; email: journals@ashgatepublishing.com

Crusades

Volume 3, 2004

Published by ASHGATE *for the*
Society for the Study of the Crusades
and the Latin East

Published by
Ashgate Publishing Limited
Gower House
Croft Road
Aldershot
Hampshire GU11 3HR
Great Britain

Ashgate Publishing Company
Suite 420
101 Cherry Street
Burlington, VT 05401–4405
USA

Ashgate website: http://www.ashgate.com

ISBN 0 7546 4099 X

ISSN 1476–5276

Typeset by N^{2}productions

The paper used in this publication meets the minimum requirements of the American National Standard for Information Sciences – Permanence of Paper for Printed Library Materials, ANSI Z39.48-1984

Printed in Great Britain by MPG Books Ltd, Bodmin.

CONTENTS

REVIEWS

Abbreviations

AOL	*Archives de l'Orient latin*
Autour	*Autour de la Première Croisade. Actes du colloque de la Society for the Study of the Crusades and the Latin East: Clermont-Ferrand, 22–25 juin 1995*, ed. Michel Balard. Paris, 1996
Cart Hosp	*Cartulaire général de l'ordre des Hospitaliers de Saint-Jean de Jérusalem, 1100–1310*, ed. Joseph Delaville Le Roulx. 4 vols. Paris, 1884–1906
Cart St Sép	*Le Cartulaire du chapitre du Saint-Sépulcre de Jérusalem*, ed. Geneviève Bresc-Bautier, Documents relatifs à l'histoire des croisades 15. Paris, 1984
Cart Tem	*Cartulaire général de l'ordre du Temple 1119?–1150. Recueil des chartes et des bulles relatives à l'ordre du Temple*, ed. Guigue A. M. J. A., (marquis) d'Albon. Paris, 1913
CCCM	Corpus Christianorum. Continuatio Mediaevalis
Chartes Josaphat	*Chartes de la Terre Sainte provenant de l'abbaye de Notre-Dame de Josaphat*, ed. Henri F. Delaborde, Bibliothèque des Écoles françaises d'Athènes et de Rome 19. Paris, 1880
Clermont	*From Clermont to Jerusalem: The Crusades and Crusader Societies 1095–1500. Selected Proceedings of the International Medieval Congress, University of Leeds, 10–13 July 1995*, ed. Alan V. Murray. International Medieval Research 3. Turnhout, 1998
Crusade Sources	*The Crusades and their Sources: Essays Presented to Bernard Hamilton*, ed. John France and William G. Zajac. Aldershot, 1998
Setton, *Crusades*	*A History of the Crusades*, general editor Kenneth M. Setton, 2nd edn, 6 vols. Madison, 1969–89
CS	*Crusade and Settlement: Papers read at the First Conference of the Society for the Study of the Crusades and the Latin East and Presented to R.C. Smail*, ed. Peter W. Edbury. Cardiff, 1985
CSEL	Corpus Scriptorum Ecclesiasticorum Latinorum
Horns	*The Horns of Hattin*, ed. Benjamin Z. Kedar. Jerusalem and London, 1992
Kreuzfahrerstaaten	*Die Kreuzfahrerstaaten als multikulturelle Gesellschaft. Einwanderer und Minderheiten im 12. und 13. Jahrhundert*, ed. Hans Eberhard Mayer with Elisabeth Müller-Luckner. Schriften des Historischen Kollegs, Kolloquien 37. Munich, 1997

Mansi. *Concilia*	Giovanni D. Mansi, *Sacrorum conciliorum nova et amplissima collectio*
MGH	Monumenta Germaniae Historica
MO, 1	*The Military Orders: Fighting for the Faith and Caring for the Sick*, ed. Malcolm Barber. Aldershot, 1994
MO, 2	*The Military Orders*, vol. 2: *Welfare and Warfare*, ed. Helen Nicholson. Aldershot, 1998
Montjoie	*Montjoie: Studies in Crusade History in Honour of Hans Eberhard Mayer*, ed. Benjamin Z. Kedar, Jonathan Riley-Smith and Rudolf Hiestand. Aldershot, 1997
Outremer	*Outremer. Studies in the History of the Crusading Kingdom of Jerusalem Presented to Joshua Prawer*, ed. Benjamin Z. Kedar, Hans E. Mayer and Raymond C. Smail. Jerusalem, 1982
PG	Patrologia Graeca
PL	Patrologia Latina
PPTS	Palestine Pilgrims' Text Society Library
RHC	*Recueil des Historiens des Croisades*
Darm	*Documents arméniens*
Oc	*Historiens occidentaux*
Or	*Historiens orientaux*
RIS	Rerum Italicarum Scriptores
NS	New Series
ROL	*Revue de l'Orient latin*
RRH	Reinhold Röhricht, comp., *Regesta regni hierosolymitani*. Innsbruck, 1893
RRH Add	Reinhold Röhricht, comp., *Additamentum*. Innsbruck, 1904
RS	Rolls Series
WT	William of Tyre, *Chronicon*, ed. Robert B. C. Huygens, with Hans E. Mayer and Gerhard Rösch, CCCM 63–63A. Turnhout, 1986

Co-operation between Constantinople and Rome before the First Crusade: a Study of the Convergence of Interests in Croatia in the late Eleventh Century[1]

Peter Frankopan

Oxford University

While Urban II's call for the knights of western Europe to rise up and take part in what later became known as the First Crusade has provoked a great deal of interest from modern historians, the eastern context for this phenomenon has been largely ignored. It was after all Jerusalem which was the goal of the crusaders themselves – something which is made abundantly and categorically clear from the contemporary charter evidence from France – and, moreover, it was the deteriorating situation in the Holy Land and in Asia Minor which had provided the impetus for Urban's call to arms in the first place.[2]

Certainly Urban himself must have been aware that passage to Jerusalem was becoming increasingly difficult in the 1080s, for several leading figures in early medieval Europe had reached and returned from Palestine in the years immediately before the First Crusade. We know, for example, that Robert of Flanders and Peter the Hermit had visited the holy places in the decade before the crusade.[3] What we can establish from a wide collection of primary sources – particularly in the form of church charters – makes it plain that the level of contact between western Europe and the East in general and with Jerusalem in particular had become extensive indeed by the end of the eleventh century.[4]

---

[1] I am extremely grateful to the Dean of the Fellows and to the Program in Hellenic Studies at Princeton University for awarding me a Stanley J. Seeger Visiting Fellowship in 2002–3, when this piece was written.

[2] Marcus Bull, *Knightly piety and the lay response to the First Crusade: The Limousin and Gascony* (Oxford, 1993); Hans E. Mayer, *The Crusades* (Oxford, 1972), pp. 39ff; Jonathan Riley-Smith, *The First Crusade and the Idea of Crusading* (London, 1986), pp. 13–30; John France, *Victory in the East* (Cambridge, 1993), pp. 1–25; Sylvia Schein, "Jérusalem. Objectif original de la première Croisade?", in *Autour*, pp. 119–26.

[3] R. Ganshof, "Robert le Frison et Alexis Comnène", *Alexiad*, ed. D. Reinsch and A. Kambylis, (Berlin, 2001), X.6.1, p. 299; E. Blake and C. Morris, "A Hermit Goes to War: Peter and the Origins of the First Crusade", *Studies in Church History* 22 (1985), 79–93.

[4] Jonathan Riley-Smith, *The First Crusaders 1095–1131* (Cambridge, 1997), pp. 23–52; Peter Frankopan, "Levels of contact between West and East: pilgrims and visitors to Constantinople and Jerusalem in the 9th –12th Centuries", in *Travellers in the Levant: Voyagers and Visionaries*, ed. S. Searight and M. Wagstaff (Durham, 2001), pp. 87–108.

In spite of the worsening political situation in the East in the 1090s, however, it took the involvement of another individual to prompt the pope to take action. According to the chronicle of Bernold, envoys arrived from Constantinople at the Council of Piacenza in March 1095 with a desperate plea to the pope for aid. After listening to what the Byzantine ambassadors had to say, Urban II resolved to do what he could, promising that he would find knights to help fight against the pagans.[5] This led inexorably to the moment six months later when the pope stood in a field at Clermont in central France, issuing a call to arms to the knighthood of western Europe.[6] It is worth stressing that the six months prior to this had seen Urban canvassing widely for support in central and northern Italy, and, above all, in France.[7]

No less important to note, therefore, is that this was not the first time that the Byzantine emperor, Alexius I Comnenus, had approached the pope for military assistance. Confronted by a series of increasingly dangerous raids by Pecheneg steppe nomads in Thrace and on the area to the north of Constantinople in the late 1080s and at the start of the following decade, Alexius had sent to Urban to see if the latter would be prepared and able to send reinforcements to swell the ranks of the imperial forces.[8] Although we cannot be sure that any such reinforcements arrived, the principal source for this period, the *Alexiad* of Anna Comnena, makes it plain that the emperor was waiting for the imminent arrival of help from Rome before he began his final, successful, assault on the nomads.[9]

This earlier contact between Alexius and the pope is of course of some significance – even if we know little about what the envoys said on this occasion, or about what Urban's response to them was. However, the fact that the emperor was prepared – and seemingly able – to seek military help from Rome provides an important precedent for his appeal only a few years later at Piacenza. Certainly, we know that there had been other appeals by Byzantine emperors to the papacy, most notably that of Michael VII Doukas to Gregory VII in the early 1070s.[10] But what makes Alexius' appeal different is that fact that it was part of a pattern where western Europe was used and seen as a pool of resources for the Byzantine emperor to draw on, provided, of course, that he could couch his appeals and requests for help in a way which could be both easily understood and well received by the target(s).

It was not only the pope with whom Alexius made contact in his search for support and above all military assistance in the years leading up to the crusade. We

---

[5] Thus "ad hoc ergo auxilium dominus Papa multos incitavit, ut etiam jurejurando promitterent, se illuc Deo annuente ituros et eidem imperatori contra paganos pro posse suo fidelissimum adjutorium collaturos", *Bernoldi Chronicon*, in MGH SS, 5:461–62.

[6] Robert Somerville, *The councils of Urban II* (Amsterdam, 1972), pp. 143–50.

[7] See for example, Herbert J. Cowdrey, "Pope Urban II's preaching of the First Crusade", *History* 55 (1970), 177–88; Alfons Becker, *Papst Urban II 1088–99*, 2 vols. (Stuttgart, 1964–88), 1:272ff.

[8] *Bernoldi Chronicon*, p. 450.

[9] *Alexiad*, 8.5.1, p. 245.

[10] See Herbert J. Cowdrey, "Pope Gregory VII's 'Crusading' Plans of 1074", in *Outremer*.

know for example that the Byzantine emperor was in direct contact with a number of magnates throughout western Europe, cajoling, requesting and imploring for help. The chronicle of Frutolf tells us that Alexius sent a series of letters to (unspecified) aristocrats in western Europe immediately before the First Crusade, reporting on the increasingly bleak and difficult situation in the East – by which we should understand not only the Holy Land, but also Asia Minor too.[11] Ekkehard of Aura says much the same in his chronicle, as does Guibert of Nogent.[12]

The most famous piece of evidence here, of course, is the letter sent by Alexius to Count Robert I of Flanders some time at the start of the 1090s, and certainly well before the crusade.[13] The authenticity of this letter has been much debated, and it has been regularly claimed that the missive is a (later) forgery.[14] There seems little reason, however, to dismiss the letter out of hand, and as has been shown convincingly in recent years, much of the content of the letter strikes a chord with what we know about Byzantium's contact with the West in this period. Crucially too, the fact that it provides an accurate and reliable summary of Byzantium's predicament in the early 1090s suggests clearly that it might very well have originated from Constantinople around this time. As such, the letter provides an important insight into the thinking and the workings of the emperor immediately before the First Crusade.[15]

There is some significance therefore to the fact that we know that Alexius had previously enjoyed personal contact with Robert of Flanders. Robert had met the Byzantine emperor on his way back from Jerusalem at the end of the 1080s, and had promised to send Alexius support in the form of armed knights on his return home.[16] Although we cannot be sure what form the emperor's request for help took, this clearly occurred against a backdrop of sustained pressure on Byzantium, apparently in Asia Minor, and certainly in Thrace and to the area north of Constantinople.

---

[11] Frutolf in *Frutolfs und Ekkehards Chroniken und die anonyme Kaiserchroniken*, ed. and trans. Franz-Josef Schmale and Irene Schmale-Ott (Darmstadt, 1972), p. 106.

[12] *Frutolf*, p. 462; Guibert of Nogent, *Dei gesta per Francos*, ed. R. B. C. Huygens, CCCM 127A (Turnhout, 1996), pp. 100–101.

[13] Heinrich Hagenmeyer, *Epistulae et chartae ad historiam primi belli sacri spectantes: Die Kreuzzugsbriefe aus den Jahren 1088–1100* (Innsbruck, 1901), pp. 130–36.

[14] E.g. Ferdinand Chalandon, *Essai sur le règne d'Alexis I Comnène* (Paris, 1900), pp. 330–36, Einar Joranson, "The problem of the spurious letter of Emperor Alexius to the Count of Flanders", *American Historical Review* 50 (1950), 811–32; Peter Schreiner, "Der Brief des Alexios I Komnenos an den Grafen Robert von Flandern und das Problem gefälschter byzantinischer Kaiserschreiben in den westlichen Quellen", in *Documenti medievali Greci e Latini. Studi comparativi*, ed. Giuseppe de Gregorio and Otto Kresten (Spoleto, 1998), pp. 111–40; Christian Gastgeber, "Das Schreiben 'Alexios' I. Komnenos an Robert I. Flandern. Sprachliche Untersuchung", in idem, pp. 141–85.

[15] Michel de Waha, "La lettre d'Alexis Comnène à Robert Ier le Frison", *Byzantion* 47 (1977), 113–25; Jonathan Shepard, "Aspects of Byzantine attitudes and policy towards the West in the 10th and 11th Centuries", *Byzantinische Forschungen* 13 (1988), 103ff.

[16] *Alexiad*, 6.6.1, p. 218. For some comments about the date of this meeting, see Ganshof, "Robert le Frison", pp. 59–61.

It is worth stressing, too, that knights duly *did* arrive from Flanders at the start of the 1090s, and played an important part in the emperor's dealings with the Pechenegs and, for that matter, in the defence of Nicomedia against the Seljuk Turks.[17] Although it is not clear whether Alexius had followed up his meeting with Robert with any correspondence, the level of contact between the two certainly points to a possibility, if not a likelihood, that the Byzantine emperor would look again to Flanders and to Robert – who had helped him in the past – for armed men to bolster the imperial forces at a time of need.

This alone is an important indicator of the fact that Alexius was not slow to see the value, as well as the possibilities, of tapping into the resources of western Europe at a time when concepts like knightly piety and military service as devotion were fast establishing the vibrant momentum which would in turn fuel and feed the crusade movement. It goes without saying that his desire to attract knights from the West came at a time when life was becoming increasingly difficult in Byzantium, where economic, social and military resources were spread thin indeed by the late eleventh century. What makes his contact with Robert of Flanders particularly interesting, therefore, are the methods to which the emperor resorted in order to attract knights to make the journey to Constantinople and beyond.

The letter to Robert makes great play, for example, of the damage being done by pagans – evidently not only Muslim Turks and Turkomen, but also Pecheneg steppe nomads too. The letter also stresses that knights would be performing a specifically Christian duty by offering their service to the Byzantine emperor, by driving out the infidels from churches and from other holy places.[18] In this way, the letter offers an invaluable precursor of the insight into the level of understanding which Alexius had of the prevailing knightly mentality of the West and, as such, provides an important example of the emperor seeking to elicit support directly from magnates in Europe without going through the papacy.

Alexius' attempt to deal directly with individuals with whom he had previously had personal contact is also useful here, for it puts the emperor's appeal to the pope into the more appropriate light of being a measure of some desperation. That is to say, that the dispatch of envoys to Urban II resulted from the fact that Alexius' other measures and other efforts to rally support had either not been effective, or, simply, that he needed considerably more men and more support than could be gathered from individuals such as Robert of Flanders.

In this respect, it is worth underlining the fact that for all the comments of the author of the *Alexiad* that the emperor had been caught by surprise by the arrival of the first wave of crusaders in Byzantium, he does not seem to have been under-prepared for the even larger numbers who were to follow in the second half of 1096 and the first half of 1097. Indeed, there are few, if any, indications that the various expeditions which converged on the imperial capital, led by Godfrey of Bouillon,

---

[17] *Alexiad*, 7.7.4, pp. 221–22, 8.3.5, p. 242.

[18] Hagenmeyer, *Epistolae*, p. 134.

Robert of Normandy, Raymond of Toulouse, Robert II of Flanders, Hugh of Vermandois or Bohemond, experienced any problems of supply during their journey across the western part of Byzantium – nor, for that matter, on their way from Nicaea to Antioch. This provides a telling indication of the fact that Alexius had been expecting large numbers of men, and that he had made the logistical arrangements accordingly.[19]

The letter to Robert of Flanders is therefore of crucial importance in establishing how Alexius went about trying to muster support before the crusade, in showing the ways in which he sought to do so, and, no less importantly, in placing the crusade itself in a fuller context – at least from a Byzantine perspective. It is worth noting, then, that there is another analogous piece of evidence which has often been overlooked, which sits very neatly with what we know about Alexius' contacts with individual magnates in the West in general, and with the letter to Robert of Flanders in particular. This comes from an episode which appears in the Croatian version of the *Letopis Popa Dukljanina* (known in Croatian as the *Ljetopis Popa Dukljanina*) and which is worthy of our attention.

In a section of the text which perhaps dates to the early fourteenth century, but certainly written no later than the first half of the sixteenth century, there is a reference to a delegation which arrived in Croatia during the reign of King Zvonimir, some time before the crusade.[20] Although it is not easy to date the arrival of this embassy with any accuracy, an obvious *terminus ante quem* is provided by the death of the king, some time between the fall of 1087 and the summer of 1089.[21]

According to the source, emissaries arrived from the pope and from the (Byzantine) emperor bearing letters ("Contigit enim ut Roma, caesaris pontificisque legati ad Zvonimerum regem missi cum binis litteris venirent").[22] The ambassadors went on to address the Croatian king using a direct and explicitly Christian formula, urging him to provide help for the pope and for the emperor.[23] The pleas of the envoys had an immediate effect, for shortly after their interview, Zvonimir called an

---

[19] For the journeys of the various crusade armies and their respective leaders through Byzantium, France, *Victory* (see above, n. 2), pp. 80ff.

[20] For some comments on the composition of this section of the text, see Ferdinand Ŝiŝić, *Povijest Hrvata u vrijeme narodnih vladara* (Zagreb, 1925), pp. 586–87, n. 81; Nikola Radojĉić, "Legenda o smrti hrvatskog kralja Dimitrija Zvonimira", *SKA Glasnik* 171 (1936), 49–51; Vladimir Môsin, *Ljetopis Popa Dukljanina: latinski tekst sa prijevodom i 'Hrvatska kronika'* (Zagreb, 1950), pp. 23–27; Ivo Goldŝtein, *Hrvatski rani srednji vijek* (Zagreb, 1995), p. 431, n. 8.

[21] Zvonimir endowed the monastery of St Mary in Zadar on 8 October 1087: Franjo Raĉki, *Documenta historiae chroaticae periodum antiquam illustrantia* (Zagreb, 1877), no. 119, p. 145. In September two years later, he is referred to as recently dead by his successor, Stephen II: ibid., no. 124, p. 148; Ferdinand Ŝiŝić, *Priruĉnik Izvora Hrvatske Historije* (Zagreb, 1914), pp. 285, 287–88; Goldŝtein, *Srednji vijek*, p. 430.

[22] *Letopis Popa Dukljanina*, ed. Ferdinand Ŝiŝić (Belgrade, 1928), p. 413; Môsin, *Ljetopis*, p. 67; see Appendix, below, pp. 12–13.

[23] The appeal was aimed at seeking Zvonimir's help for the Christian people as a whole: Ŝiŝić, *Letopis*, p. 413; Môsin, *Ljetopis*, p. 67.

assembly in order to address his knights and to urge them to lend their support as requested.[24]

The text leaves little doubt as to what the king had been told by his visitors, for he went on to announce this to his own followers. Jerusalem and the holy places where Christ had lived and died had fallen to pagans, who were destroying and abusing these sites with their profanity and desecration ("ab infidelibus … possidedutur possessaque polluantur prophanenturque et … derisionique habeantur").[25] He therefore called on the Croatian knighthood to rise up to offer their help and to embark on an expedition to liberate the East. Zvonimir's appeal met with short shrift, however, to the point that not only did it fall on deaf ears but, according to the interpolation, was responsible for the king's murder at the hands of the Croatian nobility.[26]

Many of the elements which appear in this episode also feature in the letter to Robert of Flanders. For example, the fact was emphasized that Zvonimir was not simply a king, but "regum christianorum piissime" – something which has a natural parallel with the way in which Robert of Flanders was addressed.[27] So too are there obvious similarities between the way in which Zvonimir and Robert were exhorted to offer help as a result of their love of Christ and as a mark of their faith. Zvonimir was urged to act "pro amore Christi ecclesiaeque sanctae utilitate."[28] This compares neatly with the letter to Robert, where the Flemish leader's faith was appealed to in strikingly similar terms.[29]

The stress placed on the respective leaders' membership of a wider, specifically Christian, community, is of great interest and importance given the mechanics of the response to Urban II's canvassing of support at and in the build-up to Clermont, not least since we appear to have two independent, separate pieces of evidence which suggest that this was an appropriate way to address and appeal to secular leaders at the end of the eleventh century. It also reveals how much Alexius knew about the West at a time when the manner in which appeals were couched was paramount – and, consequently, has some significance to our understanding of what the emperor was expecting and seeking with his later dispatch of envoys to the Council of Piacenza in 1095.

The bond between the potentates and Alexius was also accentuated in both cases, implicitly in the case of the letter to Robert of Flanders (and explicitly in the argumenta), and more directly still in the case of the appeal to Zvonimir, where the Croatian leader was referred to as brother ("frater").[30] This marked a major change from the tenth century when Byzantine emperors in particular were reluctant (if not

24 Ibid.
25 Ŝiŝić, *Letopis*, p. 414; Mosin, *Ljetopis*, p. 67.
26 Ibid. See also F. Ŝiŝić, "O smtri hrvatskoga kralja Zvonimira", *Vjesnik* n.s. 8 (1905), 1–29.
27 Ŝiŝić, *Letopis*, p. 413; Mosin, *Ljetopis*, p. 67; below, pp. 12–13; c.f. Hagenmeyer, *Epistolae*, p. 134.
28 Ŝiŝić, *Letopis*, p. 413; Mosin, *Ljetopis*, p. 67; below, pp. 12–13.
29 Hagenmeyer, *Epistolae*, pp. 133–36.
30 Ŝiŝić, *Letopis*, p. 413; Môsin, *Ljetopis*, p. 67; below, pp. 12–13; Hagenmeyer, *Epistolae*, p. 130.

indignant) to accord parity to any other ruler.[31] The change presumably reflects the fact that, by the end of the 1080s, the eastern Empire was exposed to the point that it could no longer afford to assert its hegemony and primacy quite so categorically as had been the case a hundred years earlier.

The most significant similarity of all, however, is the stress on Jerusalem and on the loss of the holy places which appears in both sources. In both cases the abuse of the main Christian sites was highlighted as the principal reason for military help to be sent to the East – although in the case of the letter to Robert of Flanders this was not the only encouragement on offer.[32] The stress on Jerusalem and on the abuses of Christians and of holy sites in the east is a theme which runs through almost all of the primary sources which talk about the origins of the First Crusade.

The dating of the appeal to Zvonimir is therefore important since the embassy which was sent to him was not dispatched in the middle of the 1090s or even, like the letter to Flanders, at the start of that decade, but rather towards the end of the 1080s. This would seem to point to the fact that while Jerusalem was in Muslim hands (as it had been for several centuries), the liberation of that city and of the other (unspecified) holy places was the incentive for knights to begin their journey, and not necessarily the true, or at least not the only, purpose. For just as with the crusade itself, the arrival of armed men in Byzantium had an important impact on the efforts of the Empire to deal with the Seljuks in Asia Minor.

The logical context for the appeal to Zvonimir, on the other hand, involves Alexius' struggles with the Pechenegs, which pre-occupied the emperor in the later 1080s. Given the problems which Alexius experienced in dealing with the steppe nomads at this time, it is difficult to see that he would have been thinking seriously about gathering support for projects far removed from those which were so pressing and so close to the capital in this period.[33]

In other words, it would make sense to see the true intention of the embassy to the Croats as seeking help against the Pechenegs, and not elsewhere. It is no coincidence then that the ambassadors who arrived at Zvonimir's court are reported not to have come from the pope or from Alexius alone, but rather that these were representing both.[34] We know too that this was a time of increasing co-operation on other levels between Constantinople and Rome on ecclesiastical, theological and political grounds: from the Latin sources as well as from an invaluable portfolio of letters centering on the figure of Basil of Reggio.[35] These all point to the fact that

---

31 *De Cerimoniis aulae Byzantinae libri duo*, ed. Johann Reiske, 2 vols. (Bonn, 1829–30), 2, ch. 47.

32 Ŝiŝić, *Letopis*, p. 414; Mosin, *Ljetopis*, p. 67; below, pp. 12–13; Hagenmeyer, *Epistolae*, pp. 131–32.

33 For the problems facing Alexius in the later 1080s, see for example, Chalandon, *Essai*, pp. 95ff, and Petre Diaconu, *Les Pétchénègues au Bas–Danube* (Bucharest, 1970), pp. 112–34.

34 Ŝiŝić, *Letopis*, p. 413; Mosin, *Ljetopis*, p. 67; below, pp. 12–13.

35 Above all, Becker, *Urban II*, 1:108ff. For the Basil of Reggio documents and a useful commentary, see Walther Holtzmann, "Die Unionsverhandlungen zwischen Kaiser Alexius I und Papst Urban II im Jahre 1089", *Byzantinische Zeitschrift* 28 (1928), 38–67.

Rome and the new pope Urban II, who had acceded the pontifical throne in 1088, were more than willing to co-operate with Byzantium as long as there was a chance of mending the divide (or schism) between the two Churches. In this way, then, a combined approach to Zvonimir ties in well with the wider geo-political context of the late 1080s. It is also consistent with what we know about other efforts by the Byzantine emperor to canvas support in the West immediately before the First Crusade which played on a combination of spiritual and secular rewards – as shown clearly from the Cormery text recently highlighted by Jonathan Shepard.[36]

This makes the episode extremely significant to any study of the Byzantine Empire on the eve of the crusade, above all in terms of Alexius' understanding of the mentality of the West at this time, in terms of his readiness and willingness to look for support overseas, and perhaps most important of all, in terms of his use of Jerusalem as a means – rather than an end – of attracting military assistance in the first place. The importance of these three elements cannot be over-stated.

Of course, the fact that the Croats were being gathered to liberate Jerusalem and the holy places does not necessarily mean to say that they could not have continued their journey after reaching Byzantium – just as the knights of the First Crusade were to do – although there is no evidence in the Croatian sources or elsewhere for that matter which suggests that they ever did so. That the context involved a Pecheneg (pagan), rather than a Seljuk threat to the Empire, and that the threat was posed to Byzantium in the first place, rather than to Jerusalem alone, however, certainly does tie in with what we know about the increasingly frantic appeals which Alexius was making at the end of the 1080s. As we have already seen, the emperor had approached Rome directly for help, and assistance was expected in the build-up to the decisive battle of Lebounion.[37] We know too that as Alexius closed in on the nomads, he issued instructions for men to be recruited from anywhere and everywhere ("ἁπανταχόθευ").[38]

Indeed, the *Alexiad* is even more explicit soon after, stating that the emperor ordered that cavalry and foot soldiers be raised from the western towns ("τὰς πόλεις … τῆς ἑσπέρας"), which may have included locations as far away as Croatia. The fact that Alexius had sent out men not only to recruit among the Bulgar and Vlakh populations of Byzantium but also to gather the support of "τοὺς ἄλλοθεν ἐξ ἁπασῶν τῶν χωρῶν ἐπχομένους ἱππέας τὲ καὶ πεζούς", suggests that the emperor was casting his net as wide as possible in order to muster sufficient, and experienced, troops with which to confront and fight the Pechenegs.[39]

---

[36] Jonathan Shepard, "Cross-purposes: Alexius Comnenus and the First Crusade", in *The First Crusade: Origins and Impact* (ed.) Jonathan Phillips (Manchester, 1997), pp. 107–29, esp. pp. 117–20; Jonathan Riley-Smith, *The First Crusaders 1095–1131* (Cambridge, 1997), p. 61.

[37] Above, p. 2.

[38] *Alexiad*, 8.3.3, p. 242.

[39] *Alexiad*, 8.3.4, p. 242.

It would seem that the appeal to the Croats came at a time when the Byzantine Empire was having trouble dealing with the problems posed by the steppe nomads. While it is true that the late eleventh century also saw important gains in Asia Minor by the Seljuk Turks – such as the town of Nicaea and various towns on the western coast – in the 1080s and even in the early 1090s, the attentions of the Byzantine military and of the emperor himself appear to have been directed almost exclusively at affairs to the north of the capital. While it is not possible to be certain about precisely when the envoys requested help from Zvonimir, nor where such support was deployed, or even whether support was ever sent from Croatia, the manoeuvring of the emperor and the condition of the Empire at the end of the 1080s certainly makes the appeal to Zvonimir plausible.

The fact that it is possible to provide a context for the contacts with Zvonimir also goes some way towards making the episode credible. After all, the Croatian version of the *Letopis* was not written until several centuries after the events in question, and it would be reasonable to ask whether the author's evidence was reliable here. It is not hard to see that later historians might seek to embroider on the role which the Croats might have played during the First Crusade – particularly given the incursions and pressures of the Ottoman Turks in Europe and the Croatians' own attempts to harness support from elsewhere to stem the tide of the Muslims.[40] There is the danger, therefore, that interpolation of this episode might be a fiction, rather reflecting political desires and attitudes at the time of writing than being an addition centred on historical fact.

Several elements, however, make this unlikely. First, while the *Letopis* as a whole is firmly focused on Duklja and the regions immediately surrounding it (and not on goings-on in Constantinople, Rome, Venice or other centres further afield), the fact that this later interpolation is set in a local rather than a wider political and geographic context, means that this episode is not out of place. What is more, it suggests that the interpolation was drawn from local material rather than simply being a case of an overzealous or interventionist copyist. The fact that there are no other places in the Croatian version of the *Letopis* which add to or modify the original should persuade us that there may be some substance to this hypothesis.

Of course, the fact that a natural and credible context can be suggested if not established for the appeal for help is also significant, since this too means that the report of the contact between the Croats and the pope and the Byzantine emperor cannot be dismissed out of hand as fictitious. Moreover, if this episode was fabricated, it would be plausible to suppose that it would seek to show Zvonimir and the Croats in the best possible light, as supporters of Christianity against Islam, as defenders of the West against an aggressive invader, as being faithful and reliable supporters of the pope and of the emperor during a time of need, and therefore

---

40 E.g. *Govori protiv Turaka*, ed. Vedran Gligo (Split, 1983), pp. 1–46.

promoting a positive portrayal of the Croats with the intention of drumming up sympathy and support for the Croats themselves against the Ottomans.

The fact that it is by no means clear that this is implied directly or indirectly in this part of the text is significant; but so too is the fact that the Croats do not come out of this section well: in fact, they spurn the pleas of both the pope and of the emperor, and turn on their own sovereign for suggesting the liberation of Jerusalem and the holy places.[41] What is more, they proceed to reject the advice of their own king, turning against him in the process, and committing regicide. In other words, it is not immediately clear what benefits or motives the author of this additional section might have had here and, as such, this should point us towards considering that the report of the imperial and papal approach to Zvonimir was in fact genuine.

It is true that we do not know of any Croatian involvement in the First Crusade, and none of the Latin, Greek or Arabic sources mention knights from this region during the build-up to the capture of Jerusalem and the establishment of the "crusader states" of *Outremer*. However, this may well say more about the limitations of the source material than it necessarily does about the participation of contingents which might have been merged within those of the more important magnates.[42]

In this respect, it is worth noting that Raymond of Toulouse passed through Croatia and Dalmatia on his way to Constantinople and the East.[43] Given Raymond's position on the crusade, it is tempting to think that he had been asked to pass this way by the pope or by the emperor, or by both, perhaps in order to gather more knights from this region – particularly if help had been forthcoming in the past. There must have been some reason why Raymond chose this route, rather than that followed by all those originating in western Europe – such as Robert of Normandy, Robert of Flanders and Hugh of Vermandois (as well as Bohemond) – who travelled down the length of Italy along the Via Egnatia to Bari and Brindisi before making the crossing by sea to Durazzo (Byzantine Dyrrachium, modern Dürres) and continuing along the old Roman road to Constantinople.[44]

---

41 Ŝiŝić, *Letopis*, pp. 416–17; Môsin, p. 67; below, pp. 12–13.

42 Sizeable contingents could and clearly were subsumed within at least the larger contingents. The case of the army of Raymond of St Gilles offers a good example of the diversity within at least one contingent during the crusade, and where at least seven coinage systems were used by those accompanying the Count of Toulouse: France, *Victory* (see above, n. 2), p. 86. We know too that Raymond was also joined by a substantial number of Normans when he went south from Antioch after the capture of that town in 1098: *Gesta Francorum et aliorum Hierosolimitanorum*, ed. and trans. Rosalind Hill, (London, 1962), p. 80. The lack of further reference to these, or indeed to any mention of ethnic and cultural diversity by the various chroniclers, suggests that this was simply not considered important by contemporary commentators – rather than as a clear sign that others did not and had not joined the crusade as it made its way eastwards.

43 Raymond of Aguilers, *Historia Francorum qui ceperunt Jerusalem*, 1.1 in *RHC Oc* 3:235.

44 Peter the Hermit and Godfrey of Bouillon did not pass along the Via Egnatia, nor did they go through Croatia and Dalmatia, instead journeying to Constantinople via Hungary and Bulgaria. For the journeys of all these individuals to Constantinople, see France, *Victory* (see above, n. 2), pp. 80–121.

Neither Raymond's chronicler, nor other sources which report the route taken by the count of Toulouse – such as William of Tyre and Orderic Vitalis – comment on why he chose to journey this way rather than passing through Italy. While we do learn about Raymond's dealings with the Serbs and with Constantine Bodin from at least these three crusade historians, there is nothing in any of the accounts which is relevant to any contact or recruiting which may have gone on north of Duklja.[45] For Raymond of Aguilers – as indeed for the contemporary and near contemporary historians of the First Crusade as a whole – what was most important was explaining the capture of Jerusalem and of the holy places, and as a result, useful insights and information that might prove interesting for the modern scholar are often frustratingly left out by those writing at the start and during the course of the twelfth century.[46]

Even if Raymond's journey cannot be explained by his instructions or desire to recruit Croatians because they had previously helped the Byzantine emperor and the pope in Rome (and the lack of evidence makes this conjectural either way), the most convincing reason to think that the episode which appears in the Croatian version of the *Letopis* is genuine comes precisely from the fact that it is *not* dateable or related to the First Crusade itself. As we have seen, Zvonimir of Croatia was certainly dead by the summer of 1089, when he was succeeded by Stephen II.[47] What would have been much harder to explain, of course, would be if the Croatian *Letopis* had associated an appeal from Alexius and Urban II – and the dispatch of knights – with the crusade itself. However, by linking the embassy with Zvonimir, and consequently plainly and clearly making this independent of the crusade, it provokes the conclusion that the report was based on original accounts and that the appeal was genuine and that it happened at the time that the source says that it did. Moreover, given that a credible context for this appeal can be suggested, it stands to reason that there are good grounds for taking the source at its word here, and for thinking that the evidence which it provides – at least on this occasion – is genuine and reliable.

As such, therefore, the episode is of some importance to an analysis of Alexius' foreign policy in general terms, as well as to any assessment of the contacts which the emperor had and sought in the wider Mediterranean at the end of the eleventh century. And it has great value, of course, to the assessment of the First Crusade itself, since it serves as an invaluable example of a "trial run" where papal and imperial interests coincided to seek the dispatch of knights to the East, and more specifically, where awareness of and interest in Jerusalem and the holy

---

45 Raymond of Aguilers, 1.1, p. 235; WT 2.17–18, 1:182–85; Orderic Vitalis, *Historia Ecclesiastica* 9.4,5, ed. and trans. Marjorie Chibnall, 6 vols. (Oxford, 1967–80), p. 34.

46 In this respect, Raymond of Aguilers' focus of attention is similar to that of Fulcher of Chartres, the *Gesta Francorum* and its various derivatives, and to later writers such as William of Tyre, and even Albert of Aachen, who provides the fullest account of all of the routes to and passage through Byzantium.

47 Above, p. 5.

places were exploited in order to lure military support to Byzantium.[48] This in turn provides a useful insight into the background to the First Crusade, and specifically, to co-operation between Constantinople and Rome in the years before Urban II's proclamation at Clermont in 1095. That papal and imperial interests appear to have elided and corresponded (albeit without success) some time before this allows an important marker as to how and why Alexius' and Urban's initiative in the last decade of the eleventh century was to prove so potent.

Appendix

From *Летопис Попа Дукљанина*, ed. F. Ŝiŝić, (Belgrade, 1928), ch. 27, pp. 413–16:

Contigit enim, ut Roma, caesaris pontificisque legati ad Zvonimerum regem missi cum binis litteris venirent; primas regi tantum legendas dederant, quarum haec sententia erat: "Rogamus obsecramusque, te Zvonimere frater, regum christianorum piissime, ut coacto procerum tuorum populisque concilio, alteram epistolam coram resignari coramque legi iubeas et una cum ipsis deliberes his de rebus, quas nos, deo bene iuvante, aggredi meditamus pro amore Christi ecclesiaeque sanctae utilitate; cum demum quicquid communi concilio decretum fuerit, ut nobis nihil moratus rescribas, efficiasque certiores. Vale." Zvonimirus igitur naviter, sicut regebatur, accersitis omnibus regni sui praefectis decurionibusque civitatum, coniunctimque habito ad quinque ecclesias in campo, qui Cossovus nuncupatur, concilio, litteras aperiri fecit et cunctis cum silentio audientibus, publice recitari, quae in haec fere verba scriptae errant: "Romanus pontifex et caesar augustus Zvonimiro regi populoque eius salutem. Rem certe indignam et christianorum principum ignaviae adscribendam existimamus, ut Hyerosolyme sanctaque loca, in quibus Christus dominus pro nobis nasci, pro nobis mori voluit, ab infidelibus tam diu possideantur possessaque polluantur prophanenturque, et ab iisdem illa sacra, illa domini misteria, quae nobis venerationi sunt, probro derisionique habeantur. Idcirco vos, sicut et reliquos per orbem fideles hortamur, ut nobiscum socia arma iungentes, ad res christiano nomini repetendas, in libertatemque vindicandas, proficisci statuatis, huic rei caeteros reges ac nationes, quibus itidem scripsimus, consensuros speramus. Nobis autem tam praeclarum facinus conantibus, domini opem affuturam, nemo diffidat, quando quidem non nisi eius nutu atque instinctu talis menti nostrae incidere potuit cogitatio. Quid ergo consilii vobis sit, hoc est utrum, quod rogamini, facturi estis quamprimum nosse cupimus. Valete in domino." Id audientes nequissima Crovatorum gens protinus indignari coepit, ita ut vix litteras

---

48 For the attraction of Jerusalem in the later eleventh century, see for example, Carl Erdmann, *The Origins of the Idea of Crusade*, trans. M. Baldwin and W. Goffart (Princeton, 1977), pp. 355–71; Riley-Smith, *First Crusaders* (see above, n. 36), pp. 23–52.

perlegi pateretur. Non solum itaque non consenserunt litteris et hortationi pontificis et caesaris, verum etiam in regem suum insurgentes magno tumultu et vociferatione conquesti sunt illum huiusce rei auctorem, ut ipsi relictis coniugibus, liberis patrioque solo procul per alienas domos errant, aliena sequantur imperia, et non sibi expedire loca illa sancta, si liberentur; atque ita infesta concio, pessimis usa consiliis, nequivit inhiberi, quin repente, sanctissimum regem Zvonimerum invadentes, multis conficerent vulneribus atque interimerent, eadem quippe illa perfidae mentis ferocia, quae ipsos impiissimi Seisalvi partes sequi fecit et Radoslavum patrem, omni laude dignum virum, regno pellere, in Zvonimerum quoque compulit saevire; non aliter furibundi circumstetere, quam cum rabidi venatorum canes, imbellem cervum nacti, nunc latratibus terrent, nunc dentibus laniant. Rex autem, dum adhud spiraret, tantae perfidiae immanitate commotus, eos devovisse fertur, ne unquam sui generis dominum habeant, sed semper alienigenis regibus principibusve subiecti sint. Ex illo ad hanc usque diem tempore, isthaec maledictio tam certum eventum habuit, ut non ab irato prolatum, quod tunc dixit, crediderim, sed [uti est] praenuntiatum, deo volente palam fieri, quanto gravius luituri errant supplicium criminis auctores, si sic posteri quoque eorum essent afficiendi. Post haec verba Zvonimerus continuo animam exhalavit et relicto corpore ad coeleste regnum transferri meruit, cum terrenum tam bene rexisset per annos quinque et triginta; tam diu enim cum potestate vixit.[49]

---

[49] Ŝiŝić, *Letopis*, pp. 413–16.

The Jerusalem Massacre of July 1099 in the Western Historiography of the Crusades

Benjamin Z. Kedar

Hebrew University of Jerusalem

The massacre the First Crusaders perpetrated in Jerusalem upon the city's conquest on 15 July 1099 occupies a central place in almost all Western histories of crusading written over the centuries. Yet they disagree on many counts: on factual issues like the massacre's duration or totality, on the crusaders' motives in committing it, on the extent to which it conformed to, or deviated from, contemporary norms, and on much more. The purpose of the present longitudinal examination, which starts with reports by eyewitnesses and concludes with contemporary depictions and assessments, is to expose the reasons for these disagreements and to put on view the range of variance among the Latin primary sources, the modes in which details supplied by early western chroniclers were selected, amplified or suppressed by later ones, the salience of specific western chronicles in various periods and the gradual absorption of information contained in oriental sources. The utilization of all presently available primary sources on the massacre should clarify some facets of the event. In addition, the longitudinal approach should throw light on the massacre's typical perception and interpretation in different periods and ideologies, on the persistence or resurgence of motifs that transcend these ideologies or periods, on the changing aesthetics of massacre reporting, on the tacit or acknowledged dependence of a historian on predecessors and, last but not least, on the relative importance of exposure to new sources on the one hand and of fundamental attitudes towards crusading on the other in his treatment of the massacre. A close observation of interactions between source material and attitude – from sanctimonial (not to be confused with sanctimonious) to impartiality-oriented to condemnatory – may fine-tune our understanding of the dynamics of crusade historiography in general.[1]

An early version of this paper was read at the fifth SSCLE conference, Jerusalem and Acre, July 1999.

[1] For previous attempts to employ the longitudinal approach see my "The Forcible Baptisms of 1096: History and Historiography", in *Forschungen zur Reichs-, Papst- und Landesgeschichte. Peter Herde zum 65. Geburtstag*, ed. Karl Borchardt and Enno Bünz, 2 vols. (Stuttgart, 1998), 1:187–200; "Crusade Historians and the Massacres of 1096", *Jewish History* 12 (1998), 11–31, and "La *Via sancti Sepulchri* come tramite di cultura araba in Occidente", in *Itinerari medievali e cultura europea. Atti del Congresso Internazionale, Parma, 27–28 febbraio 1998*, ed. Roberto Greci (Bologna, 1999), pp. 181–201. For surveys of the historiography of the crusades in general see Heinrich von Sybel, *Geschichte des ersten Kreuzzugs* (Düsseldorf, 1841), pp. 148–80; Laetitia Boehm, "'Gesta Dei per Francos' – oder 'Gesta Francorum'? Die Kreuzzüge als historiographisches Problem", *Saeculum* 8 (1957), 43–81; Jonathan Riley-Smith, "The Crusading Movement and Historians", in *The Oxford Illustrated History of the*

The eyewitnesses

The anonymous author of the *Gesta Francorum* writes that when Godfrey of Bouillon's men burst into Jerusalem, they chased the town's defenders, killing and lopping off heads as far as Solomon's Temple; "and at that place there was such a slaughter (*occisio*)[2] that our men were wading up to their ankles (*ad cauillas*) in blood". Shifting his attention to Raymond of Saint Gilles, he then relates that the commander of David's Tower surrendered to him and opened the town's gate, whereupon Raymond's men entered the town, chasing and killing the Saracens up to Solomon's Temple. There the Saracens fought hard for the entire day, "so that their blood was flowing throughout the Temple". When resistance ceased, the crusaders seized many men and women in the Temple, killing some and leaving others alive. A large number of Saracen men and women sought refuge on the Temple's roof; Tancred and Gaston of Béarn gave them their banners, evidently signifying the grant of protection. Then the crusaders turned to plunder Jerusalem and finally "all came rejoicing and weeping from excess of gladness to worship at the Sepulchre of our Saviour Jesus". On the next morning they cautiously ascended the Temple's roof, rushed upon the Saracens and beheaded men and women alike with naked swords, some Saracens choosing to fling themselves headlong from the roof. These killings took place to Tancred's great chagrin. By that time almost all of Jerusalem was full of Saracen corpses and the leaders of the crusade ordered the surviving Saracens to drag the dead outside the walls, where they were piled up in heaps as large as houses. The anonymous author concludes by asserting that "no-one has ever heard of, or seen, such slaughters of pagans … and no-one save God alone knows their number". Raymond, however, permitted the commander of David's Tower "and others who were with him" to leave for Ascalon unharmed.[3]

We learn thus of two massacres, the first on 15 July in the town, especially in Solomon's Temple – that is, the Mosque al-Aqsa – and the second on 16 July, on the mosque's roof. On 15 July some of the Muslims seized in the mosque were

Crusades, ed. Jonathan Riley-Smith (Oxford, 1995), pp. 1–12; Christopher Tyerman, *The Invention of the Crusades* (London, 1998), pp. 99–126; Giles Constable, "The Historiography of the Crusades", in *The Crusades from the Perspective of Byzantium and the Muslim World*, ed. Angeliki E. Laiou and Roy P. Mottahedeh (Washington, D.C., 2001), pp. 1–22.

2 To avoid repeating the Latin terms *occisio*, *cedes* and *strages* in direct quotations and close paraphrases, *occisio* will henceforward be consistently translated as slaughter, *cedes* as carnage, and *strages* as massacre. This does not mean, of course, that all chroniclers employed these terms in the same way, or that the same chronicler necessarily ascribed them the same shade of meaning throughout his account.

3 *Gesta Francorum et aliorum Hierosolimitanorum*, cc. 38–39, ed. Rosalind Hill (London, 1962), pp. 91–92. Tancred's behaviour may be contrasted with that of Bohemond at Maʿarrat al-Nuʿman, who promised to keep alive the Saracens who would take refuge in a palace above the gate, but later killed some and sold others as slaves: ibid., c. 33, pp. 79–80. On the impact of the *Gesta* see most recently John France, "The Use of the Anonymous *Gesta Francorum* in the Early Twelfth-Century Sources for the First Crusade", in *Clermont*, pp. 29–42.

left alive; the massacre of 16 July on the mosque's roof on the other hand is depicted as total. In all, the scale of the killings is emphatically presented as without precedent.

The second eyewitness account is that by Peter Tudebode, a priest who participated in the First Crusade and is believed to have used the *Gesta Francorum* or to have relied on a lost source used also by the *Gesta*. Peter presents a simpler story, with more emphasis on Raymond of Saint Gilles' doings, the sequence being: Godfrey's irruption into the city and the chasing and killing of the defenders; Raymond's irruption; surrender of the commander of David's Tower; opening of the town's gate; the commander allowed to leave with his men for Ascalon; chasing and killing of Saracens and other pagans as far as the Temple of Solomon and the Lord's Temple. From here on Peter's sequence, and much of his wording, is identical with that of the *Gesta*, but his factual statements differ on two issues. First, although he has mentioned – like the *Gesta* – that Tancred and Gaston of Béarn gave their banners to the Saracens huddling on the roof of Solomon's Temple, Peter asserts that on the morning of 16 July it was Tancred who ordered all crusaders to kill the Saracens in the Temple: some crusaders drew their bows and killed many, others ascended the roof and beheaded males and females with their naked swords. Far from being chagrined by the killings, Tancred is thus presented here as the instigator of the second massacre. Second, whereas the author of the *Gesta* writes that almost the whole of Jerusalem was full of Saracen corpses, Peter omits the modifier "almost", going on to spell out that the order to throw the corpses out of the town was issued by the bishops and priests, and to specify that the house-high heaps which the surviving Saracens piled up outside the walls were set on fire. It is also noteworthy that Peter, who – unlike the *Gesta* – does not relate that Godfrey's men chased the fleeing Saracens as far as Solomon's Temple, likewise does not repeat the *Gesta*'s subsequent statement that the victors waded there in blood up to their ankles. Yet when Peter later comes to describe the end of the Saracens' last stand, he writes – like the *Gesta* – that their blood "was flowing throughout the Temple". And, using almost the same words as the *Gesta*, he concludes the account of Jerusalem's conquest by emphasizing the unprecedented scale of the killings.[4]

The third eyewitness, unlike the *Gesta* and Peter Tudebode, gives the impression that the massacre was well-nigh total throughout Jerusalem. This is Raymond of Aguilers, chaplain to Raymond of Saint Gilles, whose much more detailed account of the killings leaves little to the imagination. Once the crusaders took possession of the town's walls and towers, he writes, wondrous scenes could be seen: some Saracens whose fate was easier merely had their heads cut off; others, wounded by arrows, were forced to leap from towers; still others were tortured for a long time

---

[4] Petrus Tudebodus, *Historia de hierosolymitano itinere*, ed. John H. Hill and Laurita L. Hill, Documents relatifs à l'histoire des croisades 12 (Paris, 1977), pp. 140–42; Peter Tudebode, *Historia de Hierosolymitano Itinere*, trans. John H. Hill and Laurita L. Hill, Memoirs of the American Philosophical Society 101 (Philadelphia, 1974), pp. 118–20.

and then burnt to death. Throughout the town's quarters and streets one could see piles of heads, hands and feet, with men and horses making their way over corpses. All this pales, however, in comparison with the scene at Solomon's Temple and its portico, where one rode in blood up to one's knees (*ad genua*) and up to the bridles (*ad frenos*) of the horses – a statement far more extreme than that by the author of the *Gesta*. Raymond, unlike the *Gesta* and Peter Tudebode, sees fit to justify the massacre. It was by indisputably just judgement, he asserts, that the place that had suffered the blasphemies of the Saracens for so long, should now receive their blood. The only Saracens whom Raymond mentions as having emerged alive from the blood-and-cadaver-filled town were those who fled to David's Tower and surrendered to Raymond of Saint Gilles. Having thus concluded his description of the conquest, Raymond dwells at considerable length on the crusaders' worshipping in front of the Sepulchre.[5] He says nothing about a second massacre on the following day or about surviving Saracens dragging corpses out of the town.

A further source that may be classified as an eyewitness account is the letter that the leaders of the First Crusade sent the pope in September 1099, within two months of the conquest of Jerusalem. The letter contains just one sentence about the fate of the town's inhabitants: "If you wish to know what was done unto the enemies found there, rest assured that in Solomon's portico and in his Temple our men rode in the Saracens' blood up to the knees of the horses (*ad genua equorum*)." The similarity to Raymond's statement is striking (although, as we have seen, Raymond goes so far as to say that the blood reached the horses' bridles).[6]

There are, then, considerable discrepancies among the eyewitness accounts: two massacres on two consecutive days (*Gesta* and Peter Tudebode) vs. a single massacre on one day (Raymond); a battle at the Mosque al-Aqsa culminating in a partial massacre (*Gesta* and Peter Tudebode), or massacre pure and simple (Raymond and the leaders' letter); the blood in the mosque reaching men's ankles (*Gesta*) vs. horses' knees (the leaders' letter) or men's knees and horses' bridles (Raymond); Tancred giving banners of protection to the Saracens on the mosque's

---

5 Raymond of Aguilers, *Historia Francorum qui ceperunt Iherusalem*, in *RHC Oc* 3:300; *Le "Liber" de Raymond d'Aguilers*, ed. John H. Hill and Laurita L. Hill, Documents relatifs à l'histoire des croisades 9 (Paris, 1969), pp. 150–51 (the edition in the Recueil is preferable: see the introduction of Huygens to WT, pp. 94–95). For the translation of *equitabatur in sanguine usque ad genua, et usque ad frenos equorum* I follow Fulcher of Chartres, *Historia Hierosolymitana* 1.27, ed. Heinrich Hagenmeyer (Heidelberg, 1913), p. 301, n. 39.

6 "... in porticu Salomonis et in templo eius nostri equitabant in sanguine Saracenorum usque ad genua equorum", Heinrich Hagenmeyer, *Die Kreuzzugsbriefe aus den Jahren 1088–1100. Eine Quellensammlung zur Geschichte des Ersten Kreuzzuges* (Innsbruck, 1901), ep. 18, p. 171. Cf. Raymond of Aguilers, *Historia*, p. 300: "... in templo et portico Salomonis equitabatur in sanguine ad genua, et usque ad frenos equorum". Hagenmeyer (*Die Kreuzzugsbriefe*, p. 389) assumes that Raymond composed the letter; see also John France, "The Anonymous *Gesta Francorum* and the *Historia Francorum qui ceperunt Iherusalem* of Raymond of Aguilers and the *Historia de Hierosolymitano itinere* of Peter Tudebode: An Analysis of Textual Relationship between Primary Sources for the First Crusade", in *Crusade Sources*, pp. 42–43.

roof and chagrined upon their massacre (*Gesta*), vs. Tancred first giving the banners and then ordering that the Saracens in the mosque be killed (Peter Tudebode); Saracen survivors in the Mosque al-Aqsa (*Gesta*) and dragging corpses out of Jerusalem (*Gesta* and Peter Tudebode) vs. an almost total massacre of the town's inhabitants, with the people who fled to David's Tower being the only survivors mentioned (Raymond).

Contemporaries

The picture becomes still more variegated when we turn to the accounts of contemporaries who were not present at the conquest of Jerusalem. Fulcher of Chartres, who arrived in Jerusalem more than five months after the conquest, offers many new details, including two numbers. He relates that first Godfrey and then Raymond forced their way into the city, chasing and killing the enemy, with some Arabs and Ethiopians fleeing into David's Fortress. Others, he reports, shut themselves up in the Lord's Temple and in Solomon's Temple and were fiercely attacked in their courts. Many of those who fled to the roof of Solomon's Temple were shot to death with arrows and thrown down headlong. About 10,000 were beheaded within the Temple, with the blood of the killed reaching men's anklebones (*ad bases*). No one was left alive; neither women nor children were spared. And while in his prose account Fulcher thus presents the massacre in the Temple as total, he claims in his verses that this is also what happened elsewhere in Jerusalem:

> With drawn swords our people moved quickly throughout the town
> Nor did they spare anyone, even if he begged for mercy.

Accordingly, Fulcher says nothing about Saracen survivors dragging corpses out of Jerusalem, but he does mention that the squires and poorer foot soldiers among the crusaders split open the corpses' bellies in order to extract bezants from the intestines, having learned that the Saracens, in their shrewdness, had swallowed their gold coins; several days later, when a great heap of corpses was set on fire, the gold was found more easily in the ashes. Fulcher writes also that after this great massacre (*post stragem tantam*) the crusaders plundered the town and everyone took possession of the house he entered first; "thus, many indigent became wealthy". He, too, concludes with a description of the worshipping at the Sepulchre, adding that it took place also at the Lord's Temple. In stating that the place where Christ was born, died and rose was now cleansed from the pollution of the heathen inhabitants who for so long had contaminated it by their superstition, he provides his justification for the well-nigh total, single-day massacre. Finally, after having related that Godfrey of Bouillon was elected to govern the nascent Kingdom of Jerusalem, Fulcher reports that the 500 or so Turks, Arabs and black Ethiopians who shut themselves in David's Fortress offered Raymond, encamped nearby, to keep the money located there and let them go unharmed; Raymond agreed and they left for Ascalon. Fulcher thus insinuates that an act of self-ransom took place a day or two after the conquest.[7]

Fulcher himself arrived in Jerusalem in December 1099 in the retinue of Baldwin of Boulogne, who came to celebrate Christmas at the holy places. Fulcher reports that the rotting cadavers of the Saracens whom his fellow crusaders had butchered at the conquest of Jerusalem set off such a stench around the city walls, both inside and outside, that he and his companions were constrained to hold their noses and cover their mouths.[8] Here Fulcher speaks as an eye – and nose – witness; his testimony appears only in the first redaction of his chronicle and has been almost totally overlooked in discussions of the massacre.

A chronicler often identified as Bartolf of Nangis, who appears to have been in Jerusalem in 1101 and in 1108 (or 1109) summarized Fulcher's first redaction while adding several details of his own, speaks likewise of an almost total, single-day massacre. In Solomon's Temple the carnage was so immense that blood reached almost up to the crusaders' calves (*tenus suras*); no man, woman or child was spared, and Bartolf voices his belief that the crusaders did so because they remembered how King Saul, who spared Agag, had aroused God's anger and perished. Bartolf thus provides a further justification for the massacre. He goes on to relate that of the innumerable Saracens, Turks, Arabs and Ethiopians who came to defend Jerusalem on the orders of the ruler of Egypt, only the few who shut themselves up in David's Tower survived; they delivered the Tower to Raymond and fled. Like Fulcher, Bartolf dwells on the cleansing motif, but does so more emphatically: "The holy city Jerusalem was purged of infidels on that day", he writes; and a few sentences later he reiterates that the conquered city was "cleansed of unbelievers". He then describes the worshipping at the Sepulchre (but not, like Fulcher, at the Lord's Temple) and adds that the following night, while the crusaders were tranquilly asleep in the houses they had seized, only Jerusalem's Greeks and Syrians were posted to keep watch. Another new piece of information pertains to the burning of Saracen corpses. While Fulcher ascribes this deed to the squires and poorer foot soldiers of the crusader army, Bartolf claims that the Provençals carried it out. Having arrived at Solomon's Temple when the Saracen corpses had already been stripped of precious possessions by the crusaders who had stormed the shrine earlier, the Provençals, learning that the Saracens had swallowed coins,

[7] Fulcher, *Historia* 1.27.10–1.30.3, pp. 299–309; idem, *A History of the Expedition to Jerusalem, 1095–1127*, trans. Frances R. Ryan, ed. Harold S. Fink (Knoxville, 1969), pp. 68–71. Fulcher's account appears to have influenced that of William of Malmesbury, who, however, does not mention that the crusaders, in their search of gold, split open the Saracen corpses and burnt them: William of Malmesbury, *Gesta regum Anglorum*, cc. 369–70, ed. and trans. R.A.B. Mynors, R.M. Thomson and M. Winterbottom, 2 vols. (Oxford, 1998), 1:648–51, 2:327.

[8] Fulcher, *Historia* 1.33, p. 332. The words "unde nares nostras et ora oppilare nos oportebat" are replaced in the second redaction with "ubicumque eos adsecuti fuerant".

disembowelled numerous corpses and found money in many viscera. Later they burnt the corpses and searched the ashes for gold.[9]

Two contemporaries who went to the East within a decade of the massacre left behind succinct references that contain no new information. Abbot Ekkehard of Aura, who visited Jerusalem in 1101 but wrote his chronicle in about 1115, merely repeats the sentence in the letter of the leaders of the crusade claiming that the blood in Solomon's Temple reached the horses' knees.[10] Evidently this stirring sentence, lifted from a written source, eclipsed whatever Ekkehard himself might have heard about the massacre during his sojourn in Jerusalem. And Raoul of Caen, who arrived in Outremer in 1108 and wrote his eulogy of Tancred a few years later, speaks of the "horrible massacre of infidels", maintains that the carnage exceeded well-known cases in Antiquity, and that "everything was blood, nothing was to be seen but blood".[11]

The contemporary whose account of the massacre is the longest, most vivid, and replete with many new details, never travelled to the East. This is Albert of Aachen,[12] who appears to have relied on oral reports Godfrey's men made upon their return to the West. Albert relates that when the Gauls – this is how he refers to the crusaders – irrupted into Jerusalem, about 400 Egyptian cavalry fled to the fortress of David's Tower; Raymond besieged them there but, "corrupted by greed", he allowed them to depart unharmed in return for an enormous sum of money, with their weapons, food and equipment left behind.[13] (Thus, what Fulcher has insinuated, Albert bluntly spells out.) A large number of Jerusalem's defenders fled to King Solomon's palace – that is, the Mosque al-Aqsa – and attempted to put up a resistance, but the crusaders "struck them down with cruel death. There was such great bloodshed that streams even flowed out across the very floors of the royal court, and the stream of spilt blood rose up to the ankles (*ad talos*)."[14] Many Saracens fled into the royal cistern, which was in front of the palace, and perished there alongside their Christian pursuers.[15] Like Fulcher, Albert gives the number of slain as 10,000. He goes on to relate that the Christians subsequently turned to chase the Saracens who were fleeing for their lives throughout the town, and spared

[9] *Gesta Francorum Iherusalem expugnantium*, cc. 35–37, in *RHC Oc* 3:515–16.

[10] Ekkehard of Aura, *Hierosolymita*, c. 17, in *RHC Oc* 5:24; *Frutolfi et Ekkehardi Chronica necnon Anonymi Chronica imperatorum*, ed. and trans. Franz-Josef Schmale and Irene Schmale-Ott (Darmstadt, 1972), p. 154. Ekkehard appears to have copied the sentence verbatim from the version of the letter that appears in Frutolf's chronicle: see ibid., pp. 112–13 with n. 69.

[11] Radulph of Caen, *Gesta Tancredi in expeditione Hierosolymitana*, c. 134. in *RHC Oc* 3:699. The description of Jerusalem's conquest starts in c. 127, p. 694.

[12] For the time being, see Albert of Aachen, *Liber christianae expeditionis pro ereptione, emundatione et restitutione sanctae Hierosolymitanae ecclesiae* 6.20–23, 25, 28–30, in *RHC Oc* 4:477–84. My thanks to Dr Susan Edgington for having put at my disposal the typescript of her forthcoming critical edition of Albert's chronicle, as well as of her translation, which I basically use below.

[13] Albert, 6.20, 28.

[14] Ibid., 6.21.

[15] Ibid., 6.22.

absolutely no one, "seizing sucklings by the soles of their feet from their mothers' bosoms or their cradles and dashing them against walls or door lintels and breaking their necks".[16]

For Albert, Godfrey of Bouillon was the shining hero of the day. He claims that while a greed-driven Tancred rushed to the Lord's Temple to seize its riches, while others pursued fugitives to the David's Tower, while all Christian chiefs gazed eagerly at the town's possessions and turreted edifices, and while the common people cut down the Saracens at Solomon's palace "with excessive cruelty",[17] Godfrey soon kept away from the massacre;[18] he took off his coat of mail and shoes, went outside Jerusalem's walls and humbly circled the town accompanied by just three of his men. Having re-entered the town through the eastern gate, he made his way to the Church of the Holy Sepulchre, where he prayed in tears for a long time, thanking God for having earned to see what had always been his utmost desire. Unlike the *Gesta*, Peter Tudebode, Raymond, Fulcher or Bartolf, Albert does not say that the other crusaders concluded the day by worshipping at the Sepulchre: he presents Godfrey's deed as a singular act of devoutness that takes place while the massacre is in full swing. The other crusaders are portrayed as simply falling asleep at the day's end.

Turning to the events of 16 July, Albert relates that about 300 Saracens fled to the roof of Solomon's palace and dared not descend before receiving Tancred's banner as a sign of protection. "But it did these wretches no good at all. For many people were angry about this, and the Christians were incensed with rage, so not a single one of them escaped with his life."[19] Like the *Gesta*, Albert reports that Tancred was furious; the other leaders appeased him by pointing out that it would be imprudent to spare enemies because of greed, sluggishness or compassion, for if the king of Egypt were to attack the town, the spared enemies would join the attackers and bring Christian rule to an end. Therefore, all Saracens, whether held for ransom or already ransomed, must be killed without delay.[20] Thus Albert provides a further justification, a military one, for the massacre.

On the third day after the victory, the Christians fell "with a pitiable carnage" on all the remaining Saracens, beheading imprisoned ones and butchering in the streets those who had been spared earlier because of money offered or out of human pity. Albert describes the Christians' doings with an intensity that suggests he had witnessed some such scenes somewhere:

> Girls, women, matrons, tormented by fear of imminent death and horror-struck by the violent murder, wrapped themselves around the Christians' bodies in the hope to save

---

[16] Ibid., 6.23.

[17] "nimia crudelitate", ibid., 6.25. Cf. "in nimia gentilium occisione perseuerant", ibid., 6.20; "crudeli funere sternentes", ibid., 6.21; "post nimiam et cruentam cedem Sarracenorum", ibid., 6.23.

[18] "ab omni mox strage se abstinens", ibid., 6.25.

[19] Ibid., 6.28.

[20] Ibid., 6.29.

> their lives, even as the Christians were raving and venting their rage in the murder of both sexes. Some threw themselves at their feet, begging them with pitiable weeping and wailing for their lives and safety. When children five or three years old saw the cruel fate of their mothers and fathers, of one accord they stepped up the weeping and pitiable clamour. But they were making these signals for pity and mercy in vain. For the Christians gave over their whole hearts to murder, so that not a suckling little male-child or female, not even an infant of one year would escape alive the hand of the murderer.[21]

Albert is the only chronicler to describe this third, final massacre. His account, largely told from the victims' viewpoint, plainly reveals his compassion for the victims. It is hardly accidental that Albert, unlike all the other chroniclers, does not have his murderous crusaders ending the day of conquest by an act of devoutness at the Holy Sepulchre.

The chronicles of the First Crusade by Guibert of Nogent, Baudri of Bourgueil and Robert the Monk are also the works of contemporaries writing in the West. Guibert, who relies for his facts on the *Gesta Francorum* and on conversations with returned crusaders, adds only one new detail: in Solomon's Temple, he relates, the crusaders left some Saracens alive for a while, so that they might remove the corpses from the building and, when this was done, killed them.[22] The account leaves the impression that the massacre was well-nigh total, with Guibert stating that he had rarely read about, and had never seen, such carnage of "Gentiles", and explaining that this was God's retribution for the pain and death they had brought upon his pilgrims.[23] Just once does he refer to the slain Saracens as wretches.[24] On the other hand, he speaks twice of crusaders wading through Saracen blood: writing about the Franks' irruption into Solomon's Temple he remarks that the wave of blood almost reached the ankles (*talos*) of the advancing men; later, describing the massacre that took place there, he observes that the blood almost exceeded their shoe tops (*oras calceorum*).[25]

Baudri, like Bartolf, has the blood in Solomon's Temple reaching men's calves (*ad suras*); like Guibert, he implies that the massacre was almost total throughout Jerusalem, yet unlike Guibert he justifies it by pointing to the Saracens' pollution of the holy places. Baudri, too, provides some new information. Some of those who escaped to the roof of Solomon's Temple, he relates, and were spared for some time

---

[21] Ibid., 6.30. The scene of Saracen women clutching at the crusaders' bodies in the hope of saving their lives recalls Albert's earlier account of how Frankish girls, during the Turkish irruption at Dorylaeum, offered themselves to the enemy: Albert, 2.39, in *RHC Oc* 4:330.

[22] Guibert de Nogent, *Dei gesta per Francos* 7.8, ed. Robert B.C. Huygens, CCCM 127A (Turnhout, 1996), p. 281.

[23] Ibid., 7.10, p. 283.

[24] Ibid., 7.8, p. 281.

[25] Ibid., 7.7, 7.8, pp. 279, 281. This replication led the chronicle's recent translator into French to exclaim: "Notre auteur revient pour la seconde fois sur ce détail abominable qui ne cessera, depuis lors, de hanter la mémoire collective des trois civilisations du Livre." Guibert de Nogent, *Geste de Dieu par les Francs. Histoire de la première croisade*, trans. Monique-Cécile Garand (Turnhout, 1998), p. 243, n. 39.

so they could remove the corpses, were later sold or killed. Later, describing the cleansing of the entire town, he reports that the Saracen survivors were too few to throw all the corpses beyond the walls and poor Christians had therefore to be paid for joining in the work.[26]

Robert, in contrast to Albert, has Godfrey of Bouillon slitting many Saracens from head to loins, in retribution for the Christian blood spilt around Jerusalem and the insults hurled at the crusaders during the siege. In Solomon's Temple, Robert envisages a wave of blood that drives forward corpses rolling on the floor, while arms and cut-off hands float on the blood until they haphazardly join some corpse. Yet he relates also that in the wake of the massacre the crusaders "yielded a little to nature", sparing many young men and women and enslaving them. Likewise, Robert says that many of the Saracens who fled to the roof of Solomon's Temple were enslaved.[27]

The contemporary accounts, then, significantly expand the range of possibilities for later reconstructions of the massacre (see Table 1, pp. 28–29). It is either total or well-nigh so (Fulcher, Bartolf, Albert, Guibert, Baudri) or partial (Robert). It takes place on a single day (Fulcher, Bartolf, Baudri) or on two (Guibert, Robert) or on three (Albert). The final massacre is said to have taken place on the explicit orders of the crusade leaders and to have brought death both to Saracens being held in prison and on those who had previously ransomed themselves (Albert). There are figures: 500 fugitives in David's Tower (Fulcher) or 400 cavalry taking refuge there (Albert); 10,000 killed in Solomon's Temple (Fulcher and Albert), 300 Saracens on that shrine's roof (Albert). Raymond is accused, with varying degrees of explicitness, of letting the Muslims in David's Tower depart unharmed in return of ransom money (Fulcher, Albert). Godfrey is portrayed as keeping away from the massacre, making a procession around Jerusalem's walls and finally praying at the Sepulchre (Albert), or as hacking down Saracens in vengeance for their misdeeds (Robert). The blood in Solomon's Temple is said to have reached anklebones (Fulcher, Albert, Guibert), calves (Bartolf, Baudri), or shoe tops (Guibert), or to have formed a wave on which cut-off limbs floated (Robert). Squires and poorer foot soldiers (Fulcher) or Provençals (Bartolf) split open Saracen corpses in search of swallowed gold coins and later burnt the corpses and searched the ashes for gold. The Saracens' corpses were dragged out of Solomon's Temple by captured survivors who were killed upon completing their task (Guibert) or sold or killed (Baudri); the corpses were dragged out from Jerusalem by captive survivors

---

[26] Baudri of Bourgueil, *Historia Jerosolimitana*, in *RHC Oc* 4:102–3. For other pieces of information on the massacre and its aftermath in an adaptation of Baudri's chronicle dating from the late twelfth century see ibid., apparatus, MS G; and see Joshua Prawer, *The History of the Jews in the Latin Kingdom of Jerusalem* (Oxford, 1988), pp. 24–25. Orderic Vitalis incorporated a slightly abridged version of Baudri's account into his chronicle: see *The Ecclesiastical History of Orderic Vitalis* 9.15, ed. and trans. Marjorie Chibnall, 6 vols. (Oxford,1968–80), 5:168–75.

[27] Robert the Monk, *Historia Iherosolimitana*, 9.7–9, in *RHC Oc* 3:866–69.

(Guibert, Robert) or by captive survivors as well as by poor Christians paid for their work (Baudri). Several reasons are given in justification of the massacre: it cleansed the holy places of Saracen pollution (Fulcher, Bartolf, Baudri); it saved the crusaders from the fate that befell Saul for having spared Agag (Bartolf); it precluded the possibility that surviving Saracens would join an attacking Saracen army (Albert); or it was in retribution for the pain, death and insults the Saracens had inflicted on the crusaders (Guibert, Robert). Finally, there are some expressions of compassion for the massacred Saracens (Albert).

An early homily on the conquest of Jerusalem, which contains several factual details that may go back to an account by some returned Provençal crusader, exemplifies the imaginative use and amplification of some of these motifs. The anonymous author of the homily points out that the resort of the Saracens to David's Tower and the Temple was intrinsically futile: they were fighting Him who was an offspring of David according to the flesh; by entering the Temple they violated a house of prayer and thereby deserved death. In fact, their concentration in these two places rendered simpler the task of the crusaders, who could easily kill all of them there together. Since the Saracens had shed much Christian blood around Jerusalem, it was fitting that their own blood was shed inside Jerusalem, to the point that crusaders entering Solomon's Temple would wade through it almost up to their knees. Here the Christian author remarks that "fitting was the sight of their little ones, and of some of their oldest, tumbling down to their death". Later he reports that the bishops and clerics ordered that the crusaders, in penance for their sins, have the task of throwing the Saracens' corpses out of the town.[28]

Chronicles instigated by kings of Jerusalem

Two chronicles sponsored by twelfth-century kings of Jerusalem have come down to us: one is the renowned work of William of Tyre, written at the suggestion of King Amaury and universally regarded as one of the masterpieces of twelfth-century historiography in general; the other is the pedestrian, unimaginative and largely neglected compilation that Amaury's older brother, King Baldwin III, instigated in 1146 when he was just sixteen or seventeen years old.

The brief description of the massacre in Baldwin III's compilation closely follows Fulcher's account, abbreviating it drastically. The Saracens fled to David's Fortress, where they shut themselves in, and to the Lord's Temple and Solomon's Temple, in which almost 10,000 were slain; no person was spared on account of age or sex. After this great massacre the crusaders took possession of Jerusalem's houses

---

28 John France, "The Text of the Account of the Capture of Jerusalem in the Ripoll Manuscript, Bibliothèque Nationale (Latin) 5132", *English Historical Review* 103 (1988), 649–50; idem, "An Unknown Account of the Capture of Jerusalem", ibid. 87 (1972), 771–83.

and many who had been indigent became wealthy. Then all went to worship in the Sepulchre and in the Lord's Temple.[29]

It is worth noting which elements in Fulcher's account do *not* re-appear in Baldwin III's compilation: the blood in Solomon's Temple reaching men's anklebones; the scene on the Temple's roof, with Saracens shot to death and thrown down headlong, which takes place on 16 July; the claim that the massacre was total throughout Jerusalem; and the story about crusaders splitting open Saracen corpses and later burning them in search of gold coins. The omissions are consistent: evidently the compiler chose to suppress the more gory passages in Fulcher's relation. Thus his single-day massacre is relatively moderate.

The compiler's jejune account contrasts starkly with the complex, ambivalent description of the massacre in William's chronicle, which wavers between justification and revulsion. William bluntly asserts that the mass of crusaders was "thirsting for the infidels' blood and utterly prone to carnage". In the two chapters that deal with the irruption into Jerusalem he employs the term *strages*, massacre, no less than six times; on four occasions he refers to the horridness of the killings.[30] The two motifs combine in the startling statement that "the *strages* of the enemy throughout the town was of such a magnitude, and the shedding of blood was so great, that it could imbue even the victors with disgust and horror".[31] Yet somewhat later he remarks (using words similar to those of Raymond, whose chronicle he knew)[32] that the killings came about by God's just judgement, in retribution for the Saracens' profanation of the Lord's sanctuary. It is remarkable that the Jerusalem-born William speaks of a single Temple, combining facts that elsewhere pertain to the Lord's Temple on the one hand and to Solomon's Temple on the other. He dwells on the cut-off limbs, decapitated bodies, and the blood spattered all over the Temple, representing them as scenes of horror, and observes that the sight of the victors, "dripping with blood from the soles of their feet to the tops of their heads", was terrifying. Like Fulcher and Albert, William gives the number of the slain in the Temple as about 10,000, adding that the number of those killed throughout the town was not smaller. (This would mean that the total was about 20,000; an anonymous Syriac chronicler, possibly William's contemporary, gives the total as 30,000.)[33] Thereupon William turns to the killings in the town, vividly describing how the crusaders would snatch poor wretches trying to hide in the town's narrow alleys and behead them in public like sheep, or how a group of crusaders would enter a

[29] Baldwin III, *Historia Nicaena vel Antiochena necnon Jerosolymitana*, c. 60, in *RHC Oc* 5:175–76. According to the prologue (p. 140), "Balduinus tertius ... compilavit simul et conscribere fecit hoc opus".

[30] "stragem operati sunt horrendam", "tanta ... strages ... ut etiam victoribus posset tedium et horrorem ingerere", WT 8.19, p. 411; "horror erat denique cesorum intueri multitudinem", "et ipsos victores ... periculosum erat conspicere et horrorem quendam inferebant occurrentibus", WT 8.20, p. 412.

[31] WT 8.19, p. 411.

[32] See Gerhard Rösch's remarks in Huygens' introduction to WT, p. 93.

[33] Arthur S. Tritton and Hamilton A.R. Gibb, trans., "The First and Second Crusades from an Anonymous Syriac Chronicle", *Journal of the Royal Asiatic Society* (1933), 73.

house, grab the head of the family with his wives, children and entire household (the wording attests to William's familiarity with Muslim polygamy), and either transfix them with swords or hurl them headlong to their deaths.[34] Then William mentions how the crusaders took possession of Jerusalem's houses and goes on to dwell at very great length on the joyful worshipping at the holy places; in fact, the description of the worshipping occupies almost as much space as that of the massacre. Later on, William relates that Jerusalemites who remained alive by chance were forced, in shackles, to remove the corpses from town and Temple and, since their numbers were insufficient, were joined by poor crusaders who worked for daily wages. (William evidently found the latter detail in Baudri's chronicle.) The corpses were burnt or buried. Finally William mentions that the enemies who found refuge in David's Fortress and realized they were unable to endure the siege any longer, surrendered to Raymond, encamped nearby,[35] and left with their wives, children and all property (which conflicts with Albert's assertion that they left behind their weapons, food and equipment). Unlike Fulcher and Albert, William does not mention, or even hint, that the surrender amounted to an act of self-ransom.[36]

William's account, then, is decidedly superior to the one in Baldwin III's compilation. It is far more detailed, characterizes the crusader multitude as bloodthirsty, contains vivid depictions of the killings, repeatedly stresses their horridness and stands out for the remark that the massacre could imbue even the victors with disgust and horror, which comes very close to an explicit critique of the crusaders' doings. Nevertheless, there is a basic similarity between the account in William's chronicle and that in King Baldwin's compilation. Since William knew the chronicles of Albert, Fulcher and Baudri,[37] it is evident that he chose to suppress the claim that the blood in the Temple reached ankles or calves; the splitting and burning of Saracen corpses in search of gold; the massacre on the Temple roof of Saracens to whom Tancred had given his banners; and the decision of the crusading leaders to kill, on the third day after the victory, all Saracens, whether imprisoned or already ransomed. In fact, William's massacre, like that in Baldwin III's compilation, takes place only on the day of the conquest.

One may conjecture several reasons for William's suppressions. His account of the massacre amply demonstrates that he was not averse to gory details, but the picture of blood reaching ankles or calves may have struck him as an exaggeration; in any case, he preferred to speak of blood spattered all over the place. A mention of the search for gold in Saracen corpses, and of the self-ransom of the Saracens shut up in David's Tower, might have depicted the crusaders as greedy and

---

[34] WT 8.20, pp. 411–12.

[35] Ibid. 8.24, p. 418: "qui circa partes illas turri vicinior hospitatus erat". The wording is the same as Fulcher's, who writes: "qui prope turrim illam hospitatus erat", Fulcher, *Historia* 1.30, p. 309.

[36] WT 8.24, pp. 417–18.

[37] See Gerhard Rösch's remarks in Huygens' introduction to WT, p. 93.

Table 1: Chroniclers' accounts of the Jerusalem Massacre

	Gesta	Tudebode	Raymond	Fulcher	Bartolf	Albert	Guibert	Baudri	Robert	Baldwin III	William
1-day massacre			+	+	+			+		+	+
2-day massacre	+	+					+		+		
David's Tower										+	
surrender to Raymond	+	+	+	+	+		+	+	+		+
Raymond allows Saracens to depart	+	+		+		+	+	+			+
number of enemy				500		400					
Solomon's Temple											
number of killed				10,000		10,000				10,000	10,000
none spared				+						+	+
blood	ad cavillas		ad genua et ad frenos equorum	ad bases	tenus suras	ad talos	prope talos; calceorum oras	ad suras	unda sanguinis		sanguine replentes universa
survivors mentioned	+	+							+		
survivors drag away corpses, are killed							+				
Temple roof											
Tancred gives banners to Saracens	+	+				+	+	+			
massacre:											
enrages Tancred	+					+	+	+			
on Tancred's orders		+									
number of killed				multi		300					
survivors mentioned								+	+		
Massacre in Town								+			
town full of corpses	+	+									+
massacre described			+			+	+				+

	Gesta	Tudebode	Raymond	Fulcher	Bartolf	Albert	Guibert	Baudri	Robert	Baldwin III	William
number of killed											c.10,000
survivors mentioned											+
none spared				+		+	+	+			
Devotion at Sepulchre	+	+	+	+	+	only Godfrey	+	+	+	+	+
Corpses											
split up and burnt in search of gold				+	+						
by poor				+							
by Provençals					+						
Survivors											
drag corpses out of town	+	+					+	+	+		+
killed afterwards							+				
enslaved or killed								+			
Massacre on unprecedented scale	+	+					+				
Massacre of people held prisoner or ransomed, ordered on 3rd day after victory by crusade leaders						+					
Crusader cruelty						+					+
Justification of massacre			Saracen blasphemies	cleansing pollution	cleansing of infidels; Saul & Agag	elimination of potential enemy	retribution for crusader suffering	pollution of churches	retribution for bloodshed and insults		profanation of sanctuary

undermined William's basic argument that they were of impeccable character.[38] And the massacre of Saracens to whom Tancred had granted protection, especially the massacre of Saracens who had been taken captive or had already been ransomed, might have cast a shadow on the crusaders' probity.

According to the conventions of the age, a town or fortress taken by assault was at the victor's mercy and its population could expect massacre or enslavement.[39] But the ratio between massacred to enslaved inhabitants varied from one case to another, with a well-nigh total massacre or a well-nigh total enslavement representing the extremes of a continuum. Therefore, the massacre that followed the storming of Jerusalem, which must have accorded with the first extreme, since eyewitnesses described it as unprecedented, posed no fundamental moral problem. Nevertheless, William hardly veils his disapproval of the extent of bloodshed. The fate of the Saracens to whom Tancred and Gaston of Béarn had given their banners did present a moral problem; for although other crusaders perpetrated the massacre and Tancred (according to two of William's sources, Albert and Baudri) objected to it, the promise of a crusader leader was nevertheless broken. Indeed, when Baudri describes this massacre and immediately afterward reports that Raymond ordered that the commander of David's Fortress and his men be escorted to Ascalon so as to keep his word unbroken,[40] he obliquely contrasts Raymond's success with Tancred's failure. It is understandable, therefore, why William chose to suppress the story about the massacre of Tancred's protégés. Still more problematic was the massacre that, according to Albert, took place on the third day after the conquest: here the crusader leaders decreed in cold blood that all survivors, women and children included, must be put to death. It is plausible to assume that, for William, this premeditated massacre of imprisoned, and even of already ransomed, people two days after the storming of Jerusalem, was a flagrant transgression of prevailing custom.

William of Tyre's variegated impact

Of the massacre descriptions surveyed above, three have proved to be most influential. The first was the claim of the crusade leaders, in their letter of September 1099, that in Solomon's Temple the crusaders rode in Saracen blood up to their horses' knees. Very soon afterward Frutolf of Michelsberg (d. 1103) incorporated it

---

38 See WT 21.7, p. 969.

39 See Joseph F. O'Callaghan, "The Mudejars of Castile and Portugal in the Twelfth and Thirteenth Centuries", in *Muslims under Latin Rule, 1100–1300*, ed. James M. Powell (Princeton, 1990), p. 13; Benjamin Z. Kedar, "The Subjected Muslims of the Frankish Levant", ibid., pp. 143–44; Jim Bradbury, *The Medieval Siege* (Woodbridge, 1992), pp. 317–24.

40 "Ita enim eis pepigerat pactumque suum illibatum conservare volebat", Baudri of Bourgueil, *Historia Jerosolimitana*, p. 103. Orderic Vitalis' paraphrase is a shade more definite: "pactumque suum illibatum conservavit", *The Ecclesiastical History* (see above, n. 26), 9.15, 5:172–73.

in his chronicle[41] and a few years later Sigebert of Gembloux (d. 1112) paraphrased it in his widely known work, which served as the basis for numerous continuations. The paraphrase, which lets the crusaders "rage without control in so great a carnage", has a ring of censure about it; its inclusion into the *Speculum Historiale* of Vincent of Beauvais (d. 1264) gave it still further vogue.[42] Ekkehard of Aura, as already noted, copied Frutolf in about 1115. A further paraphrase of the crusade leaders' claim appears in another highly influential work, the *History of the Two Cities* by Otto of Freising (d. 1158).[43] Thus the image of the crusaders' horses wading in blood up to their knees came to epitomize the conquest of Jerusalem for generations of Westerners.

The second was the chronicle of Robert the Monk, which, as we have seen, stands out for mentioning Saracen survivors both within Solomon's Temple and on its roof. The more than ninety manuscripts of the chronicle that have come down to us attest to its widespread diffusion. A versified version was composed in the twelfth century. The chronicle was printed in Cologne in about 1471, in Basel in 1533, in Frankfurt in 1583; Jacques Bongars re-edited it in his *Gesta Dei per Francos* which appeared in Hanau in 1611. A German translation was published in 1482 and an Italian one in 1552.[44]

Still more influential was William of Tyre's account. Yet whereas the claim of the crusade leaders and Robert's chronicle were transmitted virtually unchanged, William's description produced several mutations over the centuries.

The first author to use William's chronicle was Guy de Bazoches, a Third Crusader who died in 1203. In his *Cronosgraphia* he severely abbreviates William, often reproducing solely his rubrics.[45] Thus Guy's account of Jerusalem's conquest consists largely of abbreviated and slightly rearranged versions of William's rubrics of Book 8, Chapters 19–21. Consequently, all the reader can learn from the *Cronosgraphia* about the fate of Jerusalem's population is that Godfrey and his men wrought a numberless massacre among the enemy; that the citizens took refuge in the Fortress and in the Temple; that infinite blood was shed in the Temple's forecourt; and that the enemies of the true faith were driven out of the holy city.

---

41 *Frutolfi et Ekkehardi Chronica* (see above, n. 10), pp. 114–15.

42 "... et in templo Salomonis et in portico ejus Christiani cum paganis quinto bello conserto, tanta in eis cede debaccati sunt, ut in sanguine occisorum equitarent usque ad genua equorum", Sigebert of Gembloux, *Chronica*, ed. L.C. Bethmann, in MGH SS 6:368; Vincent of Beauvais, *Speculum Historiale*, 25.102 (Douai, 1624; repr. Graz, 1965), p. 1037b. Vincent was used by Felix Fabri, who went on pilgrimage to Jerusalem in the 1480s and included in his itinerary a long treatise on the crusades: *Fratris Felicis Fabri Evagatorium in Terrae Sanctae, Arabiae et Egypti peregrinationem*, ed. Conrad D. Hassler, Bibliothek des literarischen Vereins in Stuttgart 2–4 (Stuttgart, 1843–49), 3:266. The text is modified here to "ut in sanguine occisorum equitarent in nonnulis locis atrii usque ad genua equorum".

43 Otto of Freising, *Chronica sive Historia de duabus civitatibus*, 7.4, ed. Adolf Hofmeister in MGH Scr. rer. germ. 45:314.

44 See the preface in *RHC Oc* 3:li; Max Manitius, *Geschichte der lateinischen Literatur des Mittelalters*, 3 vols. (Munich, 1911–31), 3:424–26.

45 See Huygens' introduction to WT, p. 76.

William's vivid descriptions of the killings, his insistence on their horridness, his remark on the disgust they could evoke, all go unutilized in this dull rendition.[46] Alberic of Troisfontaines (d. after 1252), who incorporated Guy's account into his well-known chronicle, probably regarded it as too dry; in any case, he saw fit to add the sentence on the horses wading in blood up to their knees, which he found in Sigebert.[47]

Jacques of Vitry, bishop of Acre in the years 1216–28, who in his *Historia Orientalis* made use of William's chronicle, described the Jerusalem massacre even more succinctly than Guy of Bazoches. All Jacques says is that the crusaders "slayed, by God's just judgement, almost all the Saracens they found in the city".[48] The only words of this statement that go back to William are *iusto Dei iudicio*,[49] and even these are not reproduced in the translation of Jacques' work into Old French, done later in the thirteenth century.[50]

William's account was utilized much more extensively by two St Albans chroniclers, Roger of Wendower (d. 1236) and Matthew Paris (d. c.1259). In their chronicles, the massacre's description occupies an entire chapter, which consists of almost literal reproductions of many of William's sentences.[51] Yet a detailed comparison reveals that the English chroniclers abridged William's text and that the abridgements affect the original's tenor. They omit William's two remarks that the crusaders spared no one; William's *stragem horrendam* becomes *stragem non modicam*, while *stragem innumeram* is turned into *stragem multiplicem* or *multam*. William's scenes of cut-off limbs and decapitated bodies; of victors dripping with blood; of Saracens killed like sheep; and the characterization of the crusader mass as thirsting for blood, are all skipped. Instead there appears (only in the *Historia*

---

46 "Dux itaque cum suis per civitatem discurrens dat innumerabilem de hostibus stragem. Tholosanus ab australi parte legiones suas inducit. Civium pars se recipit in presidium civitatis, pars plurima civium in templi se conferrt atrium. Tancredus illuc eos persequitur, ibidem sanguis hostium funditur infinitus. Civitate sue libertati deletis invasoribus restituta, sedato tumultu et armis depositis, loca venerabilia circueunt, orationis gratia diem agentes sollempnem. Sic inimicis vere fidei triumphatis et fugatis a civitate sancta Iherusalem infidelibus et ab eius territorio profligatis, quia post tot immensos labores emensos christianus exercitus et devota deo militia metam obtinuit tam gravis et longe peregrinationis optatam." BNF lat. 4998, fol. 62r.

47 *Chronica Albrici monachi Trium Fontium*, ed. P. Scheffer-Boichorst in MGH SS 23:811.

48 "omnes fere Saracenos, quos in civitate repererunt, iusto Dei iudicio trucidantes", Jacques of Vitry, *Historia Orientalis*, c. 26, in his *Libri duo* (Douai, 1597), p. 53.

49 WT 8.20, p. 412.

50 "et ocisent tous les Sarrasins qu'il i troverent", *La traduction de l'*Historia Orientalis *de Jacques de Vitry*, c. 20, ed. Claude Buridant (Paris, 1986), p.81.

51 Matthew Paris, *Chronica majora*, ed. Henry R. Luard, RS 57, 7 vols. (London, 1872–83), 2:101–2; idem, *Historia Anglorum*, ed. F. Madden, RS 44, 2 vols. (London, 1866), 1:146–47. Roger's chronicle is represented by the relevant text of the *Chronica majora* without Matthew's insertions from William of Tyre, which Luard printed in letters of a larger size; Matthew's definite text, with some further insertions from William of Tyre (in our case, the sentence on the massacre as God's just retribution for infidel profanation) appears in his *Historia Anglorum*. For a detailed discussion see Huygens' introduction to WT, pp. 78–87.

Anglorum) the rather banal image of crusaders wading through rivulets of blood. The enemy are described as Turks, a mistake William would never have committed. On the other hand, Roger of Wendower and Matthew Paris do repeat William's oblique criticism of the massacre and even slightly intensify it. Yet, on the whole, the abridgements evoke a less frenzied massacre.[52] Thus we discern a trend: William chose to omit extreme or problematic statements he encountered in his sources; later chroniclers who used his account preferred to tone it down still further.

The Old French adaptation of William's chronicle known as the *Eracles* presents another variation of this trend. The anonymous adapter, a cleric writing in the first third of the thirteenth century,[53] drastically modifies William's sentence on the disgust and horror the bloodshed could have instilled in the victors, claiming instead that the heaps of cadavers could have evoked one's pity if the slaughtered had not been "enemies of Our Lord".[54] Thus William's *tedium et horror* is replaced with *pitié* and his slightly veiled critique of the massacre is branded as misplaced. The adapter is evidently unable, or unwilling, to translate abstract nouns such as *strages*, *cedes* or *horror*, choosing to convey their meaning through the portrayal of concrete scenes: for instance, William's *tantaque erat ubique interemptorum strages* is rendered by *tant en i avoit là d'ocis parmi les rues*.[55] All along, the adapter abbreviates William's descriptions: thus the drawn-out sentence on the horror-inspiring cut-off limbs, decapitated bodies and blood spattered all over the Temple is replaced with the terse statement that *hideuse chose estoit à veoir si grant plenté de gent ocise*.[56] William's scenes of crusaders snatching Jerusalemites from their hideouts and beheading them in public like sheep, and of crusaders forcing their way into a house and butchering an entire family, are omitted altogether. On the other hand, the adapter boosts William's justification for the massacre in the Temple by dwelling on the "ordures of unbelief" with which *li desloial mescréant*, adherents of "Mahomet's false law", had defiled it.[57] He does mention that the crusaders spared

---

52 Roger and Matthew reproduce William's description of how crusaders put to death an entire family but, obviously baffled by William's reference to a polygamous family (*patremfamilias cum uxoribus*) they speak either of *patremfamilias cum uxore* or of *patresfamilias cum uxoribus*: see *Chronica majora* 2:101; *Historia Anglorum* 1:147 with nn. 1–2.

53 See John H. Pryor, "The *Eracles* and William of Tyre: An Interim Report", in *Horns*, pp. 270–93; Bernard Hamilton, "The Old French Translation of William of Tyre as an Historical Source", in *The Experience of Crusading*, 2: *Defining the Crusader Kingdom*, ed. Peter Edbury and Jonathan Phillips (Cambridge, 2003), pp. 93–112.

54 "Tout estoit jonchié de genz mortes, si que pitié en peust prendre, se ce ne fust des anemis Nostre Seigneur", *Guillaume de Tyr et ses continuateurs. Texte français du XIIIe siècle*, 8.19, ed. Paulin Paris, 2 vols. (Paris, 1879), 1:290. Beugnot and Langlois, in their edition of the *Eracles*, commented at this point: "Nous ferons ici une remarque qui est applicable à divers autres passages de cette traduction, savoir: que le traducteur s'éloigne presque toujours de son auteur quand celui-ci témoigne quelque pitié pour les infidèles", *RHC Oc* 1:354, n. a.

55 WT 8.19, pp. 410–11; *Guillaume de Tyr*, ed. Paris, 8.19, 1:289.

56 Ibid., 8.20, 1:291.

57 Loc. cit.

neither women nor children, that to cry mercy helped no one, and that the crusader foot were most willing to kill;[58] but this is distant indeed from William's statement that the mass of crusaders was "thirsting for the infidels' blood and utterly prone to carnage". On the whole, the adapter's tone is matter-of-fact; he misdates, though, the conquest to 15 June.[59] Since he describes the enemy as Turks and reports that large rivulets of blood were streaming in the streets of Jerusalem,[60] it is plausible to assume that when Matthew Paris was writing the *Historia Anglorum*, he had before him, alongside William's Latin text, the Old French *Eracles*.

The *Eracles* was more widely known, and far more influential, than William's Latin original. Just nine manuscripts of William's chronicle, and a small fragment of a tenth, have come down to us, whereas no less than sixty-four manuscripts of the *Eracles* (of which nine are fragmentary) are known to exist.[61] William's chronicle was printed in Basel by Philibert Poyssenot in 1549 and reprinted in 1560, 1564 and 1583; Jacques Bongars re-edited it in his *Gesta Dei per Francos* in 1611. Gioseppe Horologgi's translation into Italian was printed in Venice in 1562, while Gabriel Du Préau's French translation was published in Paris in 1573. On the other hand, the *Eracles* was translated into Castilian already in the late thirteenth century and printed in Salamanca in 1503. Early in the fourteenth century the Dominican Francesco Pipino rendered the *Eracles* into Latin and incorporated the translation into his vast chronicle, while other Latin translations appear in manuscripts of the fifteenth and sixteenth centuries. (These retranslations into Latin indicate that William's original Latin text was not widely known; in fact, no less a man than Vespasiano da Bisticci, the major bibliophile of his times, wrote in the late fifteenth century that Godfrey of Bouillon's expedition had hitherto "never been described except in French".)[62] In 1348 Lorenzo Fiorentino translated the *Eracles* into Italian, and in 1481 William Caxton printed his Middle English translation of it. The *Eracles* served the Florentine chancellor Benedetto Accolti as the main source for his Latin-written history of the First Crusade, completed in 1464. Accolti's work in its turn enjoyed a very wide diffusion: printed four times between 1532 and 1623, it was translated into Italian in 1543, into German in 1551, into French and into Greek in 1620.[63]

---

58 Ibid., 8.19, 1:289; see also 8.20, 1:291.

59 Ibid., 8.24, p. 296.

60 "... tant y ot de sanc espandu que li ruissel en coroient granz parmi les voies", ibid., 8.19, 1:290.

61 Huygens' introduction to WT, pp. 3–32; Jaroslav Folda, "Manuscripts of the *History of Outremer* by William of Tyre: A Handlist", *Scriptorium* 27 (1973), 90–95.

62 Vespasiano, *Renaissance Princes, Popes, and Prelates*, trans. William George and Emily Waters (New York, 1963 [1926]), pp. 371–72.

63 See Paul Riant, "Inventaire sommaire des manuscripts de l'*Eracles*", *AOL* 1 (1881), 253 (appendix); A. Petrucci, "Benedetto Accolti, il Vecchio", in *Dizionario biografico degli Italiani* 1:99–101. For a recent edition of Caxton's translation, together with a rendering into modern English, see *A Middle English Chronicle of the First Crusade: The Caxton Eracles*, ed. and trans. Dana Cushing, 2 vols. (Lewiston, NY, 2001); the description of the conquest and the massacre appears in vol. 2, pp. 674–97.

An examination of some of the latter-day offspring of William's chronicle reveals that the dilution of its original tenor continued, while on one occasion it was unwittingly regained. The Castilian translation of the *Eracles*, known as *La gran conquista de Ultramar*,[64] omits altogether the Old French sentence about the pity that the slaughtered Turks might have evoked if they had not been the Lord's enemies, which in itself is a radical modification of William's original statement on the disgust and horror the bloodshed could have instilled in the victors. The justification of the massacre, and the remark that the crusader foot were most willing to kill, are also wholly omitted. William's emphasis on the horridness of the massacre reverberates only in the statement that it was frightening to see the large number of dead in the streets;[65] but William's subsequent remark that the sight of the victors, too, was terrifying – translated in the *Eracles* – was skipped. In brief, the Castilian translation is even more confined to the recounting of facts than its Old French model. The anonymous translator did take over, though, the image in the *Eracles* of the rivulets of blood streaming in the streets[66] and, like the *Eracles*, misdated the conquest to 15 June.[67]

In the historical part of his *Secreta Fidelium Crucis*, written in Latin in the 1310s, the Venetian crusade promoter Marino Sanudo Torsello dedicates a few lines to the Jerusalem massacre of 1099. The account, which depends on the *Eracles* down to misdating the conquest to 15 June, is extremely succinct. "In revenge for the injuries done unto Christ", writes Sanudo, "the Pilgrims spared no one on account of sex or age; so many were killed in the roads that they had to go over corpses; rivulets of blood streamed in the streets." Thus the *Eracles*' verbose justification of the massacre as retaliation for infidel profanations is condensed into four words, *in vindictam iniuriarum Christi*. The fighting in the Temple – the only scene dealt with – is described in the same laconic fashion; yet the Venetian merchant sees fit to reproduce the one number figuring in the *Eracles*' account, that of the 10,000 killed.[68] Here, again, the original timbre of William's description of the massacre is totally absent.

The *De bello a Christianis contra barbaros gesto pro Christi sepulchro et Iudaea recuperandis libri IV*, the history of the First Crusade which Benedetto Accolti concluded in 1464, was written in support of a crusade against the Turks who had conquered Constantinople just eleven years earlier. Hence the works of the Florentine chancellor and the Venetian merchant share the same intent. But Accolti was a prominent humanist who, according to Vespasiano da Bisticci, "had a

64 *La gran conquista de Ultramar*, ed. Pascual de Gayangos, Biblioteca de autores españoles 44 (Madrid, 1877). The massacre and its aftermath are described in Book 3, chs. 44–53, pp. 347–49.

65 "Espantosa cosa era é fea de ver la gran mortandad de los que estaban muertos por las plazas é por las calles". Book 3, ch. 45, p. 347b.

66 "... tantos de los turcos hobo allí muertos, que corria la sangre por las calles", ibid., p. 347a.

67 Book 3, ch. 53, p. 349b.

68 Marino Sanudo Torsello, *Liber secretorum fidelium crucis*, 3.5.8, ed. Jacques Bongars in *Gesta Dei per Francos* (Hanau, 1611; repr. Jerusalem, 1972), p. 148.

wide knowledge of sacred history and literature".[69] Though Accolti relies on the *Eracles* for his facts about the Jerusalem massacre, he presents them in a strict chronological order that improves not only on his immediate model but also on William himself, whose chronicle he had not seen: for instance, while William and the *Eracles* assert, well after their description of the conquest, that many crusaders attested to have seen Bishop Adhémar of Le Puy (who had died in Antioch a year earlier) being the first to scale Jerusalem's walls, Accolti mentions this apparition even as he describes that scaling.[70] Unlike the *Eracles*' Old French, Accolti's erudite Latin is packed with abstract nouns, and when he employs the terms *caedes* and *strages*, he unwittingly reverts to the words William himself used.[71] Moreover, Accolti succeeds in conjuring up a picture of the massacre which resembles that of William: he describes the crusaders as "fired with slaughter" (*caede calentes*) and full of rage (*ira*), relates twice (whereas the *Eracles* did so just once) that they did not spare anybody on account of age or sex, and characterizes the slaughter as "incredible".[72] Even his terse justification of the massacre – the Barbarian enemy polluted the Sepulchre and other shrines[73] – is closer to that of William than to the *Eracles*' crude denunciation of the adherents of *la fausse loi Mahomet*. Thus, from the embers of William's account that smoulder in the *Eracles*, the Florentine humanist succeeds unknowingly in resuscitating William's glow. This is all the more remarkable as Accolti found no use for the *Eracles*' sentences on the rivulets of blood in the streets or the pity the killed could have evoked. Instead, Accolti underlines his disapproval of the massacre by adding a scene of his own making. When the crusaders entered the Temple area, he writes, the Barbarians stretched out their hands in supplication, threw down their arms, and prostrated themselves after the manner of the vanquished, but the crusaders killed them all.[74] Accolti goes on to point out that, in the Temple itself, "neither tears nor entreaties, nor the sanctity of the place, were of use for the Barbarians".[75] He implies thus that presence in the inherently sacred Temple should have vouchsafed safety even to the Barbarians who had polluted it – an unprecedented thought that must reflect Accolti's own values.

[69] Vespasiano, *Renaissance Princes* (see above, n. 62), p. 371. On Accolti's work in general and on the place of his *De bello* in the humanist literature on the crusade see Robert Black, *Benedetto Accolti and the Florentine Renaissance* (Cambridge, 1985), pp. 184–329; for the date of the *De bello*, its source and parallels see pp. 225–26, 322.

[70] WT 8.22, pp. 414–15; *Guillaume de Tyr*, ed. Paris, 8.22, 1:293–94; Benedetto Accolti, *Historia Gotefridi* [=*De bello*] 4.11, in *RHC Oc* 5:608.

[71] Indeed, where William writes "stragem operati sunt horrendam" and the *Eracles* has "tous metoient à l'espée", Accolti says "stragem ingentem faciebant". WT 8.19, p. 411; *Guillaume de Tyr*, ed. Paris, 8.19, p.290, Accolti 4.11, p. 608.

[72] Loc.cit.

[73] Accolti 4.11, p. 609.

[74] In the earlier chronicles, the closest to this scene is the description of Baudri: "sed postquam viderunt se nihil proficere, gladiis projectis colla neci submisere" (*RHC Oc* 4:102). However, Accolti did not know Baudri's chronicle.

[75] Accolti 4.11, p. 608.

It is also noteworthy that Accolti repeatedly presents the crusaders' adversaries as Barbarians. The term reappears in several subsequent descriptions.[76]

By inventing the scene of Barbarians killed even as they are begging for their lives, Accolti was probably taking issue with the papal secretary Flavio Biondo who, in his *Decades* completed in about 1453, offers quite a different story. A carnage took place in the Temple to the point that blood reached men's ankles, he writes, but with night approaching the crusaders suspended their attack. The town was given over to pillage, but the crusaders were sternly forbidden to vent their rage on the inhabitants. When the attack on the Temple was renewed on the next day and the enemy asked for mercy, the crusaders resolved to spare the leaders. Thus by two strokes of his pen Biondo reduced the massacre's scale and portrayed the crusaders as magnanimous in triumph! His story was repeated time and again in humanist historiography.[77]

In sum, by 1500 an assortment of Williamesque texts was afloat in Catholic Europe, reaching a far larger audience than William's original chronicle. An author intending to write about the First Crusade could embroider on one or more of these texts according to his lights. For instance, Sébastien Mamerot, who in 1518 brought out a history of the crusades, basically follows the account of the *Eracles* about the conquest of Jerusalem, but chooses to characterize the massacre as "horrible".[78]Antonio Mossi, who in 1601 published a history of the First Crusade largely based on Accolti, expresses his discontent with the massacre by remarking that Tancred shed the blood of the Barbarians in the Temple *che doveva esser più che Asilo*, and by subsequently observing that Raymond of Saint Gilles behaved at David's Tower *più humanamente*.[79] Similarly, Yves Duchat, who in 1620 translated Accolti into French, expands Accolti's "armati pariter et inermes pueri, foeminae

76 Paolo Emili (d. 1529), who dedicated one of the nine books of his well-known history of France to the First Crusade, describes the massacre succinctly: "Cędes barbarorum tota urbe capta. Ad templum Solomonis eorum proceres refugere, ubi paulisper prelium recrudescens tenuit. Ab Aegyptiorum nullo temperatum. Quarto Nonas Iulias urbs sancta recepta. Postridie humandis corporibus purgandaque urbe opera insumpta." Paulus Aemilius, *De rebus gestis Francorum libri IIII* [recte: IX] (Paris, c.1517), p. 123a–b. The same text, slightly expanded, is offered by the Magdeburg Centuriators: Mathias Flacius Illyricus, *Undecima Centuria ecclesiasticae Historiae* (Basel, 1567), col. 762.

77 Blondus Flavius, *Historiarum ab inclinatione Romanorum libri XXXI* (Basel, 1559), liber XIV, p. 226. Aeneas Silvius Piccolomini, *Supra Decades Blondi, ab inclinatione Romani imperii usque ad tempora Ioannis vicesimi tertii pontificis maximi, Epitome* in his *Opera omnia* (Basel, 1551), pp. 213–14; Platyna Historicus, *Liber de vita Christi ac omnium pontificum (aa. 1–1474)*, ed. Giacinto Gaida in RIS NS 3.1:200; M. Antonius Sabellicus, *Historiae rerum Venetarum ab urbe condita libri XXXIII* (Basel, 1556), pp. 150–51; Hartmann Schedel, *Weltchronik* (Nürnberg, 1493; repr. Cologne, 2001), p. cxcvi. On Biondo's influence, and on other humanist writers on the crusades, see Ludwig Schmugge, *Die Kreuzzüge aus der Sicht humanistischer Geschichtsschreiber*, Vorträge der Aeneas-Silvius-Stiftung an der Universität Basel 21 (Basel, 1987).

78 Sébastien Mamerot, *Les passages de Oultre Mer* (Paris, 1518), p. 32v. Cf. Nicole Le Huen, *Des croisées et entreprinses faictes par les roys et princes crestiens pour le recouvrance de la Terre Saincte* (Paris, 1517), p. 107.

79 Antonio Mossi, *Breve descrizione dell'aquisto di Terra Santa* (Florence, 1601), p. 65.

mactabantur" into "car confusement pesle mesle ceux qui sont en armes, & ceux qui ne le sont, femmes et enfans, ieunes & vieillards sont mis au fil de l'espee". Later, when Duchat comes to speak of the massacre in the Temple, Accolti's "Barbari" become "ces miserables".[80] Adding or changing a word here, expanding a sentence there, an author would alter the drift of the text he was using.

The advent of Albert of Aachen

In 1584, in Helmstädt, Reiner Reinecke printed Albert's chronicle for the first time. In 1611, in Hanau, Jacques Bongars reprinted it in his *Gesta Dei per Francos*, alongside many other chronicles of the First Crusade. In 1636 Christoph Besold, professor of law in Tübingen and – after his conversion to Catholicism – in Ingolstadt, published a history of the Kingdom of Jerusalem in which he quoted verbatim several twelfth-century descriptions of the conquest of 1099, one of them being that by Albert.[81] Thus from the late sixteenth century onwards, Albert's singular account of an organized massacre of imprisoned and previously ransomed Saracens on the third day after the conquest, as well as his vivid description of the killings and expression of compassion for the victims, could reach an ever larger audience.

Soon after Besold printed Albert's account in Strasbourg in 1636, Thomas Fuller, the Anglican rector of Broadwindsor (Dorset), utilized it in his iconoclastic and witty *Historie of the Holy Warre*, first published in 1639 in Cambridge. Fuller, who forcefully rejects the crusade idea, presents William of Tyre and Matthew Paris as the sources of his description of the Jerusalem massacre; but the depiction of the enemy as Turks and the claim that after the slaughter in Solomon's Temple "none could go but either through a rivulet of bloud, or over a bridge of dead bodies" reveal that he is basically following Matthew Paris' *Historia Anglorum*. Fuller invents a detail of his own: "Next morning", he writes, "mercie was proclaimed to all those that would lay down their weapons. For though bloud be the best sauce for victorie, yet must it not be more then [*sic*] the meat." But this flare-up of crusader mercy conjured up by Fuller was short-lived. On the basis of Albert's account as printed by Besold, Fuller then retells the story of the massacre that took place on the third day after the conquest, implanting into it Tancred's anger at the slaughter of the Saracens to whom he had given his protection:

---

80 Yves Duchat, *Histoire de la Guerre Saincte, faite par les François & autres Chrestiens, pour la deliurance de la Iudee & du S. Sepulchre* (Paris, 1620), pp. 448, 450. Similarly, the Jesuit Pierre d'Oultreman speaks of "l'effroyable carnage des Barbares": Pierre d'Oultreman, *La vie du venerable Pierre l'Hermite, Aucteur de la premiere Croisade & Conqueste de Jerusalem, Pere et Fondateur de l'Abbaye de Neuf-Moustier & de la maison de l'Hermites* (Valenciennes, 1632), p. 78.

81 Christophorus Besoldus, *Historiae urbis et regni Hierosolymitani regum item Siculorum et Neapolitanorum* (Strasbourg, 1636), pp. 115–16 (William of Tyre), pp. 116–20 (Albert of Aachen), pp. 120–21 (*Gesta Francorum*), pp. 121–23 (Guibert of Nogent), pp. 123–25 (Robert the Monk).

> Three dayes after[,] it was concluded, as a necessarie piece of severitie for their defense, to put all the Turks in Jerusalem to death; which was accordingly performed without favour to age or sex. The pretense was for fear of treason in them, if the Emperour of Persia should besiege the citie .... But noble Tancred was highly displeased hereat, because done in cold bloud, it being no slip of an extemporary passion, but a studied and premeditated act; and that against pardon proclaimed, many of them having compounded and paid for their lives and libertie. Besides, the execution was mercilesse, upon sucking children, whose not-speaking spake for them; and on women, whose weaknesse is a shield to defend them against a valiant man. To conclude; Severitie hot in the fourth degree is little better than poyson, and becometh crueltie itself: and this act seemeth to be of the same nature.[82]

Thus Albert – whom Fuller does not mention by name – plays a major role in the first outspoken condemnation of the Jerusalem massacre.

Yet reliance on Albert's account by no means predetermined an author's view of the massacre. The widely known *Histoire des croisades pour la délivrance de la Terre Sainte*, which Louis Maimbourg – a Jesuit who stood out for his intense hostility to Protestantism – first published in Paris in 1675–76, is a case in point.[83] In the side-notes to his account Maimbourg refers to the *Gesta Francorum*, Peter Tudebode, Raymond, Robert, Baudri, Guibert, William of Tyre, Marino Sanudo and especially to Albert, disclosing thereby his indebtedness to Bongars' vast collection of chronicles; his assertion that "le sang couloit par les ruisseaux des ruës" suggests that he read the *Eracles* or one of its derivations. However, he did not use – or was unaware of – an Oriental chronicle printed fifty years earlier in Leiden. This was the *Historia Saracenica* by the Coptic chronicler Djirdjis al-Makin b. al-ʿAmid (1205–73), which Thomas Erpenius published both in the Arabic original and in Latin translation. Here Maimbourg could have read that the crusaders rounded up Jerusalem's Jews in their synagogue and burnt them in it, and that they killed about 70,000 Muslims.[84] But al-Makin's chronicle was to impact on Western historiography of the crusades only from the mid-eighteenth century onward.

While at one point Maimbourg refers to the "horrible boucherie de ces miserables", which amounted to a "lamentable spectacle", he emphatically and

---

82 Thomas Fuller, *The Historie of the Holy Warre* (Cambridge, 1639), p. 41.

83 The first edition appeared in 1675–76, the second in 1676, the third likewise in 1676 (with further printings in 1677, 1684 and 1685), the fourth in 1687. I use the four-volume second edition of 1676, in which the conquest of Jerusalem is described in 1:336–44. It should be noted that Maimbourg makes use of the term "massacre".

84 Georgius Elmacinus, *Historia Saracenica*, ed. and trans. Thomas Erpenius (Leiden, 1625), p. 293. On al-Makin's chronicle see Claude Cahen and R.G. Coquin, "al-Makin b. al-ʿAmid, Djirdjis", *Encyclopaedia of Islam*, 2nd ed., 6:143–44. The first to report the story about the burning of the Jews in their synagogue is the Damascene chronicler Ibn al-Qalanisi (d. 1160): H.A.R. Gibb, *The Damascus Chronicle of the Crusades, Extracted and Translated from the Chronicle of Ibn al-Qalanisi* (London, 1932), p. 48; see also Claude Cahen, "La chronique abrégée d'al-Azimi", *Journal asiatique* 230 (1938), 373. The claim that more than more than 70,000 Muslims were slain in the Mosque al-Aqsa appears for the first time in the chronicle of Ibn al-Athir (1160–1233): *RHC Or* 4:198; see also Abu 'l-Fida (1273–1331) in *RHC Or* 1:4. For an English translation and discussion of most of these sources see Carole Hillenbrand, *The Crusades: Islamic Perspectives* (Edinburgh, 1999), pp. 64–66.

unreservedly justifies the massacre. Victory, he claims, gave the right to proceed rigorously against the enemy who had committed outrages against Christ and barbarous cruelties against Christians. Reporting that the crusaders killed even infants held in the arms of their mothers, he remarks that this was done in order to exterminate that accursed race similarly to the God-willed annihilation of the Amalekites of old. Dealing with the killings in the Palace and in the Temple, he points out that it was God's vengeance that concentrated the enemy in these two places[85] in order to allow the crusaders to implement more easily the decrees of His justice. Speaking of Tancred's anger at the slaughter of the 300 to whom he had promised protection, Maimbourg relates approvingly, on the basis of Albert's account, how the other leaders appeased Tancred by pointing out the threat such people might have constituted during the impending war with "the sultan of Babylon". It is noteworthy that Maimbourg presents the massacre of the 300 as having taken place on the day of the conquest and not – like Albert and other chroniclers – as occurring on the morning after the prayer at the Sepulchre. Presumably he considered such a deed understandable in the heat of battle. It is still more significant that Maimbourg does not mention at all the subsequent event related by Albert, that is, the organized, total massacre on the third day after victory. Evidently Maimbourg was unable to extend his sanctimonial, reverential attitude towards crusading to the final massacre as reported by Albert. His massacre remains a single-day event.

There are three new elements in Maimbourg's account, all of which will enjoy a considerable vogue. First, he relates that the poor local Christians who stayed in Jerusalem pointed out the Saracens' houses to the crusaders and thus brought death on them. Second, he retells Albert's story about the barefooted, unarmed Godfrey who circled the walls with just three of his men and then offered his devotions at the Sepulchre; but while Albert says that Godfrey did so while keeping away from the massacre, Maimbourg – who considers the massacre commendable – asserts that Godfrey did so while others were engaged in plunder. He goes on to say that Godfrey's pious example touched the hearts of the entire army, who together with the local Christians went in procession to prostrate themselves before the Holy Sepulchre. Thus Maimbourg combines Albert's story about Godfrey's singular act of devoutness with the report, appearing in the other chronicles, about the crusaders joyfully worshipping in the Church of the Holy Sepulchre in the wake of the massacre. (I shall henceforth refer to this combination as Maimbourg's Godfrey Story.) Third, Maimbourg is struck by the impact of Godfrey's example on the crusaders and, attempting to explain their sudden transition from one extreme to another, makes the following observation: "One could say that these men, who took a city by assault and made a furious carnage among their enemies, emerged from a lengthy seclusion and from a profound meditation of our Mysteries, that caused their

---

85 The notion that Muslim concentration rendered the crusaders' task easier appears already in the twelfth-century homily referred to in note 28 above.

hearts to undergo one of those changes of grace, that can render, in a single instant, a great sinner into a very great saint."[86]

Even after Albert's account had become readily available, it was not utilized by all writers. For instance, the Abbé Claude Fleury, who in 1713 dealt with the conquest of Jerusalem within the framework of his multi-volume, highly influential history of the Church, chose to rely on William of Tyre. His account is succinct. Upon the irruption of the crusaders a "horrible massacre" took place in the streets, in the mosque erected on the site of the Temple – where about 10,000 were killed – and elsewhere in the town. "Everything weltered in blood", he writes, "and the victors themselves, tired of the carnage, were horrified by it." This is, of course, a tendentious restatement of William's remark that the massacre *could* have imbued the victors with disgust and horror: while William speaks of the possibility of crusader revulsion at their own deeds, Fleury turns that revulsion into fact, implying his own disapproval of the massacre. Still, Fleury devotes much more space to describing how the crusaders marched barefoot and in tears to the holy places. The devoutness with which they kissed the vestiges of the Saviour's sufferings, he says, presented a *spectacle merveilleux*.[87]

The Abbé René Aubert de Vertot, who earned his reputation by describing internal political upheavals in several countries, was asked by the Knights Hospitaller to write a comprehensive history of their order. His account of the Jerusalem massacre appears in the first of the five volumes of that history, first published in Paris in 1726 and reprinted several times thereafter. De Vertot copies verbatim Fleury's sentence, "Everything weltered in blood and the victors themselves, tired of the carnage, were horrified by it." Later he repeats verbatim Fleury's sentence on the devoutness with which the crusaders kissed the vestiges of the Saviour's sufferings, the only difference being that Fleury's *spectacle merveilleux* becomes a *spectacle très-touchant*. Faithful to the conventions of his times (and perhaps also of more recent ones), de Vertot does not acknowledge his debt to Fleury. Yet his disapproval of the massacre is far more pronounced than Fleury's. He claims – probably relying on Accolti or Duchat – that the crusaders killed even those who laid down their arms; that "more than 10,000 inhabitants who had been promised quarter were afterwards massacred in cold blood"; and that sucklings were mercilessly killed in their mothers' arms. The statement about the 10,000 probably constitutes a misunderstanding of Albert's account, or of Fuller's summary of it. In addition, de Vertot quotes in a side-note Sigebert of Gembloux's paraphrase of the claim of the crusade leaders that in Solomon's Temple the crusaders rode in Saracen blood up to their horses' knees, a paraphrase that represents the crusaders as raging out of control. All this suggests a sharply critical attitude towards the massacre. Then de Vertot goes on to relate how this "fureur militaire" was replaced by more Christian sentiments and, like Maimbourg, dwells on the crusaders' surprisingly

---

86 Maimbourg, *Histoire* 1:343.

87 [Claude] Fleury, *Histoire ecclésiastique*, vol. 13 (Paris, 1713), pp. 686–87.

swift transition from cruelty to piety, giving the opinion that "men often behave according to quite contrary principles".[88]

Thus the diffusion of Albert's chronicle did serve to enhance criticism of the massacre. Yet such criticism could also arise independently of Albert. As the example of Benedetto Accolti demonstrates, even a watered-down adaptation of William's chronicle could prompt a Christian humanist to express disapproval of the massacre. On the other hand, the case of Louis Maimbourg proves that a sanctimonial approach towards crusading was impervious even to Albert's poignant scenes. An author's values rather than his sources determined his attitude.

Varieties of condemnation in the Age of Enlightenment

Emphatic condemnation of crusading in general is a well-known feature of the Enlightenment; censure of the Jerusalem massacre is one of its obvious upshots. Voltaire, who presents the First Crusade as the earliest instance of the "fureur épidémique" that made millions of Europeans lose their lives in Asia, writes that the Jerusalem massacre was total and lasted for several days. He depicts just one scene: some local Christians, whom the Muslims had allowed to live in Jerusalem, guide the crusaders to the Muslims' hiding places. The scene resembles the one described by Maimbourg and most probably depends on it: but while Maimbourg has the local Christians merely indicating the Saracens' houses to the crusaders and justifies the subsequent killing of infants in the arms of their mothers by pointing to the precedent of the Amalekites, Voltaire renders the scene into a veritable woman-hunt by claiming that these Christians "led the victors to the most remote cellars where mothers were hiding with their infants, and none was spared". Voltaire implies moreover that these local Christians behaved in an ungrateful manner towards the Muslims. It should also be noted that, unlike the pre-Enlightenment writers and several post-Enlightenment ones, Voltaire speaks here of Muslims, not Saracens. Having presented his single but powerful tableau of the massacre, he goes on to remark that almost all historians agree that in the wake of the carnage the crusaders went in procession to the purported [*sic*] sepulchre of Christ, where they shed their tears. Voltaire expresses his scepticism: "This tenderness made manifest by weeping is not much compatible with the spirit of giddiness, rage, lewdness and violence. The same man can be raging and tender, but not at the same time." In other words, he rejects Maimbourg's ornate explanation of the crusaders' swift transition from killing to worshipping. He rounds out his description by noting that Elmacim – that is, the Coptic chronicler Djirdjis al-Makin b. al-ʿAmid – reports that the crusaders shut Jerusalem's Jews in the synagogue and burned all of them in it, and gives his opinion that this report is credible. Thus we witness here for the first time a

---

88 [René Aubert] de Vertot, *Histoire des Chevaliers Hospitaliers de S. Jean de Jérusalem, appellés depuis Chevaliers de Rhodes et aujourd'hui Chevaliers de Malthe*, 5 vols., 4th ed. (Paris, 1755), 1:57–58.

western writer on the crusades using in his account of the massacre – and boosting it with – an oriental chronicle that had existed in Latin translation since 1625.[89]

In the widely known biography of Saladin which François-Louis-Claude Marini, known as Marin, published in 1758 on the basis of Eastern as well as western sources, the massacre is condemned in still harsher terms. Marin, who was close to Voltaire in his early years, asserts that "one reads with horror" about the cruelties the crusaders committed. Paraphrasing Voltaire without saying so, Marin states that the massacre was total, embroiders the woman-hunt scene with the original claim that the crusaders "cut the throats of women and girls after having raped them" and reports that they subsequently went "to cry at the tomb of their [*sic*] God, that God of peace who abhors injustice, murder and infamy".[90] The moral indignation is patent. So is its anachronism. As the Scottish historian William Robertson was to observe about a decade later, modern authors of histories of the crusades "are apt to substitute the ideas and maxims of their own age in the place of those which influenced the persons whose actions they attempt to relate".[91] This observation, as we shall see, applies also to some much later authors.

The most detailed description of the massacre in Enlightenment literature appears in Jean-Baptiste Mailly's *L'esprit des croisades* of 1780. His scenes are largely based on chronicler accounts, to which he refers in ample side-notes, but more than other writers he expands these accounts according to his imagination. Unlike Voltaire, he considers the crusades "a grand and magnificent spectacle" and the First Crusade a just, legitimate war, yet he censures the crusaders for the atrocities by which they disgraced it.[92] The Jerusalem massacre is for him a major case in point. The carnage, he says, was dreadful: "never, perhaps, did war show itself more horrible than on that day". (Here he echoes the *Gesta Francorum*, one of the many sources he mentions.) Tancred, Gaston of Béarn, Godfrey and the other leaders dishonoured themselves by the multitude of infidels they put to death: this is the first occurrence of a theme that will recur in later years. In his description of the killings in the Temple, Mailly fleshes out Robert the Monk's scene of cut-off arms floating on a wave of blood, adds on his own that all columns, altars and walls dripped with blood, and reports that the blood reached the murderers' ankles while

---

89 Voltaire, *Histoire des croisades* (Berlin, 1751), pp. 14–36; idem, *Essai sur les mœurs et l'esprit des nations*, ed. René Pomeau, 2 vols. (Paris, 1963 [1756]), 1:558–67, with the quotations appearing on pp. 560, 566.

90 [François-Louis-Claude] Marin, *Histoire de Saladin, sulthan d'Egypte et de Syrie*, 2 vols. (Paris, 1758), 1:61. A second edition appeared in 1763; a German translation in 1761. Lessing used Marin while working on his *Nathan der Weise*.

91 William Robertson, *The History of the Reign of the Emperor Charles the Fifth*, 2 vols. (London, 1809 [1769], 1:457–58.

92 Jean-Baptiste Mailly, *L'esprit des croisades, ou histoire politique et militaire des guerres enterprises par les Chrétiens contre les Mahométans, pour le recouvrement de la Terre Sainte pendant les XIe, XIIe et XIIe siècles*, 4 vols. (Amsterdam, 1780), 1:3, 3:192–93. For a detailed discussion of Mailly's career and work see Jean Richard, "Jean-Baptiste Mailly et l'*Esprit des croisades*", *Mémoires de l'Académie des sciences, arts et belles-lettres de Dijon* 136 (1997–98), 349–59.

some, undeserving of belief, claim that it reached even the horses' knees. Turning to the massacres committed in the town, Mailly repeats – without acknowledgement – Voltaire's woman-hunt scene, but, coming to describe the killings of the infants, he utilizes Albert's depiction of sucklings seized by their feet and hurled against walls, then adds on his own that the crusaders were pleased to see their arms and clothes covered with streams of blood and pieces of brain. Later he describes in similar detail the second-day massacre of the 300 on the Temple roof, and opines that this cold-blooded killing rendered the crusaders perhaps even guiltier than they had been before. He reports with obvious disdain that the crusaders believed they were acting like the Hebrews of old against the Amalekites (this goes back to Maimbourg) and feared that by sparing a single Saracen they would arouse God's anger, as Saul did by sparing Agag (this goes back to Bartolf). He brands the slaughter of the 300 as an "act of inhumanity" and "a barbarism suggested by the poison of fanaticism". Still later he turns to describe – closely following Albert – the general massacre ordered on the third day after the conquest and expands Albert's description of women and girls throwing themselves at the feet of the crusaders by asserting that they were "deaf to their crying and wailing, insensible to their tears and caresses". Then he relates that the few Saracen slaves ordered to remove corpses out of Jerusalem were weeping as they gathered scattered members into baskets – this goes back to Robert the Monk – and recognized among them those of a friend, relative or co-citizen – a detail that springs from Mailly's imagination. Finally, he tells the story, which goes back to Bartolf, that the greedy Provençals, who were the last to force their way into Jerusalem, disembowelled corpses in search of coins and later burnt them hoping to find some gold or silver in the ashes.[93] Mailly thus culls from numerous sources, old and new, precisely those scenes of the massacre that must have struck an enlightened reader as particularly revolting. And he lets this reader know how much he disapproves of the massacre, performed by men whom he repeatedly describes as acting like madmen. Tancred trying to protect the 300 is the only hero of the story, but even he is depicted as dishonouring himself by having taken part in the initial killings.

Mailly paraphrases and expands Maimbourg's Godfrey Story, without acknowledging that he is doing so. But he combines Albert's report that Godfrey left his companions engaged in slaughter with Maimbourg's claim that he did so while they were engaged in plunder, writing that they were "occupés au massacre ou au pillage". Mailly then turns to Maimbourg's theme of the swift transition from massacre to devoutness at the Sepulchre, which he presents as *un spectacle bien étonnant*. He considers this transition plausible and indeed quite in character with the crusaders. Differing explicitly from Voltaire on this issue, he argues that "it is possible to be pious as well as fanatical, raging and tender at the same time, with superstition rendering a man's heart susceptible to all extremes".[94] Despite the

93 Ibid., 4:423–25, 429–37, with the quotations appearing on pp. 423, 430, 431, 432.

94 Ibid., pp. 425–29, with the quotation appearing on. p. 427.

horror that the crusaders' atrocities so evidently evoke in him, his basic attitude to the crusade is, unlike that of Voltaire, positive, and he definitely attempts to understand the crusaders.[95]

Across the Channel, attitudes similar to those of Voltaire, Marin and Mailly were expressed by David Hume, Edward Gibbon and Charles Mills. Hume, today better known as a philosopher and political economist, dealt with the massacre in his *History of England*, originally published between 1754 and 1762. Closely paraphrasing the Abbé de Vertot – and referring to him in a footnote – Hume relates that about "ten thousand persons who had surrendered themselves prisoners, and were promised quarter, were butchered by those ferocious conquerors". He paints a picture more grisly than de Vertot's: where the French abbot writes that "on tuoit impitoyablement les enfans à la mamelle, & dans les bras de leurs meres", the Scottish philosopher states that "infants on the breast were pierced by the same blow with their mothers, who implored for mercy". Also, de Vertot's "fureur militaire" becomes "a mixture of military and religious rage". Hume does not however repeat de Vertot's claim that the crusaders themselves were horrified by the blood they had shed. Finally, he describes the demonstration of devoutness at the Sepulchre and dwells on the theme of the swift transition from – as he puts it – "fury" to "soft and tender sentiment". Unlike Voltaire, but like Mailly, he considers the transition plausible: "So inconsistent is human nature with itself! and so easily does the most effeminate superstition ally, both with the most heroic courage and with the fiercest barbarity!"[96] Nevertheless, Hume's negative view of the massacre, though not explicitly stated, is unmistakable.

Edward Gibbon's account of the crusades appears in the part of *The History of the Decline and Fall of the Roman Empire* that was published in 1788. In a telling footnote, Gibbon brands the title *Gesta Dei per Francos* of Guibert and Bongars as fanatical and observes that some critics prefer to speak of *Gesta Diaboli per Francos*. In the same footnote Gibbon states that he accepts most of Mailly's judgements.[97] He does not acknowledge his indebtedness to Voltaire, though his comment on Urban II's Clermont Address to the effect that "war and exercise were

---

[95] A German translation of Mailly's work appeared in Leipzig in 1783. In 1808, Johann Christian Ludwig Haken published a description of the massacre which amounts to an overstatement of that by Mailly: Johann Ch.L. Haken, *Gemälde der Kreuzzüge nach Palästina zur Befreiung des heiligen Grabes*, 3 vols. (Frankfurt an der Oder, 1808–20), 1:392–99.

[96] David Hume, *The History of England from the Invasion of Julius Caesar to the Revolution in 1688*, 8 vols. (new ed., London, 1802), 1:311–12. Between Hume's death in 1776 and 1894 about 50 editions of his *History* appeared.

[97] Edward Gibbon, *The Decline and Fall of the Roman Empire*, ch. 58, ed. J.B. Bury, 7 vols., 2nd ed. (London, 1897–1902), p. 266 n. 20. (The original volume appeared in 1788.) Gibbon does not mention Mailly's name, referring to him as "a late French historian, the author of *Esprit des Croisades*". Elsewhere he refers to him as "the French author of the *Esprit des Croisades*": ibid., p. 309, n. 113. See also pp. 270, 273, 278, 280, nn. 30, 35, 44, 50. On Gibbon's sources on crusading history in general see Elizabeth Siberry, *The New Crusaders. Images of the Crusades in the Nineteenth and Early Twentieth Centuries* (Aldershot, 2000), pp. 3–5.

the reigning passions of the Franks or Latins; they were enjoined, as a penance, to gratify those passions, to visit distant lands, and to draw their swords against the nations of the East" is evidently a tedious rendering of Voltaire's dictum that at Clermont "le Pape leur proposait la remission de tous leurs péchés, et leur ouvroit le Ciel, en leur imposant pour penitence de suivre la plus grande de leur passions, d'aller faire la guerre".[98]

Gibbon explicitly condemns the Jerusalem massacre. "A bloody sacrifice", he writes, "was offered by his mistaken votaries to the God of the Christians: resistance might provoke, but neither age nor sex could mollify, their implacable rage: they indulged themselves three days in a promiscuous massacre." The reference to three days suggests that Gibbon is following here Albert's narrative, whether directly or in Mailly's rendition. In a footnote he points out that he is relying on the Latin authors, "who are not ashamed of the massacre" (a statement doing less than justice to Albert), as well as on the Arabic-writing ones, Elmacin, Abulpharagius and Aboulmahasen.[99] It is from the latter authors that Gibbon learned that "seventy thousand Moslems had been put to the sword, and the harmless Jews had been burnt in their synagogue"; but, accepting Mailly's view that Jerusalem had more than 200,000 inhabitants at the time, he states that the crusaders "could still reserve a multitude of captives whom interest or lassitude persuaded them to spare". Thus Gibbon's massacre is far from total; neither does he describe any specific scene of it. He does single out two crusaders who emerge from the massacre relatively untarnished: "Of these savage heroes of the cross, Tancred alone betrayed some sentiments of compassion; yet we may praise the more selfish lenity of Raymond, who granted a capitulation and safe conduct to the garrison of the citadel."

The one scene Gibbon does describe is the crusaders' devoutness at the Sepulchre. He then turns to discuss the transition from massacre to piety, which as we have seen was on the agenda ever since Maimbourg dwelled on it more than a century earlier, and notes that Hume and Voltaire differed with regard to this "union of the fiercest and most tender passions", the first regarding it as "easy and natural", the second as "absurd and incredible". Gibbon offers a compromise, down-to-earth solution: "Perhaps", he writes, "[this union] is too rigorously applied to the same persons and the same hour: the example of the virtuous Godfrey awakened the piety of his companions; while they cleansed their bodies they purified their minds; nor

---

98 Gibbon, ibid., p 271; Voltaire, *Histoire des croisades*, p. 17; idem, *Essai sur les moeurs*, 1:559 (where "d'aller faire la guerre" is replaced with "de courir au pillage"). A similarly downbeat paraphrase appears in the *Encyclopédie* of Diderot and d'Alambert: "L'Europe se trouvait pleine de gens qui aimoient la guerre, qui avoient beaucoup de crimes à expier, & qu'on leur proposait d'expier en suivant leur passion dominante: ils prirent la croix & les armes". "Jérusalem", in *Encyclopédie, ou dictionnaire raisonné des sciences, des arts et des métiers* 4 (Paris, 1765), p. 511a.

99 That is, al-Makin (see above, n. 84), Bar-Hebraeus (1226–86), and Abu ʾl-Mahasin Jamal al-Din Yusuf Ibn Taghribirdi (1409–70).

shall I believe that the most ardent in slaughter and rapine were the foremost in the procession to the holy sepulchre."[100]

To read a detailed description of the massacre in English one has to turn to Charles Mills, a modest epigone and part-time critic of Gibbon, who in 1820 published a two-volume history of the crusades. Mills, who regards crusading as a "romantic superstition",[101] emphasizes that the Jerusalem massacre differed from the excesses that a victorious soldiery ordinarily commits. The crusaders acted out of insatiable, remorseless fanaticism: "Under the mental delusion that they were the ministers of God's wrath on disobedient man", they undoubtedly "murdered the Muselmans from principle".[102] In his description of the slaughter in "the Mosque of Omar [*sic*]", Mills slightly overdoes Robert the Monk, relating that "the mutilated carcasses were hurried by the torrents of blood into the court; dissevered arms and hands floated into the current that carried them into contact with bodies to which they had not belonged". In a footnote he quotes the statement of the leaders of the First Crusade that the crusaders rode in the Saracens' blood up to their horses' knees. Then he paraphrases William of Tyre, claiming that "it was not only the lacerated and headless trunks which shocked the sight, but the figures of the victors themselves reeking with the blood of their slaughtered enemies". Yet the sources were evidently not gory enough for Mills, and he saw fit to add a scene of his own: some of the vanquished, he claims, "were thrown from the tops of the churches [*sic*] and of the citadel". Neither does Mills empathize with Godfrey's shift from massacre to devoutness. Having stated that on the irruption into Jerusalem Godfrey "murdered the helpless Saracens", he remarks that his devotion, as well as that of the other crusaders, at the Sepulchre, was an act of piety, "unchristian as it may appear to enlightened days".[103] Later he reports on the subsequent decision of the crusade leaders to kill all remaining "Muselmans" in order to avoid their possible collusion with those of Egypt and, relying on Albert, describes compassionately this latter massacre. He quotes approvingly Fuller's view that, unlike the earlier one, this was a premeditated act.[104]

A variant of the Enlightenment view of the massacre appears in the first volume of Friedrich Wilken's monumental *Geschichte der Kreuzzüge nach morgenländischen und abendländischen Berichten*, published in 1807. Wilken, the Heidelberg professor who – as the title of his book indicates – lays emphasis on the importance of Oriental sources for the history of the crusades, describes the crusaders who committed the massacre as "wild murderers", speaks of the cruelties

---

[100] Gibbon, ibid., pp. 311–12, with n. 117. For Gibbon's acceptance of Mailly's estimate of Jerusalem's population in 1099 see p. 309 n. 113.

[101] Charles Mills, *The History of the Crusades for the Recovery and Possession of the Holy Land*, 2 vols., 4th ed. (London, 1828 [1820]), 1: vi. On Mills' historical work see Siberry, *The New Crusaders* (see above, n. 97), pp. 10–14.

[102] Mills, *History* 1: 257, 259 n. 1.

[103] Ibid., *History* 1:253–54 with n. 1 on p. 253.

[104] Ibid., *History* 1:258–59 with n. 1 on p. 258.

they perpetrated and claims that Raymond's description demonstrates that they delighted in tormenting the infidels before killing them. He writes that according to Fulcher more than 10,000 Muslims were slain in Solomon's Temple, adding in a footnote that Abu 'l-Fida even speaks of 70,000;[105] he then quotes Raymond's sentence on the blood that reached the horses' bridles. Once the crusaders were satiated with Muslim blood, their murderousness led them to round up the Jews in their synagogue and set it on fire – an act of cruelty, Wilken remarks in a footnote, known only from an Oriental author, Elmazin (that is, al-Makin).

Wilken modifies Maimbourg's Godfrey Story. Albert's claim that Godfrey kept away from all killing must be discarded, given that Robert the Monk writes that he hacked down Saracens in vengeance for their misdeeds. Wilken's solution is to portray Godfrey as leaving the "murderous turmoil" while it was still in full swing, circling the walls barefoot with just three followers and then praying at the Sepulchre. All the other crusaders, tired of murdering – "des Mordens müde", possibly a translation of the Abbé de Fleury's "fatiguez du carnage" – then followed his example and "shed tears of devotion at places where the still warm flowing blood reminded them of their cruelties". Where, asks Wilken – probably aware that he is following in Maimbourg's footsteps – has one seen so swift a transition, and he answers that Voltaire was wrong to assume that the transition was impossible: he forgot that the crusaders were warriors who acted out of religious zeal and believed to come closer to heaven with every Muslim head they cut off and to serve God through murder.[106] In other words, the transition that baffles the modern observer was, for the crusaders, merely a shift from one form of devotion to another. Thus Wilken attempts to understand the inner spirit of the crusaders even as he makes abundantly clear that he does not approve of the massacre.

Enlightenment authors were the first to use Oriental chronicles for their accounts of the massacre. From al-Makin they learned about the burning of the Jews in their synagogue; in the chronicles of Abu 'l-Fida and Ibn Taghribirdi they came upon the claims that 70,000 or 100,000 Muslims perished in Jerusalem.[107] But this information was not of central importance. For the most part the Enlightenment authors based their reconstructions of the massacre on the Latin chronicles that were readily available after Bongars printed them in 1611, that is, on the very same sources that had served Maimbourg for his sanctimonial account. Yet they read these sources through the prism of their own values.

---

[105] See n. 84 above.

[106] Friedrich Wilken, *Geschichte der Kreuzzüge nach morgenländischen und abendländischen Berichten*, 7 vols. (Leipzig, 1807–32), 1:293–300; ibid., Beylage (Appendix) 9, pp. 48–49.

[107] Utilization of these Oriental chroniclers by Voltaire, Gibbon and Wilken has been mentioned above. In addition, Mills brings in a footnote the figures of the slain as given by Ibn Taghribirdi and Abu 'l-Fida, but rejects them as unreliable; he also mentions that according to Abu 'l-Fida the massacre lasted seven days: Mills, *History* 1:260, note.

Michaud: *atténuer ou cacher*

Joseph-François Michaud (1767–1839) was an avowed royalist most of his life. Still, many royalist and ecclesiastical readers of his immensely influential *Histoire des croisades* complained that the work, even in its later editions, was coloured by Voltairean attitudes.[108] The objection was not groundless. Michaud's description of the Jerusalem massacre, in the fourth edition of 1825, contains references to crusader fanaticism and barbarism, which are indeed stock Enlightenment denigrations. However, Michaud differs fundamentally from Voltaire. He regards the crusades as a major, heroic chapter of medieval history and attempts to understand the motivations of the crusaders. Having mentioned, like so many before him, that the crusaders entered Jerusalem on the same day of the week and at the same hour as Jesus expired on the cross, he goes on to comment that this coincidence should have evoked feelings of mercy in the crusaders' hearts. Evidently this is what Michaud's own religiosity would have called for; but as the crusaders behaved quite differently, he goes on to explain – echoing Guibert and Robert – that they were irritated by the Saracen menaces, insults and resistance during the siege. This explanation notwithstanding, Michaud expresses his disapproval of the massacre in terms far more pronounced than that of the Christian humanists. At the Mosque of Omar, writes Michaud (meaning the Mosque al-Aqsa), the crusaders "renewed the deplorable scenes that stained the conquest of Titus"; somewhat later he speaks of the "terrible spectacle" that took place there. In a remarkable footnote he is the first to call attention to the differences between the statements of Fulcher, Robert, Raymond and the crusade leaders on the height to which the blood of the slain Saracens had purportedly risen and, commenting on Raymond's claim that the blood reached the horses' bridles, observes that this is a hyperbole which proves "that the Latin historians exaggerated things which they should have toned down or concealed".[109] This singular statement throws light on Michaud's conception of how atrocities should be reported; as we shall see, he himself was to act in conformity with it.

Michaud decries as barbarous the decision of the crusade leaders to kill all surviving Saracens and describes the subsequent massacre in some detail, combining elements of Albert's account of it with those of Raymond's narrative about a single-day massacre. Yet, faithful to his conception, he presents a watered-down version of Albert's account, candidly admitting in a footnote to having done

108 [Valentin] Parisot, "Michaud (Joseph-François)", in *Biographie universelle, ancienne et moderne*, Supplément 74 (Paris, 1843), p. 38; see also p. 33. For a recent appreciation of Michaud that brings in full one of Parisot's remarks see Jean Richard, "De Jean-Baptiste Mailly à Joseph-François Michaud: un moment de l'historiographie des croisades (1774–1841)", *Crusades* 1 (2002), 1–12.

109 Joseph-François Michaud, *Histoire des croisades*, 4th ed., 5 vols. (Paris, 1825–28), 1:442–44, with n. 1 on pp. 443–44, which reads inter alia: "Ces paroles de Raymond d'Agiles sont évidemment une hyperbole, et prouvent que les historiens latins exagéraient les choses qu'ils auraient dû atténuer ou cacher."

so.[110] He goes on to point out that the contemporaneous chroniclers present so many revolting details without any expression of horror or pity – a remark that does less than justice to Albert or William of Tyre. He believes that the carnage lasted a week[111] and though he does not say so, he must be relying for this on some oriental author; we know today that Ibn al-Athir (d. 1233) is the earliest Muslim chronicler to have made this claim.[112] Michaud writes also that oriental historians, in accordance with their Latin counterparts, give the number of Muslims killed in Jerusalem as more than 70,000[113] (this is a mistake – no Latin chronicler mentions this figure, which, too, appears for the first time in Ibn al-Athir's chronicle). It is ironic that Michaud, who militates against exaggerated descriptions of the massacre, uncritically accepts the allegation of Oriental authors writing a century or more after the event that the massacre lasted for a week – that is, more than twice as long as is claimed by Albert, the only western author to assert that it went on for more than two days.

Elsewhere Michaud – true to his conception – is reluctant to dwell on the killings. Speaking of the initial massacre he chooses to paraphrase sentences from Josephus Flavius' account of the Roman conquest of Jewish Jerusalem; later he states that "imagination turns aside with dismay from these scenes of desolation" and thus shields his readers from confronting the sights themselves. He prefers to dwell on the touching scene – *tableau touchant* – in which the crusaders break the chains of Jerusalem's Christians. Then comes Maimbourg's Godfrey Story about "le pieux Godefroy, qui s'était abstenu du carnage après la victoire". The subsequent transition of all crusaders from horrible carnage to tender devotion makes Michaud quote approvingly Maimbourg's observation that they appeared to have "emerged from a lengthy seclusion and from a profound meditation of our Mysteries". Michaud is aware of the discussion about these "inexplicable contrasts" and remarks that "some writers believed to find in them a pretext for blaming the Christian religion, others – no less blind and no less passionate – tried to excuse the deplorable excesses of fanaticism; the impartial historian is satisfied with narrating them, and groans in silence over the weaknesses of human nature".[114] In other words, Michaud positions himself at midpoint between a sanctimonial Maimbourg and a derogatory Voltaire; but having witnessed how he chose to narrate some of the excesses in question, one may assume that he was closer in spirit to the former.

Michaud's *Histoire des croisades*, the first volume of which appeared in 1812, went through several editions and many printings, the latest of which came out in

[110] Ibid., p. 447 n. 1: "Le récit fait par le même Albert d'Aix, des massacres qui durèrent pendant une semaine, et dont nous avons affaibli plutôt qu'exagéré la peinture ...."

[111] Ibid., p. 447 n. 1, p. 449.

[112] Ibn al-Athir, *RHC Or* 4:198; Abu 'l-Fida, *RHC Or* 1:4.

[113] Michaud, *Histoire* 1:450.

[114] Ibid., 1:443–47.

1978.[115] Many authors followed in Michaud's footsteps, usually presenting a picture much less nuanced than his. Indeed, Michaud himself did this in the abridged version of his book, aimed at young readers, that he and his collaborator Jean-Joseph-François Poujoulat published in 1836. Its young readers are not offered even a watered-down description of the massacre scenes; all they are told, in the single relevant paragraph, is that "history has narrated with dismay the carnage of the Muslims in the conquered city"; that it went on for a week; and that 70,000 were killed. Then follows the rather cryptic statement that a barbarous policy, prompted by the difficulty of guarding a large number of prisoners, brought to conclusion the work of vengeance and fanatic fury. The rest of the paragraph deals with the devotion at the Sepulchre, calling attention to the "mysterious contrast" within the self-same men as they turned from slaughter to prayer.[116] Evidently Michaud believed that the young deserve a simpler fare.

Fréderic Delacroix in 1835 and François Valentin in 1837 published short histories of the crusades that depend heavily on, and sometimes literally copy, Michaud. Delacroix, convinced that the preceding, impious century was unable to comprehend the noble nature of the crusades and the solely religious motivation of the crusaders, has little to say about the massacre but copies verbatim Michaud's account about "le pieux Godefroi, qui s'était abstenu du carnage après la victoire" and about the ensuing devotion at the Sepulchre, concluding with Michaud's quote of Maimbourg's observation on the crusaders appearing as if having emerged from seclusion and meditation. Valentin, whose book had gone through thirteen printings by 1868, summarizes Michaud's account of the massacre, adopting his explanation that the crusaders committed it because of their irritation with the Saracens during the siege. Having related that the massacre went on for about a week, with more than 70,000 Muslims slaughtered and the Jews burned in their synagogues [*sic*], Valentin adds that the crusaders spared a multitude of captives, whether out of fatigue with killing – *la fatigue du carnage*, a phrase that goes back to the Abbé Fleury – or out of avarice. The data on the massacre depend on Michaud; the remark on the spared captives most probably goes back to Gibbon; a mistaken identification of the Mosque of Omar with the Temple of the Resurrection is of the author's own making.[117]

Varying degrees of Michaud's influence can be detected in other nineteenth-century French histories of the crusades. The unacknowledged loans from the Master's work may be literal or merely conceptual; disapproval of the massacre may exceed his formulations or be omitted altogether; exact rendering of his factual

---

115 For details on the editions, and for a discussion of their differences, see Richard, "De Jean-Baptiste Mailly à Joseph-François Michaud" (see above, n. 108), pp. 4–8, 11.

116 Joseph-François Michaud and Jean-Joseph-François Poujoulat, *Histoire des croisades abrégée pour la jeunesse*, Bibliothèque de la jeunesse chrétienne (Tours, 1860 [1836]), p. 56.

117 Fréderic Delacroix, *Histoire des croisades* (Paris, 1835), pp. 1–3, 105–7; François Valentin, *Abrégé de l'histoire des croisades (1095–1291)* (Paris, 1837), pp. 79–81.

assertions is not always considered important; in almost all instances his views are presented partially and simplified.[118] Yet despite Michaud's great influence, not all French writers of that period followed in his footsteps. A notable exception is the original, well-documented and unjustly neglected history of the First Crusade by the *ancien magistrat* Jean-François-Aimé Peyré, who describes and condemns the massacre in terms closely recalling those of the age of the Enlightenment.[119] On the other hand, Michaud's disapproval of the massacre and his aversion to dwelling on its gory details reverberate, sometimes in intensified fashion, well into the twentieth century: for instance, Ethel Mary Wilmot-Buxton writes in 1919 that "from the horrors of bloodshed that followed the capture of Jerusalem we can but turn away with disgust"; René Grousset maintains in 1934 that the massacre "est une tache dans l'histoire de la Croisade"; Gennaro Maria Monti asserts in 1940 that "l'eccidio … costituì una vera vergogna per l'esercito cristiano"; Robert Lopez in 1962 remarks that the crusaders "ternirent leur victoire par des massacres dont des rapporteurs sadiques ont d'ailleurs exagéré l'importance"; Zoé Oldenbourg, in 1965, refers to the massacre as a "monstrous act" and a "disaster"; and Régine Pernoud speaks in 1977 of the "page de sang et d'horreur" on which the Jerusalem massacre is inscribed and exclaims: "On souhaiterait, pour l'honneur des croisés, qu'elle n'ait pas été écrite".[120]

Source criticism, aesthetics of massacre reporting, new and old interpretations

Heinrich von Sybel's *Geschichte des ersten Kreuzzugs* of 1841, a landmark in the critique of the sources pertaining to the First Crusade, occupies a prominent place also in the historiography of the Jerusalem massacre. One would have expected von Sybel, who in 1837 participated in Ranke's *Übungen* on the sources of the First

---

[118] See Auguste Gruson, *Histoire des croisades racontée à la jeunesse* (Paris, 1844), pp. 122–25; Charles Farine, *Histoire des croisades*, 4th ed. (Paris, 1863 [1853]), pp. 71–73; J. Lingay, *Histoire des croisades* (Paris, 1861), pp. 25–26; A. de Laporte, *Les croisades et le royaume latin de Jérusalem* (Limoges-Paris, 1863), pp. 48–49; Félix Delacroix, *Histoire de la première croisade* (Limoges, 1876), pp. 75–78.

[119] Jean-François-Aimé Peyré, *Histoire de la première croisade*, 2 vols. (Paris-Lyon, 1859), 2:375–92. Peyré mentions (p. 391) that Matthew of Edessa [d. c. 1136] relates that 65,000 Muslims were killed in the Temple. See now *Armenia and the Crusades, Tenth to Twelfth Centuries: The Chronicle of Matthew of Edessa*, trans. Ara E. Dostourian (Lanham, MD, 1993), p. 173.

[120] Ethel M. Wilmot-Buxton, *The Story of the Crusades* (New York, 1919), p. 98; René Grousset, *Histoire des croisades et du royaume franc de Jérusalem*, 3 vols. (Paris, 1934–36), 1:161; Gennaro M. Monti, *Storia delle crociate* (Genoa, 1988 [1940]), p. 79; Robert S. Lopez, *Naissance de l'Europe* (Paris, 1962), p. 259; Zoé Oldenbourg, *The Crusades*, trans. Anne Carter (London, 1966 [1965]), pp. 137–38; Régine Pernoud, *Les Hommes de la Croisade* (Paris, 1977), p. 80. More recently, Henri Platelle wrote that "malheuresement le succès [of the crusader assault] fut suivi d'un affreux massacre". Henri Platelle, *Les croisades*, Bibliothèque d'histoire du Christianisme 33 (Bruges, 1994), p. 46.

Crusade, to present a carefully annotated attempt at describing the massacre *wie es eigentlich gewesen*, yet he announces that he is refraining from this and that he does so all the more willingly seeing that highly detailed accounts about it can be found everywhere. All he does is to quote Raymond's sentence on the blood in Solomon's Temple reaching the knees of the horsemen and the horses' bridles.[121] Thus in place of Michaud's reluctance to reproduce fully the chroniclers' gory accounts we encounter here their total exclusion.

Von Sybel makes three contributions to the study of the massacre. First, he claims that Albert's account that Godfrey abstained from all murder and was the first to pray at the Sepulchre[122] is contradicted by both Robert and Raymond, who depict Godfrey as amply shedding Saracen blood. Wilken, the first to note the discrepancy between the accounts of Albert and Robert, tried to harmonize them; von Sybel summarily rejects Albert's account as historically untrue. Second, he calls attention to the disagreement between the *Gesta Francorum* and Peter Tudebode with regard to Tancred's role in the killing of the captives on the roof of Solomon's Temple early on 16 July, and leaves the issue undecided. In any case, he claims, Tancred did not give his protection to these people only out of humaneness but also out of an expectation of ransom money. Von Sybel remarks that with regard to both Godfrey and Tancred he must, unfortunately, discard stories that portray them as more humane.[123] Third, von Sybel casts doubts on the reliability of Albert's chronicle in general. Consequently, the most detailed description of the Jerusalem massacre and the only account about the decision of the crusade leaders, on the third day after the conquest, to slaughter all surviving Saracens, lost its credibility.

An examination of subsequent histories of the crusades reveals that von Sybel had a remarkable influence, especially on more learned works. Maimbourg's Godfrey Story disappears altogether. Albert is rarely cited and when he is, the reader is told that his reliability is problematic.[124] The total massacre on the third day after the conquest is no longer mentioned. On the other hand, the reputation of Tancred goes unaffected, probably because von Sybel found the evidence inconclusive.

Whether because of von Sybel's example or not, subsequent descriptions of the Jerusalem massacre do not mention severed limbs floating on waves of blood or sucklings seized by their feet and dashed against walls. Usually some variation of the statement about blood having reached ankles, knees or bridles in Solomon's Temple, or an account of men walking over corpses is considered sufficient for visualizing the massacre – a visualization at one remove from the actual killings and therefore less upsetting.

---

121 Von Sybel (see above, n. 1), p. 490.

122 Here von Sybel unwittingly conflates Albert's account with Maimbourg's Godfrey Story.

123 Ibid., pp. 490–91.

124 See for instance Steven Runciman, *A History of the Crusades*, 3 vols. (Cambridge, 1951–54), 1:286 n. 1.

Bernhard Kugler, an erstwhile student of von Sybel, dedicates to the massacre just one sentence of his history of the crusades published in 1880. "In wildest murder-lust did princes and knights take revenge for plight and dangers endured", he writes, proffering a secularized version of Robert's explanation of the massacre, and immediately provides a single visualization: "'up to the knee of the horsemen and up to the bit of the horses' extended the heaps of corpses and flowed the blood of the killed". Thus, he appears to understand Raymond's statement as meaning that horses waded among bloodied corpses rather than in a sea of blood that reached up to their bridles. More explicitly, Reinhold Röhricht wrote in 1898 that the horses are said to have stood up to their knees, or even up to their bridles, among the corpses.[125] About the same time Auguste Molinier wrote that "the blood in the Church of the Holy Sepulchre [*sic!*] reached the horses' hocks". Ferdinand Chalandon, in 1925, also paraphrasing Raymond, speaks of blood reaching a knight's knees; he adds, on the basis of Fulcher, a scene of cadavers lying in the streets, mostly disembowelled in search of gold coins. In 1928, Louis Bréhier's horses have blood up to their breastband, while Paul Alphandéry in his pathbreaking *La Chrétienté et l'ideé de la Croisade*, published posthumously in 1954, visualizes the massacre by quoting in full Raymond's sentence, which he represents as "renowned". Recently Jean Flori has cited the same sentence.[126] Other historians have preferred to envisage the massacre through the more restrained version of the *Gesta Francorum*, according to which the blood reached only the crusaders' ankles. Among these are René Grousset in 1934, Robert Bossuat in 1937, Paul Rousset in 1957 (who unjustly accuses Albert of cynically describing the slaughter of women and infants), Cécile Morrison in 1969, and Hans Eberhard Mayer in 1965.[127] Ernest Barker, in his long entry on the crusades that was published in the 1910 edition of the *Encyclopaedia Britannica*, and later appeared in book form, chose to create an original scene

---

125 Bernhard Kugler, *Geschichte der Kreuzzüge* (Berlin, 1880), p. 60; Reinhold Röhricht, *Geschichte der Kreuzzüge im Umriss* (Innsbruck, 1898), p. 50. It may be noted that de Laporte understood Raymond's sentence in a similar manner, for he wrote "les rues, au rapport d'un chroniqueur, étaient tellement jonchées de cadavres, que les chevaux avaient du sang jusqu'au poitrail". A. de Laporte, *Les croisades* (see above, n. 118), p. 48.

126 Auguste Molinier, "Croisade", in *La Grande Encyclopédie. Inventaire raisonné des sciences, des letters et des arts* 13 (Paris, n.d.), p. 442; Ferdinand Chalandon, *Histoire de la première croisade jusqu'à l'élection de Godefroi de Bouillon* (Paris, 1925), p. 275; Louis Bréhier, *L'Eglise et l'Orient au moyen âge: Les croisades* (Paris, 1928), p. 82; Paul Alphandéry and Alphonse Dupront, *La Chrétienté et l'idée de croisade* (Paris, 1995 [1954–59]), p. 123. Jean Flori, *La Première Croisade. L'Occident chrétien contre l'Islam (Aux origines des ideologies occidentales)* (Brussels, 1997 [1992]), pp. 101–2; idem, *Pierre l'Ermite et la première croisade* (Paris, 1999), p. 419. Dana Munro opted for the version of the letter of the crusade leaders, adding some sentences from the *Gesta*: Dana C. Munro, *The Kingdom of the Crusaders* (New York and London, 1936), pp. 55–56.

127 René Grousset, *Histoire des croisades et du royaume franc de Jérusalem*, 3 vols. (Paris, 1934–36), 1:158; Robert Bossuat, *Les croisades* (Paris, 1937), p. 48; Paul Rousset, *Histoire des croisades* (Paris, 1957), pp. 104–5; Cécile Morrison, *Les croisades* (Paris, 1992 [1969]), p. 32; Hans E. Mayer, *Geschichte der Kreuzzüge* (Stuttgart, 1976 [1965]), p. 67.

based on Raymond as well as on the *Gesta*. "The slaughter was terrible", he wrote, "the blood of the conquered ran down the streets, until men splashed in blood as they rode".[128]

What lies behind this consistent avoidance from direct descriptions of the massacre and the opting for less disturbing visualizations of it? One possible explanation is that graphic scenes like that of infants seized by the soles of their feet and hurled against door lintels, or of girls throwing themselves at the crusaders' feet and begging them, weeping and wailing, for their lives, were no longer considered aesthetically appropriate; in some cases they might also have been at odds with an author's sanctimonial vision of crusading. An alternative explanation is that the most explicit scenes appear in the chronicles of Albert and Robert, neither of whom was present at the massacre, and therefore lost importance once the critical study of sources led to a preference for eyewitness reports. Fortunately it is possible to test the relative validity of these two explanations, because the account of Raymond – undoubtedly an eyewitness – not only contains the sentence about blood reaching knees and bridles, but also tells about wounded Saracens forced to leap from towers and others subjected to prolonged torture and burnt to death. Yet Raymond's graphic scenes of killing are almost totally absent from academic histories of the crusades written in post-von Sybel times. Thus whereas Raymond's account is quoted in full in the popular history of the crusades published by Thomas Andrew Archer and Charles Letheridge Kingsford in 1894, in the *Atlas of the Crusades* of 1991, which quotes sentences from the self-same account, the passage depicting actual scenes of killing is not reproduced.[129] Hence it is plausible to assume that the reluctance to display such scenes indeed reflects a new aesthetic sensibility.

Of the above-mentioned historians, only Röhricht, Archer and Kingsford and Chalandon mention briefly the second-day massacre of the 300 Saracens on the roof of Solomon's Temple on 16 July. Archer and Kingsford relate that "the rumour went about that Tancred had been luring the fugitives to their destruction", and Chalandon claims that the *Gesta Francorum* (in reality it is Peter Tudebode) presents Tancred as responsible for that massacre. Several historians mention the surrender of the Fatimid commander, with Archer and Kingsford regarding Raymond of Saint Gilles' acceptance of that surrender as a unique sign of "an honourable compassion for the conquered"; on the other hand, Nicolae Iorga, evidently misunderstanding Fulcher, claims that even the Turks, Arabs and Ethiopians who believed they were protected by the agreement between the commander and Raymond were

---

[128] Ernest Barker, "Crusades", *Encyclopaedia Britannica*, 11th ed., 29 vols. (Cambridge, 1910–11), 7:529a; idem, *The Crusades* (New York, 1971 [1923]), p. 23. Similarly, Claude Conder wrote: "The feet of the palfreys trod deep in blood, as the knights rode in upon the pavement of the Temple". Claude R. Conder, *The Latin Kingdom of Jerusalem, 1099 to 1291 AD* (London, 1897), p. 67.

[129] Thomas A. Archer and Charles L. Kingsford, *The Crusades: The Story of the Latin Kingdom of Jerusalem* (London and New York, 1894), p. 91; *Atlas of the Crusades*, ed. Jonathan Riley-Smith (New York and Oxford, 1991), p. 30.

massacred.[130] The motif that recurs time and again is the one first highlighted by Maimbourg in 1675: the prayer in the Church of the Holy Sepulchre in the wake of the massacre. The swift transition is for the most part no longer a moral problem to be pondered upon, but the temporal sequence is underscored. For instance, Archer and Kingsford write that the crusaders, "weary with slaughter", went to the Sepulchre, whereas Chalandon says that, "fatigués de tuer", they went there still covered with blood. In both cases, the expression ultimately goes back either to the Abbé Fleury's "fatiguez du carnage", or to the Abbé de Vertot's "fatigués du carnage", or to Wilken's "des Mordens müde". On the other hand, Adolf Waas, in an innovative book of 1956, presents an ingenious though totally unfounded description of the transition: the knights, he claims, were ultimately filled with disgust by their own blood-stained hands and formed a large penitential procession![131]

It is René Grousset who provides, in his unjustly neglected trilogy of 1934–36, a novel analysis of the massacre. In an attempt to explain its reasons, he points to the acts of desecration the Muslims had committed "in cold blood" during the siege, like covering crosses with spittle. As for the burning of the Jews in the synagogue, Grousset reminds his readers that, under Fatimid rule, the Jewish element (*l'élement juif*) had taken part in Muslim massacres of Jerusalem's Christians. This is a strange argument, one that assumes the crusaders were knowledgeable of details in Jerusalem's history under Muslim rule.[132] As for the massacre of the Muslims, Grousset provides what he considers to be proof that not all were slaughtered: the establishment of the suburb of al-Salihiyya near Damascus by Muslim refugees who left Jerusalem at the time of the conquest.[133] (In reality, however, al-Salihiyya was founded in 1161 by the Banu Qudama, Muslims who left the Frankish-ruled area of Nablus from 1156 onward.)[134] Nevertheless, Grousset concludes that the massacre of 15–16 July did stain the crusade. Moreover, it was a political blunder, for it horrified the world of Islam and, in Palestine, rendered the coastal towns unwilling

---

130 Röhricht, *Geschichte*, p. 50; Archer and Kingsford, *The Crusades*, p. 92; Chalandon, *Histoire*, p. 277; Nicolae Iorga, *Brève histoire des croisades et de leurs fondations en Terre Sainte* (Paris, 1924), p. 66.

131 Adolf Waas, *Geschichte der Kreuzzüge*, 2 vols. (Freiburg, 1956), 1:153. Waas explains: "So nahe können die Gegensätze an Tagen solcher Steigerung des religiösen Gefühls und Kampfeswillens liegen."

132 Grousset, *Histoire* (see above, n. 127), 1:161. Zoé Oldenbourg, obliquely referring to Grousset's argument, believes that although the crusaders may have been aware of those massacres, they were avenging Christ not local Christians: Oldenbourg, *The Crusades* (see above, n. 120), pp. 137–38.

133 Grousset, *Histoire* 1:160 n. 5. Grousset – who relies on an inexact summary of sources by René Dussaud in 1927 – was to be followed by Joshua Prawer in 1963 and 1969, by Zoé Oldenbourg in 1965, by Jacques Heers in 1995 and by Jean Richard in 1996 and 1999.

134 See Henri Laoust, *Le précis de droit d'Ibn Qudama* (Beirut, 1950), pp. xi–xii; the author relies on two works on al-Salihiyya edited by Muhammad A. Duhman. On the exodus of the Banu Qudama see Emmanuel Sivan, "Refugiés syro-palestiniens au temps des croisades", *Revue des études islamiques* 35 (1967), 138–39; Joseph Drory, "Hanbalis of the Nablus Region in the Eleventh and Twelfth Centuries", *Asian and African Studies* 22 (1988), 93–112. See also Postscript.

to submit peacefully to Frankish rule and hence having to be conquered in a prolonged process. Raymond's acceptance of the Muslim governor's surrender and Tancred's protection of the Muslims on the roof of al-Aqsa attest, according to Grousset, that several crusade leaders understood that for political reasons the massacre should be limited. But the *esprit croisé* proved to be stronger than the incipient *esprit colonial*. William of Tyre's statement that the massacre could have imbued the victors themselves with disgust and horror shows that he was instilled with the latter *esprit* and fully comprehended the necessities of a colonial situation.[135] Grousset's reasoning was echoed by Gennaro Maria Monti, who in 1940 wrote that the massacre was a veritable disgrace besides having rendered impossible a non-violent conquest of Palestine, and by Paul Rousset, who in 1957 stated, in a formulation obviously rooted in Talleyrand's famous dictum, that the massacre "was not only a crime but still more a serious political mistake".[136] Yet the indebtedness to Grousset was not spelled out.

Steven Runciman, in the first volume of his *History of the Crusades*, which appeared in 1951, perhaps unwittingly follows Grousset on the latter issue when he claims that in the long run the massacre was detrimental to Frankish rule in the Levant: "Amongst the Moslems, who had been ready hitherto to accept the Franks as another factor in the tangled politics of the time, there was henceforward a clear determination that the Franks must be driven out. It was this bloodthirsty proof of Christian fanaticism that recreated the fanaticism of Islam. When later, wiser Latins in the East sought to find some basis on which Christian and Moslem could work together, the memories of the massacre stood always in their way." At the same time Runciman claims that "many even of the Christians were horrified" by the massacre[137] – a sweeping statement that, soothing as it may be to some readers, is unsubstantiated, and unsubstantiable, by any source. Indeed, it should be pointed out that Runciman's trilogy, which is undoubtedly the most popular twentieth-century history of the crusades and has stimulated cohorts of history students to do research on them, contains some glaring examples of misunderstanding or plain error. [138]

---

135 Grousset, *Histoire* 1:161–63. Grousset's paraphrase of William's renders it more forceful than it really is; where William writes, "Tanta autem per urbem erat strages hostium tantaque sanguinis effusio, ut etiam victoribus *posset* tedium et horrorem ingerere" (WT 8.19, p. 411), Grousset translates, "La ville présentait en spectacle un tel carnage d'ennemis, une telle effusion de sang, que les vainqueurs *ne pouvaient qu'être* frappés d'horreur et de dégout" (p. 161).

136 Monti, *Storia delle crociate* (see above, n. 120), pp. 78–79; Rousset, *Histoire des croisades* (see above, n. 127), p. 104. Likewise, Henri Platelle writes in 1994 that the massacre "était à la fois un crime et une faute politique". Platelle, *Les croisades* (see above, n. 120), p. 46.

137 Runciman, *History* (see above, n. 124), 1:287.

138 See Kedar, "Crusade Historians" (see above, n. 1), pp. 19–20; idem, "The Forcible Baptisms" (see above, n. 1), pp. 192–94; idem, "On the Origins of the Earliest Laws of Frankish Jerusalem: The Canons of the Council of Nablus, 1120", *Speculum* 74 (1999), 323 n. 59. See also Susan Edgington, "The First Crusade: Reviewing the Evidence", in *The First Crusade: Origins and Impact*, ed. Jonathan Phillips (Manchester, 1997), pp. 66–71; Thomas F. Madden, *Enrico Dandolo and the Rise of Venice* (Baltimore and London, 2003), p. 68.

Runciman bases his account on the eyewitnesses and on Fulcher and therefore the massacre, as that in Grousset, takes place only on 15 and 16 July. The account is devoid of graphic details. Like so many of his predecessors, Runciman uses Raymond's statement on the blood reaching men's knees – but he manages to turn the sentence into a personal account, writing that "when Raymond of Aguilers later that morning went to visit the Temple area, he had to pick his way through corpses and blood that reached up to his knees".[139] Evidently we are confronted with a master storyteller. Runciman then turns his attention to Jerusalem's Jews. He knows – but does not tell his readers whence – that "they were held to have aided the Moslems" and goes on to relate that the crusaders burnt them all in the chief synagogue, to which they had fled. The reader cannot fail to understand that the help the Jews extended to the Muslims brought upon them the crusaders' harsh punishment.[140] (The reasoning recalls Grousset's remark, at precisely the same juncture, that in Fatimid times *l'élement juif* had taken part in massacres of Jerusalem's Christians.) Yet nothing of this – Jewish help, Jewish flight, chief synagogue – does one find in the account of Ibn al-Qalanisi, the twelfth-century Damascene chronicler, to whom Runciman refers in the relevant footnote.

The detached tone characteristic of academic references to the massacre in the post-von Sybel era is not shared by authors, mostly non-academic, who adopt a condemnatory stance resembling or exceeding that of Fuller and Voltaire. For example, George W. Cox, the author of an important work on comparative mythology whose history of the crusades appeared in London in 1874 and reached a seventh edition in 1887, observes sarcastically that "the forms of Christian knights hacking and hewing the bodies of the living and the dead furnished a pleasant commentary on the sermon of Urban in Clermont". In the same vein he goes on to comment that "from the duties of slaughter these disciples of the Lamb of God passed to those of devotion". Cox maintains that a second, deliberate and total massacre was resolved upon on 16 July; he paraphrases Albert's description of the killings and refers to them acidly as "this great act of faith and devotion".[141] Some critics of the Catholic Church writing after World War II go still further in their appraisals of the massacre. The Viennese publicist and historian Friedrich Heer, writing in 1969, indignantly observes that it did not occur to the author of the *Gesta Francorum* or to Raymond, "who saw with their own eyes mounds of women's and children's corpses", that they were witnessing the shedding of innocent blood. This insensitivity to pain and disregard of murder corresponds to that of erstwhile Nazi

[139] Runciman, *History* 1:287. The personalization of the account allows Runciman to steer clear of Raymond's claim that the blood reached the horses' bridles. Probably following Runciman, Friedrich Heer writes: "Raimund von Aguilers muß sich seinen Weg zum Tempelviertel durch Leichen und Blutströme bahnen, die ihm bis an die Knie reichen". Friedrich Heer, *Kreuzzüge –gestern, heute, morgen?* (Luzern and Frankfurt/M, 1969), p. 56.

[140] Loc. cit.

[141] George W. Cox, *The Crusades* (New York, 1889 [1874]), pp. 74–76. On the author see Siberry, *The New Crusaders* (see above, n. 97), pp. 21–22, 28.

killers who, years after their defeat, placidly consider themselves innocent; like the crusaders, they do not regard the Other as human. Moreover, denominational historians who played down or glossed over past atrocities, may have contributed to the obfuscation of conscience in our times.[142] And the author and translator Hans Wollschläger, mounting a frontal attack on the Christian Church in his 1973 history of the crusades, evokes the massacre with a string of harrowing quotations from the chronicles and introduces the most startling of them, that of Albert of Aachen on the final killings, with the wry remark: "Vor dieser Ausbreitung des Christentums gab es kein Entrinnen." Wollschläger, who accepts at face value the claim of oriental chroniclers that the crusaders killed in Jerusalem between sixty to seventy thousand people, concludes his account of the massacre by assigning Pope Urban II a perpetual place among humanity's mass murderers.[143] And the East German author Martin Erbstösser in 1977 quotes an unnamed – and, as far as I know, unnameable – Christian chronicler who purportedly reports that the patriarch [*sic!*] murdered all infidels he encountered on his way to the Sepulchre; there he washed his hands, celebrated Mass and remarked that never had he offered God a more pleasing sacrifice![144] It is noteworthy that writers of this persuasion do their best to conjure up the massacre with graphic accounts of killings that their academic contemporaries tend to shun. The scene of the Jews being burnt alive in their synagogue (repeatedly upgraded to "chief synagogue") often gets pride of place here – as it did in Voltaire's *Histoire des croisades*.[145]

The Cairo Geniza, Albert of Aachen and Apocalypse 14:20

In 1952, after centuries of dependence on the same accounts about the massacre, historians were confronted with new contemporary evidence: two letters written about nine months after the crusader conquest of Jerusalem were discovered by Shelomo Dov Goitein in the Cairo Geniza. The first of these was sent by the elders of the Jewish community of Ascalon to their coreligionists in Alexandria. In it the elders report about the ransoming of Jerusalemite Jews in which they have been engaged and call for further funds. It is possible to deduce from their letter that a few

---

142 Heer, *Kreuzzüge*, pp. 55–58.

143 Hans Wollschläger, *Die bewaffneten Wallfahrten gen Jerusalem: Geschichte der Kreuzzüge* (Zurich, 1973), pp. 37–41; see also pp. 224–25. Wollschläger appears to be the first author to have noted Fulcher of Chartres' important eyewitness report, hidden in Hagenmeyer's apparatus, on the stench of the rotting Saracen cadavers more than five months after the massacre. Walter Zöllner speaks likewise of "mass murder", but – with the exception of placing the liberation of Jerusalem between inverted commas – his account is factual: Walter Zöllner, *Geschichte der Kreuzzüge* (Berlin, 1979 [1977]), pp. 83–84.

144 Martin Erbstösser, *Die Kreuzzüge: Eine Kulturgeschichte* (Leipzig, 1977), p. 96. English and French translations appeared in 1978; I have not seen the revised German edition of 1996.

145 The burning in the synagogue has become central also in mainstream works, replacing the blood-up-to-heels scene as the single visualization of the massacre. See for instance Michel Balard, *Les Croisades* (Paris, 1988), p. 30.

Jews escaped on the second and third days after the conquest and managed to leave Jerusalem in the retinue of the Fatimid governor to whom Raymond of Saint Gilles had granted safe conduct; that a few others were captured by the Franks but later succeeded in escaping while others remained in captivity. Of the latter, some were killed by various kinds of torture "out of sheer lust to murder" in front of others who were left alive; a few were taken to Antioch; some chose to gain freedom by turning Christian, but most were ransomed by the community of Ascalon and sent on to Egypt. The number of the ransomed ones must have been sizeable, for after several groups had left Ascalon for Egypt, more than twenty such people remained in Ascalon. Also ransomed were 230 Bible codices, 100 other volumes and eight Torah scrolls. The elders of Ascalon point out that they have not heard that "the accursed ones who are called Ashkenaz violated or raped women, as others do"; Goitein identified these Ashkenazi crusaders as Lotharingians, followers of Godfrey, who – unlike Raymond of Saint Gilles and his Frenchmen – purportedly refrained from raping women. The second Geniza letter was written by a Jew from the Maghrib who was waiting in Egypt for a chance to go on pilgrimage to Jerusalem. His account of the crusader conquest of Jerusalem is succinct and ties in with the one that can be pieced together from the letter of the Ascalon elders: "The Franks arrived and killed everybody in the city, whether of Ishmael or Israel; and the few who survived the slaughter were made prisoners. Some of these have been ransomed since, while others are still in captivity in all parts of the world".[146]

These two letters written so shortly after the crusader conquest of Jerusalem, and especially the letter of the Ascalon elders who must have had detailed knowledge about it, make possible the resolution of some of the issues on which the crusader eyewitnesses and later Latin and Arabic chronicles diverge. First, the massacre was not total; there were some Jews – and one may assume also some Muslims – who managed to escape. Others were taken captive but succeeded in getting away. Still others turned Christian, probably under crusader pressure. (Indeed, Albert recounts that during the siege the crusaders took a Muslim nobleman prisoner, tried to convert him to Christianity and, when he refused, decapitated him in front of David's Tower.)[147] Some captives were ransomed by their coreligionists. Second, a captive could not be sure that his life would be spared. Some captives were tortured

---

[146] Goitein first edited the letters, written in Arabic but using the Hebrew alphabet and interspersed with Hebrew or Aramaic phrases, in a Hebrew article published in *Zion* 17 (1951–52), 129–47. For an English version that gives only the translation of the letters see Shelomo D. Goitein, "Contemporary Letters on the Capture of Jerusalem by the Crusaders", *Journal of Jewish Studies* 3 (1952), 162–77, with the quotation from the second letter appearing on p. 176. For a re-edition of the letters with some additions see idem, *Palestinian Jewry in Early Islamic and Early Crusader Times in the Light of the Geniza Documents*, ed. Joseph Hacker (Jerusalem, 1980), pp. 231–53 [in Hebrew]. The letters were re-edited once again, with several divergences in text and translation, by Moshe Gil, *Palestine during the First Muslim Period (634–1099)*, 3 vols. (Tel Aviv, 1983), 3:440–43, 445–55 [in Hebrew]. For the first letter I use Goitein's final translation (see below, n. 160).

[147] Albert of Aachen 6.5 in *RHC Oc* 4:469.

and killed. (This is corroborated by the Muslim sources which relate that the Franks took captive Abu ʾl Qasim Makki b. ʿAbd al-Salam al-Rumayli al-Maqdisi, an author of tracts on the praises of Jerusalem and Hebron. The crusaders were ready to set him free for a ransom of 1,000 dinars; but when the sum was not forthcoming, they stoned him to death near Beirut on 1 September 1099.)[148] Third, Jerusalem's inhabitants faced danger not only on the day of the conquest but also on the second and third days after it. Fourth, the Fatimid governor and garrison left for Ascalon not on 15 July but two days later. This revision of the accepted narrative ties in with the temporal sequence in Fulcher's account, where the garrison leaves *after* Godfrey's election as ruler of Jerusalem; with William of Tyre's remark that the garrison surrendered when it was unable to endure the siege any longer; and with Ibn al-Athir's report that the garrison fought for three days before surrendering.[149]

The second and third points are partially congruent with Albert's account that the crusader leaders decided, on the third day after the conquest, to kill all remaining Saracens and Gentiles, whether captive or already ransomed. The letter of the Ascalon elders proves that some captives were indeed put to death, though not necessarily on the third day. It indicates also that on the third day Jerusalemite Jews still felt endangered and attempted to flee. In other words, the letter may be regarded as supporting Albert's three-day-massacre scenario. On the other hand, the letter refutes Albert's claim that all captives were put to death – unless one assumes that the decision of the crusader leaders pertained only to Saracens.

How did historians of the crusades deal with this new information from the Geniza? The first major history of the crusades to appear after Goitein's discovery was Joshua Prawer's *History of the Crusader Kingdom in the Land of Israel*, published in Hebrew in 1963. Although Prawer dwells at length on the fate of Jerusalem's Jews during the crusader conquest, he barely utilizes the recently discovered Geniza letters. Tacitly summarizing articles he published in 1946 and 1947,[150] Prawer relates that Jerusalem's Jewish quarter was situated just to the south of the stretch of the wall attacked by Godfrey of Bouillon and he claims that Jews

---

148 Franz Rosenthal, *History of Muslim Historiography*, 2nd ed. (Leiden, 1968), pp. 464, 468; Emmanuel Sivan, "The Beginnings of the Fadaʾil al-Quds Literature", *Israel Oriental Studies* 1 (1971), 264; Moshe Gil, *A History of Palestine, 634–1099*, trans. Ethel Broido (Cambridge, 1992), pp. 424–25 (but Gil's account of the 1099 conquest [ibid., pp. 827–28] is faulty on many counts). Mujir al-Din, writing in 1496, reports that the captive was clubbed to death near Antioch; as he gives 432H (=AD 1040–41) as his date of birth, he must have been about sixty years old: *Histoire de Jérusalem et d'Hébron*, trans. Henry Sauvaire (Paris, 1876), p. 65.

149 Fulcher, *Historia* 1.30.1–3, pp. 306–9; WT 8.24, p. 418; Ibn al-Athir in *RHC Or* 1:198. In addition, Caffaro – who was in Jerusalem in 1101 but wrote in the 1150s – relates that David's Tower surrendered after twenty days: Caffaro, *De liberatione civitatum Orientis*, ed. Luigi T. Belgrano in *Annali Genovesi di Caffaro e de' suoi continuatori*, 5 vols. (Genoa and Rome, 1890–1929), 1:110.

150 Joshua Prawer, "The Jews in the Latin Kingdom of Jerusalem", *Zion* 11 (1946), 38–82; idem, "The Vicissitudes of the Jewish Quarter of Jerusalem in the Arabic Period", *Zion* 12 (1947), 136–48 (both in Hebrew). The argument, based on pre-1099 Geniza passages and on the poem of Gilo of Toucy, is repeated in 1988 in idem, *The History of the Jews* (see above, n. 26), pp. 17–22.

were among the defendants of that stretch. When Godfrey and his men irrupted into the city, he writes, the Muslims and the Jews retreated to the Temple Mount, probably intending to make their last stand there. When this hope was lost, the Jews decided to follow the example of their ancestors: they gathered in their synagogue (or synagogues) to plead with their celestial father. The crusaders locked them in and burnt them alive. (It is instructive to compare Prawer's fighting and retreating Jews with those of Runciman, who were "held to have aided" the Muslims and "fled in a body to their chief synagogue".) Prawer then turns his attention to Tancred's conquest of al-Aqsa and Raymond's advance on the citadel and goes on to say that the crusaders acted in frenzy for two days, committing a massacre the city had not witnessed since its conquest by Titus. "It seems that on the morrow of the victory no Muslim remained alive. He who was not killed fell into captivity, but such were few" – a *non sequitur* resembling the statement in the letter of the Maghribi Jew found in the Geniza, which, however, Prawer does not utilize. The Jews who remained alive were sold into slavery. Italian and Egyptian Jews attempted to ransom them, and the latter brought the redeemed captives to Ascalon and thence to Egypt.[151] Only the last statement is based (somewhat inaccurately and without reference) on the letters Goitein had published more than a decade earlier. In a detailed review published in 1964, Goitein took Prawer to task for this "incredible" neglect.[152] Nevertheless, Prawer did not utilize the Geniza letters in the French translation of his book that appeared in 1969–70, though he did so, and in great detail, in his last book, which came out in 1988.[153]

Goitein's discoveries were utilized more thoroughly by Hans Eberhard Mayer in his widely known short history of the crusades that first appeared in 1965. Mayer, who stands out for his dispassionate, critical attitude – at one point he mentions rather approvingly the enlightened sceptics who regard crusading as "the folly to fight for 200 years for what is after all an empty hole in a rock"[154] – considers the massacre "an atrocious bloodbath" and "a mass murder", asserting that, with the

151 Joshua Prawer, *History of the Crusader Kingdom in the Land of Israel*, 2 vols. (Jerusalem, 1963), pp. 141–42. Prawer's account of the fate of the Jews was reproduced, without acknowledgement and with some embellishments, by Amin Maalouf, *Les croisades vues par les Arabes* (Paris, 1983), pp. 8–9.

152 *Speculum* 39 (1964), 743–44. The neglect was shared by other authors of works on the crusades, like Zoé Oldenbourg in 1965, Friedrich Heer in 1969, Hans Wollschläger in 1973, Walter Zöllner and Martin Erbstösser in 1977, Jacques Heers and Gerhard Armanski in 1995, and Giosuè Musca in 1999. For an early utilization of Goitein's discovery see Lopez, *Naissance de l'Europe* (see note 120 above), p. 129.

153 Joshua Prawer, *Histoire du royaume latin de Jérusalem*, trans. Gérard Nahon, 2 vols. (Paris, 1969–70), 1:230–32; idem, *The History of the Jews* (see above, n. 26), pp. 26–33, where on p. 28 Prawer rightly observes that the Geniza letter corroborates the three-day-massacre scenario and, in footnote 35, calls attention to the agreement, with regard to the date of the garrison's departure, between the Geniza letter, Fulcher of Chartres and Ibn al-Athir. (However, Fulcher does not "clearly imply" that it departed on the third day after the conquest).

154 Mayer, *Geschichte* (see above, n. 127), p. 261; for a somewhat different English translation see idem, *The Crusades*, trans. John Gillingham (New York and Oxford, 1972), p. 281. The chapter containing this passage does not appear in the book's later version: *Geschichte der Kreuzzüge*, 6th rev. ed. (Stuttgart, 1985); *The Crusades*, 2nd ed., trans. John Gillingham (Oxford, 1988).

exception of the Fatimid governor and his retinue, no Jerusalemite Muslim was spared. He presents two details derived from the letter of the Ascalon elders as interpreted by Goitein: first, that the Lotharingian crusaders stood out for not having violated any Jewish woman; second, that the Franks sold "the valuable library of the Jewish community" to Ascalon. Interestingly, Mayer does not mention that the Ascalon elders ransomed quite a number of captive Jerusalemite Jews.[155]

In contrast, Jean Richard in his *L'Esprit de la croisade* of 1969 claims – evidently on the basis of Goitein's discoveries – that the Jews of Jerusalem were "systematically" directed to Ascalon.[156] Richard, who presents the crusade as "the touchstone of a Christian faith whose liveliness and depth provide moving lessons for today's Christian",[157] attempts to play down the extent of the Jerusalem massacre. He concedes that Saracens were massacred, especially in the Haram al-Sharif, which was taken by force, but he regards this massacre as normal for a town taken by assault. Since the burning of the Jews in their synagogue reported by Ibn al-Qalanisi is not mentioned in the letters published by Goitein, Richard assumes that one may now discard the "legend" of the synagogue massacre.[158]

Richard's assumption is congruent with Goitein's own initial view. In his 1964 review of Prawer's book Goitein remarks that not only does the burning go unmentioned in the two Geniza letters, but the plunder of the large number of synagogue books that were later ransomed by the Jews of Ascalon renders the story of the burning unlikely.[159] But in 1975 Goitein discovered a further Geniza letter, written by a Rabbanite Jew, describing the reaction of the Nagid Mevorakh b. Seᶜadya, the head of Egypt's Jewry, to the news about the crusader conquest of Jerusalem. The letter suggests that the conquest took place just two weeks earlier; if so, it is the earliest account on the conquest in any language. According to this account as interpreted by Goitein, a "great disaster" befell the Rabbanite Jews of Jerusalem: their synagogue was burnt, many members of the community lost their lives, Torah scrolls and some members were captured, and captives were subjected to manifold vexations while awaiting ransom.[160] Thus it becomes evident

155 Mayer, *Geschichte*, pp. 66–67; 6th ed., pp. 57–58; idem, *The Crusades*, pp. 60–61; 2nd ed., p. 56. In this later version the Lotharingians continue to be singled out for refraining from rape and not, as Goitein claimed in his 1982 article (see below, n. 159), the crusaders in general. In the other well-known brief history of crusading the massacre goes unmentioned: see Jonathan Riley-Smith, *The Crusades: A Short History* (New Haven and London, 1987), p. 34. In a recent short history the massacre is briefly described, but Raymond of Saint Gilles is presented as having condemned it: Thomas F. Madden, *A Concise History of the Crusades* (Lanham, Maryland, 1999), p. 36.

156 Jean Richard, *L'Esprit de la croisade* (Paris, 1969), p. 32.

157 Ibid., p. 53.

158 Ibid., p. 32.

159 *Speculum* 39 (1964), 743.

160 Partial text (Arabic interspersed with Hebrew phrases) and modern Hebrew translation in Goitein, *Palestinian Jewry* (see above, n. 146), pp. 254–56; partial English translation in idem, "Geniza Sources for the Crusader Period: A Survey", in *Outremer*, pp. 309–11; full text with modern Hebrew translation in Gil, *Palestine during the First Muslim Period* (see above, n. 146), 3:433–36.

that a Jerusalem synagogue was indeed burnt, but it was the Rabbanite one; the letter neither corroborates nor disproves Ibn al-Qalanisi's report that Jews were burnt in it. Later Goitein realized that the Ascalon elders were Karaite Jews, a fact that casts light on why their letter does not mention the burning of the Rabbanite synagogue.[161]

In addition, an examination of other sources led Goitein to the conclusion that the "Ashkenaz" in the letter of the Ascalon elders are not Lotharingians but crusaders in general; that is, the elders point out that the *crusaders*, unlike previous Muslim conquerors, did not rape Jewish women. In the only humorous remark in the vast literature on the massacre, Goitein remarks: "I apologize to Raymond and his Frenchmen".[162] He believes that in Jerusalem the crusaders brought to an end a Jewish community that was dwindling even before their arrival. He also supposes that the crusaders did not run berserk but methodically plundered Jewish – and probably also Muslim – books. Yet he does not play down the killings. "There was a gruesome massacre, no doubt", he writes, "but it was not as all-embracing as the summary reports of the chroniclers led us to believe."[163]

The discovery of the Geniza letters was one of three twentieth-century developments that are of import for the historiography of the massacre. The second was the rehabilitation of Albert of Aachen, whose credibility had been assailed, back in 1841, by Heinrich von Sybel and whose chronicle had thenceforward been much neglected. In 1966, Peter Knoch forcefully argued that, contrary to von Sybel's opinion, Albert's chronicle constitutes one of the best-informed sources on the First Crusade, because Albert relied on a lost Lotharingian chronicle written by an eyewitness as well as on oral reports by returning crusaders. More recently, Susan Edgington persuasively contended that Albert's chronicle is of critical importance inasmuch as it is entirely independent of other Latin sources and provides a Lotharingian point of view that countervails their "Frankish" bias.[164] As for Albert's

---

[161] Goitein, *Palestinian Jewry*, pp. 238, 250; idem, "Geniza Sources", pp. 311–12. Goitein's final translation of the full letter of the Karaite elders of Ascalon (which differs on several points from the translation he published in 1952) appeared posthumously in 1988: idem, *A Mediterranean Society: The Jewish Communities of the Arab World as Portrayed in the Documents of the Cairo Geniza*, 6 vols. (Berkeley, 1967–93), 5:374–79.

[162] Goitein, "Geniza Sources", p. 312 n. 30. It should be noted, though, that some Muslim poets accuse the crusaders of having violated Muslim women: see the anonymous poet quoted by Carole Hillenbrand, "The First Crusade: The Muslim Perspective", in *The First Crusade*, ed. Phillips (see above, n. 138), p. 137 and, more obliquely, al-Abiwardi (d. 1113), quoted by Ibn al-Athir in *RHC Or* 1:200–1 and translated in Francesco Gabrieli, *Arab Historians of the Crusades*, trans. E.J. Costello (Berkeley, 1969), p. 12.

[163] Goitein, *Palestinian Jewry* (see above, n. 146), p. 229; idem, "Geniza Sources", p. 308; idem, "al-Kuds", in *Encyclopaedia of Islam*, 2nd ed., 5: 330.

[164] See Peter Knoch, *Studien zu Albert von Aachen. Der erste Kreuzzug in der deutschen Chronistik* (Stuttgart, 1966); the hypothesis about a lost Lotharingian chronicle was first proposed by Bernhard Kugler in 1880. Susan Edgington, "The First Crusade" (see above, n. 138), pp. 61–73; the author doubts the lost-Lotharingian-chronicle hypothesis, arguing instead that Albert gathered oral and written information from returning crusaders and fused them into a narrative of his own. See also eadem, "Albert

account of the Jerusalem massacre, disregarded by historians since 1841, the Geniza evidence, as we have just seen, is partially congruous with it.

The third noteworthy contribution to the historiography of the massacre was made in 1969 by John Hugh Hill and Laurita L. Hill. The two pointed out that Raymond's oft-quoted statement that in Solomon's Temple the crusaders rode in blood "usque ad frenos equorum" is based on Apocalypse 14:20, which reads: "et calcatus est lacus extra civitatem et exivit sanguis de lacu usque ad frenos equorum".[165] In 1974 the Hills expressed their amazement at the recurrence of this statement in recent historical works: "We cannot understand why writers of modern textbooks repeat this story without indicating its source, unless they are ignorant of it."[166] The context of their observation leaves no doubt that, in their view, historians have mistakenly regarded Raymond's statement and others similar to it as proof of the massacre's totality.

The Hills' discovery that Raymond's mention of the blood reaching the horses' bridles amounts to a quotation from the Apocalypse is important. Yet should one conclude that when the anonymous author of the *Gesta Francorum* writes that the blood touched the crusaders *ad cavillas*, Fulcher – *ad bases*, Albert – *ad talos* (all meaning "up to the ankles"), Bartolf – *tenus suras* (as far as the calves of the leg), Raymond himself – *ad genua* (up to the knees), and the crusade leaders in their letter – *ad genua equorum* (up to the horses' knees), they are all presenting nothing but a downgraded version of the apocalyptic image? This is what the Hills (who are however aware only of the formulations in the *Gesta* and in the letter of the crusade leaders) seem to suggest. But is it not more likely that blood puddles in the Mosque al-Aqsa were indeed ankle-high at some points and that the ecstatic Raymond – and only he – chose to lend grandeur to the scene by using the words of the Apocalypse?

900 years after the event

The ninth centennial of the First Crusade gave rise to a spate of scholarly works on that expedition, most of them dealing with the Jerusalem massacre at some length. As they demonstrate the present-day gamut of attitudes, it is worthwhile to discuss them one by one.

Giosuè Musca, the Bari historian well known for his studies of Norman Italy, published an essay in 1999 on Christians and Jews during the First Crusade that deals also with the Jerusalem massacre. He quotes at length the accounts of the *Gesta Francorum*, Raymond, William of Tyre, Ibn al-Athir and, more briefly, of

---

of Aachen Reappraised", in *Clermont*, pp. 55–67; eadem, "Albert of Aachen and the *Chansons de Geste*", in *Crusade Sources*, pp. 23–37.

165 *Le "Liber" de Raymond d'Aguilers*, ed. Hill and Hill (see above, n. 5), p. 150 n. 2.

166 Peter Tudebode, *Historia*, trans. Hill and Hill (see above, n. 4), p. 119 n. 27.

Fulcher, Bartolf and Albert; unaware of the Geniza evidence, he argues that the total massacre on 17 July reported by Albert could not have taken place, since no contemporary chronicler alludes to it.[167] Musca's view of the Jerusalem massacre (and of the earlier massacres of Jews in the Rhineland) recalls that of earlier critics of crusading: he who massacres innocents cannot be regarded a Christian; historians should not idealize the massacres or write them off as marginal incidents of a glorious enterprise; they should identify them as the outcome of a narcissistic culture of violence that pretends to be the only possessor of truth. Aware that he might be accused of an anachronistic approach, Musca argues that not all Christians of that age justified the killings; as he sees it, many were horrified by them. Among those he names not only Albert and William of Tyre but also Fulcher, Raymond, the *Gesta Francorum* and Raoul of Caen.[168] Musca does not spell out his reasons for believing that the last four chroniclers were appalled by the massacres. One notes with some perplexity that Robert Lopez – in the same section from which Musca quotes approvingly a statement on a related subject[169] – considered them to be sadists who delighted in exaggerating the massacre.

Gerhard Armanski, the Frankfurt social and cultural historian, offers a more radical version of this approach in his *Es began in Clermont* of 1995. For him, the First Crusade was the first ideological war in European history, a collective neurosis of the Christian faith, the genesis of European violence. The Jerusalem massacre, originating in matchless bloodlust, was totally unprecedented; Armanski's description of it is replete with quotations from the *Gesta Francorum*, Raymond, Fulcher and Albert, including the latter's account about infants smashed against walls. Unlike Musca, Armanski believes that the chroniclers report the atrocities with satisfaction and he accepts Albert's report about the deliberate massacre on the third day after the conquest, although he does not think it was total. Surprisingly, Armanski resuscitates Maimbourg's issue of the swift transition from massacre to prayer and attempts to explain it by pointing to the vehemence of emotions, the release from tension, a possibly bad conscience, and – last but not least – Friedrich Wilken's remark in 1807 that the crusaders believed to serve God through murder.[170]

While Musca and Armanski offer variants of the condemnatory stance toward the Jerusalem massacre and towards crusading in general, the book on the First Crusade published by the well-known social and economic historian Jacques Heers in 1995 may be regarded as a radical specimen of works on the subject by medievalists who do not specialize in the crusades. In his discussion of the massacre Heers refers to only three western writers – Robert, Guibert, Raoul of Caen – of whom

---

[167] Giosuè Musca, *Il Vangelo e la Torah: Cristiani ed ebrei nella prima Crociata* (Bari, 1999), pp. 81–88. An earlier version appeared under the same title in *Quaderni medievali* 45 (June 1998), 63–128.

[168] Ibid., pp. 91–98.

[169] Ibid., p. 197. See Lopez, *Naissance de l'Europe* (see above, n. 120), p. 258.

[170] Gerhard Armanski, *Es began in Clermont. Der erste Kreuzzug und die Genese der Gewalt in Europa*, Geschichte der Gewalt in Europa 1 (Pfaffenweiler, 1995), esp. pp. viii–x, 100, 120–24, 136–38.

none was an eyewitness, and to the fourteenth-century Muslim author Abu ʾl-Fida; moreover, for Robert and Raoul he chooses to rely on Guizot's translation of 1825. In addition, he refers the reader to Guibert's autobiography instead of his *Dei gesta per Francos*, and attributes to him statements appearing in the *Gesta Francorum*! Heers repeats Grousset's erroneous statement that Muslim fugitives from Jerusalem founded the Damascene suburb of al-Salihiyya, but on the whole he is certain that the "murderous madness" of the victorious crusaders induced them to commit a veritable massacre. He also asserts that crusade leaders attempted unsuccessfully to preserve parts of the conquered town intact, while small people engaged in pillage and, once enriched, went in procession to the Sepulchre.[171] Like Musca and Armanski, he appears to be unaware of the Geniza documentation, the Hills' argument and the rehabilitation of Albert of Aachen.

Three works by crusade specialists published during the ninth centennial share a tendency to play down the massacre's scale and exceptionality, probably in reaction to sweeping assertions like that of Zoé Oldenbourg in 1965 that "the massacre perpetrated by the Crusaders in Jerusalem has long been reckoned among the greatest crimes in history".[172] John France, in his military history of the First Crusade published in 1994, starts his discussion of the massacre by stating that "this notorious event should not be exaggerated".[173] First, he asserts, "many Jews survived". He does not ask, though, what share of Jerusalem's Jewish population these survivors constituted. The only source on this issue, the letter of the Maghribi Jew written within a year of the conquest, squarely states, as we have seen, that the massacre was total "and *the few who survived* the slaughter were made prisoners". Second, France claims that "many Muslim refugees from the city later took refuge at Damascus bringing with them the celebrated Koran of Uthman". The statement on the refugees reproduces Grousset's mistake with regard to al-Salihiyya; that on the Koran is based on the popular book by Amin Maalouf. (In reality ʿUthman's book was brought to Damascus from Maʿarrat al-Nuʿman in 1098, not from Jerusalem in 1099.)[174] Third, France argues that "however horrible the massacre at Jerusalem, it was not far beyond what common practice of the day meeted [*sic*] out to any place

[171] Jacques Heers, *Libérer Jérusalem: La première croisade (1095–1107)* (Paris, 1995), pp. 225–27. For a scathing review see Jean Flori, "De Clermont à Jérusalem. La première croisade dans l'historiographie récente (1995–1999)", *Moyen Age* 105 (1999), 440–42.

[172] Oldenbourg, *The Crusades* (see above, n. 120), p. 137. In her fictional, well-researched account of the massacre, Oldenbourg may well have recaptured the way many crusaders experienced it: see Zoé Oldenbourg, *The Heirs of the Kingdom*, trans. Anne Carter (London, 1972; 1970), pp. 418–81. On the value of fictional works for historians see the perceptive discussion by Susan Edgington, "The First Crusade in Post-War Fiction", in *The Experience of Crusading* 1: *Western Approaches*, ed. Marcus Bull and Norman Housley (Cambridge, 2003), pp. 255–60; Oldenbourg's book is discussed on pp. 265–66.

[173] John France, *Victory in the East: A Military History of the First Crusade* (Cambridge, 1994); the discussion of the massacre appears on pp. 355–56.

[174] Maalouf, *Les croisades* (see above, n. 151), p. 9; Hillenbrand, *The Crusades* (see above, n. 84), p. 305. France speaks also of "the shock expressed by Ibn al-Athir" in his description of the conquest; but the tone of that description is matter-of-fact.

which resisted". While this may perhaps be true of the massacre on the day of Jerusalem's conquest, it is less so of the killing of the Muslims to whom Tancred had given protection, and much less so of the total massacre of Saracens, whether held for ransom or already ransomed, that Albert reports. France, who accepts Albert's account at face value, regards the slaughter of Tancred's protégés as "repellent" and the total massacre as "cold-blooded murder", "horror", and "atrocious killing". But these expressions of disapproval reflect France's own values; from the vantage point of 1099, he regards all three phases of the massacre as a single event that did not overly exceed the ordinary customs of war. He points also to other roughly contemporary instances of brutality that, like the Jerusalem massacre, should be considered exaggerations of the common practice of that age. For example, he writes, "in 1057 the entire population of Melitene was slaughtered or enslaved by the Turks". Now, the sources leave no doubt that Melitene did undergo a terrible sack and that a great number of its inhabitants were slaughtered, including children on the laps of their mothers, with some citizens hiding under corpses. The same sources relate, however, that a large part of the population escaped from the city before the Turkish assault and that the numerous inhabitants who were led into captivity regained their freedom when an Armenian prince routed the Turks; indeed, the Melitene captives took part in massacring their captors.[175] Another of France's examples of eleventh-century savagery is William the Conqueror's sack of Mantes in 1087. But was it that savage? Orderic Vitalis writes that William's enraged squires burnt the castle of Mantes together with churches and houses and that "it is said that a great number of men (*multitudo hominum*) perished in the fierce fire"; later William sent gifts to the town's clergy to enable them to rebuild the burnt churches.[176] Thus, when the fates of Melitene in 1057 and of Mantes in 1087 are set alongside that of Jerusalem in 1099, the distinctiveness of the latter clearly emerges. This distinctiveness becomes apparent also when one compares the other conquests-by-storming that took place during the First Crusade or immediately afterward: namely those of Antioch and Maʿarrat al-Nuʿman in 1098, Haifa in 1100 and Caesarea in 1101. These conquests are not only in close chronological proximity to that of Jerusalem but were carried out by largely the same warriors. In all these places a massacre took place, but only with regard to Jerusalem do eyewitnesses present the killings as totally unprecedented (*Gesta*, Peter Tudebode) or hardly credible (Raymond). Only with regard to Jerusalem do some chroniclers feel the need to justify them.

---

[175] See *Matthew of Edessa*, trans. Dostourian (see above, n. 119), pp. 92–93; *Chronique de Michel le Syrien, patriarche jacobite d'Antioche (1166–1199)*, ed. and trans. Jean-Baptiste Chabot, 4 vols. (Paris, 1899–1924), 3:158–59. Speros Vryonis, in his authoritative *The Decline of Medieval Hellenism in Asia Minor and the Process of Islamization from the Eleventh through the Fifteenth Century* (Berkeley, 1971), writes that in Melitene "great numbers of the inhabitants were either killed or enslaved" (p. 88). Incidentally, France's reference (p. 355, n. 66) to Matthew of Edessa appears to apply to an edition other than that cited in his bibliography and list of abbreviations.

[176] *The Ecclesiastical History of Orderic Vitalis* (see above, n. 26), 7.14, 4:78–81.

Jean Richard, who in his *Histoire des croisades* of 1996 gives the opinion that the description of the massacre has been repeated to the point of wearing out the reader, chooses to deal with it very briefly. Unlike France, he states that the massacre did leave an impression on contemporaries, yet he notes only the killings in the Mosque al-Aqsa, the massacre in the streets of those who attempted to flee to David's Tower, the slaughter of those who were granted protection by Tancred and Gaston of Béarn, and the burning of Jews in a synagogue of their quarter.[177] The gory scenes throughout the town that Raymond and other chroniclers describe, and their emphasis on the massacre's extraordinariness, go unmentioned. Instead, Richard underlines that the massacre was not systematic: "Hebrew letters" found in the Cairo Geniza relate, he claims, that a party of Jews was led under escort to Ascalon where they and their books were ransomed by Egyptian Jews; local Christians were expelled from Jerusalem by the Fatimid governor; it has been said that Muslim refugees started to populate the Damascene suburb of al-Salihiyya (which is a further repetition of Grousset's assertion). Moreover, two remarks may be understood as playing down the massacre's magnitude. First, Richard states that, in order to describe the killings in the Mosque al-Aqsa, "the historians, and in particular Raymond of Aguilers, made use of an image borrowed from the text of the Apocalypse that speaks of 'blood reaching the horses' bridles'". Yet only Raymond used this image; the claim that the other chroniclers did so as well, albeit to some lesser degree, gratuitously casts doubt on the factuality of their accounts about the blood shed in the mosque. Second, mentioning the killings in the mosque, Richard comments that they were a repeat of the scenes that had occurred there in 1077, alluding thereby to the massacre that the Turkish ruler Atsiz perpetrated when he reconquered a rebellious Jerusalem. The reader cannot but conclude that the crusader massacre in the mosque twenty-two years later was not that exceptional.[178] The sources on Atsiz's doings on the Haram al-Sharif in 1077, however, offer a more nuanced picture. Ibn al-Athir (d. 1233) asserts that Atsiz killed those who took refuge in the Mosque al-Aqsa but not those who were near the Dome of the Rock[179] – a situation evidently different from that of 1099. Moreover, Sibt b. al-Jawzi

---

[177] Jean Richard, *Histoire des croisades* (Paris, 1996), p. 79; idem, *The Crusades, c.1071–c.1291*, trans. Jean Birrell (Cambridge, 1999), p. 66. Unfortunately this important work of synthesis is not annotated; yet the last detail demonstrates that Richard – who in 1969 believed that the massacre in the synagogue did not take place – has duly taken into account Goitein's discovery of the Rabbanite letter.

[178] For the mention of Atsiz's massacre see Richard, *Histoire des croisades*, p. 26. Similarly, in his discussion of the 1096 persecutions, Richard – who still believes that Jewish usury was one of their reasons – remarks that explosions of anti-Jewish violence were not limited to the Christian West: "The first great movement of hatred of which Jews were victims in the eleventh century occurred in about 1066 in Muslim Spain, at Granada." Ibid., p. 53. For recent discussions of the usury thesis see Michael Toch, "Wirtschaft und Verfolgung: Die Bedeutung der Ökonomie für die Kreuzzugspogrome des 11. und 12. Jahrhunderts", in *Juden und Christen zur Zeit der Kreuzzüge* (Sigmaringen, 1997), pp. 256–72; Kedar, "Crusade Historians" (see above, n. 1), pp. 18–19.

[179] Ibn al-Athir, *al-Kamil fi al-ta'rikh* (Beirut, 1965), 10:103; Goitein, "al-Kuds" (see above, n. 163), p. 328. For the background see Gil, *A History of Palestine* (see above, n. 147), p. 412.

(d. 1256) writes that Atsiz's men killed 3,000 Jerusalemites, but those who took refuge in the Dome of the Rock and in the Mosque al-Aqsa were merely ordered to pay ransom.[180] Evidently, the sources allow for more than one way of juxtaposing the happenings on the Haram al-Sharif in 1077 with those in 1099. Indeed Mustafa Hiyari, who describes Atsiz's doings only on the basis of Sibt b. al-Jawzi, offers a mirror image of Richard's remark when he writes that in 1099 the Muslims fled to the Haram "hoping to be spared, as was the custom on previous occasions", but the crusaders massacred most of them.[181]

In an article on the conquest of 1099 published in 2001, Kaspar Elm adopts the view that the behaviour of the crusaders in conquered Jerusalem basically followed prevailing norms, quotes approvingly (and verbatim) John France's conclusion that the massacre "was not far beyond what common practice of the day meeted [*sic*] out to any place which resisted", and adds (on the basis of an unpublished paper by G. Cochlovius) that those who died in the first attack on the Haram al-Sharif were by no means only women and children but also armed Muslims who viewed the enclosure as a fortress of sorts and attempted to defend it. Arguing that when Muslims had the upper hand they acted in the same manner, he adduces two examples: the total slaughter or enslavement of the population of Melitene in 1057 (for which he depends on France) and the massacre that took place upon the fall of Frankish Acre in 1291 (he dispenses though with mentioning what happened at the fall of Frankish Jerusalem in 1187 and does not consider whether an event of 1291 can be taken to exemplify eleventh-century mores). Elm then goes on to ask whether in fact all of Jerusalem's population was massacred in 1099 and answers: "Definitely not!" pointing out that (a) the defenders of the citadel were allowed to leave for Ascalon, although there was reason to fear they would join the advancing Fatimid host; (b) Jews were ransomed by the communities of Ascalon and Cairo; (c) local Christians who remained in Jerusalem survived the conquest; and (d) "it is certain that, at the beginning of the twelfth century, accommodations were made available in Damascus in order to shelter Muslim refugees from Jerusalem and Palestine".[182] The last statement is purportedly based on Emmanuel Sivan's pioneering article on Palestinian refugees at the time of the crusades – but nothing in that work supports Elm's assertion.

Having stated his case for the relative normality of the conquest of 1099, Elm goes on to ask why the chroniclers of the First Crusade chose – with a few exceptions, one being Albert – to exaggerate and indulge in descriptions of cruelty

---

[180] Sibt b. al-Jawzi, *Mir'at al-zaman*, ed. ʿAli Sevim (Ankara, 1968), p. 185. My thanks to my colleagues Etan Kohlberg and Amikam Elad for their help with this and the previous passage.

[181] Mustafa A. Hiyari, "Crusader Jerusalem 1099–1187 AD", in Kamil J. Asali, *Jerusalem in History* (London, 1989), pp. 136, 138.

[182] Kaspar Elm, "Die Eroberung Jerusalems im Jahre 1099. Ihre Darstellung, Beurteilung und Deutung in den Quellen zur Geschichte des Ersten Kreuzzzugs", in *Jerusalem im Hoch- und Spätmittelalter: Konflikte und Konfliktbewältigung – Vorstellungen und Vergegenwärtigungen*, ed. Dieter Bauer, Klaus Herbers and Nikolas Jaspert (Frankfurt, 2001), pp. 42–46.

and murder rather than to express regret, compassion or shame. His answer is that because of the extraordinary nature of the crusade and the many precedents and prototypes that were on the crusaders' minds, the chroniclers describe the 1099 conquest with images offered by literary tradition. Thus when Raymond and others speak of blood reaching the horses' bridles, conquered Jerusalem is portrayed as the blasphemous Babylon of the Apocalypse. Fulcher's description of the smashing of infants' heads and of the search for gold pieces in cut-up bellies originates in nothing else but the account of Josephus Flavius about the atrocities committed by Roman legionaries. The main reservoir of images drawn upon in the description of the massacre is however the Old Testament precept to completely annihilate the population of a conquered town like Jericho. Buttressing his case by references to anthropological literature, Elm argues that this precept may be considered as just one instance of a universal pattern of God-willed purification of the sacred through the shedding of the polluters' blood, a purification in which raging bloodlust and fervent devoutness occur simultaneously and violence and sanctity draw shockingly close. The chroniclers, who perceive the crusade as the cleansing of the Holy Land, the Holy City and the holy places through the blood of the Gentiles who had defiled them, describe the conquest of Jerusalem in accordance with this pattern.[183]

This argument calls for several comments. First, Elm provides a persuasive solution to the swift-transition issue originally raised by Maimbourg. Second, Elm's hypothesis that the chroniclers chose to exaggerate the massacre *ad maiorem purificationis gloriam* is not inherently implausible, but the fact that Albert of Aachen, the author of the most gruesome and detailed account of the killings, refrains from emphasizing the purification motif, presents the crusaders as murderous and reveals compassion for their victims, tends to militate against it. Third, given that since with the crusader conquest the Muslim and Jewish communities of Jerusalem undoubtedly ceased to exist, that there is no evidence for their members' expulsion, that the Geniza evidence indicates that only few Jews outlived the killings and that the references to Muslim survivors are scant and the only Muslim known to have been held for ransom was ultimately stoned to death, the unavoidable conclusion is that the Jerusalem massacre was in fact immense. This is also borne out by Fulcher, who in the description of his pilgrimage to Jerusalem in December 1099 observes that the stench of rotting Saracen cadavers around the city walls forced him and his companions to cover their nostrils and mouths. This accidental – and therefore trustworthy – eyewitness remark, unrelated to his description of the killings and omitted from the chronicle's second redaction, amounts to an unintended confirmation of the massacre's extraordinary nature. Fourth, Elm is right in assuming that the chroniclers may have used literary models.

183 Ibid., pp. 46–54; idem, "*O beatas idus ac prae ceteris gloriosas!* Die Eroberung Jerusalems 1099 und der Erste Kreuzzug in der Geschichtsschreibung Raouls von Caen", in *Es hat sich viel ereignet, Gutes wie Böses. Lateinische Geschichtsschreibung der Spät- und Nachantike*, ed. Gabriele Thome and Jens Holzhausen (Munich, 2001), pp. 156–64.

Yet the existence of a description in earlier literature surely does not preclude the possibility that its recurrence is based on actual observation. For instance, the fact that the image of infants' heads hurled against stones appears in Psalms 137:9 does not render unrealistic the very many accounts about Germans killing Jewish infants in this way during World War II. Incidentally, Fulcher does not mention the smashing of infants' heads at all; as for his account about the search for gold coins in cut-up bellies, we should note that he relates having seen in Caesarea in 1101 how the conquerors burnt heaps of Saracen cadavers in order to expose swallowed gold coins (here, too, Fulcher remarks on the stench) and that the author of the *Gesta* and Peter Tudebode report that poor crusaders cut up Saracen cadavers in Maʿarrat al-Nuʿman in 1098 for the same purpose.[184] We therefore have good reasons to believe that Fulcher's description of the crusaders' doings in Jerusalem was rooted in reality. Bringing Josephus Flavius into the discussion, then, tends to obscure rather than enhance our understanding of the events at hand. As R.C. Smail once remarked in a different context, too much knowledge may on occasion be detrimental to a historian's work.

While France, Richard and Elm highlight their doubts about the massacre's exceptionality, Jean Flori, in a book published in 1999, maintains that the Geniza evidence, the departure of the garrison and the mention of survivors burying the dead do not detract from the massacre's horror and extent, even if it was not as total as previously believed.[185] Thus Flori's assessment is about the same as that of Goitein. Flori, who rightly insists that a historian's duty is to explain not to excuse, distinguishes between the initial massacre and the subsequent total extermination, and offers different explanations for combatants' actions and chroniclers' accounts. The combatants irrupting into Jerusalem, he thinks, massacred out of a visceral, feverish furor, experiencing a liberating explosion of violence after having endured much fear, anguish, suffering and doubt; besides, they knew that the Christian inhabitants had been expelled and that all whom they confronted were God's enemies.[186] On the contrary, the subsequent total extermination, decreed upon by the crusade leaders, was done in cold blood. Flori accepts Albert's account about it at face value; surprisingly, he believes that Albert claimed it was Tancred who proposed this massacre. The reason for it, Flori thinks, was not only the military one mentioned by Albert but also the wish of at least some crusaders to liberate

---

[184] Fulcher, *Historia* 2.9, pp. 403–4; *Gesta Francorum* (see above, n. 3), c. 33, p. 80; Petrus Tudebodus, *Historia*, ed. Hill and Hill (see above, n. 4), p. 124.

[185] Jean Flori, *Pierre l'Ermite* (see above, n. 126); the massacre is discussed on pp. 419–22, 587 n. 73.

[186] Flori remarks (p. 420) that the crusaders perpetrated a similarly general massacre in Maʿarrat al-Nuʿman in 1098. Now, Fulcher – not an eyewitness – relates that the crusaders killed there all Saracens, but the *Gesta Francorum* and Peter Tudebode mention that Bohemond sold some of those whom he promised to save, Raymond writes that his men took many captives, while Ibn al-Qalanisi emphasizes the plundering and the demand for exorbitant payments: Fulcher, *Historia* 1.25, p. 267; *Gesta Francorum*, c. 33, pp. 79–80; Petrus Tudebodus, *Historia*, ed. Hill and Hill, p. 124; Raymond in *RHC Oc* 3:270, and ed. Hill and Hill (see above, n. 5), p. 98; Ibn al-Qalanisi, trans. Gibb (see above, n. 84), p. 47.

Jerusalem by an ethnic cleansing [*sic*] of the illegitimate and idolatrous occupiers, thereby paving the way for the Second Coming. As for the chroniclers, they all wrote after the event and knew that History did not come to an end with the conquest of Jerusalem.[187] Offering an intricate argument, Flori rejects the view that the chroniclers dwelt on the shedding of Infidel blood because, influenced by Apocalypse 14:19–20, they interpreted the events *ex post facto* according to such eschatological notions as God's wrath and vengeance and the cleansing of the holy places with blood. He believes instead that they suppressed these notions and justified the massacres not as a sign of things to come but as prophecy already fulfilled – the prophecy about the recovery and cleansing of the holy places. "Hence, perhaps, the emphasis of some chroniclers on the blood shed in the Temple, in a language inspired by the Apocalypse".

Enter Ibn alʿArabī

In 1993, four decades after Goitein published his initial version of the Geniza letters, a further source relevant for the understanding of the massacre came to light when Joseph Drory translated into Hebrew a number of excerpts from the copious writings of Ibn al-ʿArabī (1076–1148). This author was a Muslim from Seville who studied in Jerusalem in the years 1092–95, and passed through Palestine again in December 1098 on his way from Baghdad to Egypt, where he spent most of his time in Alexandria. In late 1099 he was still in Egypt, mainly in Alexandria; during the next two years he lived in Tlemcen and Fez and then returned to Seville. Late in his life he moved to Fez, where he died.[188] In other words, here is a man who knew pre-crusader Jerusalem very well and who most probably followed with interest, while in Egypt in 1099, the news about the town's conquest. Unfortunately, the account about his stay in the Muslim East was lost during his lifetime; yet in the treatise *al-ʿAwasim min al-Qawasim*, completed in 1142 but referred to already in a work concluded in 1110,[189] he does briefly mention the massacre. Misdating it to 11 July but giving the correct day of the week, he writes that on the morning of that Friday 3,000 men and women, "including God-fearing and learned worshippers", were killed in the Mosque al-Aqsa. A learned woman from Shiraz, Persia, was killed at the Dome of the Chain – just east of the Dome of the Rock – along with other women.[190]

---

187 On this point Flori differs from Guy Lobrichon, who believes that the author of the *Gesta Francorum*, Peter Tudebode and especially Raymond regarded the conquest of Jerusalem as prelude to the Last Judgement, while later chroniclers suppressed this notion: Guy Lobrichon, *1099, Jérusalem conquise* (Paris, 1998), pp. 123, 130–33.

188 See Joseph Drory, *Ibn al-ʿArabi of Seville: A Journey in Palestine (1092–95)* (Ramat Gan, 1993), pp. 11–12, 18 [in Hebrew].

189 Ibid., pp. 12, 36, 50, 51.

190 Ibid., p. 112; and see Drory's article in *Crusades* 3:101–24, below. It is noteworthy that Sibt b. al-Jawzi gives 3,000 as the total number of Jerusalemites killed in 1077 (see above, n. 180).

Thus while Fulcher, Albert and William of Tyre relate that 10,000 were killed in the mosque, Matthew of Edessa says 65,000, and Ibn al-Athir 75,000, Ibn al-ʿArabī, a contemporary who may be regarded as well informed and who hardly intends to minimize the massacre's extent, gives the much smaller figure of 3,000. Adherents of the sanctimonial approach to the crusades, who may be tempted to seize upon Ibn al-ʿArabī's figure in order to play down the massacre's magnitude, should, however, remember that it is by no means negligible. It still exceeds that of the victims of 11 September 2001 and it pertains not to a multimillion megalopolis but to a town of perhaps 20,000–30,000 inhabitants.

Some concluding remarks

The Latin, Judeo-Arabic and Arabic sources support the following scenario: after the crusader irruption into Jerusalem on 15 July, the Mosque al-Aqsa was the scene of fighting and massacre; about 3,000 Muslim men and women found their death there; Muslims on the mosque's roof, who had been promised protection by Tancred and Gaston of Béarn, were massacred early on 16 July; the Fatimid garrison, besieged in David's Tower for three days, surrendered on 17 July and left for Ascalon; some Jews and probably some Muslims succeeded in leaving Jerusalem with it. Albert's report that the crusader leaders decreed a total massacre on 17 July is uncorroborated, yet the letter of the Ascalon elders indicates that on that day inhabitants were trying to flee and sustains Albert's assertion that crusaders put captives to death. If the leaders did issue the decree in question on 17 July, it may have been related in some way to the garrison's departure. In general, the sources' emphasis on the killings and the scant evidence for survivors enslaved or held for ransom suggest that the massacre in Jerusalem was considerably more extensive than in other towns of that time that were taken by storming. The stress of the eyewitnesses on the massacre's extraordinariness is supported by Fulcher's remark on the stench of cadavers in December 1099.

Perusal of later medieval works attests to the vast, centuries-long preponderance of William of Tyre's chronicle. Neither William nor the author of the other widely known chronicle, Robert the Monk, were eyewitnesses, but readers evidently preferred works of literary distinction to cruder accounts by participants. (Similarly, literary merit goes a long way to explain the popularity of Michaud in the nineteenth century and of Runciman in the twentieth.) A comparison of William's account of the massacre with those in his sources reveals which details he chose to select, suppress or amplify. A comparison of his account with its many derivations testifies to a progressive attenuation of the original's ambiguity and complexity.

Scrutiny of post-medieval works has disclosed cases of surprising persistence and resurgence. Thus the issue of swift transition from slaughter to devotion, first raised by the Jesuit Maimbourg in 1675, was of major interest throughout the Enlightenment and beyond, virtually disappeared from sight in the era of academic history, but recently resurfaced in the works of Armanski and Elm. Again, the characterization of the crusaders at the end of the first-day massacre as "fatiguez du carnage", first used by the Abbot Fleury in 1713, was echoed – possibly unwittingly – in 1997 when Jean Flori depicted them at the same juncture as "fatigués de tuer".[191] Indeed, attention to what one may call "the lost generations of secondary literature" – that is, historical works much too recent to qualify as sources but too outdated to enter the run-of-the-mill scholarly apparatus – lays bare otherwise imperceptible processes of intergenerational dialogue, continuity and disjunction. Also, the impact of religious and ideological background on the authors of these works is often more easily perceptible than in the case of more recent historians.

The longitudinal approach has also highlighted the extent of unacknowledged borrowing, the uncritical acceptance of a flawed argument, and the disquieting amount of faulty craftsmanship, especially with regard to oriental sources. More importantly, it has demonstrated how, for a historian's perception of the massacre, basic values and attitudes may be more important than exposure to sources old and new, with critics of the crusades tending to present the massacre as the prime example of the horrors to which religious fanaticism can lead and admirers of crusading often attempting to play down the massacre's extent or to stress mitigating circumstances. Having observed the damaging impact of prejudice and passion on some of our predecessors' works, we may sensitize ourselves to notice it more readily in the products of our contemporaries – and, hopefully, in our own as well.

---

[191] Flori, *La Première Croisade* (see above, n. 126), p. 102. As we have seen, in the intervening years these figures of speech were employed by the Abbé de Vertot in 1726, Wilken in 1807, Valentin in 1837, Archer and Kingsford in 1894 and Chalandon in 1925.

Postscript: For a detailed discussion of the settlement of Muslim refugees in al-Salihiyya see Daniella Talmon-Heller and Benjamin Z. Kedar, "Did Muslim Survivors of the 1099 Massacre of Jerusalem Settle in Damascus? The True Origins of the al-Salihiyya Suburb", *Al-Masaq* (in the press).

Eyewitnessing in Accounts of the First Crusade: the *Gesta Francorum* and Other Contemporary Narratives[1]

Yuval Noah Harari

Jerusalem

Historians have been arguing for generations about the reliability of the accounts of the First Crusade. Up till now, most of these arguments focused on examining whether the authors of these accounts were eyewitnesses to the crusade, and what alternative sources of information they relied upon. Susan Edgington has concluded her recent article on Albert of Aachen's *Historia* by suggesting what she defines as "a new set of questions" for historians. Edgington argues that aside from examining the authors' sources of information, historians should devote more attention to understanding the authors' literary purposes.[2]

I would like to take up Edgington's suggestion, and re-examine in its light the very idea of "eyewitness accounts" in the historiography of the First Crusade. I would like to argue that not every account produced by an eyewitness is an "eyewitness account". For eyewitness accounts are defined by their purposes as much as by their sources. They are a distinct type of writing, which displays particular values and characteristics, and a text lacking these values and characteristics can hardly be considered an eyewitness account, even if it was written by an eyewitness. I hope to show that, for example, what has often been considered the most important eyewitness account of the First Crusade, the *Gesta Francorum*, is not an eyewitness account at all.

Eyewitness accounts are texts whose main purpose is to narrate what their authors have seen and experienced and that accordingly privilege factual accuracy over skill of writing and breadth of interpretation. Authors of eyewitness accounts are rarely professional historians. They are often lacking in literary and scholarly

[1] I would like to thank Susan Edgington for providing me with extracts from her forthcoming new edition-cum-translation of Albert of Aachen's *Historia*.

[2] Susan B. Edgington, "Albert of Aachen and the *Chansons de Geste*", p. 37. In their edition of Walter the Chancellor's *The Antiochene Wars* Edgington and Thomas Asbridge accordingly devote considerable attention to Walter's purposes in writing this work: Thomas S. Asbridge and Susan B. Edgington, eds., *Walter the Chancellor's The Antiochene Wars* (Aldershot, 1999), pp. 11–42. However, they limit themselves to a rather traditional discussion of Walter's political purposes, arguing that he presented the events and characters of his history in such a way as to "explain the principality [of Antioch]'s varying fortunes on the basis of divine will": Ibid., p. 73. They devote very little attention to discussing Walter's literary purposes. A more thorough examination of the literary purposes of a crusader chronicler is to be found in Epp's study of Fulcher of Chartres: Verena Epp, *Fulcher von Chartres: Studien zur Geschichtsschreibung des ersten Kreuzzuges* (Düsseldorf, 1990), pp. 140–52.

skills, and their narratives are usually considered inferior according to the literary and scholarly standards of their day. Hence their main way of justifying why they wrote these texts and why they are worthy of being read is by emphasizing that they saw what they write, and that eyewitnessing is the most reliable source of information, and that therefore their texts are more trustworthy than texts written at second hand. Thus authors of eyewitness accounts often couple an apology for their limited skills and rude style with a redeeming reference to their value as eyewitnesses.[3] In later centuries authors went even further, taking pride in the fact that they write without eloquence, as if lack of eloquence in itself guarantees truthfulness.[4]

Texts that justify themselves in such a way, and whose very *raison d'être* is therefore the connection between truthfulness and eyewitnessing, are geared to remind the audience of the importance of truthfulness and eyewitnessing and of their own status as eyewitness accounts. In consequence such texts tend to display the following four characteristics:

1 They are aware of the possibility that the audience may not believe them and, indeed, they often draw the audience's attention to the importance of factual truthfulness in historical accounts and admonish it not to believe uncritically in every such account.
2 They repeatedly remind the audience that a report based on eyewitnessing is more trustworthy than second-hand reports.
3 The authors explicitly say that they eyewitnessed what they are writing and occasionally mention themselves as protagonists, thereby further establishing their status as eyewitnesses. This point deserves special notice in a period like the high Middle Ages, when authors were usually expected to say little or nothing about themselves.
4 In order to preserve their credibility, whenever they recount something that they did not eyewitness, the authors tend to make this explicit, and even explain

[3] See Odo of Deuil, *De profectione Ludovici VII in orientem*, ed. and trans. Virginia Gingerick Berry (New York, 1948), p. 4; Robert de Clari, *La Conquête de Constantinople*, ed. Philippe Lauer (Paris, 1924), section 120; Gunther of Pairis, *The Capture of Constantinople: The "Hystoria Constantinopolitana" of Gunther of Pairis*, ed. and trans. Alfred J. Andrea (Philadelphia, 1997), p. 65; George Gordon Coulton, *From St. Francis to Dante: Translations from the Chronicle of the Franciscan Salimbene (1221–1288)* (London, 1907; repr. 2nd ed., Philadelphia, 1972), p. 4. Note though that an apology for a rude style coupled with a promise to tell only the truth was a standard medieval formula, used even by the most scholarly and eloquent of authors. In their treatment of Walter the Chancellor, Asbridge and Edgington discuss only once the status of eyewitnessing, when arguing that Walter "showed some desire to establish the credibility of his sources, commenting on his own eye-witness status and on one occasion noting that he received his knowledge from 'reliable intermediaries'": Asbridge and Edgington, *Walter the Chancellor*, p. 7.

[4] Yuval Noah Harari, "History and I: War and the Relations between History and Personal Identity in Renaissance Military Memoirs, c. 1450–1600", unpublished D.Phil. Thesis, University of Oxford, 2001, p. 58.

what alternative source they relied upon. Otherwise, if no clear distinction is made between what does rely on eyewitnessing and what does not, a suspicious audience may doubt the truthfulness of everything it is being told, once it realizes that not all the text is based on eyewitnessing.[5]

I would like first to exemplify these four characteristics and the connections between them by briefly examining two accounts of the First Crusade, those of Fulcher of Chartres and of Raymond of Aguilers.

Fulcher of Chartres

Fulcher of Chartres draws the audience's attention to the importance of truth and its connection with eyewitnessing in his prologue, where he says that "I have recounted in a style homely but *truthful* what I deemed worthy of remembrance as far as I was able or just as *I saw things with my own eyes* on the journey itself" (my italics).[6] He repeats this idea again in book 2 chapter 34, where he says that though he is "rude in skill and weak in ability" he is writing about events "as far as I have seen them with my own eyes or have learned by diligently seeking out reliable information". He then asks the reader to correct his rude style, but "let him not change the arrangement of my history for the sake of pompous eloquence lest he deceitfully confuse the truth of events".[7]

---

[5] The theory presented here regarding eyewitness accounts is based on extensive research I conducted during my doctoral studies on medieval, Renaissance and twentieth-century memoirs and eyewitness accounts. The medieval texts I examined include accounts of later crusades, in particular accounts of the Second Crusade by Odo of Deuil; of the Third Crusade by Ambroise; of the Fourth Crusade by Robert de Cléri, Geoffroy de Villehardouin, and Henri de Valenciennes; of the Fifth Crusade by Oliver of Paderborn; of the crusade of 1228–29 by Philip of Novara; and of crusades of King Louis IX by Jehan de Joinville. Other accounts relating to the crusades include the memoirs of Usāma ibn Munqidh and those of the thirteenth-century Armenian prince Hetoum, and Gunther of Pairis's history of the Fourth Crusade. Other medieval texts I examined include Gerald of Wales's *Expugnatio Hibernica*; Fernan Alvarez de Albornoz's *Memorias*; the chronicles of Salimbene of Parma, Muntaner, and Kings Jaume I and Pere III of Aragon; the chronicles of the Valenciennes school (particularly those of Jean le Bel and Froissart); and the writings of the *caballero* school in late medieval Castile, in particular Pedro López de Ayala's *Crónicas de los reyes de Castilla*. Some of the relevant material can be found in Harari, "History and I", part 2, chapter 2.

[6] "Stilo rusticano, tamen veraci, dignum ducens memoriae commendandum, prout valui et oculis meis in ipso itinere perspexi, diligenter digessi": Fulcher of Chartres, *Fulcheri Carnotensis historia Hierosolymitana (1095–1127)*, ed. Heinrich Hagenmeyer (Heidelberg, 1913), Prologue 2 (hereafter cited as Fulcher).

[7] "Malui ego Fulcherus scientia rudis, ingenio debilis, temeritatis naevo notari quam haec opera non propalari, prout oculis vidi vel a relatoribus veridicis perscrutans diligenter didici. Precor autem haec legentem, ut nescientiae meae caritative indulgeat et dictamen istud nondum a quolibet correctum oratore locatim, si velit, corrigat; veruntamen historiae seriem propter pulchritudinem partium pompaticam non commutet, ne gestorum veritatem mendaciter confundat": Fulcher, 2.34.1–2. For the importance of truthfulness for Fulcher see Epp, *Fulcher von Chartres*, pp. 143–44.

Other references to the problem of truth are scattered throughout the text, as for example when he fears that the audience will not believe his description of some sea battle,[8] or when, while speaking of the siege of Aleppo, he reassures the audience that "I who tell it do not depart from the truth."[9] Perhaps the most illuminating example occurs in his description of the battle of ʿAzaz (1125), where he dedicates two sections to discussing the failings of historians who are in the habit of deceitfully magnifying the losses of the enemy and minimizing those of their own side. He then assures the audience that the numbers he quotes regarding this battle are accurate, because they were reported by those present at the battle, and later verified by enemy survivors.[10]

In addition to being concerned with the question of its own truthfulness, Fulcher's text also dwells on examples in which protagonists were deceived by false reports. For instance, he tells at some length how the Holy Lance, in which many people believed, was disclosed as a fraud; how the garrisons of Jaffa and Antioch were mistakenly led to believe that Baldwin I was defeated at Ramla in 1101; and how the Franks in the Levant were repeatedly deceived by false rumours about the coming of Bohemond the younger.[11]

Having thus alerted the audience to the importance of truthfulness, Fulcher also emphasizes the importance of eyewitnessing as a basis for truth and the fact that he eyewitnessed much of what he tells. In addition to the two examples quoted above, in book 1 he says that "I, Fulcher of Chartres, who went with the other pilgrims, afterwards diligently and carefully collected all this in my memory for the sake of posterity, just as I saw it with my own eyes".[12] When describing Baldwin of Edessa's first journey to Jerusalem, he says that "I saw many people who had no tents die from chills from the rains. I, Fulcher of Chartres, who was with them, saw many persons of both sexes and a great many beasts die one day because of these freezing rains".[13]

When describing Baldwin's campaign to the Dead Sea and Transjordan area, Fulcher reports the wonders they found there, assuring the audience that he personally experienced them. Thus after reporting how salty the Dead Sea is, he says that "This I, Fulcher, learned by experience when I dismounted from my mule into the water and took a drink with my hand, testing it by the taste and finding it to be more bitter than hellebore".[14] He then recounts that "I saw there among the trees

---

[8] Fulcher, 3.20.6.

[9] "Sed qui hoc narro, a veritate non devio": Ibid., 3.39.5.

[10] Ibid., 3.43.1–2. See also Epp, *Fulcher von Chartres*, p. 147.

[11] Lance: Ibid., 1.18; Ramla: Ibid., 2.13–14; Bohemond: Ibid., 3.57.4.

[12] "Ego Fulcherus Carnotensis cum ceteris iens peregrinis, postea sicut oculis meis perspexi, diligenter et sollicite in memoriam posteris collegi": Ibid., 1.5.12.

[13] "Vidi tunc plures tabernaculis carentes imbrium algore exstingui. Ego Fulcherus Carnotensis, qui his intereram, vidi quadam die plures utriusque sexus, bestiasque quamplurimas hac pluvia mori algidissima": Ibid., 1.33.12.

[14] "Quod ego Fulcherus experimento didici, cum in illum de mula mea descendens et ori meo manu haustum inmittens gustu probavi et elleboro amariorem esse inveni": Ibid., 2.5.1.

some bearing a fruit. I gathered some of it wishing to know what it was. When I broke its shell I found a black powder inside".[15] Finally, wishing to convince the audience how much water there is at Wadi Musa, despite its being in the middle of the desert, he tells them that "I watered my horses in this brook".[16] Other references to eyewitnessing occur when he describes the capture of Caesarea, the battle of Ramla in September 1101 and the Holy Land's fauna and flora.[17] Lastly, when after describing the 1101 battle of Ramla he reflects on the nature of war and wishes to convince the audience that his negative verdict on war is not a clerk's idle musing, he exclaims: "I saw the battle, I wavered in my mind, I feared to be struck".[18]

In order to strengthen his status as eyewitness in the minds of the audience, Fulcher repeatedly mentions himself as protagonist throughout the narrative, in religious, military, and political contexts. Thus he tells of his inability to understand the language of Breton and Teuton crusaders; of how he went with Baldwin to Edessa and how he served as the latter's chaplain during the conquest of the said city; of how he later accompanied Baldwin in his journey to Jerusalem; of his visits on that occasion to Jerusalem and Bethlehem; of how he prayed barefooted in Jerusalem during the 1105 battle of Ramla; and of how he accompanied King Baldwin I in the 1111 campaign.[19] These references to himself as protagonist serve not only to establish Fulcher's qualifications as an eyewitness, but also to enable the audience to have a fair idea of Fulcher's whereabouts at any particular time, thereby indicating which events he witnessed himself and which events he describes from second hand. When this is not clear enough, he usually clarifies matters further by describing events in which he did not take part in the third person, while reserving the first person plural to describe events in which he did participate.[20] Thus the sieges of both Antioch and Jerusalem, from which he was absent, are described in the third person, whereas the journey through Asia Minor or Baldwin of Edessa's journey to Jerusalem are described in the first person plural.

Lastly, when describing events to which he was not an eyewitness, Fulcher frequently informs the audience on which alternative source he is relying. For instance he says that the size of the crusader armies at the outset of the crusade and at Nicaea is based on "those skilled at reckoning".[21] When identifying biblical places in the Holy Land and when explaining why the Dead Sea is so salty, he

---

15 "Illic inter arbores ceteras vidi quasdam poma terentes, de quibus cum collegissem, scire volens cuius naturae essent, inveni, rupto cortice, interius quasi pulverem atrum et exinde inanem prodire fumum": Ibid., 2.5.6.

16 "In qua aquula ego meos adaquavi equos": Ibid., 2.5.8.

17 Ibid., 2.9.8, 2.11.11, 3.47.

18 "Bellum cernebam, mente nutabam, ictus timebam": Ibid., 2.12.1. For the importance of eyewitnessing in Fulcher's text see also Epp, *Fulcher von Chartres*, p. 144.

19 Language: Fulcher, 1.13.4; Baldwin: Ibid., 1.14.2; chaplain: Ibid., 1.14.15; journey: Ibid., 2.2.4; Bethlehem: Ibid., 1.33.15–18; 1105: Ibid., 2.31.7–12; 1111: Ibid., 2.45.9.

20 For an unusual exception see Ibid., 2.32.6.

21 "De numero callebant": Ibid., 1.10.4–5.

makes it clear that these are only his conjectures. He explicitly says that his sources for the capture of Bohemond are those who managed to escape the defeat; that his source for Godfrey's death is the messenger who brought the news; that on events at the battle of Carrha (1104) he learned when he later visited Antioch; and that on Baldwin's expedition to the Red Sea he learned from participants whom "I myself very eagerly questioned".[22] When telling how Belek besieged and recaptured King Baldwin II he explains that "Because these things happened far from us we were with difficulty able to learn with any certainty of the affair. Nevertheless as exactly as I was able I have written down what others have told me".[23] Of Belek's later defeat by Joscelin he learned from the messenger that brought Belek's head to Jerusalem, who, Fulcher assures us, was present with the combatants in this battle.[24] Epp's study further indicates Fulcher's diligence in verifying facts he did not eyewitness himself. She particularly emphasizes that Fulcher did not rely only on information that came his way accidentally, but rather conducted intentional inquiries to learn and verify the facts, and in the second redaction of his work he corrected various factual mistakes he had committed while writing the first redaction.[25]

Raymond of Aguilers

Raymond of Aguilers presents a somewhat different picture to Fulcher. His general awareness of the problem of truth is already apparent in the prologue, where he says that he wrote the text in order to tell the truth about the crusade and correct lies which were spread by deserters,[26] whereas after reporting the death of his co-author Pons of Balazun, he goes much further than that, imploring the audience to believe in the truth of what he tells, and wishing that God will send him to Hell and blot him from the Book of Life if he does not tell the truth.[27] However, unlike Fulcher, Raymond shows concrete interest in the problem of truth only when dealing with

---

[22] Conjectures: Ibid., 1.34.4; 2.v.3; Bohemond: Ibid., 1.35.1–3; Godfrey: Ibid., 1.36; Carrha: Ibid., 2.26.11–12; Red Sea: "ego ipse avido corde ... rimabar": Ibid., 2.56.4.

[23] "Et quia procul a nobis facta haec aberant, vix certitudinem rei addiscere poteramus; verumtamen quem verius potui, a relatoribus mihi intimatum chartae commendavi": Ibid., 3.26.5.

[24] "Cum proeliantibus praesens fuit": Ibid., 3.31.6. The fact that Fulcher never mentions his reliance on the *Gesta Francorum* and on Raymond of Aguilers is of little importance. For I am interested here in the *attitude* of Fulcher's text to truth, rather than in its truthfulness.

[25] Epp, *Fulcher von Chartres*, pp. 144–45.

[26] Raymond of Aguilers, *Le 'Liber' de Raymond d'Aguilers*, ed. John H. Hill and Laurita L. Hill (Paris, 1969), p. 36 (hereafter cited as Raymond).

[27] "Oro igitur et obsecro omnes qui hec audituri sunt, ut credant hec ita fuisse. Quod si quicquam ego preter credita et visa studio, vel odio alicuius aposui, aponat michi Deus omnes plagas inferni, et deleat me de libro vite. Etenim licet ut plurima ignorem, hoc unum scio quia cum promotus ad sacerdotium in itinere Dei sim, magis debeo obedire Deo testificando veritatem, quam in texendo mendatia, alicuius muneris captare dispendia": Ibid., pp. 107–8.

the Holy Lance and the visions seen during the crusade, and perhaps his most important concern while writing his text was proving their authenticity. Raymond is constantly aware that there is a contradictory version of events regarding the Lance and the visions, a version which the audience may well be acquainted with, and that therefore there is a real danger that the audience will not believe what he says. In contrast, when relating military and political affairs, Raymond seems almost oblivious to the question of truth.[28]

Consequently, it is only in connection with the visions, the Lance and the other miracles that we find the three other abovementioned characteristics of eyewitness accounts, namely the emphasis on the importance of eyewitnessing; the appearance of the author as an eyewitness and a protagonist; and the distinction between eyewitnessing and other sources of information. When dealing with other issues, Raymond's text displays none of these characteristics.

Thus, when describing a miracle that occurred during the battle of Dorylaeum, Raymond admits that he did not see it himself, specifies as his source some apostate Turks who joined the crusader ranks, and then hastens to add that he has some first-hand supporting evidence for this, namely that for two days after the battle the crusaders saw dead riders and dead horses on the way.[29] That this supporting evidence has little to do with the miracle in question only goes to show how important it was for Raymond to provide some first-hand evidence in support of the miracle's veracity. The next appearance of the eyewitnessing theme is again in a miraculous context, this time when reporting the appearance of a comet.[30] Later on, when some crusaders are killed by the Muslims and a sign of a cross is discovered on their right shoulders, one of these unfortunates, who is still in his last agonies, is dragged back to the crusader camp to convince those who stayed there of the miracle's authenticity – an act which implies that eyewitnessing is the surest basis of truth.[31] The same point is later put into Peter Bartholomew's mouth, who is quoted as saying that he desires to pass the fire ordeal because no one believes what he tells, but, he implies, they will believe what they themselves see.[32] When he then describes the fire ordeal, Raymond recounts at length some miraculous visions seen by three respectable witnesses, supporting the authenticity of Peter's visions, and he then remarks that many more visions were seen at the time, but that "three capable witnesses are sufficient for all judgements".[33] After the ordeal is over the sceptics among the crusaders are gathered so that they can examine Peter themselves and be convinced of the miracle – again implying the superiority of eyewitnessing to other sources of information.[34]

28 Except for two minor occasions: Ibid., pp. 55–56, 110–11.

29 Ibid., pp. 45–46.

30 Ibid., p. 74.

31 Ibid., p. 102.

32 Ibid., p. 120.

33 "Cum ad omnem causam tres idonei testes sufficiunt": Ibid., pp. 121–22.

34 Ibid., p. 123.

Not surprisingly, the first appearance of Raymond as a protagonist coincides with the report of the first doubts cast on Peter Bartholomew's visions: Raymond of Saint Gilles, who believes Peter, places him in the custody of his chaplain, Raymond.[35] From now on Raymond constantly appears as a protagonist, but solely in connection with the question of the authenticity of the visions and the Holy Lance. He next appears together with his co-author Pons of Balazun among the twelve men who dug out the Holy Lance, and, he says, "I who write this kissed the point of the Lance as it barely protruded from the ground".[36] Some months later, when the question of the Lance's authenticity is discussed in an assembly of priests, Raymond testifies before them and repeats the story of his participation in the Lance's excavation in almost the same words, although this time it is told to the assembled priests rather than directly to the audience.[37] This double account of his participation in the Lance's excavation conveys to the audience a double message: first, that not only Raymond personally, but also the Church in general, considers eyewitnessing as a sure basis for truthfulness; and secondly, that since the priests on that occasion accepted Raymond's testimony, the audience can do the same without hesitation.

Raymond again appears as a protagonist when he and the bishop of Orange together question Peter Bartholomew about the truthfulness of his visions.[38] He then mentions that he took part in the great battle of Antioch, but the only thing he tells about his participation in this momentous battle is that he carried the Holy Lance and that this Lance protected the force led by Bishop Adhémar, so that no one in that force suffered any harm. He then goes out of his way to squash a rumour that Heraclius, standard-bearer of the bishop, was wounded there, saying that actually Heraclius gave the standard to someone else and was not in Adhémar's force at the time.[39]

Other appearances as protagonist include Raymond's witnessing the death of the saintly Adhémar; a story of how he and some other priests saw in a tent at Chastel-Rouge several visions which confirmed the authenticity of the Holy Lance; his participation in Peter Bartholomew's fire ordeal; a vision told to him by Peter Desiderius; and his participation in the excavation of some relics, in which Raymond infuriated St George by nearly causing the saint's bones to be left in Antioch instead of being taken along with the crusaders to Jerusalem.[40] Perhaps the

---

[35] Ibid., p. 72.

[36] "Et ego qui scripsi hec cum solus mucro adhuc appareret super terram, osculatus sum eam": Ibid., p. 75.

[37] Ibid., p. 119.

[38] Ibid., p. 76.

[39] "Vidi ego hec que loquor, et dominicam lanceam ibi ferebam. Quod si quis dicat Heraclium vicecomitem vexilliferum episcopi in hoc bello vulneratum fuisse, sciat quod et vexillum suum alii tradiderat, et ordinem nostrum longe reliquerat": Ibid., pp. 81–82.

[40] Adhémar: Ibid., p. 84; Chastel Rouge: Ibid., pp. 89–90; fire ordeal: Ibid., pp. 120–21; Peter Desiderius: Ibid., pp. 131–32; St George: Ibid., p. 132.

most interesting of all these examples is a private conversation Raymond had with Peter Bartholomew, in which the latter accused Raymond of causing him to pass the fire ordeal even though Raymond believed in Peter's visions, just in order to convince the others too of their truthfulness.[41]

It is also noteworthy that while discussing the Holy Lance and the visions, Raymond is always careful to differentiate between what he himself saw and what he heard from others, and to explain who said what, when and on what basis. In contrast, he shows no such care when treating non-religious matters, except perhaps on two occasions when he says he bases what he narrates on letters captured from the enemy, one on which his estimate of enemy casualties relies on reports by deserters, and one on which he names hearsay as his source.[42]

It is interesting to note here that Raymond's example shows that an author could be well aware of the connection between truth and eyewitnessing in one context while ignoring it in others. Indeed, it appears that in the high Middle Ages the eyewitnessing theme was more prominent in accounts of visions and miracles than in accounts of military and political events.

Gesta Francorum

So far, the present examination has largely confirmed the established opinion that views Fulcher's and Raymond's texts as comparatively reliable eyewitness accounts. Things are very different when we come to examine the *Gesta Francorum*. This text has long been considered, for better or worse, the most important and influential eyewitness account of the First Crusade. Recently, scholars have begun to question the *Gesta*'s relative importance and reliability, and John France in particular rightly argues that the modern research of the First Crusade has been over-influenced by the *Gesta*, whose framework, prejudices and interests have been built into almost all modern writings about the crusade.[43]

However, a close reading of the *Gesta* reveals that though its agenda and concerns indeed came to dominate scholarly attention in some respects, in other respects they are completely ignored. And if reading the *Gesta* as the main eyewitness account of the First Crusade does some injustice to our understanding of the crusade, it does at least equal injustice to our understanding of the *Gesta*,

---

[41] Ibid., pp. 123–24.

[42] Letters: Ibid., pp. 110, 135–36; deserters: Ibid., p. 57; hearsay: Ibid., p. 158.

[43] John France, "The Anonymous *Gesta Francorum* and the *Historia Francorum qui ceperunt Iherusalem* of Raymond of Aguilers and the *Historia Hierosolymitano itinere* of Peter Tudebode: An Analysis of the Textual Relations between Primary Sources of the First Crusade", in *Crusades Sources*, p. 59; John France, *Victory in the East: A Military History of the First Crusade* (Cambridge, 1994), pp. 378–79. See also Susan Edgington, "The First Crusade: Reviewing the Evidence", in *The First Crusade. Origins and Impact*, ed. Jonathan Phillips (Manchester, 1997), pp. 57–77.

for it is not an eyewitness account at all. By that I do not mean that the *Gesta*'s anonymous author was not present at the First Crusade. Rather, I mean that he had no intention of writing "an eyewitness account", and that the text he produced lacks the main characteristics of eyewitness accounts, as well as their main merits and faults.

Though the *Gesta* includes several incidents in which some protagonists are concerned by the problem of truth – most prominently in connection with Peter Bartholomew's visions and Stephen of Blois's false report to Emperor Alexius about the situation in Antioch[44] – the only occasion when we have some hint that the *Gesta* itself is subject to the same problem is when the Anonymous reports that a host of saints came to the help of the crusaders at the great battle of Antioch, and remarks that "This is credible, for many of our men saw it".[45] In no other place is there the slightest hint that his account is open to doubt. Thus when reporting the visions of Peter Bartholomew and another priest, and the crusaders' reaction to them, the Anonymous indeed says that some did not believe the accounts of these visions, but he seems oblivious to the possibility that some may refuse to believe his own account as well.[46] Unlike Fulcher and Raymond, he never implores the audience to believe what he says, never assures it that he is telling the truth, and never brings forward evidence in support of what he says. Characteristically, the text does not open with a promise to tell only the truth, but plunges straight into the matter. Likewise, despite having a much ruder style than either Raymond or Fulcher, the Anonymous nowhere apologises for it, nor does he wave his credentials as an eyewitness in defence.[47]

He is even less concerned with eyewitnessing and apart from the abovementioned occasion there is only one other occasion in which he refers to eyewitnessing and makes a connection between it and truth. When Tancred reports the arrival of a large Egyptian army in 1099, Raymond of Saint Gilles and Robert of Normandy do not believe him and order some of their own knights to go reconnoitre. Only when these knights confirm Tancred's report from first hand are Raymond and Robert convinced.[48] In contrast, the Anonymous at one point draws attention to the limitation and narrowness of eyewitness accounts, saying with regard to the siege of

---

[44] *Gesta Francorum et aliorum Hierosolimitanorum*, ed. and trans. Rosalind Hill (London, 1962), pp. 59–60, 64–65 (hereafter cited as *Gesta*).

[45] "Hec uerba credenda sunt, quia plures ex nostris uiderunt": Ibid., p. 69.

[46] Ibid., pp. 57–60.

[47] Colin Morris, "The *Gesta Francorum* as Narrative History", *Reading Medieval Studies* 19 (1993), 56–57.

[48] *Gesta*, p. 94. It is noteworthy that in those occasions when the protagonists are concerned with the problem of truth – for example, in the disputed visions and Stephen of Blois's report of the situation in Antioch – neither the protagonists nor the Anonymous appeal to eyewitnessing as a test of truth. Rather, the visionaries try to establish their truthfulness by oaths and ordeals, whereas Stephen's account is discredited on the grounds that he is a coward, without the fact that he is an eyewitness being disputed: Ibid., pp. 57–60, 65.

Antioch that "there is in this land neither clerk nor layman who could write down the whole story or describe it as it happened".[49]

It is therefore not surprising that the Anonymous never appears as a protagonist, and never refers to himself as an eyewitness. Nowhere in the text is there an explicit statement that the author participated in the crusade. Moreover, as Colin Morris has shown in a recent article, even his use of the first person plural is not necessarily self-referential, and it is unsafe to assume that whenever he uses the first person plural he indicates his personal participation in or eyewitnessing of the described events. Clear examples of this are the cases in which he uses the first person plural to refer to two different forces which operated at the same time at a great distance from one another.[50] The Anonymous ignores his own actions to such an extent, that we know almost nothing about him, not even his name; we cannot be sure where he was at each stage of the crusade; and as recent articles have suggested, we cannot even be certain whether he was a knight or a clerk.[51]

We see then that the Anonymous makes absolutely no attempt to establish his status as an eyewitness in the minds of the audience. He displays the same disregard by failing to distinguish between events he eyewitnessed and events he did not, and by almost never specifying what alternative sources of information – if any – he relied upon. For example, he tells of the "peasants' crusade", in which he did not participate; of the secret councils of the Byzantine emperor; of numerous secret meetings of the crusader leaders; of the Turks' thoughts and plans during the siege of Nicaea; of an apocryphal discussion between the Turkish leader Kerbuqa and his mother; of the meeting between Count Stephen of Blois and Alexius's council; of what Kerbuqa thought during the battle of Antioch; or of how the Egyptian commander viewed his defeat at the battle of Ascalon.[52] He recounts some of these events – which he surely did not eyewitness – with such great familiarity and vividness, that it makes it difficult to be certain whether the equal familiarity and vividness with which he recounts events like the storming of Antioch prove that he participated in them personally.

It is particularly important to note here his repeated efforts to describe events from the enemy's viewpoint, a viewpoint about which he had little first-hand information. Throughout the narrative the Anonymous never ceases to oscillate between the viewpoints of crusaders, Greeks and Muslims, as collectives and as individuals, and there is scarcely a battle or a skirmish in which he does not give the audience at least a glimpse of what was going on on the other side of the hill.

---

49 "Nemo est in his partibus siue clericus siue laicus qui omnino possit scribere uel narrare, sicut res gesta est": Ibid., p. 44.

50 Morris, "*Gesta Francorum*", 67–68.

51 Ibid., 61, 66–67; Edgington, "First Crusade", p. 55.

52 Peasants' Crusade: *Gesta*, pp. 2–4; Byzantine councils: Ibid., p. 11; crusader leaders: see for example Ibid., pp. 44–45; Nicaea: Ibid., pp. 14–15; Kerbuqa: Ibid., pp. 53–56; Stephen of Blois: Ibid., pp. 63–65; Antioch: Ibid., pp. 68–69; Ascalon: Ibid., pp. 96–97.

Indeed, there are quite a few events which are described in greater detail from the Muslim than from the crusader viewpoint.

Not only the Muslims' actions, but also their plans, emotions, hopes, and fears, receive his attention, and it is not always evident that he privileges the crusaders' viewpoint. On one occasion in particular his contrast of crusader and Muslim viewpoints is almost ironic, and can be interpreted as tacit criticism of the narrowness of eyewitness viewpoints. In his description of the battle of Dorylaeum he says that the crusaders were astounded by the numbers of the attacking Turks, "for nearly all the mountains and hills and valleys, and all the flat country within and without the hills, were covered with this accursed folk".[53] Yet when he afterwards quotes the description of the battle as told by the Turkish leader Suleiman to a group of Arabs, he has Suleiman describing the crusader army in exactly the same words, saying that it was so huge "that if you or anyone else had been there you would have thought that all the mountains and hills and valleys and all the plains were full of them".[54]

Another illuminating case is the report of how the Egyptian commander viewed his defeat at Ascalon. While describing the battle from the crusader viewpoint, the narrator confesses that he does not know how many soldiers the Egyptians had there, but then the Egyptian commander is quoted giving a precise number.[55] This creates the impression that the readers are given direct access to the Egyptian's mind, unmediated by the narrator. Though this is most probably an accidental slip by the author, the fact that he could commit such a slip is itself very telling.

It is noteworthy that in contrast to the Anonymous, Fulcher, who is committed to factual truthfulness and eyewitnessing, very rarely describes events from the Muslim viewpoint,[56] and though he relied extensively on the *Gesta*, he rarely if ever plagiarizes the episodes in which events are described from that viewpoint. Raymond, who cares about factual truth and eyewitnessing only in the religious context, shows more willingness to describe military and political events from the Muslim viewpoint,[57] though he does so to a much lesser extent than the Anonymous. It is characteristic that in their respective descriptions of the second siege of Antioch, Raymond tells us about a dialogue between Christ and His mother witnessed by the priest Stephen, whereas the Anonymous chooses to recount a dialogue between Kerbuqa and his mother, which he probably invented himself.

Whatever may have remained of his credibility as an eyewitness the Anonymous happily destroys by giving free rein to the most dreaded enemy of anyone who wishes to write an eyewitness account – his imagination. For what worse accusation

---

[53] "Quia pene omnes montes et colles et ualles et omnia plana loca intus et extra undique erant cooperta de illa excommunicata generatione": Ibid., p. 19.

[54] "Ut si uos aut aliquis illic adesset, putaret quod omnes montes et colles uallesque et omnia plana loca plena essent illorum multitudine": Ibid., p. 22.

[55] Ibid., pp. 95–96, 96–97.

[56] For two rare exceptions see Fulcher, 1.22.4–8, 1.31.5.

[57] E.g., Raymond, pp. 80, 101, 155, 157.

can one direct at an eyewitness than that he relies on his imagination? The Anonymous's use of the imagination is especially evident when he tries to give an account of events from the Muslim viewpoint. Since he often had no information about the Muslims' thoughts and actions, he turned to his imagination instead, as he does for example in reporting the dialogues between Suleiman and the Arabs or Kerbuqa and his mother.

The Anonymous did not intend to deceive the audience by such inventions. These were merely the medieval equivalent of modern analysis. When historians today want to fill in unknown factual gaps by conjectures or to interpret known facts, they normally do so in analytical sections, the style of which clearly distinguishes them from "the facts". In contrast, twelfth-century historians (like classical historians) rarely wrote analytical sections, perhaps for fear of boring the audience, and instead they incorporated their conjectures and interpretations into the narrative as integral parts of it. They did so by extrapolating or inventing incidents and episodes.[58]

Inventing speeches and dialogues was a particularly favourite means of conjecturing and interpreting without becoming boring. Such direct speech episodes were not meant to be factually true. Even when an author had reliable information about what a particular protagonist said, he could hardly have expected to report his exact words. (Thus when Guibert of Nogent quotes Urban's speech at Clermont, he explicitly asserts that he conveys only Urban's meaning, not his exact words.)[59] Instead, such direct speech episodes were meant to represent what was probably said, or what should have been said. Even more importantly, they were often meant to serve as mouthpieces for the author's own views. For they allowed the author to reflect on events and analyse them, but because the words were put into the mouth of protagonists rather than that of the narrator, it did not break the continuity of the narrative. Indeed, when read aloud by a skilled performer, such speeches and dialogues may well have been among the most dramatic and entertaining parts of the narrative.

Thus in the *Gesta Francorum*, the fanciful dialogue between Kerbuqa and his mother is at one and the same time both the most important interpretative part of the entire text, and one of its most entertaining parts. Kerbuqa's old mother, who is a skilled astrologer and fortune-teller, comes to Kerbuqa before the battle of Antioch to warn him of his impending disaster. She explains to Kerbuqa what the crusade is, who the crusaders are, what is their place in the divine scheme, and why he will be

---

58 It is interesting to note that analogous techniques have been re-adopted in present day military memoirs. Late-modern military memoirs, though written by eyewitnesses of wars, make extensive use of the imagination for interpretative purposes. Indeed, some of the most influential twentieth-century "eyewitness accounts" of wars are either partially or completely fictional (for example, *All Quiet on the Western Front*, *The Good Soldier Švejk*, and *Catch-22*).

59 "His ergo etsi non verbis, tamen intentionibus usus est": Guibert de Nogent, *Dei gesta per Francos et cinq autres textes*, ed. Robert B. C. Huygens, CCCM 127A (Turnhout, 1996), p. 111 (hereafter cited as Guibert). About interpretation and facts, see also Guibert, p. 303.

defeated despite his overwhelming military superiority. Through her voice, we can hear the Anonymous's own opinions.

It may be asked why the Anonymous chose such an unlikely mouthpiece to express his version of crusader ideology. He could have invented a speech by Bishop Adhémar of Le Puy – as Albert of Aachen does[60] – and put the things into Adhémar's mouth. But instead he chooses to put them into the mouth of an elderly Muslim sorceress, who is also the mother of the enemy commander. The reason is, first, to add magical colour and a touch of epic to the narrative. The appearance of a sorceress before a great battle to prophesy catastrophe – in this case for Kerbuqa – was a favourite topos in history and legend. Walter the Chancellor has a moonstruck woman prophesy doom before the Battle of the Field of Blood in 1119 and Ernoul has a Saracen sorceress do the same before Hattin.[61] Kerbuqa, like Roland and the Nibelungen, is going to battle though he (and the audience) knows beforehand that he is doomed.

But equally important is the Anonymous's bid for "objectivity". He does not want to write a narrow eyewitness account, but rather an authoritative story. Therefore he chooses as his mouthpiece the most radical "other" he can think of. Instead of speaking in his own name – a Christian male knight (or cleric) – he puts his views into the mouth of an old Muslim female sorceress. The message to the reader is that if even such an unlikely person upholds this view, it must be the right view. For this end, the Anonymous renounces his potential authority as an eyewitness.

The Anonymous nowhere implies that this episode and others like it are factually true and, indeed, it seems that the question whether they are factually true or not was irrelevant in the eyes of both the Anonymous and his intended audience. It is this that distinguishes him from Fulcher and Raymond. They too must have relied occasionally on their imagination for interpretative ends, but they make every effort to hide this and to convince the audience that everything they say is factually true.[62]

Hence, the Anonymous was not writing an eyewitness account. His focus on the Muslim viewpoint coupled with his extensive use of the imagination indicate that the reason why he made no attempt to write an eyewitness account, and even de-emphasized on purpose his status as an eyewitness, is that he intended to write a general and fully rounded history of the crusade, including a Muslim as well as a crusader viewpoint, and such a history cannot be written from the narrow viewpoint of an eyewitness. For it should be remembered that justifying one's text by emphasizing the importance of factual truth and eyewitnessing has a price. An

---

[60] Albertus Aquensis, "Historia Hierosolymitana", 3.36 in *RHC Oc* 4 (hereafter cited as Albert).

[61] Walter the Chancellor, *Bella Antiochena*, ed. Heinrich Hagenmeyer (Innsbruck, 1896), pp. 83–84; *Chronique d'Ernoul et de Bernard le Trésorier*, ed. Louis de Mas Latrie (Paris, 1871), pp. 163–64.

[62] An interesting case is Fulcher's account of a dream which the Turkish leader Belek had. Fulcher puts this dream into a factual context, and hints how he got wind of it, by informing the readers that when he woke up Belek told the dream to his priests, and on their advice sent men to kill Joscelin: Fulcher, 3.24.1.

author who justifies his text in such a way and who emphasizes his status as an eyewitness, makes it very hard for himself to oscillate between contradictory viewpoints or to write about matters which he did not eyewitness and about which he has little or no alternative reliable sources. Not only would he thereby fail to stand up to his own standards, but, displaying contradictory viewpoints of the same events would also sap the foundation of his approach by showing that an eyewitness account is necessarily partial and subjective (something of which, as was shown above, the Anonymous was aware).

We can conclude then that in contrast to Fulcher and Raymond, the Anonymous was not attempting to write a factually true eyewitness account of the crusade, but rather a general history of the crusade, which would give a fully rounded view of events, and in order to achieve this aim he was willing to rely on his imagination and on the wildest pieces of gossip as much as on his own first-hand experience. The concerns and the agenda of the *Gesta* are therefore very different from those of an eyewitness account, and consequently reading it as such an account is a misunderstanding. Indeed, the *Gesta* is closer in spirit to eleventh-century epics than it is to an eyewitness account. Its interest in the enemy's viewpoint and its admiration of enemy warriors certainly reminds one much more of the *Chanson de Roland* and its like than of Fulcher's *Historia*.[63] Seeing the *Gesta* as an epic account may also explain why it dominated the perception of the First Crusade from the twelfth century to this day, for the spirit of the *Gesta* captures better than any other contemporary account what the First Crusade really was – an epic.

Guibert of Nogent

The method of analysis used above can also be applied to second-generation accounts of the First Crusade. In these accounts too the attitude towards truth and eyewitnessing is central to understanding the authors' purposes and reliability. I would like to exemplify this by examining two second-generation works, those of Guibert of Nogent and Albert of Aachen.

Guibert of Nogent wrote a mirror image of the ideal eyewitness account. He himself did not participate in the crusade and he had before him accounts written by participants, above all the *Gesta Francorum*. He frankly admits that he relies heavily on the *Gesta*, and he is therefore afraid that the audience may value his own work less than the *Gesta* (which was indeed the case both in his own day and today).[64] Hence Guibert is hard pressed to justify the value of his own project, and

---

63 For similarities between the *Gesta* and *chansons de geste* see Morris, "*Gesta Francorum*", 61–63. See also: Kenneth Baxter Wolf, "Crusade and Narrative: Bohemond and the *Gesta*", *Journal of Medieval History* 17 (1991), 207–16.

64 Guibert, p. 80.

he attempts to do so by taking the traditional arguments that support eyewitness accounts and turning them on their head.

First he emphasizes the importance of eloquence. He argues that "honesty nourishes eloquence"[65] and that the bad Latin and style of both the *Gesta* and Fulcher's work would cause their audience to discount them, especially because such an important matter as the crusade demands high style.[66] He says that the story of the crusade is hidden in the *Gesta*'s artless speech like a precious gem in the lowest dust.[67] In contrast, he praises his own Latin and writing skill,[68] and promises to rescue and clean this gem and turn the crude materials provided by the Anonymous and Fulcher into a worthy history.[69] He goes as far as boasting in his highly polished and complicated style, warning that if people find it obscure and difficult, it only testifies to the weakness of their intellect.[70] Fulcher's fears that some readers may "confuse the truth of events for the sake of pompous eloquence" were well founded.

Secondly, Guibert downplays the problems of writing from second-hand information. Like a modern historian, he says that he learned the facts from different unrelated sources, namely the *Gesta* and various oral eyewitness accounts, and that he compared the *Gesta*'s version to that of the eyewitness accounts and found them completely in accord. He admits that he might nevertheless have made some mistakes, but only because he wrote about things he did not see himself and not because of an intention to deceive.[71] Later Guibert takes a stronger stand, saying that "If anyone objects that I did not see, he cannot object on the grounds that I did not hear, because I believe that hearing is in a certain way almost as good as seeing." He defends this awkward position rather clumsily, arguing that nobody dares doubt the veracity of hagiographies written on the basis of hearsay. He likewise cites the Bible, arguing that stories based on reliable witnesses should be accepted as truth.[72]

Thirdly, in what is a seemingly contradicting and self-defeating manoeuvre, Guibert casts doubt on the reliability of eyewitness accounts, as if forgetting that he himself relied on them. He takes particular delight in exposing "miraculous" frauds. He thus doubts Fulcher's account of how when a crusader ship drowned, the bodies washed ashore were found with signs of crosses over them, and lists various occasions when people fabricated such signs.[73] He narrates earlier how a certain

[65] "Pabulum eloquentiae ... honestas": Ibid., p. 79.

[66] Ibid., pp. 79–80, 329.

[67] Ibid., pp. 80–81.

[68] Ibid., p. 80.

[69] Ibid., pp. 81–82.

[70] Ibid., pp. 81–82, 200.

[71] Ibid., p. 82. See also pp. 277, 351.

[72] "Si michi plane id obicitur quia non viderim, id obici non potest quod non audierim, cum visui auditum quodammodo supparem profecto crediderim": Ibid., p. 166.

[73] Ibid., pp. 329–30.

abbot chiselled the sign of the cross into his forehead, pretending it was a miracle, and was believed by many who saw it.[74] He gives another example from his own experience, telling how one day in Beauvais he saw clouds in the sky in the shape of a crane or a stork, when suddenly many people began crying that they saw a cross in the sky.[75]

He accuses Fulcher of a more serious mistake, ridiculing his numerical estimates. He thus says that Fulcher's estimate that six million pilgrims set out for Jerusalem is preposterous, noting that he would be surprised if the whole Occident together contains such a number of people.[76] He becomes downright vicious when saying that Fulcher's doubts about the Holy Lance's authenticity should not be believed, given that when the Lance was found by the crusaders who were starving and dying in Antioch, Fulcher was feasting at his ease in Edessa.[77]

However, a more careful reading of Guibert reveals that he has an interesting strategy to extricate himself from this seemingly self-defeating position. Guibert rarely doubts the facts told by eyewitnesses. He doubts either facts told by those who did not witness them (e.g. Fulcher and the Lance) or the *interpretations* given by eyewitnesses. Thus he does not doubt that eyewitnesses saw bodies with the sign of the cross on them. He doubts only Fulcher's interpretation that this is a miracle rather than a fraud.

Accordingly, Guibert offers a division of labour that every modern historian would love to accept, between the crude uneducated producers of "bare facts", and the professional scholar who alone knows how to interpret them correctly and set them into an eloquent narrative. He explicitly says regarding Fulcher's narrative that he took from it only "the naked limbs of the deeds", rescuing them from Fulcher's inadequate style.[78]

This approach is also evident in his claim to be collating different accounts, and in his awareness that even a true eyewitness account is always partial. He thus takes the Anonymous's remark about the siege of Antioch that "there is in this land neither clerk nor layman who could write down the whole story or describe it as it happened", and sharpens the point further, saying that "We believe that no-one can relate what was done in the siege of Antioch, because among those who were there none could really be found who could have seen everything that happened

[74] Ibid., p. 197.

[75] Ibid., pp. 330–31.

[76] Ibid., p. 344. Epp (*Fulcher von Chartres*, p. 148) argues that indeed Fulcher's earlier numerical estimates were grossly exaggerated, but later, when he developed his skills as a historian, his estimates became far more realistic.

[77] Guibert, p. 332. It is noteworthy that Guibert knew that Fulcher was at Edessa during the siege of Antioch thanks to the careful way in which Fulcher's text distinguishes between events Fulcher eyewitnessed himself and events he did not.

[78] "Cum enim vir isdem ampullas et sesquipedalia verba proiciat et luridos inanium scematum colores exporrigat, nuda michi rerum gestarum exinde libuit membra corripere meique qualiscumque eloquii sacco potius quam pretexta contegere": Ibid., p. 329.

around that city, nor could have understood it entirely in the order in which the deeds were done".[79]

Hence Guibert clearly distinguishes between eyewitness accounts and histories, believing that each has different aims and privileges. In particular, the privilege of embellishing and interpreting facts is something he denies eyewitness accounts while gladly exercising himself. He often adds colour to the stories he extracts from the *Gesta*, as well as lyrical verses, biblical quotations, allegories, and theological interpretations. At times he invents whole episodes, as for example when he tells about the martyrdom of a certain knight and invents for him a fitting "last words" scene.[80]

Yet ironically, Guibert falls victim to his own game. Since he covets the role of the interpretative historian, he depicts the previous works as "crude and partial eyewitness accounts" rather than as such histories. He therefore fails to notice that the Anonymous also intended to write a history and incorporated into his text many fanciful conjectures and interpretative details. Consequently Guibert believes in the factual truthfulness of all the details provided by the Anonymous.

For instance, Guibert incorporates Suleiman's fabricated speech after Dorylaeum into his own narrative, embellishing it to the best of his ability.[81] He similarly falls victim to the story of Kerbuqa's mother. He closely copies the Anonymous's story, though with a more polished style, more quotation from the Bible, and more theological finesse, which make the whole episode almost comical. Whereas the Anonymous has the mother speak as a Muslim should, referring to the Frankish god as "their god" ("deus eorum"), in Guibert's narrative the Christian theologian shows all too easily through the disguise of the Muslim sorceress. For he has the woman speaking about "God" and "Christ", and even making hair-splitting distinctions between God the Father and God the Son.[82] Yet Guibert appears to have believed that "the bare limbs" of the original story in the *Gesta* were factually true. Thus he later tells of a prophecy heard by Robert of Flanders twelve years before the crusade, and to establish its authenticity he remarks that this prophecy accords with the words of Kerbuqa's mother, which he quoted earlier.[83]

We can conclude then that Guibert clearly wanted to write a history rather than to just collect and preserve eyewitness accounts. He therefore explains the differences between eyewitness accounts and histories in terms of their respective style, aims, opportunities, and limitations, and repeatedly emphasizes the superiority of the

---

[79] "Quae facta sunt in Antiochena obsidione nemini relatu possibilia existimamus, quia inter eos qui ibidem interfuerunt nullus profecto potuit repperiri qui *cuncta*, quae circa eandem urbem agi potuerunt, valuisset pervidere vel ita comprehendere ad integrum, sicut se habet ordo gestae rei": Ibid., p. 200; and see pp. 227, 312.

[80] Ibid., p. 199; and see pp. 323–27.

[81] Ibid., pp. 159–60.

[82] Ibid., pp. 213–16.

[83] "Quibus gentilis hominis verbis illa quae superius relata sunt Curbaran matris dicta concordant": Ibid., p. 320.

latter over the former. However, he used his primary sources in a cavalier fashion, which makes his text a valuable source for crusader ideology, but a dubious one for hard facts.

Albert of Aachen

Albert of Aachen was a less pretentious author. In spite of Claude Cahen's opinion, it is quite clear from the narrative that Albert was not an eyewitness to the crusade, as Edgington shows.[84] Thus he never mentions himself as a protagonist and he always uses the third person when speaking of the crusade and the crusaders. Therefore Albert faced the same problem as Guibert in justifying his work. Yet he chose a different course. Whereas Guibert glorifies in the role of the interpretative and eloquent historian producing a learned and polished history, Albert seems to have chosen the more humble role of a compiler, collecting various oral accounts and writing them down as a sort of hotchpotch history.[85]

The difference between his chosen aim and that of Guibert is evident already in Albert's prologue. Whereas Guibert's declared aim is to improve upon existing written narratives, Albert's states that his main aim is to preserve for posterity oral accounts that he has heard and that may otherwise be lost ("I decided to commend to posterity at least some of the things which were made known to me by listening to those who had been there and from their reports").[86] And whereas Guibert boasts of his interpretative and writing skills, Albert nowhere speaks of interpretation and apologizes for his lack of writing skills.[87]

Since Albert presents himself as a compiler, the self-proclaimed value of his work depended on the value of the accounts he compiled. Consequently, Albert stresses both the value of eyewitnessing and the fact that he relied on accounts of "those who had been there".[88] Thus on one occasion he stresses the truthfulness of what he writes, saying that "We have heard, not merely from hearsay, but also from the very truthful relations of persons who themselves took part in these tribulations".[89] On another occasion, when he vividly describes the extreme misery to which even the crusader leaders were reduced at the time of the battle of Antioch,

---

84 Cahen suggests that, given the wealth of accurate details in books 7 to 12, Albert may have lived in the East for some time. Yet Albert could have gathered these details from his informers – or invented at least some of them himself. For a discussion of Cahen's argument and Albert's sources of information, see Edgington, "Albert of Aachen", pp. 23–28.

85 Ibid., p. 35.

86 "Temerario ausu decrevi saltem ex his aliqua memoriae commendare quae auditu et relatione nota fierent ab his qui praesentes affuissent": Albert, 1.1. The translation is taken from Edgington, "Albert of Aachen", p. 35.

87 Albert, 1.1.

88 "His qui praesentes affuissent": Ibid., 1.1.

89 "Comperimus etiam illic, non ex auditu solum, sed ex veridica eorum relatione qui et participes fuerunt ejusdem tribulationis": Ibid., 3.2.

Albert notes that "Only those who have never heard anything like it and those who did not see the evils which befell such eminent men in the course of so long an exile marvel at these miseries and impoverishments of the noble leaders, but those people do not marvel who bear witness that they saw Duke Godfrey himself and Robert prince of Flanders in need of provisions and horses at the last".[90] He then adds regarding Robert of Flanders that "Robert was likewise in need […] and those who were there and saw this with their own eyes claim he often used to beg in the army, and we learnt from many people's accounts that he had obtained the very horse which he mounted on the day of the great battle by begging".[91]

On about ten other occasions Albert says that he relies on the accounts of eyewitnesses, using the formulaic phrases that he wrote such and such a thing according to the accounts of "those who were present" or those "who saw with their eyes".[92] On another occasion Albert specifies his source as the reports of truthful and noble men.[93] He also stresses the importance of eyewitnessing twice in the body of his narrative. When news of the coming of Kerbuqa's army reach the crusaders at Antioch, they at first refuse to believe them and they send scouts to verify them. They believe in the news only when these scouts return, and tell the princes what they saw "with their eyes".[94] Similarly, even in the midst of his imaginative account of the Muslim war council in Samarkand, Albert repeatedly has the Khurasan Muslims refusing to believe in the reports coming from Asia Minor and Suleiman stressing that these reports are true, for they are based on what he himself has seen.[95]

Albert nowhere casts doubt on the value of eyewitnessing, yet as can only be expected from a compiler, he does say that no single eyewitness report can give an exhaustive account of everything that happened. Thus, after his account of the siege and battle of Antioch – at exactly the same point where the Anonymous and Guibert insert similar remarks – Albert writes that "the other deeds which were done in this battle, among the Christian people as well as the Gentile, and those wonderful and unbelievable things which were done during the siege of Antioch cannot, I think, be recorded by any pen, any memory, so many and such various things are reported to have happened there".[96]

---

90 "Super his miseriis et attenuationibus nobilium procerum, mirantur solummodo hi qui nunquam simile huic audierunt, nec mala viderunt quae in tam longo exsilio contigerunt tam egregiis viris, sed non mirantur qui ipsum ducem Godefridum et Robertum, principem Flandriae, ad ultimum egere rebus et equis se vidisse testati sunt": Ibid., 4.55. The translation is taken from Edgington's forthcoming edition.

91 "Eguit pariter Robertus ... quem saepius in exercitu mendicasse asserunt qui affuerunt et oculis inspexerunt; ipsumque equum quem in die belli ascenderat mendicando eum acquisisse multorum relatione didicimus": Ibid., 4.55. The translation is taken from Edgington's forthcoming edition.

92 For example, "ut aiunt qui praesentes fuerunt" (Ibid., 1.23) or "ut aiunt pro vero qui haec oculis viderunt" (Ibid., 8.21). See also Ibid., 1.24, 2.33, 3.1, 3.4, 4.34, 6.23, 6.50.

93 "Verum, ut a veridicis et nobilibus viris relatum est": Ibid., 8.46.

94 "Oculis viderant": Ibid., 4.12–14.

95 Ibid., 4.1–4.

96 "Cetera quae in hoc bello acta sunt, tam in populo Christiano quam Gentili, quae etiam in obsidione urbis Antiochiae mira et inaudita gesta sunt, nullius stylo, nullius memoria aestimo retinenda: tot tamque

However, Albert's work is far from being a compilation of eyewitness accounts. For as Edgington concludes, Albert was not particular in his choice of information sources, and took material from hearsay accounts, fables and *chansons* just as readily as from eyewitness accounts.[97] He seems to have shown restraint only when it came to accounts of miraculous events and visions. There must have been an abundance of such accounts circulating in the wake of the crusade (as Guibert complains), yet Albert records just very few of them. Similarly, he downplays the whole Holy Lance issue, mentioning it only twice and even then very briefly.[98]

There are many cases in which it is clear that Albert either relied on dubious sources of information or invented details and incidents himself. Thus he narrates in great detail how a small crusader force was completely destroyed in Asia Minor, recounting even such details as how a lady called Florine fled by herself until she was caught up with by the Turks and fell pierced with six arrows.[99] Similarly he narrates how a knight called Arnoul went hunting alone in the mountains and was killed in a Muslim ambush.[100] It is not clear what possible source of information Albert could have had for such incidents, and he volunteers no details.

This is even clearer in cases when he narrates events on the Muslim side of the hill and from a Muslim viewpoint. Like the Anonymous and Guibert, Albert felt the need to give a fully rounded account of events, from the Muslim as well as from the crusader side. Whether he heard stories about the Muslim side from his informers, or whether he wove such stories himself, is not clear. Either way, at least some of these stories are fanciful inventions. For instance, the first six chapters of Book 4 are a mostly imaginary and grossly inaccurate account of how King Yaghi-Siyan of Antioch sent the refugee King Suleiman of Nicaea to the court of his overlord in Samarkand to ask for help, and of how Suleiman was received there by Kerbuqa. Albert gives minute graphic details about the reception, and throughout the story quotes in direct speech several speeches and dialogues of Yaghi-Siyan, Suleiman, and Kerbuqa.[101] (Needless to say, the references to Suleiman and Samarkand are fanciful mistakes.) He then devotes two more chapters to describing the preparations of Kerbuqa's army.[102] On another occasion Albert quotes in direct speech what a Muslim messenger told Kerbuqa in the middle of the battle of Antioch[103] and he similarly quotes in direct speech a secret Turkish war council.[104]

---

diversa illic exsitisse referuntur": Ibid., 4.56. The translation is taken from Edgington's forthcoming edition.

97 Edgington, "Albert of Aachen", pp. 28–31, 36–37.

98 For visions see Albert, 1.4, 4.38, 5.25, 6.26, 6.33, 6.36–37; for the Holy Lance see Ibid., 4.43, 5.32; for a similar argument see Edgington, "Albert of Aachen", p. 35.

99 Albert, 3.54.

100 Ibid., 9.52.

101 Ibid., 4.1–6.

102 Ibid., 4.7–8.

103 Ibid., 4.53.

104 Ibid., 5.7. See also 1.19, 2.39, 3.30, 3.35, 3.63, 8.18–19, 9.28. It is likely that some information

Albert's imagination probably also played a role in the wording of the many letters and speeches he incorporates into his narrative.[105] He never indicates the sources he relied upon for either the letters or the speeches. In the former case, he may have used some written source, but it does not seem likely. The fact that some of these quoted letters contain standard formulas and legalistic wording proves little, for Albert could easily have invented these as well. In some cases, Albert may have used direct speech as a convenient way to present information he received from witnesses. In other cases, these speeches and letters may have been a complete invention of Albert, serving as a means of conveying his own conjectures and interpretations.

The most important thing is that with the exception of the above references to eyewitness accounts, and a few references to hearsay,[106] Albert nowhere indicates what sources he relied upon; he does not distinguish clearly between stories he heard from eyewitnesses and stories he gathered from other sources; and he never mentions his reliance on *chansons de geste*. Likewise, unlike Guibert, Albert is not critical of his sources and he makes no distinctions between the various episodes he recounts in terms of their credibility.

Hence in theory Albert was well aware of the value of eyewitnessing, and his prologue in particular gives the impression that his work is credible for it is largely based on eyewitness accounts. Yet in the body of the text eyewitnessing does not figure prominently and there is no noticeable attempt to distinguish between eyewitness accounts and other sources. Consequently the text is extremely valuable for gauging what people in Europe told and heard about the crusade, but as a source for hard facts it should be treated with caution.

Conclusion

From examining these five sources for the First Crusade, it appears that contemporary authors were well aware of the difference between writing "an eyewitness account" and writing "a history", and of the different advantages and limitations of these two genres. Which of the two they chose to write depended not only on their sources of information, but also on their envisioned aims and as the case of the *Gesta Francorum* shows an eyewitness may well have chosen to write a history rather than an eyewitness account.

Equally important is the fact that despite their theoretical awareness of the unique credibility of eyewitnessing, in practice authors such as Albert and Guibert were not

---

about the Muslim side was received from deserters, but Albert only once refers to deserters giving information: Ibid., 3.66.

[105] Letters: for example, Ibid., 2.2–3, 9.43, 9.46; speeches: for example, Ibid., 2.3, 2.35, 2.40, 3.6–7, 3.9, 3.36, 4.15.

[106] Ibid., 3.37, 4.16, 5.3, 6.14, 6.24, 6.44, 6.49, 7.32, 8.39.

necessarily either interested or skilful in sifting eyewitness accounts from other sources. Even authors who in their meta-text seem keenly aware of the importance of factual accuracy and the value of eyewitnessing may just be paying lip service. A major reason for this was that it was common to rely on imaginative inventions to convey conjectures and interpretations.

Hence in evaluating the reliability of these texts, it is not enough to gauge what sources of information they had at their disposal. It is equally valuable to examine what kind of texts they intended to produce and what they consequently did with the information at their disposal. Such examination may cast doubt on the factual reliability of alleged "eyewitness accounts" such as the *Gesta Francorum*, but on the other hand, it makes them a much richer source for exploring world-views, ideologies, and mentalities in the time of the First Crusade. Thus I would like to suggest that when reading these texts, apart from investigating "the facts" of the crusade, it could be equally valuable to investigate "factuality" in the time of the crusade; in other words to investigate what contemporaries of the crusade understood by "facts", what kinds of facts they deemed important, and what kind of importance these facts were accorded.

Note on Translations

Albert of Aachen: translations are either my own, or – where indicated – are taken from Susan Edgington's forthcoming new edition-cum-translation of Albert's *Historia*.

Fulcher of Chartres: translations are based on Fulcher of Chartres, *A History of the Expedition to Jerusalem, 1095–1127*, trans. Frances Rita Ryan (New York, 1969).

Gesta Francorum: translations are based on *Gesta Francorum et aliorum Hierosolimitanorum*, ed. and trans. Rosalind Hill (London, 1962).

Guibert of Nogent: translations are based on Guibert of Nogent, *The Deeds of God through the Franks. Gesta Dei per Francos*, trans. Robert Levine (Woodbridge, 1997).

Raymond of Aguilers: translations are based on Raymond of Aguilers, *Historia Francorum qui ceperunt Iherusalem*, trans. John H. Hill and Laurita L. Hill (Philadelphia, 1968).

Some Observations During a Visit to Palestine by Ibn al-ʿArabī of Seville in 1092–1095

Joseph Drory

Bar Ilan University, Ramat Gan

Ibn al-ʿArabī, from whose writings several excerpts whose locale is Palestine will be presented in this article, was a young Spanish scholar of distinguished origin. Born in Seville in 1076, he visited the eastern Islamic territories (*mašriq*) towards the end of his teenage years (approximately between 1092 and 1100). Contrary to common tradition, some of his personal impressions were incorporated in his various works. When older, he fulfilled several public duties in Seville, including being appointed a judge. Forced to leave following the invasion of the Almohads (*al-Muwaḥḥidūn*), Ibn al-ʿArabī went to Morocco where he spent a year in jail. He died, near Fez, in 1148.

Ibn al-ʿArabī's literary output includes some fifty items of varying length that cover a wide range of Muslim scholarship: commentary on the Qurʾān; auxiliary tools to enhance its study; elements of religious law; specific issues in prophetic tradition; commentary on al-Tirmiḏī's overall collection of traditions; the disputes of the different law schools; language and belles-lettres (*adab*); and polemical treatises (against the seekers of allegorical hints at the holy scriptures, or against people who oversimplified the interpretation of its message and contents, and against the proponents of theological innovations). A plausible conclusion from a perusal of his writings is that Ibn al-ʿArabī proved to be a prolific author and a sworn defender of the *via media* orthodoxy, who snubbed innovations and audacious opinions.

Apart from the traditional yearning to fulfill the precept of the *ḥajj* which is required of every Muslim and expected of a man of learning and means like Ibn al-ʿArabī, the motive of his journey was also to acquaint himself with further centres of the culture with which he had only a limited and marginal familiarity; he desired to complete and enrich his formal education by meeting high-ranked scholars[1] and teachers of religious law. The driving spur for his journey, accompanied by his nearly fifty year old father, was the invasion in 1091 of his town by the notorious Almoravids (*al-Murābiṭūn*). The previous political order was torn apart, giving way to a new situation which "made it impossible to remain in our land".[2]

---

[1] Ibn al-ʿArabī's success in this domain is quite remarkable. In the East he studied under such notable theologians and traditionists as Abū Ḥāmid al-Ġazzālī, Abū Bakr al-Šāšī, Abū Bakr al-Ṭurṭūšī and Naṣr al-Muqaddasī.

[2] Slīmānī, *Qānūn al-Taʾwīl* (Beirut, 1990), p. 74 (*wa-lam yumkin bi-arḍinā al-muqām*).

Ibn al-ʿArabī visited numerous sites of Muslim culture (Granada and Malaga in Andalus; Bougie (*Bijāya*) and Bone, Tunis and Mahdiyya in North Africa; Alexandria and Cairo in Egypt; Jerusalem, Hebron and Ascalon in Palestine; Damascus and Baghdad) exposing him to the cores of traditional learning and giving him an opportunity to compare his fresh Eastern impressions to his former indigenous experience. The gloomy situation at long suffering *Andalus*, on the defensive against the Christians and at the same time robbed by its Muslim north-African Berber defenders, amplified his admiration for the relatively secure East. Ibn al-ʿArabī's eyes were opened to the military, political and social upheavals in the hub of the Muslim world.

Ibn al-ʿArabī's records of his relatively long (around thirty months) stay in Palestine are available from a number of sources. He himself wrote a monograph, *Tartīb al-Riḥla*, which contained personal remarks about his journey. Regrettably, this monograph was lost in his own lifetime. However, Ibn al-ʿArabī recorded part of his description, mainly its scholarly aspects, in another work, designated to serve as an auxiliary text for Qur'ān study, entitled *Qānūn al-Ta'wīl*. Some sections derived from MS Selim Aga (in Üsküdar, Istanbul) no. 499 were first published in an article by Iḥsān ʿAbbās in *al-Abḥāṯ*[3] and were the inspiration for my own endeavours to broaden my acquaintance with this unique traveller's observations.[4] From Ibn al-ʿArabī's commentary on the Qur'ān, *Aḥkām al-Qur'ān*, which was published in various editions, I was able to collect personal utterings scattered amid discussion of exegetic questions. Annotations, entitled *ʿĀriḍat al-Aîwaḏī*, to a collection of traditions by al-Tirmiḏī (d. 892), considered to be of high rank and called *Ṣaḥīḥ al-Tirmiḏī*, was a further source of statements and passages relating to Jerusalem and Palestine. An apologetic treatise by Ibn al-ʿArabī, *al-ʿAwāṣim min al-Qawāṣim*, which attempts to exonerate the early friends of Muḥammad from harsh criticism by means of logical arguments, also provided a number of autobiographical episodes connected with his visit to the East.

The following features indicate Ibn al-ʿArabī's singularity:

(a) His is to date the only known personal testimony of a visit to Jerusalem in the last decade of Seljūq rule, a period on the threshold of the crusades. Ibn al-ʿArabī transmits first-hand information and impressions of some Palestinian towns and of indigenous Muslim residents in an era poor in documentary

[3] "The Journey of Ibn al-ʿArabī to the East as illustrated by *Qānūn al-Ta'wīl*" (*riḥlat ibn al-ʿarabī ilā al-mašriq kamā ṣawwarahā Qānūn al-Ta'wīl*), *al-Abḥāṯ* 21 (1968), 59–91.

[4] In 1987 Saʿīd Aʿrāb issued a monograph labelled *Along with the Judge Ibn al-ʿArabī* (*maʿa al-qāḍī abī bakr ibn al-ʿarabī*) (Dār al-Ġarb al-Islāmī, Beirut) which includes the autobiographic text from *Qānūn al-Ta'wīl*, derived from what was described as "private manuscript" with no further identifying details. In 1990 Muḥammad Slīmānī published the full text of *Qānūn al-Ta'wīl* (Dār al-Ġarb al-Islāmī, Beirut) based on four manuscripts. Consulting the initial MS Selim Aga 499, Slīmānī appended a slightly different version, which I take into account in the present article.

material. Moreover, his remarks were composed when he already realized the facts, form and scale of the Frankish invasion. As an immediate contemporaneous reaction they bear distinctive value.

(b) His comments are of an original nature and reflect his own experience rather than being borrowed from former writers. Ibn al-ʿArabī contributes a double innovation to conservative Muslim writing replete with plagiarism. Not only does he refrain from recycling his predecessors' observations (common, for instance, in the geographic writing tradition) but, in commenting on holy texts – literary genres where writers' individual opinions were more often than not concealed – he also dares to incorporate personal impressions and recollections of events he himself witnessed. His personality emerges far clearer than those of his contemporary colleagues.

(c) Ibn al-ʿArabī supports previous Qur'ān exegesis. Earlier commentators identified abstract names, phrases and images of the Qur'ān with real sites in the regions ruled by Islam, mostly in the Arabian peninsula or Syria and Palestine (e.g. Chapter 11 "Olive tree in the shrine"). Ibn al-ʿArabī in his turn enhances these theoretical exegetic suggestions, basing himself on his personal experience. He even takes issue with those who fail to accept them. His novelty as a commentator is not in conveying subtler concepts or more convincing etymology to Qur'ān verses but rather in supplying first-hand support to indistinct locations that formerly were considered only probable proposals.

(d) Ibn al-ʿArabī's observations and statements on phenomena of the Muslim East, against the background of the Andalusian world with which he was familiar, endow his impressions with insightful, humanistic and cultural value. Especially reliable and valuable are his descriptions of the modesty of women (Chapter 18), the indifference of the population towards war (Chapter 13), the custom of Christian pilgrims to appropriate holy relics (Chapter 15) and the taking over (perhaps continuing to hold) of the Christians of lands in Palestine in the pre-crusader epoch (Chapter 2). His discernment mirrors social conditions in his home country, Muslim Spain.

(e) The information adduced in his works on encounters between educated scholars of various Muslim sects and on their theological debates such as those held in Jerusalem, Ascalon or Acre, provides an opportunity to make direct acquaintance with their atmosphere and intrinsic norms. One can become aware of the scholars' life style, their place of study and seclusion, their stances towards colleagues of long-standing, rivals or proponents of trendy foreign ideas. Such a vivid picture alters the poor and disappointing impression of Jerusalem as a dull centre of learning, insufficient and unchallenging for inquisitive knowledge-seekers some hundred years previously. The learning activity illustrated by Ibn al-ʿArabī validates the assertion of later Muslim sources concerning the harm wrought by the crusader conquest not only to the Holy City as a religious or political symbol, but also by their uprooting of a lively, multinational Islamic cultural area. The account (in Chapter 2) of a Jewish intellectual – one among many – who took part in a Muslim study session attests to the contact and integration between Jewish sages in the East and their Muslim counterparts. Both sides shared a common platform for debate, and arguments of an adherent of one religion were likely to be acceptable to the logic of his rival from another faith. Furthermore, they present vividly and from a primary source the spiritual outlines of the Muslim literati, the issues that occupied them, their customs and their genuine reactions to daily affairs – that differ from those officially declared.

(f) The excerpts from Ibn al-ʿArabī's writings are replete with local references that extend our knowledge of the country's vistas and its toponomy. Here is a random list: Miḥrāb Zakariyyā, the Divine Immanence [area], the Dome of the Chain, al-Ġuwayr, Bāb al-Asbāṭ, Bāb Ḥiṭṭa, the eighth gate of the Ḥaram, all of which are on the Holy Shrine in Jerusalem, Ġazza Gate in Ascalon, Joseph's cave in Hebron and the guardhouse in Acre.

The collection presented here includes twenty-four out of forty-three excerpts of Ibn al-ʿArabī's oeuvres that I have managed to cull, whose setting and core of interest is medieval Palestine.[5] The overall canon of Ibn al-ʿArabī's output calls for a deeper scrutiny, to facilitate better acquaintance with this orthodox scholar, his spiritual world, agenda, reactions, world view and insights.

The titles of the excerpts are my own.

Excerpt 1 [Initial Encounter in Jerusalem]

After that, we travelled from Egypt to Syria and our hope was [to join] the Imām [Abu Bakr al-Ṭurṭūšī].[6] We entered the Holy Land (*al-arḍ al-muqaddasa*) and arrived at al-Aqṣā Mosque. The moon of learning shone on me and I benefited from its light for more than three years. When I prayed at al-Aqṣā Mosque, on entering it for the first time, I went to the *madrasa* of the Šāfiʿītes at the Gate of the Tribes (*bāb al-asbāṭ*). There I found a group of their scholars on the day they assembled for their discussion under their sage, the rightly-guided judge Yaḥyā[7] who had

---

5 The excerpts were translated and commented at length in my *Ibn al-ʿArabi of Seville – A Journey in Palestine (1092–1095)* (Ramat Gan, 1993; in Hebrew).

6 Known also as: al-Fihrī or Ibn Abī Randaqa, a Spanish Mālikī law scholar (1059–1126) who spent many years in the East (Baghdad, Basra, Damascus, Jerusalem, Alexandria). He was the most respected, estimated and inspiring of Ibn al-ʿArabī's teachers, on grounds of his pietistic virtues, puritan living standards, and extensive scope of Islamic juristic comprehension, and the author of several treatises (e.g. counsels to the perfect ruler: against undesirable innovations).

7 By all probability the Šafiʿī scholar Yaḥyā ibn al-Mufarrij al-Laḫmī al-Muqaddasī, also nicknamed "the rightly-guided judge" (*al-qāḍī al-rašīd*) al-Muqaddasī. See ʿA. Ṭālbī, *Arāʾ abī bakr ibn al-ʿarabī al-kalāmiyya* (Algiers, 1981), 2:499, n. 5. The year of his death is not indicated.

been left in charge of them by our teacher, the ascetic Imam Naṣr ibn Ibrāhīm al-Nābulsī al-Muqaddasī.[8] They conducted their discussion in their customary manner.

The first thing I heard came from one of the scholars called Mujallī[9] who said: [The *ḥaram*] is an area in which, if a killing took place there, the conditions for blood-vengeance would have been fulfilled. This would also be true if the killing occurred somewhere else. Basically the *ḥaram* is a place of exculpation. I did not understand a single letter of his words nor could I make head or tail of them from start to finish. I remained until the session had ended and began to go back to my home, but my old passion caused me to return and my striving to grasp and to learn prevailed over me. I said to my father,[10] may Allāh have mercy upon him: if you intend to go on pilgrimage to Mecca [*ḥajj*] go as is your wish. As for me, however, I will not leave this city (*balda*) until I have plumbed the knowledge of those in it, and set it as an example of knowledge and a ladder to its virtues. When my father saw that I was serious, he helped me and accompanied me, and that was one of the most important reasons for my diligence. We considered remaining there and detached ourselves from the group with whom we had arranged to go on Ḥijāz, for they were at the peak of their preparations.

We went to our mentor, Abū Bakr al-Fihrī [i.e. al-Ṭurṭūšī] , may Allāh have mercy upon him, and he used to perform his devotions in al-Aqṣā Mosque, may Allāh purify it,[11] at a place called al-Ġuwayr between the Gate of the Tribes (*bāb al-asbāṭ*) and the prayer niche (*miḥrāb*) of Zakariyyā, may they have peace. We did not find him there and followed him to another place [in al-Aqṣā Mosque] called the Divine Presence (*sakīna*) and there we met him. I was a witness to his instruction, heard his words, my ears and eyes were filled by him. My father told him of my firm intention and he was duly responsive.[12] Through his help all the doors to knowledge were opened to me and Allāh enabled me, through him, to study and to practise. By him I was enabled to achieve my greatest hope. I made Jerusalem (*bayt al-maqdis*) my dwelling place to which I adhered and where I read. I neither turned to worldly matters nor spoke to any one. We ran night into day, especially in the Dome of the Chain. From there the sun rises on the Mount [of Olives] (*al-ṭūr*) and sets on David's

---

[8] A devout, ascetic, and a Šāfiʿī Syrian scholar (1018–96), who taught in Gaza, Tyre, Jerusalem and Damascus. Al-Ġazzālī regarded him one of his teachers. He headed a circle of admiring disciples who were labelled the *naṣriyya*: Mujīr al-Dīn, *al-Uns al-Jalīl* (Amman, 1973), 1:297–98.

[9] Mujallī ibn Jumayʿ al-Maḫzūmī, a Šāfiʿī local scholar, born in the coastal town of Arsūf, composed the *al-Ḏaḫa'ir*, a book on legal themes regarded as an authority in Egypt at the time, and died in 1156: Ibn Ḫallikān, *Wafayāt al-Aʿyān*, ed. Iḥsān ʿAbbās (Beirut 1968–71), 5:154ff., no. 556.

[10] Ibn al-ʿArabī's father, ʿAbd Allāh al-Maʿāfirī (1043–99) was a learned man of his own merit, and was reckoned among Ibn Ḥazm's pupils. In his native town Seville he enjoyed esteem as a civil patrician: Fatḥ ibn Ḫāqān, *Matmaḥ al-Anfus* (Istanbul, 1302 AH), p. 62.

[11] When these texts were composed Jerusalem was no longer under Muslim rule, but was dominated by the "sinful" Franks.

[12] And he adds another clause (*wa-ṭālaʿahu bi-ʿazīmatī fa-ajāba*) reiterating actually the same.

prayer niche (*miḥrāb dāwud*),[13] followed by the moon, as it waxes and wanes over these two honoured sites. Every day I would enter the schools of the Ḥanafītes and the Šāfiʿītes to watch the dispute between the two groups. Trade did not divert our attention and ties to relatives did not distract us, nor did friendly links or fear of enemies break the bond between us.

Iḥsān ʿAbbās, "Riḥlat ibn al-ʿArabī ilā al-Šarq", *al-Abḥāṯ* 21 (1968), 79–81.

Excerpt 2 [Dispute with a Jewish scholar]

We had debates with the Karāmiyya,[14] the Muʿtazila,[15] the anthropomorphists (*mušabbiha*)[16] and the Jews. Among the Jews there was one of their learned (*habr*)[17] named al-Tustarī,[18] skilful in their reasoning. We engaged in controversy with the Christians present and [at that time] the land was theirs, they cultivated its estates, kept up its monasteries and preserved its churches. One day we were present at a long session attended by various denominations. Al-Tustarī spoke about his religion and said: "No argument exist between us that Moses was a prophet (whose prophecies) were confirmed by miracles, who taught the Commandments. Now if

[13] Nowadays: the Citadel (*al-qalʿa*) in the western part of the Old City. Other locations suggested by Muslim tradition for that ancient site are the southern wall of al-Aqsa Mosque, east of the Ḥaram, or north of the Ḥaram. Cf. A. Elad, *Medieval Jerusalem & Islamic Worship* (Leiden, 1995) pp. 131–37. The sentence may hint that he worked such long hours that he actually saw the sun rising and then the moon.

[14] A circle of learned disciples mostly of Iranian origin, named after Muḥammad ibn Karrām (b. 806 – d. 870 and buried in Jerusalem), who advocated certain flexible and moderate attitudes to exegetic and religious problems (God's nature: single utterance of the Muslim as sufficient to regard him a believer regardless of less orthodox creeds and deeds: certain legal obligations were considered mere customs by him). His preaching in the Ḥaram attracted large crowds of students which constituted for future decades a community of theologians and ascetics adhering to his teaching.

[15] A sect characterized by free theological thinking. The Muʿtazili teachers rejected the doctrine of predestination, upheld the thesis of God's obligation to do for every man what is most advantageous for him, asserted absolute responsibility of every individual for his transgressions, and maintained the obligation of God to procure Justice that could be understandable to human perception. Muʿtazili thinking had a decisive influence on Jewish theologians, mainly the Karaites.

[16] A general definition for theological circles discussing the way one should accept God's humanly-described features and attributes, and how one should understand them (symbolically, transcendentally, metaphorically). The gap between God's existence and man's need to feel accessible to Him and His divinely intangible essence occupied their thinking and writings. The mere term *mušabbiha* became derogatory for almost every group deviating from orthodoxy on theological grounds.

[17] The Arabic language uses the word *ḥabr* almost similarly to its Hebrew Mishnaic meaning *ḥaver*, an observant Jew, in contrast to non-observant: *ʿam ha-aretz*. In another treatise Ibn al-ʿArabī relates that in Jerusalem there were "from among the Jewish *aḥbar* an uncountable number": Ṭalbī, *Arāʾ*, 1:35, citing *al-ʿAwāṣim min al-Qawāṣim*.

[18] Believed to be a Karaite scholar, from the famous family of Persian origin, the Tustarīs. It has been suggested that this is Abū Saʿd, nicknamed son of the Tustarī woman, who was captured in 1099 by the crusaders and whom the Jewish community in Ascalon was not hasty to ransom: M. Gil, *A History of Palestine (634–1099)* (Cambridge and New York, 1992), p. 802, n. 15.

anyone claims that there is any prophet other than him, that person bears the onus of proof."

He aimed, by using sophistic argument, to force us to undertake the burden of (positive) proof so that his desire be fulfilled and his argument be set out at length [lit. extend its tent ropes]. Al-Fihrī[19] replied: "If you are alluding to Moses who was confirmed by miracles, who taught the commandments and announced the coming of Aḥmad[20] [i.e. Muḥammad], we agree with you about him, have faith in him and confirm him. But if you mean some other Moses, we do not know who he is". Those present considered that [response] impressive and praised him lengthily. It was a clever, convincing, argumentative ruse. His opponent was astounded and the session concluded.

Iḥsān ʿAbbās, "Riḥlat ibn al-ʿArabī ilā al-Šarq", 81–82.

Excerpt 3 [Well-read Ḫurāsānīs]

At that time, there arrived a group of Ḫurāsānī scholars, namely: al-Zawzanī,[21] al-Ṣāğānī,[22] al-Zinjānī[23] and the judge al-Rayḥānī,[24] accompanied by a group of students that included al-Biskarī[25] and Sātkīn al-Turkī.[26] Their objective was to pay a holy visit (*ziyāra*) in Hebron, Allah's blessings upon it,[27] and their intention was to pray in al-Aqṣā Mosque. When I heard their discussion I realized that it was of superior rank and praiseworthy nature,[28] a highly-valuable fabric of knowledge and

---

19 Abū Bakr al-Fihrī, alias: al-Ṭurṭūšī, Ibn al-ʿArabī's mentor in Jerusalem: see Excerpt 1.

20 Al-Fihrī (= al-Ṭurṭūšī) names his Prophet Ahmad after the wording of the Qurʾān in ch. 61 verse 5 where Jesus is made to describe his vocation which includes announcing the appearance of a messenger, who would follow him, named Aḥmad.

21 According to Ṭalbī, *Arāʾ*, 1:33, n. 3 he is to be identified as Abū Saʿd Aḥmad ibn Muḥammad al-Zawzanī, who died in 1141 and is mentioned in biographical dictionaries.

22 He must be the leading figure of the incident described in the chapter "attitude towards foreigners". It is very probable that these Ḫurāsānīs were a group of learned individuals, emerging from the same areas of origin, but with no mutual connections. It is only through the pen of Ibn al-ʿArabī that they were regarded as a "group".

23 Abū Saʿīd, Muḥammad ibn Ṭāhir al-Zinjānī, one of Ibn al-ʿArabī's Ḥanafi teachers in Jerusalem. Born apparently in eastern Persia around 1053. Since he is also nicknamed "the martyr" (*al-šahīd*) it was suggested that he fell victim to the Frankish conquest of Jerusalem in 1099.

24 I could not find biographical data on this Ḥanafi lecturer.

25 M. Slīmānī in his edition of *Qānūn al-Taʾwīl* (Beirut, 1990), p. 97 n. 5, identifies him with Abū Muḥammad ʿAbd al-ʿAzīz, the judge of the (now Algerian) town of Biskra. It is, however, an unlikely assumption. Why would a judge be mentioned as a student? Why did a prominent judge from the Mağrib join an East Persian group?

26 Slīmānī (*Qānūn*, p. 97 n. 6) contributes additional data on this person. His name is Abū Manṣūr, Sātkīn ibn Arslān al-Turkī, who composed a short opus on grammar, was of (untypical) Māliki conviction and died in Jerusalem in 487/1094.

27 Lit. " upon him" since it refers to al-Ḫalīl, which signifies both the city and Abraham.

28 A different reading has been suggested, replacing enigmatic *ṯāniya* by *ṯābita* (solid, invariable). Thus it would be rendered as "firm nature".

a lofty grade of science. Upon hearing their debate I felt as though I had not yet learned anything which can be acquired, nor anything that satisfies what is required and sufficient. By a strange providential coincidence it so happened that the topic that I heard immediately after I entered Jerusalem and failed to understand what people have said about it, was the same topic about which I heard the man of Ṣāġān talking. I saw how profound was he in responding to the Book of Allah[29] and that he [commands] reasoning incomprehensible save to those chosen by Allah. I also heard the words of al-Zawzanī on several topics including the killing of a Muslim (to counter the murder) of a non-Muslim. I saw how accurately he grasped the point of the man from Ṣāġān, and that both were of one mind[30] of what was the point of the issue. I asked Allah, may He be praised, for his guidance about my desire to go to Iraq. The form of the inquiry and the juxtaposition of the two legal claims will unveil both systems [to the reader] …

Iḥsān ʿAbbās, "Riḥlat ibn al-ʿArabī ilā al-Šarq", 82.

Excerpt 4 [Impressions of Ascalon]

At that time, wanting to reach the coast, I went to Ascalon. There I found a sea of learning (*adab*) whose waves range high and engulf and whose water channels gush freely. I stayed here approximately six months without being sated. On one occasion when I was departing from one of the brethren,[31] I came to the main road and saw that it was full of people crowding around a handmaiden singing in an alcove. I halted and looked for another way or thought of going by another route, and there she was, singing a song by al-Tuhāmī[32]

I told her when the grey camel is saddled to travel to its destination
Store in my absence what patience you can
Is it not a pity that our nights
Flow past without avail and are considered part of my life?

---

29 The reading of Slīmānī, *Qānūn*, p. 98 states: "immersed with the jewels (*ġawṣ ʿalā jawāhir* ...) of the Book of Allah".

30 Lit. "looked through one pupil". The Slīmānī edition inserts here (p. 98): "And penetrated the house of knowledge from one door" (*wa-yalijuna bayt al-maʿārif min bāb wāḥid*) which is totally omitted from Iḥsān ʿAbbās' rendering of the text.

31 Probably his colleagues, other students of holy scriptures, people who shared a similar lifestyle of scholarly dedication.

32 ʿAlī ibn Muḥammad al-Tuhāmī, a poet from the western part of the Arabian peninsula. An adherent of the Palestinian Bedouins of Banū Jarrāḥ who rebelled against the Fatimids in 415/1024, al-Tuhāmī was sent by them to other Bedouins in Egypt in a diplomatic mission, during which he was captured, jailed and killed mysteriously in prison in 416/1025: cf. Ibn Ḫallikān, *Wafayāt al-Aʿyān*, ed. Ihsān ʿAbbās (Beirut, 1968–71), 3:378–81.

I said: Muḥammad, this is, God is my witness, a Ṣūfic revelation and a divine voice of religion. You are the objective and the one around whom the song centres. Proceed at once to your initial goal and undertake something that is worthy of and befits you. I hurried home and said to my father: A journey, a journey. This is not a place to rest. This gladdened him because he had previously urged me to do it but I had [then] hindered him from doing so. I made for the sea at once and sailed to Acre and we ascended to Tiberias and Ḥawrān en route to Damascus.

Iḥsān ʿAbbās, "Riḥlat ibn al-ʿArabī ilā al-Šarq", 84.

Excerpt 5 [Attitude towards foreigners]

The Qāḍī Abū Bakr ibn al-ʿArabī said:[33] "In Jerusalem – may Allāh purify it – I attended the *madrasa* of Abū ʿUqba al-Ḥanafī[34] and the Qāḍī al-Rayḥānī[35] was giving us a lesson one Friday. While we were thus occupied a man of fine appearance, but clad in rags, entered. He greeted us in the customary manner of scholars and, in a shepherd's cloak, took his seat at the top of the room [waiting to be questioned]. Al-Rayḥānī asked "Who are you?" and the man answered him "A person whom the rabble robbed yesterday, and my intention was this holy shrine. I am a person from Ṣāġān,[36] one of those who seek knowledge". The Qāḍī said immediately, "Question him" as is the custom to honour scholars by presenting extempore questions to them. The topic chosen was the (legal) issue about an infidel[37] who seeks sanctuary in the shrine (*ḥaram*). Should he be killed or not? And he ruled not to kill him. When he was asked what were the grounds for his ruling he replied: The word of God, "Do not fight them, however, in the precincts of the Sacred Mosque (*al-masjid al-ḥarām*) until they fight you therein" (Qurʾān ch. 2 v. 191), can be read either as "Do not kill them" or "Do not fight them". If you read it as "Do not kill them" the problem is solved by an explicit text (*naṣṣ*). If you read it as "Do not fight them" this is an instruction, for if He forbids fighting which is the cause of the killing, that is a clearly revealed proof that He forbids killing.

The Qāḍī al-Rayḥānī disagreed with this, basing (his opinion) on Šāfiʿī[38] and

---

33 This experience is also told, with minor different text, in Iḥsān ʿAbbās' article "Riḥlat ibn al-ʿarabī ..." *al-Abḥāṯ* 21 (1968), 83.

34 Located opposite the Holy Sepulchre, as attested to in Excerpt 39, I am unable to date this *madrasa* or to deliver details about its (apparent) founder, and yet the very record of such an institution (with a specific name and credible location) in pre-crusader times has no parallel save in Ibn al-ʿArabī.

35 Information about him was not available to me through common biographical dictionaries.

36 Referred to also as Ṣaġāniān, in the Oxus region (cf. the geographical work of the early thirteenth-century writer Yāqūt al-Hamawi, *Muʿjam al-Buldān*, under Ṣāġān, Ṣaġāniān). Modern Sar-i-Asyā, nowadays in the republic of Uzbekistan.

37 In al-Sulaymānī, *Qānūn al-Taʾwīl* (Beirut, 1990), p. 101: "a transgressor" (*jānī*).

38 Abū ʿAbd Allāh, Muḥammad ibn Idrīs (said to be born in Gaza 767 – Fusṭāṭ 820), a theologian and traditionalist. Out of his circle of followers emerged the school of law that bears his name. Assumed to

Mālik,[39] although he does not usually take their doctrines into consideration. He maintained this verse is annulled by the words of the Qur'ān, "slay the polytheists wherever ye find them" (Qur'ān ch. 9 v. 5). The man from Ṣāġān said to him "This is not appropriate to the Qāḍī's station and learning, because this verse, with which you objected to my words, is the general rule[40] and the verse I quoted as proof is a specific case and no one is allowed to claim that the general annuls the particular." He astounded the Qāḍī al-Rayḥānī and this was a wondrous dispute.

From Ibn al-ʿArabī's Qur'ān commentary, *Aḥkām al-Qur'ān* (Cairo, 1959), 1:107.

Excerpt 6 [An hour of grace]

I had already been staying for three years in Jerusalem where there lived a devout man who would watch for the Friday hour every week. And if this is Friday, for example, he would commune with God from dawn till before noon. After that he went his way. In the second week he would commune with his Creator from before noon till after noon. In the third week he would commune with his Lord from around noon until the afternoon prayer (*al-ʿaṣr*) and then he would leave. In the fourth week he would commune with his Lord from the afternoon prayer till sunset. In this way he would find the appropriate hour during four weeks. People considered this action of his a worthy deed.

Our teacher, Abū Bakr al-Fihrī[41] said: What he does is unavailing. For it may be that on the day when he is waiting from noon till the afternoon prayer it [i.e. the hour of grace] comes between the afternoon prayer and sunset and on the day when it comes from the afternoon hour to sunset, he would have waited for it from dawn until before noon because the hour might change from one Friday to another, and not remain at one fixed hour every Friday. That this is correct is proved by the shifting of the Night of Destiny (*laylat al-qadr*) over the nights of the month, for it indeed falls every year on a specific night but its blessing does not fall on it the subsequent year.

From Ibn al-ʿArabī's Qur'ān commentary, *Aḥkām al-Qur'ān*, 3:1176.

---

oppose the rationalist influence in Islamic emergent jurisprudence, he contributed to legal thought by introducing systematization of analogical reasoning, definition of the Sunna, and critique of traditions, thus securing the status of Ḥadīṯ in establishing Islamic law. He composed the first treatise on the principles of Muslim jurisprudence.

[39] Abū ʿAbd Allāh, Mālik ibn Anas, a Muslim jurist (d. 179/796), the founder of the law school of the *Mālikī*s, which reflects and represents the ritual traditions, religious practices and law customs, concepts and reasoning which prevailed in al-Madīna.

[40] Literally: relevant everywhere, in every place (*fī al-amākin*).

[41] Better known as al-Ṭurṭūšī (1059–1126), see Excerpt 1 n. 6, above.

Excerpt 7 [The cave under the rock]

The author of *Muṯīr al-Ġarām*[42] recorded: in the book *al-Qabas fī Šarḥ Muwaṭṭaʾ al-Imām Mālik ibn Anas*[43] composed by the Imām Abū Bakr ibn al-ʿArabī I saw that he dealt with the interpretation of the Qurʾān verse "and we sent down from the heaven water in (due) measure".[44] He mentioned four interpretations of which the fourth is: the water of the whole world emerges from the rock of the mosque. This is one of the wonders of God, may he be praised, upon earth, for this is a shapeless rock in the center of al-Aqṣā Mosque that was quarried out on all sides, and nothing holds it up other than what keeps the heavens from falling onto the earth unless God permits. On the elevated part of the southern side there is the footprint of the Prophet – may God's prayer be upon him – while he rode on *Burāq* and the rock was inclined in that direction in awe [of the Prophet]. On the other side were the fingerprints of the angels who grasped the rock when it leaned over with him [i.e. Muḥammad]. Underneath the rock is the cave that is separated [from the rock] on every side. The cave has a gate that is open to people for prayers and acts of individual devotion. For some time I dreaded entering underneath because I feared that it would collapse upon me on account of my sins. But then I saw the sinners and the transgressors in public entering and leaving it unharmed and I intended to enter the cave. After a while I said: "perhaps their punishment has been postponed and mine will be advanced". I waited for some time but then I made up my mind and went into the cave and I saw wonder of wonders, that on whatever side you walked you noticed that the cave was separated from the ground and not joined to it anywhere at all. Some parts were separated further away than others.

From Mujīr al-Dīn, *al-Uns al-Jalīl* (Amman, 1973), 2:17.

Excerpt 8 [The Game of Chess]

The Ḥadīṯ asserts "Everything with which a Muslim amuses himself is forbidden except for shooting with his bow, taming his horse and sporting with his wife, all of which are permitted". Commentators add to shooting with his bow, additional martial training such as throwing the javelin, defending oneself with a leather shield and running.

To these examples Šāfiʿite scholars added the game of chess, asserting that it has to do with training for war. We [adhering to our Māliki concepts] said: "By no means, it

42 Šihāb al-Dīn al-Muqaddasī (died 1364).

43 The commentary of Ibn al-ʿArabī to the principal book of the Māliki teaching, *al-Muwaṭṭaʾ*, by Mālik ibn Anas (d. 795). See Excerpt 17 n. 66.

44 Qurʾān ch. 23 v. 18: Richard Bell, *The Qurʾān, translated, with a critical re-arrangement of the Surahs* (Edinburgh, 1937–39), 1:327.

teaches us to neglect prayer or to pray at incorrect times or it teaches obscene language and indecency". I heard al-Ṭurṭūšī say to the prime scholar of the Šāfiʿites in al-Aqṣā Mosque after he had voiced (his opinion): "Moreover, chess is able to harm warfare because the aim in war is to stalk the king and kill him, so that his army can be destroyed and his people scattered and victory will be yours, whereas in chess you say 'Check' to the king and warn him that he is about to be captured". Those present laughed.

From Ibn al-ʿArabī's commentary on *Ṣaḥīḥ al-Tirmiḏī, Āriḍat al-Aḥwadī*, ed. Jamal Marʿashli, 14 vols. in 8 (Beirut, 1997), 7:137.

Excerpt 9 [Excessive modesty]

Abū ʿĪsā[45] transmitted the tradition of Ibn ʿUmar[46] "Beware of undressing. There are those who will never leave you except when you relieve yourselves, or in the case of a husband drawing near to his wife. Be bashful of them and honour them." A remarkable[47] tradition.

[Commentary] When he said "Those who will never leave …" this refers explicitly to angels but may be taken as covering Jinn who are believers because angels write and remember, whereas the believing Jinn seek provisions [for the road] and try to enter [houses]. And even if the house is empty of people it is not devoid of angel or Jinn. I have already heard about Ibn ʿUmar from wise scholars in al-Aqṣā Mosque that he would not approach his wife when a cat was in the house; how much the more so if there was anyone else there.

From Ibn al-ʿArabī's commentary on *Ṣaḥīḥ al-Tirmiḏī, Āriḍat al-Aḥwaḏī*, 10:241–42.

Excerpt 10 [Grey hair]

A person is forbidden to pluck his grey hairs for by doing so he does away with dignity and respect. It is only his love for women and his desire for worldly success that cause him to pluck them, since white hair is considered black[48] by the pretty girls and black [is deemed] white in their hearts. During the scholarly discussion (*muḏākara*) in al-Aqṣā Mosque one of our friends recited to me

---

45 Abū ʿĪsā is al-Tirmiḏī (d. 279/892) to whose valid (*ṣaḥīḥ*) collection of traditions Ibn al-ʿArabī appended his genuine commentary in his work (*Āriḍat al-Aḥwaḏī fī Ṣaḥīḥ al-Tirmiḏī*).

46 ʿAbd Allāh ibn ʿUmar was the offspring of the second Caliph, ʿUmar ibn al-Ḫaṭṭāb, who had acquired a great reputation as a pious and god-fearing person (d. 74/694).

47 *ġarīb*, technical term for a tradition transmitted from only one companion or from a single man at a later age.

48 Black has a pejorative sense in this context.

The initial white hair appeared on my temple
I hastened to pluck it for fear that I would (soon) perish.
It said: "You overcame my weakness and scarcity
But beware of the whole army that follows me".

From Ibn al-ʿArabī's commentary on *Ṣaḥīḥ al-Tirmiḏī, Āriḍat al-Aḥwaḏī*, 10:260.

Excerpt 11 [The olive tree in the shrine]

In reference to the following Qur'ānic verse:

> Allah is the light of the heavens and the earth. His light is like a niche in which is a lamp, the lamp in glass and the glass like a brilliant star, lit from a blessed tree, an olive neither of the East nor of the West whose oil would almost give light even though no fire did touch it.[49]

In al-Aqṣā Mosque I have already seen an olive tree located between the Miḥrāb of Zakariyyā and the Gate of Repentance (*bāb al-tauba*) and Mercy (*raḥma*) which, they say, is the one referred to in the verse [Qur'ān, ch. 57 v. 13] "with a wall having a door in it; (as for) the inside of it, there shall be mercy in it", i.e. al-Aqṣā Mosque, "and (as for) the outside of it, before it, there shall be punishment", i.e. at its eastern part, outside the wall is *Wādī Jahannam* (Gehenna)[50] and above it the gathering place [of the souls on the Day of Judgement] called al-Sāhira.[51] They said: This is the tree mentioned in this verse. It is your God who knows best.

From Ibn al-ʿArabī's Qur'ān commentary, *Aḥkām al-Qur'ān*, 3:1376.

Excerpt 12 [The Egyptian invasion in 1098]

In reference to the Qur'ānic verse (ch. 34 v. 10):

> We bestowed upon David preference from Us. O ye mountains return (praises) with him, and ye birds also. And we made iron tractable for him.[52]

---

49 Sūra 24 [the Light], v. 35: Bell, *Qur'ān*, 1:340.

50 The vale separating Mount Moriah from Mount of Olives, known in Jewish tradition as the Valley of Jehoshaphat, which was distorted, by mediation of European travellers, <Joshafat- Josafat> to its actual name in Arabic Wādī Jōz.

51 Islamic tradition indicates more than one place for *al-Sāhira*, the cemetery of those awake at night, such as: Mount of Olives, The city of Jerusalem, its northern part, the expanse adjacent to Mount of Olives: see G. Le Strange, *Palestine under the Moslems* (Beirut, 1965, repr. from the original edition of 1890), pp. 218–20; Elad, *Medieval Jerusalem*, pp. 141–44.

52 Bell, *Qur'ān*, 2:422.

Ibn al-Kāzarūnī[53] used to frequent al-Aqṣā Mosque and we enjoyed his services then for three years. He used to read from Jesus' cradle (*mahd ʿīsā*) and his voice could be heard [as if, lit. from] the Mount of Olives. When he read, no one could do anything except listen to him.

It happened that the Egyptian ruler called al-Afḍal[54] entered Jerusalem in [the month of] Muḥarram in 492 [December 1098] and took it over from the ʿAbbāsids.[55] He was incensed at the city and its inhabitants because he had to besiege them and because of their waging war against him. And when he was in the city, and approached al-Aqṣā Mosque and had performed two prostrations [in his prayer], Ibn al-Kāzarūnī turned to him and read the verse "Say: O Allah, owner of the (kingly) power! Thou givest the power to whom Thou willst and withdrawest the power from whom Thou willst, and Thou exaltest whom Thou willst and abasest whom Thou willst. [In Thine hand is the good];[56] verily, Thou over all things hast power" (Qur'ān ch. 3 v. 26).[57] Al-Afḍal could not restrain himself from saying to the people, in spite of the severity of their transgressions [towards him] and his great loathing, "There is no reproach upon you to-day; Allah will forgive you; He is the most merciful of the merciful." (Qur'ān ch. 12 v. 92).[58]

From Ibn al-ʿArabī's commentary on the Qur'ān ch. 34 (*sabāʾ* i.e. Sheba) verse 10: *Aḥkām al- Qurʾān*, 4:1584–85.

Excerpt 13 [David's tower – a war zone encircled by ordinary life]

In Jerusalem I witnessed the Niche of David (*mihrāb dāwud*), may he rest in peace. It is a large edifice of hard stone on which picks could make no impression. The stone is 50 cubits[59] in length and 13 in width and the higher the building rises, the smaller the stones become. It seems to have three walls, because throughout the

53 The only detail on this loud-voiced Qur'ān reciter, available to me, is that he died out of excessive grief while al-Ġazzālī stayed, all but secluded, in Jerusalem (between 1095 and 1097). Subkī, *Ṭabaqāt al-Šāfiʿiyya*, ed. Al-Ṭannāḥī and Ḥilō, 1964, 7:48.

54 Al-Afḍal ibn Badr al-Jamālī, Egyptian commander and key statesman, who captured Jerusalem from the Seljūq Turks in 1098. He took other military initiatives against the Franks and was assassinated in 1121.

55 More precisely: From an Urtuqid officer named Suqmān: Ibn al-Aṯīr, *al-Kāmil*, 11 vols. (Beirut, 1967), 10:282 (Dār Ṣāder). The Urtuqids were given Jerusalem as appanage by the Seljūqs. As religious superiors, the Urtuqids, like the Seljūqs, paid allegiance to the ʿAbbāsid Caliph residing in Baghdad. Al-Afḍal served the rival Egyptian Fatimid aspirations for universal Islamic hegemony, and therefore was detested by the local Jerusalemites.

56 *bi-yadika al-ḫayr*, omitted from Bell's translation.

57 After Bell, *Qur'ān*, 1:47 [verse 25 according to his enumeration].

58 After Bell, *Qur'ān*, 1:226.

59 *Ḏirāʿ*, roughly 50 cm, which renders the measures of David's Niche (to-day the fortress, *Qalʿa*, in the west of Jerusalem, close to Jaffa Gate) totally imaginary.

winter it is up in the clouds and the fourth wall is unnoticeable due to the height of the site and the structure itself. It has a small gate, wide staircase and houses and dwellings in it. At the top of it is a turret [lit. a mosque] with an eastern window as big as a gate, facing al-Aqṣā. People assert: When the dove[60] went through it he [i.e. David] stared from it at the woman. Nobody can think of any way in which it could be destroyed. There the Muslims who were able to flee from the Franks (*rūm*) took refuge, when they stipulated that they hand it to them on condition that life and property were left intact. So it happened that they vacated it.[61]

I noted there the wonder of the generation [meaning: something very remarkable indeed] that occurred at a time when a rebel rose up against his ruler (*wālī*), took up his position there and provisioned it with food. The ruler besieged him for some time and sought to kill him with arrows. In spite of its small size the city carried on as usual. No market was closed because of this attempted coup. None of the common people went there, no pious man left his seclusion in al-Aqṣā Mosque for that reason. No theological discussion was interrupted and no learning terminated. The army split into two opposing camps but the rest of the people did not, for that ground, make any move [in their direction]. If only a little of that were to take place in our country the flame of war would be ignited far and near. Working for sustenance would stop, stalls would be closed and trading of merchandise would die away, due to our great immoderation (*fuḍūl*) [which differs wholly from] their scarcity of excesses.

From Ibn al-ʿArabī's commentary on the Qurʾān, *Aḥkām al-Qurʾān*, 4:1586.

Excerpt 14 [Bāb Ḥiṭṭa]

In reference to the verse:

> When we said: "Enter this town, and eat comfortably from it wherever ye please, enter the gate doing obeisance, and say 'Ḥiṭṭa' and we shall forgive you your transgressions and increase those who do well.[62]

---

60 The dove indicates the start of the trial of King David. Satan appeared to him at his niche in the figure of a golden dove, on which all the fine colours were observed. David tried to seize it but it flew and landed nearby. With the dove still flying, David continued his pursuit and thus went out of his niche and saw the lady [biblical Bathsheva] bathing, and her beauty attracted him: Ṯaʿlabī, *Qiṣaṣ al-Anbiyāʾ*, ed. Dār Iḥyāʾ al-Kutub al-ʿArabiyya, n.d., p. 248. See also: *Tales of the Prophets* by Muḥammad ibn ʿAbd Allāh al-Kisāʾī, trans. W. M. Thackston Jr. (Chicago, 1997), pp. 281–82.

61 On the surrender of the Fatimid garrison of Jerusalem see John France, *Victory in the East: A Military History of the First Crusade* (Cambridge, 1994), pp. 354–55.

62 Sūra 2 [the Cow] v. 59: Bell, *Qur'ān*, 1:9; a corresponding verse can be consulted in Sūra 7 [the Heights] v. 161: Bell, *Qur'ān*, 1:153.

The gate through which they [the Children of Israel] were ordered to enter is the eighth[63] gate of the Mosque, that is on the southern side (*qibla*) and is well known and celebrated. I entered through it in the year [4]86 [which corresponds to 1093]. I fell on my knees and prostrated and uttered: "there is no God besides Allah", God relieve me of my iniquity and pardon me. I stayed there for years and although I went through it often, I repeated this each time: "We have heard and obeyed, Praise be to God the Lord of the Universe".

From Ibn al-ʿArabī's commentary on *Sahīh al-Tirmidī*, *Āridat al-Ahwadī*, 11:78.

Excerpt 15 [Mary's tree trunk in Bethlehem]

I entered Bethlehem in the year 485 [1092] and in their place of worship I observed a cave in which there was a dry tree trunk that the resident monks unanimously assert is Mary's trunk. I came again into Bethlehem in Muḥarram [4]92 [December 1098] six months before the Christians (*rūm*) took control of it. I saw the cave in their site of worship and lo, there is no tree trunk there. I asked the monks dwelling there and they replied that it had rotted and collapsed. Furthermore, pilgrims [*ḫalq*, lit. people], used to chop off pieces of it as amulets for healing until it disappeared.

From Ibn al-ʿArabī's commentary on the Qurʾān, ch. 19 v. 25, *Aḥkām al-Qurʾān*, 3:1240.

Excerpt 16 [The graves of the Patriarchs in Hebron]

On the words of the Muslim tradition quoted by Mālik that Joseph, Peace unto him, said before his death: "I have not avenged a single wrong committed against me and these are my provisions upon departing this world. My deeds are added to those of my forefathers. I beg you to add my grave to theirs". Ibn al-ʿArabī appends the following:

Concerning his words "Add my grave to the tomb of my forefathers", we saw it in the year [4]87 [1094] and we sojourned there for many days in an atmosphere of security, delight and pleasure, able to dedicate ourselves to study and discussion. The tomb is in the village of Hebron[64] which belonged to Abraham, the Friend (*al-Ḫalīl*). Six *farsaḫ*s[65] separate it from Jerusalem,[66] on the downward ridge where

---

[63] From the term "eighth" one can perhaps conclude that there was an accepted or official enumeration of the gates to al-Aqṣā Mosque area.

[64] In print: Jayrūn.

[65] Approximately 40 km.

[66] Lit. *al-masjid al-aqṣā*, the name denotes both the holy mosque and the city of Jerusalem.

the site of Bayt Rāma,[67] the place of religious worship of Abraham, Peace unto him, was located. It overlooks the cities of Lot.

In the centre of the village there is a sturdy building of huge stones, which form a huge wall, and inside of it is a mosque. In the western wing, next to the *qibla* is [the grave of] Isaac and behind it in the wing mentioned, the grave of Abraham, the Friend. At the rear, on the inner side of the western wing, is the similarly designed [grave of] Jacob. Parallel to them in the eastern wing rest the graves of their wives in the same order. On each grave is a huge monolithic stone of [considerable] length, breadth and height as we described in the book *Tartīb al-Riḥla*.[68]

In the wing to the south of it, outside this sanctuary (*ḥaram*) lays Joseph's tomb, standing alone. It has an overseer, who comes from Ṭarṭuš,[69] who is paralysed and his [lit. he has a] mother who officiates in his stead. The design of the tomb of Joseph, may God's prayer and blessing be upon him, is like that of the other graves. This is the most trustworthy reference to his burial-place because Mālik mentions it.[70] Mālik, may God be pleased with him, gives the most likely solution that he has found.

From Ibn al-ʿArabī's Qur'ān commentary, *Aḥkām al-Qur'ān*, 3:1091.

Excerpt 17 [The document bestowed on Tamīm al-Dārī]

The learned judge Abū Bakr [ibn] al-ʿArabī al-Maʿāfirī stated in the book *al-Qabas*:[71] The descendants of Tamīm al-Dārī of Ḥabrūn[72] in Damascus[73] (the village of Abraham, Peace be upon him) have in their possession a letter of the Prophet, God's prayer on him, [written] on a piece of skin. It reads: In the name of Allah, the

---

67 The name of Bayt Rāma occurs in Islamic sources as an ancient place of legendary nature, somewhere between Jordan valley and the Balqā' (biblical Ammon, Moab and Gilead): Le Strange, *Palestine*, p. 415. However, one can hardly identify it with the place described by Ibn al-ʿArabī that should be found in the mountainous vicinity of Hebron, towards the east. The suggestion that Ibn al-ʿArabī confused Bayt Rāma with Rāma, biblical Mamre (Le Strange, *Palestine*, p. 518), nowadays Rāmet al-Ḫalīl, to the north of Hebron, is not likely either.

68 The itinerary of Ibn al-ʿArabī describing his impressions of cities, teachers, scholars and books with which he was able to acquaint himself during his journey in the East. The book was lost during his lifetime, and only those paragraphs that were interpolated into other books can attest to its original scope and value.

69 The town of Tortosa, on the estuary of the Ebro on the Mediterranean, in northeastern Spain.

70 The Muslim tradition is not unanimous as to the authentic locality of Joseph's tomb.

71 A famous book by Ibn al-ʿArabī where he comments on the principal book of the Māliki teaching, *al-Muwaṭṭa* by Mālik ibn Anas (d. 795).

72 An unusual way to signify al-Ḫalīl, after four centuries of Islamic imprint. Certainly influenced by the words of the prophetic document.

73 Damascus here means al-Ša'm or al-Šām , the traditional name for Syria. By all probability, one copyist of the text made an opposite use of the term al-Ša'm, which entails both the country of Syria and its main city Damascus. By the same token that copyist expanded the meaning of Damascus to indicate also both the city and the country. The published edition of *Kitab al-Qabas*, ed. Muḥammad ʿAbd Allāh Ould Krīm (Beirut, 1992), 2:796 omits the words "in Damascus" altogether.

compassionate, the merciful, this is what Muḥammad, the Messenger of God, bestowed on Tamīm al-Dārī, namely Ḥabrūn and ʿAynūn, the two villages of Abraham the friend, to do with as he thought fit. [The document] was written by ʿAlī ibn Abī Ṭālib[74] and witnessed by so and so. Both remained under his management and he ran them in his own manner. People saw this letter until the Rūm[75] entered in the year [4]96 [1102].

Even before that, one of the governors contested their claim [in this matter of the Dārīs' estate] and demanded to remove both villages, namely Ḥabrūn and ʿAynūn, from the ownership of Tamīm [and his heirs] while I was away in Syria. That ruler came to the seat of the judge Ḥāmid al-Harawī who purported to be a Ḥanafī but was secretly a Muʿtazilī, an infidel and Šiʿīte. The ruler (*wālī*) was Sukmān ibn Urtuq [printed: Uzbeq].[76] Tamīm's descendants produced the letter of God's Messenger to support their case. The judge, Ḥāmid, said: This letter is not binding because the Prophet bestowed something that he did not own. [The ruler] consulted the scholars. Al-Ṭūsī who then was there [i.e. in Syria] said "These are [the words of] an infidel. The Prophet, Peace be upon him, was accustomed to bestow allotments in Paradise saying: a palace to someone. How then could he not be capable of granting something in this world? God's Messenger also said: The world grew smaller (*zuwiyat lī al-arḍ*) for me [and therefore has come under my sway]. Indeed his [Muḥammad's] promise is trustworthy and the letter true". The faces of the ruler and of the judge fell and the descendants of Tamīm remained with their letter.

Al-Suyūṭī, *Itḥāf al-Aḫiṣṣāʾ*, ed. Aḥmad Ramaḍān Aḥmad (Cairo 1982–84), 2:227–28, Appendix 5.

Excerpt 18 [The modest women of Nāblus]

With reference to the Qurānic verses ch. 33 v. 32–33:

> O wives of the prophet, ye are not like any ordinary woman. If you show piety, do not wheedle in your speech, so that one in whose heart is disease grows lustful, but speak in reputable fashion. Remain in your houses, and do not swagger about in the manner of the former paganism. Observe the prayer and pay the Zakat, and obey Allah and his messenger.[77]

---

74 A close relative of Muḥammad, who later became the fourth Caliph (656–61).

75 Ibn al-ʿArabi uses *Rūm*, the common term for the Byzantine Empire which for centuries offended Islam, to define the new Latin intruders. Whether it was his failure of differentiation or an allusion to their transitory success which is doomed to miscarry as mentioned in the holy Islamic scriptures, is unsettled.

76 The name of the local ruler supplied by the published edition of *Kitāb al-Qabas*, 2:797 is, seemingly, even more perplexing y.k.m.a.n ibn a.r.t.i. d.n.k. Sukmān or Suqmān, son of Urtuq, is mentioned, for example, in *al-Kāmil fī al-Taʾrīḫ* by Ibn al-Aṯīr, 10:282 (Dār Ṣāder).

77 Bell, *Qur'ān*, 2:414.

I entered more than a thousand villages in the country and never saw women more protective of their families and more modest than the women of Nāblus, the city in which Abraham, our Patriarch, may he rest in peace, was cast into the fire.[78] I stayed there for a few months and never did I notice a woman on (any) road on any day except Friday. They would go out there until they filled the mosque. When the prayer has ended they would return home and I would not see a single one of them until the next Friday. As for the other villages you see their women preening themselves with jewellery or (going) without ornaments, and being split among themselves in every quarrel and problem.

In al-Aqṣā Mosque I have seen modest women who never left their places of seclusion until they became martyrs there [following the Frankish conquest of Jerusalem in July 1099].

From Ibn al-ʿArabī's commentary on the Qurʾān, ch. 33 (*al-aḥzāb*, i.e. the confederates), verses 32–33 *Aḥkām al-Qurʾān*, 3:1523.

Excerpt 19 [An evaluation of the Ašʿarīs][79]

In Ascalon I went one day to the guardhouse (*maḥras*) at the Gaza Gate. Before that, Ḥāmid,[80] the Muʿtazilī Ḥanafī judge, had come to us there and the Šīʿites, the Qadarīs[81] and the Sunnīs assembled around him as was their wont to look for the newcomers who are adorned by learning and relate to it. We had already become acquainted in al-Aqṣā Mosque. One of his disciples asked him: "Should the Ašʿarīs be considered as infidels for saying that the Creator sees?"[82] Judge Ḥāmid replied to him: "They should not be condemned as infidels because they say 'He sees' without [anthropomorphic] intention (*jiha*). They, thereby, mention something which can not be grasped by reason and one who does so[83] should not be considered an infidel."

---

78 This tradition which is conveyed here as common knowledge is not to be found in early sources (e.g. Ṭabarī's Qurʾān commentary, and the earliest version of *qiṣaṣ al-anbiyāʾ* by Kisāʾī, both locate the scene of Abraham in the furnace in southern Iraq). One can observe the Nāblus identification in books of later publication (Yaqūt's geographical dictionary s.v. *balāṭa*, but with reservation). I incline to suggest that Ibn al-ʿArabī is the earliest written source which refers to this less-accepted site.

79 The dominant school of theology in the Arabic-speaking lands of the ʿAbbasid caliphate. Their teaching almost became identical to orthodoxy. They were accused of basing their teaching on Aristotelian logic, or rational argumentation, thus distancing themselves from true, genuinely innocent credence.

80 Mentioned also as al-Harawī, in Excerpt 17. He was regarded as embracing Muʿtazilī ideas concealed by Ḥanafī outward show.

81 Defenders of free will and man's responsibility, unlimited by divine omnipotence or foreknowledge.

82 The question of the way corporeal terms applied to God should be interpreted, engaged Ašʿarīte theorists.

83 Lit. who says unreasonable things.

This statement conveys a profound philosophical speculation (*naẓar*) that will be unfolded, if sublime Allah so desires. I have mentioned it so that you can grasp how highly they appreciate us.[84]

Ṭālbī, *Arā' abī bakr ibn al-ʿarabī al-kalāmiyya* (Algiers, 1981), 2:42–43.

Excerpt 20 [Pre-crusade Syria, a territory of Islamic law]

If only you had seen Syria and Iraq in the decade of 490 you would have seen an unconcealed religion, abundant knowledge, a secure, settled and united society, too splendid and perfect to be described because of the lustre of its condition and the brilliance of its perfection. But an evil fate (*maqādīr*) brought a cold wind from the north and the south[85] which left Syria like yesterday that has passed and gone. It erased the voice of Islam from al-Aqṣā Mosque and executed there on Friday morning, the 18th of Šaʿbān 492 [11 July 1099], three thousand men and women, including God-fearing and learned worshippers, renowned for their (spiritual) state and noted for their religiosity. Then (too) the learned woman from Šīrāz was killed in the Dome of the Chain along with other women. When al-Malik al-ʿĀdil[86] died in [4]86[87] [1093] and when [the Caliph] al-Muqtadī bi-llāh passed away, a dispute (*fitna*) broke out in the land of Ḫurāsān, the Bāṭiniyya [probably Ismāʿīliyya] awakened and the sons [of Malikšāh] contended with each other. [Such a situation explains why] the Europeans (*rūm*) succeeded and invaded Syria and took control over the third holiest Moslem site (*mašhad*) and went forth and took over from "a.b.g.d."[88] to "ḥ.ṭ.i.",[89] I then learnt that they brought about [in Syria] the silent darkness.[90] I mentioned in *Tartīb al-Riḥla* something sufficient concerning the history of judges and scholars[91] and their relation to laws and statutes.

One day I was sitting in the Madrasa of al-Šāfiʿī at the Gate of the Tribes (*bāb al-asbāṭ*) in al-Aqṣā Mosque. It was being conducted according to the custom of the communities of Šāfiʿīs and Ḥanafīs, and they were (engaged) in their discussion

84 Referring to the scholastic Muʿtazilī consideration of the harmless Ašʿarīs, Ibn al-ʿArabī being one of them.

85 The Arabic text is unclear. It reads: *fa-habbat ʿalayhi min al-maqādīr j.r.j.f. min šamā'il wa-janā'ib fa-tarakat al-Ša'm ka-ams al-ḏāhib*. The unclear *j.r.j.f.* was replaced by *ḥ.r.j.f.* meaning "violent and glacial wind".

86 Al-ʿĀdil is the honorific title of the Seljuq Sultan Malikšāh, who ruled from Baghdad from 1072 to 1092.

87 Ibn al-ʿArabi gives the year 486 for the death of Malikšāh. The regular history books and biographies give it as 485/1092.

88 First Arabic letters in a list arranged according to numerical value.

89 Further letters, alluding to the gradual progress of crusader invasions aiming at making more conquests.

90 Vague term. Perhaps insinuating at the Fatimids, who ruled part of Syria when the Franks invaded it, and to whom the label "silent transgressors" penned by an orthodox scholar fits properly.

91 Needs the complement: who fell victim to the Frankish invasion.

(*naẓar*) session. There appeared a seeker of knowledge[92] who stood before us and spoke to the head of the academy (*ṣāḥib al-madrasa*) the straightforward Qāḍī Yaḥyā b. Mufarrij al-Maqdisī, the oldest disciple of Naṣr, and said to him: "I swore and said: I shall divorce my wife three times that I would not eat nuts. However, later I did so unintentionally". He looked at them and asked: "What do you say?" the Ḥanafīs replied unanimously: "He must break his vow" whereas the Šāfiʿīs were divided on the issue. The rightly-guided Qāḍī smiled and said to him, "Go [your way], you have not [transgressed]".

From "al-ʿAwāṣim min al-Qawāṣim", Talbi, *Arāʾ abī bakr ibn al-ʿarabī al-kalāmiyya*, 2:498–99.

Excerpt 21 [Flawed Šīʿi opinions]

After that I went from them [the Egyptian teachers] to Syria and reached Jerusalem, May God purify it. There I found twenty-eight study circles (*ḥalqa*) and two schools (*madrasa*). One of them, at the Gate of Tribes, was for the Šāfiʿīs and the other, opposite the Church of the Holy Sepulchre, known as the school of Abū ʿUqba was for the Ḥanafīs. Among them were many of their leading scholars together with the principal heretics (*mubtadiʿa*) of various ranks and circles as well as Jewish *aḥbār*, Christian and Samaritan sages too many to be counted. I reached the destination in the right way and acquired the knowledge in the most desirable method. I observed each group while it was debating and took part in its discussions in the presence of our teacher Abū Bakr al-Fihrī, may God have mercy upon him, and other Sunni learned men of his like.

After that, for the reasons I specified in *Tartīb al-Riḥla*,[93] I headed for the coast that was full of deviant opinions and schools [of thought] of the Ismāʿīlis[94] and the Imāmīs.[95] For the same religious reasons for five months I wandered about the coastal cities, from which I went down to Acre.

The head of the Imāmīs there at that time was Abū al-Fatḥ al-ʿAkkī, joined by a Sunni scholar called the sage al-Daybaqī. I met Abū al-Fatḥ at his place of learning and I was (then) twenty. When he saw me, of tender age yet grown up in wisdom, a fluent speaker, capable of reaching my goals, clever and well-trained, he enthused over me. There are, by Allah's life, amongst them some, who although they hold flawed opinions do possess innate ability (*inṭibāʿ*) and fair judgement (*inṣāf*),

---

92 Lit. *sāʾil*, which can signify also a beggar. If this is the right translation it sheds a different light on the social contribution and nature of these scholarly gatherings.

93 Ibn al-ʿArabī's autobiographical treatise on the voyage to the East.

94 The major branch of the Šīʿa adhering to seven *Imāms* (the last one Ismāʿīl [ibn Jaʿfar al-Ṣādiq], hence their name). In this chapter they are called *bāṭiniyya* referring to their stress on the inward (*bāṭin*) meaning behind the literal wording of sacred texts.

95 The central Šīʿi party, known also as the Twelver Šīʿa (*iṯnā ʿašariyya*).

recognition and affirmation of one's virtues – if they are evident. He did not leave me alone and hastened to interrogate and debate with me and he did not get tired of me. I spoke to him about my rejection of the Imāmī school of thought and of the idea to acquire exclusively from the impeccable Imām,[96] matters that are too long to mention in this chapter …

Talbi, *Arāʾ abī bakr ibn al-ʿarabī al-kalāmiyya*, 2:61–62.

Excerpt 22 [Excitement before a journey]

The judge Abū Bakr said: There were meetings [with Šīʿīs] apart from the one [described before] which we will portray in their place. One of these is the following. When my name became known in the town mentioned [Acre] and my case became familiar and the harm I caused them increased, there was an amir, a Šīʿī, who was very capable in debate. Though a Šīʿī, [he had] a leaning towards the Muʿtazilī school of thought and an inclination for false novelties (*bidʿa*) and erroneous ideas. Upon hearing about me he lay in wait for me but failed to succeed, except on the day of the public gathering (*tabrīz*) before setting out for Tiberias. Together with his retinue (*kawkaba*), he placed himself near me among my riding animals. By Allāh's life, we were powerless when he stopped at our place since they[97] had the authority, they were the rulers and the country was theirs.

When he had taken his place he started to talk to me. By Allāh's life, among these people [i.e. the Šīʿīs], even if they differ in opinion from us, there is pleasure at the encounter, mildness in discussion and intense patience. He said to me "It has come to my knowledge that you conducted a debate with our friends here and I heard about your aloofness. I wished to meet you so that I could find out all about you and ascertain what are your good qualities". I recovered my spirits and calmed my soul concerning the evil about God that it may have had to confront. He spoke pleasantly to me [but] his hostility was apparent. I said to him "Some of what you heard is, indeed, correct and he is[98] worthy of my thanks for his cunning and good spirits".

[Continuing, Ibn al-ʿArabī describes how he overcame the Šīʿī amir with demonstrable proofs and also how the amir knew how to retract in time and even gave orders to the commander of the caravan to Tiberias to dare not return to Acre without a work of Ibn al-ʿArabi – a token of his appreciation for him.]

Ṭālbī, *Arāʾ abī bakr ibn al-ʿarabī al-kalāmiyya*, 2:72–73.

---

[96] The main attributes of the Imām according to the Twelvers is that he is divinely guided, immune from sin and an authoritative instructor in religion. Disobedience to that Imām is deemed infidelity.

[97] Šīʿī officeholders in Fatimid Palestine circa 1100.

[98] Polite third form to the present listener.

Excerpt 23 [Lake Tiberias]

Apocalyptic literature mentions the people of Gog and Magog who are about to reach the Lake of Ṭabariyya (Gennesaret) and drink of its water.

I descended to it in [the month of] Jumādā al-Ūlā 489 [May 1096] and stayed there for [some] days. The city (*balda*) was built by the Roman ruler Tiberius [rendered in Arabic as *Ṭabārā*]. The adjective denoting this place is Ṭabarānī whereas for Ṭabaristān in Ḫurāsān it is Ṭabarī. Its circumference, according to my estimation, is about five or six parasangs.[99] The river Jordan flows into its upper part and out of its lower part and it is like a pool between mountains. If you ascend the upper ridge (*ʿaqaba*),[100] you can set out for Ḥawrān, Baṯaniyya and Buṣrā in the center of Šām.[101]

From Ibn al-ʿArabī's commentary on *Ṣaḥīḥ al-Tirmiḏī*, 9:89–90.

Excerpt 24 [Confronting Šīʿīs in Acre]

The head of the Bāṭinīyya, known also as Ismāʿīliyya, wanted to meet me. Abū al-Fatḥ approached me at the assembly of the scholar al-Daybaqi and said thus: "The head of the Ismāʿīliyya is keen to talk to you". I replied "I am busy". He said "There is a place nearby which he attends, the guard-post (*maḥras*) of the people of Tiberias. It is a mosque in a beautiful edifice (*qaṣr*) on the shore, an elevated building perfect in design." He displayed an unfriendly attitude towards me [since I had succeeded in refuting his arguments] so I vacillated between timidity and acquiescence. The guard-post had a long fence (*rāʿiʾa*) which I managed to cross. Diffidently we entered the striking guard-post, we climbed up to where we found them segregated in its eastern corner. Their faces reflected unsociability. I greeted them and then went towards the prayer niche where I prostrated two *rakʿa*s aiming, thus, to complete speech with them and [immediately afterwards] distance myself from them. By Him who ordered me to obey [God] I shall recount that I wanted to leave this meeting (*majlis*) for good. I stared at the sea blowing at a black pointed stone under the balustrades of the guard-post and uttering "This is my tomb into which they will cast me". Within myself I sang "Behold, is there a return to this world, or is the bottom of the sea a grave and a shroud other than water".

This was the fourth grave trial in my life, from which God saved me. After my greeting, I turned to them and interrogated them about their situation in general and my soul [gradually] returned to me. I said "Death is easy [to accept] and appropriate in this respectful abode where I am fighting for the religion, thus I shall be the

99 In Arabic *farsaḫ* measured, usually, as 6.5 km.

100 Known as *ʿaqabat fiq*, roughly from Samakh to the Golan Heights.

101 The medieval Arabic name for Syria.

trusted envoy (*qayyim*) of the Muslims". Abū al-Fatḥ said to me, while pointing to a good-looking youngster, "This is the head of the party and its master". I blessed him and remained silent. He initiated the conversation, was the first to start talking and said, "The essence of your discussions has reached me and your words have come before me. Is it true that you proclaim 'God said' and 'God did'? What is the substance of God to whom you pray and increasingly mention? Please let me know and clarify it to me. Detach yourself from the falsehood (*maḫraqa*) which was imposed upon you by this poor party [Sunni theology]". He raged, his fury burned, he was filled with wrath and anger and bent on his knees. His pleasant manner of His speech vanished and I was perfectly sure that his adherents would kidnap me before he could end his words and I could reply. With God's assistance I delved into my mind and came up with a sharp retort which floored him and left him speechless [literally, I directed my hand to my quiver, pulled out a pointed dart and with it I smote the chambers of his heart as well as his hands and mouth. He remained with no adequate word worthy of writing].

Ṭālbī, *Arāʾ abī bakr ibn al-ʿarabī al-kalāmiyya*, 2:64–66.

A Notice about Patriarch Aimery of Antioch in an Armenian Colophon of 1181[1]

Michael E. Stone

Hebrew University of Jerusalem

Aimery of Limoges, who served as patriarch of Antioch from 1141 (or 1142) to 1196, is one of the better known figures of the Latin East. Although William of Tyre decried him as a man *absque litteris*,[2] there is substantial evidence for his intellectual interests. When Pope Eugenius III (1145–53) asked him for a Latin translation of John Chrysostom's commentary on the Gospel according to Matthew, Aimery procured a copy of the original Greek text and sent it to Rome. In 1176 he corresponded with the Pisan, Constantinople-based theologian, Hugh Etherianus, received his tract on the double procession of the Holy Spirit, and asked him for others of his writings, as well as for a work of John Chrysostom on Paul's epistles, and for a chronicle of the Byzantine Empire.[3] (The attribution to Aimery of *La Fazienda de Ultra Mar*, a Castilian-written work that exhibits familiarity with the Hebrew Bible and with Jewish exegesis, should however be discarded.)[4] As a prelate, Aimery brought about the union of the Maronites with Rome in about 1181 and was probably involved in the Armenian rapprochement with Rome in 1184. Furthermore, in 1178 he took the unprecedented step of inviting a leading schismatic – the Jacobite patriarch Michael the Syrian – to the Third Lateran Council. Aimery also attempted to regulate the conduct of the many hermits who lived in solitude on the Black Mountain, laying down that each of them must have a spiritual guide.[5]

Aimery's role in the politics of the Principality of Antioch was considerable. Thus, when Prince Raymond of Antioch fell in battle against Nur al-Din in 1149, and again when Prince Bohemond III was taken prisoner by Nur al-Din in 1164, Aimery temporarily took charge of the principality. His quarrel in 1153 with Prince

---

1 My thanks to Benjamin Kedar for drawing my attention to recent discussions of the tensions in Antioch.

2 WT, 15.18, p. 700.

3 Benjamin Z. Kedar, "Gerard of Nazareth, A Neglected Twelfth-Century Writer in The Latin East", *Dumbarton Oaks Papers* 37 (1983), 65, 69, repr. in idem, *The Franks in the Levant, 11th to 14th Centuries* (Aldershot, 1993), article IV, pp. 65, 69; Rudolf Hiestand, "Un centre intellectuel en Syrie du Nord? Notes sur la personnalité d'Aimery d'Antioche, Albert de Tarse et *Rorgo Fretellus*", *Moyen Age* 100 (1994), 8–16.

4 See Benjamin Z. Kedar, "Sobre la génesis de *La Fazienda de Ultra Mar*", *Anales de Historia Antigua e Medieval* 28 (1995), 131–36.

5 Bernard Hamilton, "Aimery of Limoges, Patriarch of Antioch. Ecumenist, Scholar and Patron of Hermits", in *The Joy of Learning and the Love of God. Studies in Honor of Jean Leclercq*, ed. E. Rozanne Elder (Kalamazoo, MI, 1995), pp. 269–90.

Renaud of Châtillon led to his imprisonment in Antioch's citadel and, later, to his exile in Jerusalem, and when in 1165 the Byzantine emperor Manuel imposed a Greek patriarch on Antioch, Aimery excommunicated all Latins who had accepted him.[6]

Aimery's last political clash occurred some time after Emperor Manuel's death on 24 September 1180. Prince Bohemond III repudiated his wife Theodora, a great-niece of Manuel, and married his mistress Sybilla, apparently a daughter of a noble Frankish family, who – according to William of Tyre – was said to have engaged in sorcery. Aimery repeatedly called on Bohemond to revert to his legitimate wife and, when he refused to comply, excommunicated him and imposed an interdict on Antioch. Bohemond countered by seizing church property and persecuting Aimery and his clergy; when Aimery and his followers withdrew to the fortress of Qusair, Bohemond laid siege to it. At that juncture several Antiochene nobles led by Reynald Mazoir, the lord of Margat, took the side of the church and turned against Bohemond. This internal strife threatened to place the principality's very existence in jeopardy – thus writes William of Tyre, who on this occasion unequivocally sides with Aimery. King Baldwin IV of Jerusalem and the prelates and nobles of his kingdom decided to intervene. A high-powered delegation led by Patriarch Eraclius of Jerusalem met separately with Prince Bohemond and Patriarch Aimery in Laodicea and, after some further discussions at Antioch, negotiated an agreement according to which Bohemond was to return the Church property he had seized and Aimery was to lift the interdict. Bohemond himself was to remain excommunicated as long as he did not cast away Sybilla and reinstate Theodora. When the delegation left for Jerusalem, Bohemond expelled the nobles who had revolted against him (but not their leader, Reynald Mazoir). The expellees found refuge at the court of Prince Rupen III of Cilician Armenia.[7]

William of Tyre does not give the date of this clash between Aimery and Bohemond; in Robert Huygens' 1986 edition of William's chronicle the clash is dated to 1180 and the agreement engineered by Patriarch Eraclius' delegation to 1180–81; in 1993 Hans Eberhard Mayer persuasively argued that the nobles' revolt took place in 1181 and that it was over in December of that year.[8] Now, however, we possess a contemporary, Antiochene source that, in conjunction with Mayer's analysis, allows us to date the clash to August–November 1181 and that – unlike William of Tyre – sides with Bohemond not Aimery.

This source is the colophon of an Armenian manuscript containing the Gospels, now MS Chester Beatty Armenian 624, fol. 260r–260v i.[9] The text runs as follows:

---

[6] For a detailed discussion of these and other events see Hamilton, "Aimery", pp. 274–76.

[7] The main source on these events is WT 22.5, 6, pp. 1012, 1013–16; for a detailed discussion see Hans E. Mayer, "Der Ehestreit Boemunds III., die Adelsrevolte von 1181 und die Verdrängung der Mazoir aus Margat". in idem, *Varia Antiochena. Studien zum Kreuzfahrerfürstentum Antiochia im 12. und frühen 13. Jahrhundert*, MGH Schriften und Texte 6 (Hanover, 1993), pp. 162–83.

[8] Mayer, "Der Ehestreit", pp. 162–70.

[9] Thanks are expressed to Dr Michael Ryan, Director of the Chester Beatty Library, who granted

Փառք ամենասուրբ երրորդութեանն յաւիտեանս: ամէն:

որ հասոյց զապիկար գրիչս յոհաննէս յաւարտումն աստուածախաւս տառիս սուրբ աւետարանիս քրիստոսի:

Գրեցաւ ի թվականիս հայկազեան տումարիս ՈԼ յանտիոք մայրաքաղաքիս: ընդ հովանեաւ սուրբ փրկչիս ի լեառնս ի հայրապետութեան տեառն գրիգորիոսի հայոց կաթոսի: ի թագաւորութեան կիւռ ալեքսի տղայոյ: |col. 2| եւ երուսաղեմի սիրպաղտէ մանկան: եւ ի բրընձ պէմընդին. յայսմ ժամանակի մուռտ արար հեմրի պատրիարգն ի խուսայրն եւ կապեաց բանադրանաւք զաշխարհս անտիոքու. եւ զբազումս սրահողխող առնէր:

Արդ գրեցաւ յամենալաւ աւրինակէ. խոշորութեանս անմեղադիր լերուք. եւ որք ընթեռնոյք կամ ընդաւրինակէք. յիշեսջիք ի քրիստոս. զանպիտան գրիչս յոհաննէս զծառայս ամենայն ծառայիցդ աստուծոյ. զի լի եմ ամենայն (eras 7) մեղաւք. |fol. 260v col i| զի թերեւս ողորմութիւն գտից ի ք[րիստոսէ]է աղաւթիւք ձեր. եւ որ զմեզ յիշէքդ եւ դուք յիշեալ եղիջիք առաջի ք[րիստոսի]ի զի ողորմեսցի ձեզ յիշողացդ եւ մեզ յիշատակելոցս. եւ թողցէ զյանցանս[10] մեր եւ զծնողաց մերոց եւ զեղբարց. եւ զձերտ եւ զամենայն անյիշատակ ննջեցելոցն. եւ դատեսցէ ընդ սուրբս իւր զամենեսեան ք[րիստոս] ա[ստուա]ծ որ է աւրհնեալ յաւիտեանս. ամէն:

Glory to the all-holy Trinity for ever, Amen, who caused me, the feeble scribe Yohannēs to reach the end of this divinely-spoken book of the holy Gospel of Christ. It was written in this year 630 of the Armenian calendar [1181–82] in this metropolis of Antioch, within the church of S. P'rkič' (St Saviour) in this mountain,[11] in the pontificate of Rev. Gregory, Cath(olic)os of the Armenians; in the rule of the child Kyr Alēk's and of Sir Baldwin the Younger of Jerusalem, and in (the rule of) Prince Bohemond. In this time Hemri (Aimery) Patriarch carried out riots in Qusair (*Xusayr*) and laid a ban of excommunication this land of Antioch and put many to the sword.

Now, it was written from an excellent exemplar. Do not blame my roughness (i.e., of writing). And you who read or copy (it), remember me, the feeble scribe, to Christ, Yohannēs, servant of all the servants of God, for I am full of all sins, so that, perhaps, I will find mercy from Christ through your prayers. And you who remember us, may you also be remembered before Christ so that he may have mercy on you who will remember me.

And may he forgive our sins and those of our parents and brothers, and yours and those of all those who have fallen asleep without memorial. And may Christ God judge all (of them) with his saints, He who is blessed for ever. Amen.

---

permission to publish this text. The manuscript will be fully described in the forthcoming catalogue of the additional Armenian manuscripts of the Chester Beatty Library being prepared by M.E. Stone and N. Stone.

[10] յ miniaturized, above line.

[11] Or, in the mountains.

Observations

1 630 of the Armenian era started on 11 August 1181 (Julian) and ended on 10 August 1182.[12] Therefore, accepting Mayer's reasoning, the conflict in Antioch must have taken place in the late summer and/or in the fall of 1181.

2 "In this time Hemri (Aimery) Patriarch carried out riots in Qusair (*Xusayr*) and laid a ban of excommunication this land of Antioch and put many to the sword." I interpret the Armenian *Xusayr* in the sentence as Qusair, where Aimery withdrew in the course of the conflict. The colophon adds new details of Aimery's activities while in Qusair, its chief innovation being that he "put many to the sword". He also instigated riots against Bohemond.

3 It appears that the scribe Yohannēs does not much like the patriarch, though his language about him is not very extreme. This is a nice contrast with William of Tyre's position, favouring Aimery.

4 The identification of "this mountain" where the manuscript was copied is unclear. Relatively few Armenian manuscripts known to have been copied in Antioch. Matenadaran 1526 of 1294 contains a reference to Antioch in 1190, as follows: յետ այսորիկ փութացաւ ի լեառն որ առընթեր մեծին Անդիոքու, ի վանորեայսն, որ ի Լատինացւոց եւ ի Հելլենացւոցն պայծառանային անդ (After this, he [Nersēs of Lambron] hastened to the mountain which was near the great [city of] Antioch, to the monastics who, being of the Latins and of the Greeks, were resplendent there). After "Antioch" Yovsēp'ian adds the words ի լեառն որ Ռասխանձիր կոչի (to the mountain which is called Ras-Khandzir [Ṙasxanjir]). Ras al-Khanzir is a cape west of Antioch, where a Benedictine monastery, and an Armenian one close to it, were located.[13] A Jerusalem manuscript, J1801, records that in 1187 Nersēs of Lambron translated Revelation in Antioch.

5 St Saviour monastery remains unidentified. I do not believe that this St Saviour is in the Black Mountains, a branch of the Armenian Taurus, in Cilicia, adjoining Antioch. The wording of the colophon does not favour this, as it places the copying of the manuscript in "this metropolis of Antioch".

6 Bohemond expelled the pro-Aimery nobles to the Armenian kingdom of Cilicia. Does this indicate that they were connected in some way with that kingdom and a consequent Armenian sympathy for the Latin Patriarch? If so, then the Armenian scribe Yohannēs's even muted sympathy for Prince Bohemond of Antioch seems unusual. Nothing could be found in the sources about the relationship of the Armenians to Latin Christianity in Antioch at this time but in

---

[12] Thanks are expressed to Dr Aram Topchyan of the Matenadaran, Yerevan for assistance in verifying the calendary synchronizations.

[13] Claude Cahen, *La Syrie du Nord à l'époque des croisades et la principauté franque d'Antioche* (Paris, 1940), pp. 324 n. 6, 565, and map opposite p. v.

Cilicia, Catholicos Grigor IV Tłay (1173–93) was involved in negotiations with Rome.

7 There was an Armenian archbishop of Antioch in this period, in 1179 and for some time after, he was called Grigorios.[14] Robert Hewsen's new *Armenia: A Historical Atlas* shows both Latin patriarchal and Armenian archiepiscopal sees of Antioch, but no monasteries (map 119, The Barony of Kilikian Armenia, 1080–1199).

[14] M. Ormanian, *National History* (repr. Antelias, 2001), para. 1009 (in Armenian).

Crusader Inscriptions from Southern Lebanon

Denys Pringle

Cardiff University

In his corpus of crusader inscriptions from the Holy Land, published in 1974, the late Fr Sabino de Sandoli, OFM, assembled over 400 inscriptions relating to the Crusader kingdom of Jerusalem, including lead seals and masonry marks.[1] The geographical coverage of the corpus, however, was restricted to the modern political entities of Israel, the Palestinian territories and Jordan, thus leaving out the northern part of the Crusader kingdom of Jerusalem now lying in southern Lebanon.[2] The present paper attempts to make good that omission by listing all those inscriptions from southern Lebanon that are known to the author. A comprehensive corpus of crusader-period inscriptions from Lebanon and Syria, however, still remains a desideratum.

As almost all the inscriptions listed here have been published before in some form or other, their texts are presented as editions, accompanied where possible by facsimile drawings. Two Frankish epitaphs, reportedly found respectively in Sidon[3] and in the paving of the ʿUmariyya mosque (the former crusader cathedral) in Beirut,[4] have not been traced. Also excluded are the Frankish masonry marks that have been recorded on the Sea Castle in Sidon[5] and on the crusader cathedral in Tyre,[6] as well as lead seals.[7]

The closest parallels elsewhere in the Latin Kingdom for the epitaphs from Tyre and Sidon (nos. 2–14) come from Acre, where a similar mixture of Latin and French

---

1 *Corpus inscriptionum crucesignatorum Terrae Sanctae (1099–1291): testo, traduzione e annotazioni*, ed. Sabino de Sandoli, Pubblicazioni dello Studium Biblicum Franciscanum, Collectio maior 21 (Jerusalem, 1974); cf. P. Thomsen, "Die lateinischen und griechischen Inschriften der Stadt Jerusalem und ihrer nächsten Umgebung", *Zeitschrift des Deutschen Palästina-Vereins* 43 (1920), 138–58; 44 (1921), 1–61, 90–168.

2 *Corpus*, p. lxiii.

3 C. Virolleaud, "Les Travaux archéologiques en Syrie en 1922–1923", *Syria* 5 (1924), 113–22 (p. 116).

4 M. de Vogüé, *Les Églises de la Terre Sainte* (Paris, 1860), pp. 373–74.

5 P. Deschamps, *Les Châteaux des croisés en Terre-Sainte*, 2. *La défense du royaume de Jérusalem: étude historique, géographique et monumentale*, 2 vols. (text and plates), Bibliothèque archéologique et historique 34 (Paris, 1939), p. 231; H. Kalayan, "The Sea Castle of Sidon", *Bulletin du Musée de Beyrouth*, 26 (1973), 81–89 (pl. X).

6 Denys Pringle, "The Crusader Cathedral of Tyre", *Levant* 33 (2001), 165–88 (fig. 10).

7 See Le comte Chandon de Briailles, "Trois sceaux du clergé franc de Beyrouth", *Bulletin du Musée de Beyrouth* 3 (1939), 13–24; idem, "Bulle de Clérembaut de Broyes, archevêque de Tyr", *Syria* 21 (1940), 82–89; idem, "Matrices de sceaux francs", *Bulletin du Musée de Beyrouth* 9 (1949–50), 99–106; idem, "Bulles de l'Orient latin", *Syria* 27 (1950), 284–300; G. Schlumberger, F. Chalandon and A. Blanchet, *Sigillographie de l'Orient latin* (Paris 1943).

texts is to be found.[8] In most cases these record the name and status of the deceased and the time of death. Dates given include 1190 (no. 7), 1202 (no. 8), 1266 (no. 9) and 1272/4 (no. 11). Nationalities include two from Italy (nos. 3, 7) and one apparently from France (no. 6), while the occupations represented include two knights (nos. 4, 9), a *m*(*aistre*?) (no. 5), a woollen cloth merchant (no. 6), and a deacon (no. 12). In one case (no. 2) the name of the deceased is not given; this was possibly because the stone formed part of a composite tomb, in which further details concerning the dead person were given in a separate text. Two of the epitaphs include an invitation to pray for the soul of the dead man (nos. 9, 11).[9]

The graffiti from chapel walls in Beirut and Tyre (nos. 1 and 15) are evidence of a lively pilgrim traffic from the later twelfth century onwards, though at least one of those in Tyre appears to have been left by someone who participated in the siege of Acre (1189–91) (no. 15b), as also may another which appears to refer to the squire of a knight of Jerusalem (no. 15f).

In editing the texts the following conventions have been observed:

[.] lacuna on the stone, the number of suspended stops indicating the assumed number of missing letters.
( ) expansion of an intentional contraction.
‹ › expansion of an unintentional contraction or accidental omission.
a̲ doubtful reading, where only part of the letter survives.

BEIRUT

1 Graffiti in the chapel of St Saviour or St Barbara

Various graffiti, including chrisms and monograms in Latin characters, were scratched over the wall paintings inside the excavated chapel of St Saviour, or St Barbara, in the thirteenth century and possibly later.[10] In addition, the following letters were found scratched above and to the right of the aureoled head of Christ in a representation of the Virgin and Child (Fig. 1):

---

[8] *Corpus*, pp. 299–318, nos. 404–20. Note that no. 407 is from Ascalon: see Denys Pringle, "King Richard I and the Walls of Ascalon", *Palestine Exploration Quarterly* 116 (1984), 133–47; repr. in Denys Pringle, *Fortification and Settlement in Crusader Palestine* (Aldershot 2000), ch. 3. For further discussion of no. 417, see also Joshua Prawer, "A Crusader Tomb of 1290 from Acre and the Last Archbishops of Nazareth", *Israel Exploration Journal* 24 (1974), 241–51.

[9] Cf. *Corpus*, nos. 404, 416–17.

[10] J. Lauffray, "Forums et monuments de Béryte (suite)", *Bulletin du Musée de Beyrouth* 8 (1946–48), 7–16 (pp. 8, 11–12, fig. 2); Denys Pringle, *The Churches of the Crusader Kingdom of Jerusalem: A Corpus*, 3 vols. (Cambridge, 1993–), 1:118; L. Nordiguian and J.-C. Voisin, *Châteaux et églises du moyen âge au Liban* (Beirut, 1999), pp. 371–72.

Fig. 1 Beirut: Graffito (no. 1) from church of St Saviour, or St Barbara (after J. Lauffray, *Bulletin du Musée de Beyrouth* 8 (1946–48), p. 12)

húet deaqs [...

This seems most likely to represent a name, such as *Hu*(*gu*)*et de Aq*(*ui*)*s*. Alternatively it might possibly be expanded as: *h*(*ab*)*ue*(*ri*)*t de aq*(*ui*)*s*. The meaning of such a phrase, however, appears obscure, though it is possible that the text continued on the area of missing plaster to the right.

SIDON

2 *Verse epitaph*

From the Bustan al-Franji, or garden of the Frères de Terre Sainte, on a marble arch.[11]

‡ Hic iacet in pulchro pietatis norma sepulchro
qui stud‹u›it semp(er) Domino servire libenter
et quod suppleret que lex divina iuberet
omnia quippe dabat Xpo (Christo) que danda putabat

Here lies in a beautiful tomb a model of piety, who forever strove to serve the Lord freely, and because he fulfilled those things which divine law commanded, he gave to Christ all those things indeed which he considered ought to be given.

Renan identified the deceased as an archbishop of Tyre on the basis of the double cross;[12] this argument, however, is far from convincing.

[11] E. M. Renan, *Mission en Phénicie*, 2 vols. [text + plates by M. Thobais] (Paris, 1864–74), 1:391.
[12] Ibid.

3 *Epitaph from a tomb made by or for Domenico Baronilla*

This text was noted by Renan, but its precise provenance is unknown.[13]

…]a Veneticus D(omi)nicus Baronilla nomin[e …
…] sepulcrum istud composuer(it) t[…

…the Venetian, Domenico Baronilla, by name …
…will have made that tomb …

4 *Epitaph*

This text was also recorded by Renan.[14]

…]l
…]co miles
… qui r]equie
scit …] m(ens)e

…] knight [… who] lies […] in the month [of …

Lines 3–4 might alternatively read … *qui r]equie[scat in pace* (may he rest in peace).

5 *Epitaph of Jo[sep]h Timeron*

Marble slab (33 × 29 cm), found in Sidon in 1923 and removed to the National Museum, Beirut (Fig. 2).[15]

Ici] gist mesire Jo
sep]h Timeron, fi(ls)
si]re Angorrant, m(aistre)
…, q]ui trespassa an
l'incar]nacion Ih(es)u Cr[is]t
m cc.……]i

[Here] lies Sir Jo[sep]h Timeron, son of Sir Enguerrand, m(aster of …), who passed away (in the) year of the Incarnation of Jesus Christ, [12..].

---

13 Ibid.

14 Ibid.

15 Virolleaud, "Travaux", p. 116; Camille Enlart, *Les Monuments des croisés dans le royaume de Jérusalem: architecture religieuse et civile*, 2 vols. + 2 albums of plates, Bibliothèque archéologique et historique 7–8 (Paris, 1925–28), 2:338–39, fig. 455, pl. 144; Pringle, *Churches*, 2:320.

Line 2: In the photograph published by Enlart, the first legible letter is clearly *h*, allowing the restoration of the name *Jo[sep]h*. His photograph, however, had evidently been retouched prior to publication and the reading is therefore not entirely certain. Enlart himself restored the letter as *e*, which would allow the alternative possibilities of *Jo[rg]e*, *Jo[ffr]e* or *Jo[ss]e*. *Line 3:* Enlart curiously took the letter following Angorrant (Enguerrand) to be *c*, which he interpreted as the beginning of *c[hevalier]*. His photograph, however, shows *m*, or possibly *an*, as in the following line. Furthermore, the colon following the letter indicates that it is either a complete word or a contraction of one. Possibilities might include *m(ajour)*, *m(aistre)*, or perhaps *m(aistre) / (le) roy* (majordomo). *Line 6:* Enlart recognized the final letter as *I*, but it is scarcely visible on the photograph. The text seems to have ended with a colon, of which only the upper dot remains.

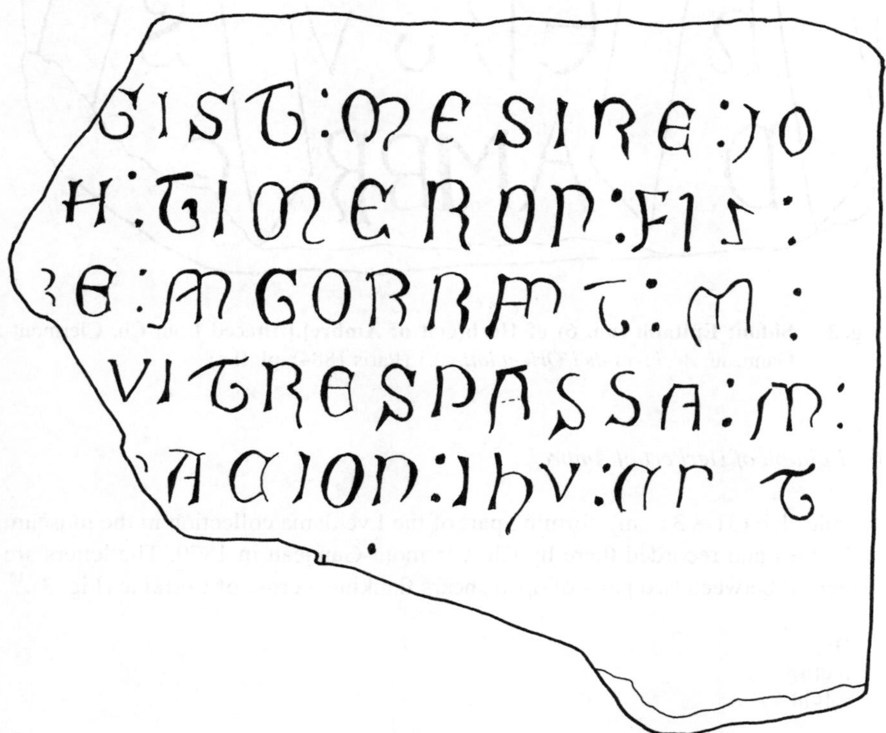

Fig. 2 Sidon: Epitaph (no. 5) of Jo[sep]h Timeron (traced from C. Enlart, *Les Monuments des Croisés* (Paris 1925–28), fig. 455

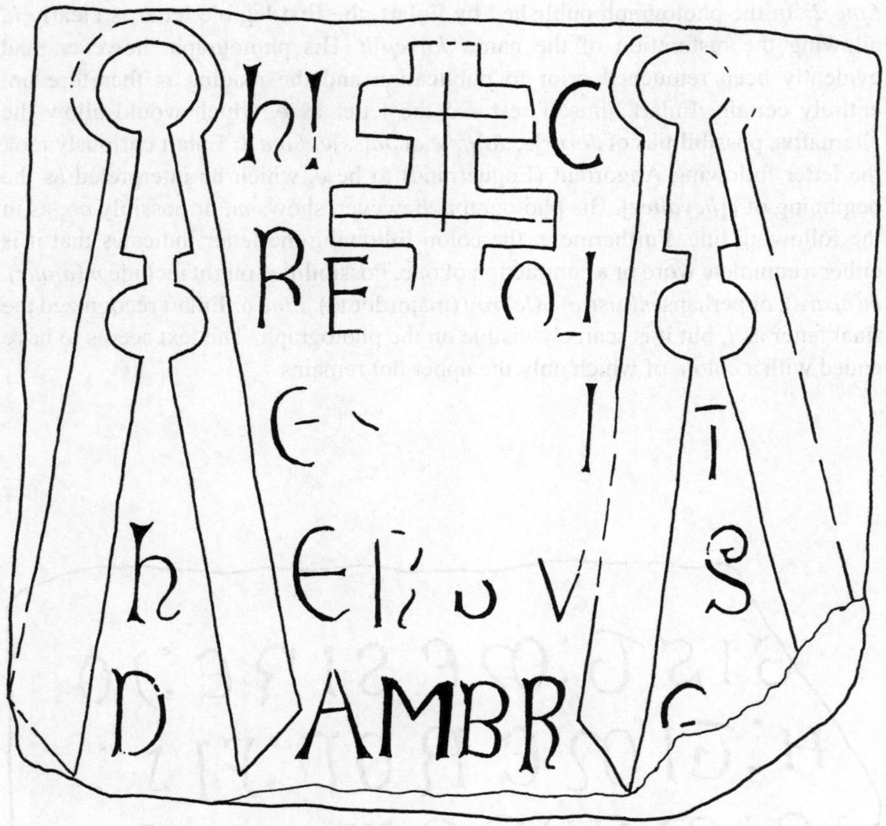

Fig. 3 Sidon: Epitaph (no. 6) of Herb(er)t of Ambre[.] (traced from Ch. Clermont-Ganneau, *Archives de l'Orient latin* 2.1 (Paris 1884), pl. II.c)

6 *Epitaph of Herbert of Ambre[.*

Marble slab (31 × 31 cm), forming part of the Lycklama collection in the museum in Cannes and recorded there by Ch. Clermont-Ganneau in 1879. The letters are dispersed between two pairs of open shears flanking a cross of Lorraine (Fig. 3).[16]

Hic
req(u)i
es̲[c]it

[16] Ch. Clermont-Ganneau, "Nouveaux monuments des croisés recueillis en Terre Sainte", *AOL* 2.1 (Paris, 1884), 457–64 (p. 462, pl. II.c); Enlart, *Monuments*, 2:339, fig. 128, pl. 139 *bis*; Pringle, *Churches*, 2:320.

Herb(ert)us
Dambre[.

Here lies Herbert of Ambre[.].

Line 5: Clermont-Ganeau read the last line as *d'Ambro* .... The last visible letter, however, seems more likely to be *e*, with sufficient space remaining for a final letter.

In early medieval England, shears appearing on tombstones appear to have reflected an earlier pagan tradition in which such artefacts were placed inside the grave; normally they indicated that the deceased was female.[17] By the thirteenth century, however, such symbols more usually indicated the dead person's trade or profession. Since Herbert d'Ambre[.] was evidently male, this also seems to be the case here. The broad shears with blunt ends illustrated on the stone may be identified as fullers' shears, used in the cloth trade for shearing the surface of newly woven cloth to give it a smooth finish.[18] They would thus appear to indicate that the dead man was involved in the woollen cloth trade. His place of origin may perhaps have been Ambert, a small town in the Auvergne south-east of Clermont-Ferrand, whose medieval industries included paper and cloth-making.[19]

TYRE

7 *Epitaph of Peter, son of Sergius of Capua (or Campania) (1190)*

Marble plaque (15 × 15 × 4 cm) (Fig. 4). Now in the Musée du Louvre, Paris.[20]

+ H[i]c [r]eq(u)ies
cit Petrus, fili(us)
S(er)gii C(a)p(u)ani. Obiit
anno d(omi)nic(ae) nat(ivitatis) m°
c° nonag(esimo) ind(i)c(tione) viii

+ Here lies Peter, son of Sergio of Capua. He died in AD 1190, indiction VIII.

Line 3 might equally read *S(er)gii C(am)pani* (Sergius of Campania).

---

17 Lawrence Butler, "Symbols on Medieval Memorials", *Archaeological Journal* 144 (1987), 246–55 (pp. 252–53).

18 E. Carus-Wilson, "The Significance of the Secular Sculptures in the Lane Chapel, Cullompton", *Medieval Archaeology* 1 (1957), 104–17 (pp. 104–9).

19 K. Baedeker, *Southern France including Corsica: Handbook for Travellers*, 6th ed. (Leipzig, 1914), p. 221.

20 Clermont-Ganneau, "Nouveaux monuments", p. 460, pl. I.c; Enlart, *Monuments*, 2:370; Pringle, "Crusader Cathedral of Tyre", p. 185.

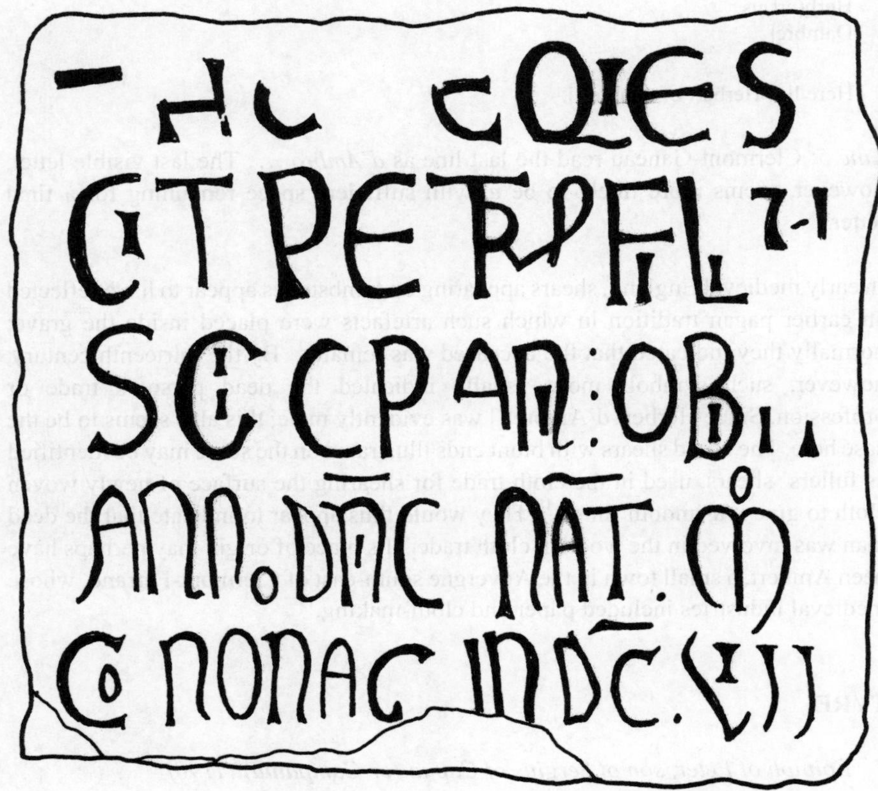

Fig. 4 Tyre: Epitaph (no. 7) of Peter, son of Sergius of Capua (or Campania) (traced from Ch. Clermont-Ganneau, *AOL* 2.1 (Paris 1884), pl. I.c)

8 Epitaph of Thomas Debontomas and his brother Obertus (1202)

This text was recorded by Renan.[21]

+ Ann° D(omi)ni m° cc° ii° m(en)se maii die xx obiit
Thomas Debontomas et fr(ater) ei(us) k(alend)is
Septe(m)br(is) Obert(us)

Thomas Debontomas died 20 May AD 1202, and his brother Obertus on 1 September.

21 Renan, *Mission en Phénicie*, 1:545.

Fig. 5 **Tyre: Epitaph (no. 9) of Bartholomew Chayn (or Caym)** (from J. N. Sepp, *Meerfahrt nach Tyrus* (Leipzig, 1879), p. 264)

9 *Epitaph of Bartholomew Chayn (or Caym), knight of Tyre (1266)*

Large marble slab, now in the Musée du Louvre, Paris (Fig. 5).[22]

> + Ici gist messire Bert-
> helme Chayn, ch(evalie)r de Sur, (qu)i
> trespassa en l'an de l'incarna-
> tion N(ost)re Seignor Ih(es)u Crist
> m cc lxvi, samadi au seir, le
> premier ior de jenvier, la-
> quel amme se[it ...

+ Here lies Sir Bartholomew Chayn, knight of Tyre, who died in the year of the incarnation of Our Lord Jesus Christ 1266, on the evening of Saturday the first day of January. May his soul ...

The *casalia* of *Farachyen* (al-Frakhiya) and *Cafardebael* (Kafar Dabʿal), which Bartholomew Chayn (or Caym) held from the king and in which the Venetians also

---

22 M. H. Chéhab, *Tyr à l'époque des croisés*, 2. *Histoire sociale, économique et religieuse* (Paris, 1979), p. 477; Clermont-Ganneau, "Nouveaux monuments", pp. 459–60; Pringle, "Crusader Cathedral of Tyre", p. 185, fig. 28; Hans Prutz, *Aus Phönizien* (Leipzig, 1876), p. 336; J. N. Sepp, *Meerfahrt nach Tyrus zur Ausgrabung der Kathedrale mit Barbarossa's Grab* (Leipzig, 1879), p. 264.

Fig. 6 Tyre: Inscribed headstone (no. 10) from a grave (from J. N. Sepp, *Meerfahrt nach Tyrus* (Leipzig, 1879), p. 261)

had a part share, are referred to in Marsilio Zorzi's survey of Venetian properties in Tyre in 1243.[23]

10 Headstone from a grave

Carved on what appears to have been the headstone for a grave capped by a rosette in relief, found at the site of the crusader cathedral in Tyre (Fig. 6).[24]

‡Hoc
est
sepulcru(m)
[…

This is the tomb [of …

[23] O. Berggötz, *Der Bericht des Marsilio Zorzi: Codex Querini-Stampalia IV3 (1064)*, Kieler Werkstücke, Reihe C: Beiträge zur europäischen Geschichte des frühen und hohen Mittelalters 2 (Frankfurt am Main–Berne–New York–Paris, 1991), pp. 155, 160; Chéhab, *Tyr à l'époque des croisés*, 2:477–78.

[24] Clermont-Ganneau, "Nouveaux monuments", p. 459 n. 7; Pringle, "Crusader Cathedral of Tyre", p. 185, fig. 27; Sepp, *Meerfahrt nach Tyrus*, p. 261.

Fig. 7 **Tyre: Epitaph (no. 11) of a knight** (from P. M. Bikai, *Bulletin du Musée de Beyrouth* 24 (1971), p. 88, fig. 1)

11 Epitaph of a knight (1272/4)

From the Greek Catholic church. White marble slab, 11 × 12 × 3.2 cm (Fig. 7).[25]

> Seignor I[…
> et lxxii[……………… pries por l'a
> rme de l̲[ui …
>
> Lord […] and 72 (*or* 73, 74) [… pray for] his soul […

If *lxxii* is part of a date, it would presumably be 1172/4 or, more likely, 1272/4.

---

[25] Patricia M. Bikai, "A New Crusader Church in Tyre", *Bulletin du Musée de Beyrouth* 24 (1971), 83–90 (p. 88, fig. 1, pl. XI.1).

Fig. 8 Tyre: Epitaph (no. 12) of Payen the Deacon (adapted from P. M. Bikai, *Bulletin du Musée de Beyrouth*, 24 (1971), p. 88, fig. 2)

12 Epitaph of Payen the Deacon

From the Greek Catholic church. Blue-white marble slab, 14.5 × 12 × 4 cm (Fig. 8). Although only the right-hand part of the inscription survives, it appears to have been set out below a two-armed cross flanked by single-arm crosses with dots in the quarters. Between the crosses, a shallow rectangular recess cut into the stone seems likely to have been intended to receive a metal insertion.[26]

\+]‡ +
ici gist …]Paien dia‹c›re
…]diemart de la
… qui t]respassa en
l'an m cc.… le …] ior en
…

[26] Ibid., p. 88, fig. 2, pl. XI.1.

Here lies ...] Payen the Deacon [...] Tuesday of the [... who] departed in [the year 12.. on the ..]day in [...

Line 2: The name could possibly read *Da(m)ien*, though the tail of the *p* is reasonably distinct. It might perhaps have been preceded by a title, such as *Frere*. Alternatively it is possible that Paien was a family name and was preceded by a first name. If so, this would raise the further possibility that the deceased was related to Godfrey Payen (see no. 13 below). A canon of Sidon named Paguanus is referred to in 1170,[27] but there is no particular reason to connect him with this man.

13 Epitaph of Godfrey Payen

From the Greek Catholic church. Stone 19 × 23 × 4.3 cm (Fig. 9).[28]

Hic re[q(uiescit)
Gaufr[i
dus Pag
anus q(ui)
obiit i]n pa
....]m

Here lies Godfrey Payen, who [died i]n ...

Lines 5–6 might have read: *q(ui)* [*obiit i*]*n pa*[*rasceve* ...] or *pa*[*scha* ...] (who died on Good Friday/at Easter), followed by the year or [*a*]*m*[*en*]. Alternatively, but perhaps less probably: *q(ui)* [*iit in paradisu*]*m* (who has passed into Paradise). Godfrey may possibly have been related to the deceased in no. 12 above.

14 Epitaph

From the Greek Catholic church.[29]

... requiesci]t i(n) pace [...

15 Graffiti in the chapel of St Saviour

The chapel of the Saviour was constructed outside the walls of Tyre soon after the fall of the city in 1128. It was built over the *spina* of the Roman circus and enclosed the base of a column upon which Jesus was supposed to have sat.[30] The internal

27 RRH, p. 125, no. 475.
28 Bikai, "New Crusader Church in Tyre", p. 88, pl. XI.3.
29 Enlart, *Monuments*, 2:373, fig. 483.
30 Pringle, *Churches*, vol. 3 (forthcoming). My investigation of this building in May 1998 was facilitated by an Archaeology Research Grant awarded by the Humanities Research Board of the British

Fig. 9 Tyre: Epitaph (no. 13) of Godfrey Payen (traced from P. M. Bikai, *Bulletin du Musée de Beyrouth*, 24 (1971), pl. XI.3)

walls are covered with smooth white plaster, into which Western pilgrims – and others literate in Greek and Arabic – have scratched graffiti. These include representations of crosses, shields, ships and a number of monograms and names (Figs. 10–14). Full publication of this important collection of graffiti will require further more detailed study. In the meantime, however, the following identifiable names may be noted:

Academy. I am also most grateful to Dr Camille Asmar, head of excavation in the Direction Général des Antiquités, for permission to examine and record the remains and to Mr Ali Badawi, the department's local officer, for his unfailing assistance.

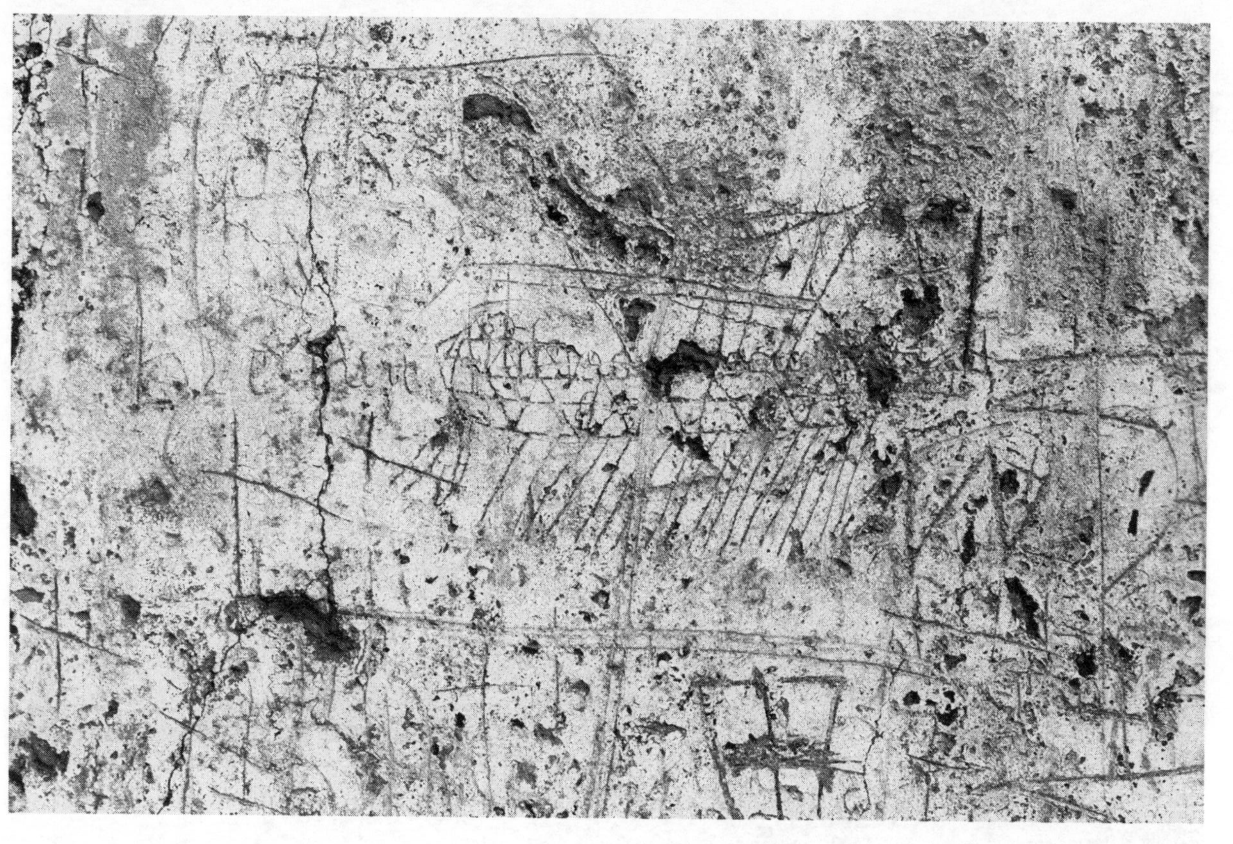

Fig. 10 Tyre: Chapel of St Saviour: graffiti representing a galley, preceded by the words *hic fuit* (photo: DP 232/18)

Fig. 11 Tyre: Chapel of St Saviour: inscription no. 15b, with part of no. 15a above it (photo: DP 222/9)

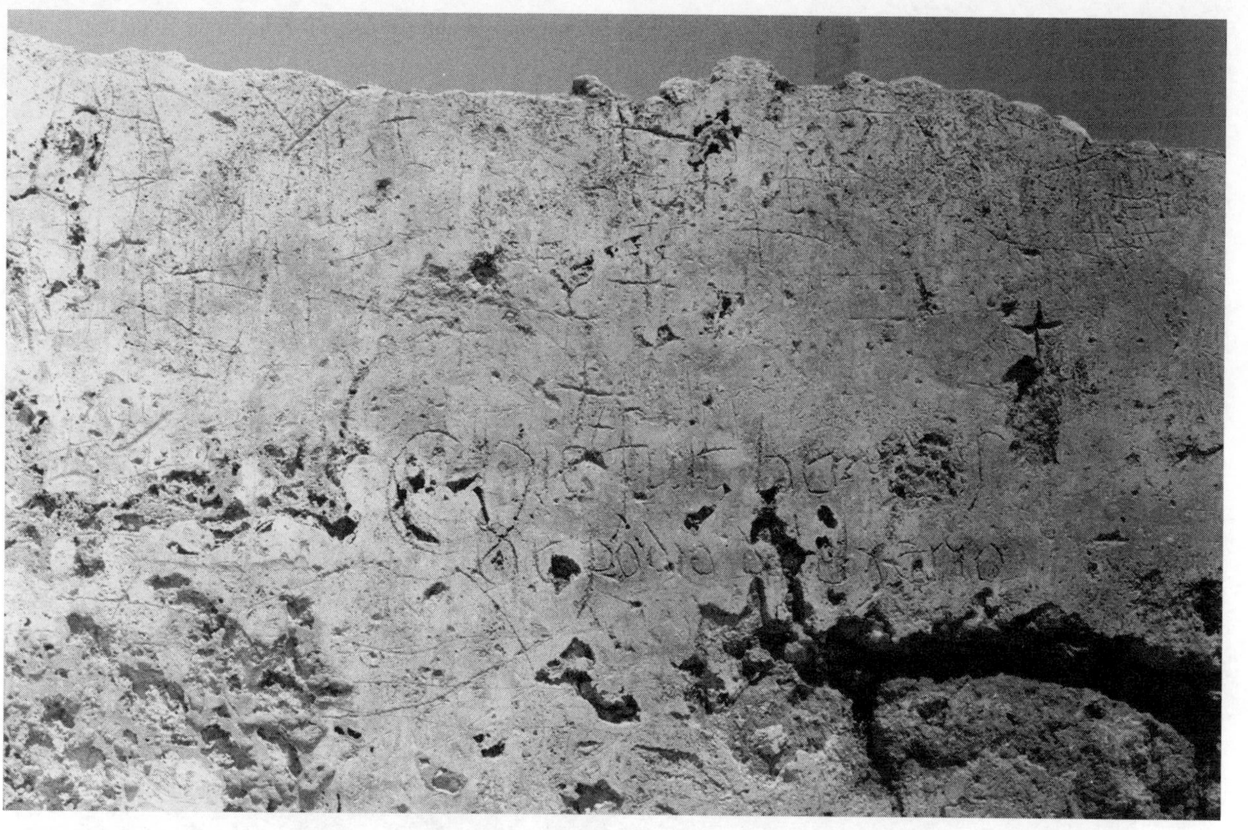

Fig. 12 Tyre: Chapel of St Saviour: inscription no. 15d (photo: DP 222/8)

Fig. 13 Tyre: Chapel of St Saviour: inscription no. 15f (photo: DP 222/10)

Fig. 14 Tyre: Chapel of St Saviour: inscription no. 15g (photo: DP 232/20)

(a) simon umlom

The significance of this name is unclear; but just below it in much smaller letters is written:

(b) hic fuit stephan(us) coch ī(n) assis[ia] accone[nse]

Stephen Coch was here in the siege (or assize?) of Acre

The word *assisa* or *assisia* usually means assize. In this context, however, the word seems more likely to refer to the siege of Acre by the army of the Third Crusade, which lasted from August 1189 until July 1191.[31] Tyre was the base from which the campaign against Acre was initially launched and the main port through which the crusaders' camp was supplied with men and materials.

(c) Georgii de […

(d) hic fuit hen(ricu)s
de podio d[..]ferio

Henry de Podio d[..]erio was here

The name could alternatively be read as *Herbe*[*rtu*]*s*, since the form of the third letter is somewhat unusual. John, son of a certain Henry de Podio (of Le Puy?), however, is listed among the knights of Roard, lord of Haifa, in an act concerning the granting of the unlocated village of *Digegie* to the Hospital in 1201.[32] It is uncertain whether he is the same as John Dupuis, sergeant of the king of France, whose tombstone was built into the Hermann Struck House in Haifa in the 1920s.[33]

(e) h(ic) fuit r[i]chi(us) d[e …]io pleba(nus)

Richius of … , parish priest, was here

It is possible that this man also belonged to the de Podio family.

(f) hic fuit jacob[us] sc(ut)ifer
Ih[eru]s[a]l(im)it(an)i Will[elmi …

---

[31] *Itinerarium Regis Ricardi*, 1.26; 3.17–18, ed. William Stubbs, RS 38.1 (London, 1864), pp. 62, 231–33; trans. Helen J. Nicholson, *Chronicle of the Third Crusade* (Aldershot, 1997), pp. 70, 218–21.

[32] RRH, pp. 208–9, no. 784.

[33] + *Ici : gist : Iohan : / dou : Puis : serga /* (*n*)*t : dou : puissa*(*n*)*t : / roy : de : Fra*(*n*)*ce : / Proies : por : / lame* (Here lies John Dupius, sergeant of the powerful king of France. Pray for his soul). This text only came to light after the publication of Fr de Sandoli's *Corpus*. See *Jerusalem Post* (26 Feb. 1976), p. 3; *Journal d'Israël* (16 April 1976), p. 8; Anon., "Epitaffo del sergente Giovanni di Le-Puy", *La Terra Santa* 53 (1977), 15–16; Pringle, *Churches*, 1:222.

James, squire of William of Jerusalem, was here.

This text is written in small letters, similar to (b), below a shield. Unfortunately a larger inscription in Greek letters, which has still to be deciphered, partly obscures the second line, the reading of which is therefore not at all certain. It is possible that *Willelmus*, or a contraction of the same name, was followed by a noun such as *militis* or *equitis* indicating his position; however, it would perhaps be over-speculative to attempt to identify him, for example, with one of the marshals of Jerusalem of that name, who are mentioned in charters between 1159 and 1179[34] and in 1273[35] respectively, or with the constable of Jerusalem mentioned in 1263.[36]

(g) hic fuit fĩ

This text is preceded by a triangle containing three roundels below a line and surmounted by a cross. It appears to be incomplete, as though the writer was interrupted in the middle of a word.

---

[34] RRH, pp. 87–88, no. 336 (1159), and passim; RRH Ad, pp. 36–37, no. 590b (1179).

[35] Gulielmus de Caneta, mareschalcus regni Iherosomitani: *Tabulae Ordinis Theutonici: ex tabularii regii Berolinensis codice potissimum*, ed. Ernest Strehlke, introduction by Hans E. Mayer (Toronto, 1975), p. 118, no. 126.

[36] Guillelme, seignor dou Boutron et conestable dou dit reyaume [de Jerusalem]: ibid., p. 114, no. 123.

Pilgrimage, Crusade, Trade and Embassy: Pre-Elizabethan English Contacts with the Ottoman Turks

Gregory O'Malley

Emmanuel College, Cambridge

Over the last century the foundations, development and ideological justifications of English mercantile and diplomatic contacts with the Ottoman Turks in the reign of Elizabeth and later have been the subject of a number of scholarly studies, while the English "image of the Turk" during the Elizabethan and Jacobean Renaissance has been explored by both literary critics and historians.[1] Despite their variant approaches, both economic historians and literary and cultural scholars have tended to downplay evidence of earlier English contacts with the Ottomans in order to stress the novelty and scope of those occurring after 1570. They usually relate that during the reign of Elizabeth I changing economic and political conditions in the Low Countries and Mediterranean, coupled with royal support for the tentative contacts undertaken by London merchants with the Porte, laid the foundations for

---

[1] M. Epstein, *The Early History of the Levant Company* (London, 1908); H. G. Rawlinson, "Early Trade between England and the Levant", *Journal of Indian History* 2/1 (1922), 107–16; idem, "The Embassy of William Harborne to Constantinople, 1583–88", *Transactions of the Royal Historical Society*, Fourth Series 5 (1922), 5–6; Warner G. Rice, "Early English Travellers to Greece and the Levant", *Essays and Studies in English and Comparative Literature by Members of the English Department of the University of Michigan* (Ann Arbor, 1933), pp. 205–60; Alfred C. Wood, *A History of the Levant Company* (Oxford, 1935); Samuel C. Chew, *The Crescent and the Rose: Islam and England during the Renaissance* (New York, 1937), esp. section 3; A. L. Horniker, "William Harborne and the Beginning of Anglo-Turkish Diplomatic Relations", *Journal of Modern History* 14 (1942), 306–15; Franklin L. Baumer, "England, the Turk and the Common Corps of Christendom", *American Historical Review* 50 (1944–45), 26–48; idem, "The Conception of Christendom in Renaissance England", *Journal of the History of Ideas* 6 (1945), 131–56; T. S. Willan, "Some Aspects of English Trade with the Levant in the Sixteenth Century", *English Historical Review* 70 (1955), 399–410; G. D. Ramsay, *English Overseas Trade during the Centuries of Emergence* (London, 1957), pp. 34–62; Ralph Davis, "England and the Mediterranean, 1570–1670", in *Essays in the Economic and Social History of Tudor and Stuart England*, ed. F. J. Fisher (Cambridge, 1961), pp. 117–37; C. A. Patrides, "'The Bloody and Cruell Turke': the Background of a Renaissance Commonplace", *Studies in the Renaissance* 10 (1963), 126–35; A. C. Wood, *A History of the Levant Company* (London, 1964); Andrew P. Vella, "A Sixteenth Century Elizabethan Merchant in Malta", *Melita Historica* 5/3 (1970), 197–238; idem, *An Elizabethan-Ottoman Conspiracy* (Malta, 1972); S. A. Skilliter, *William Harborne and the Trade with Turkey, 1578–1582: A Documentary Study of the First Anglo-Ottoman Relations* (Oxford, 1977); G. V. Scammell, *The World Encompassed: The First European Maritime Empires c. 800–1650* (London, 1981), chap. 9; Kenneth R. Andrews, *Trade, Plunder and Settlement: Maritime Enterprise and the Genesis of the British Empire, 1480–1630* (Cambridge, 1984), pp. 87–100; Nabil Matar, *Islam in Britain, 1558–1685* (Cambridge, 1998).

a regular and substantial commerce between England and the Levant. Some years later, in the 1580s, the English government's search for allies against the Spanish led it to retain a permanent ambassador in Constantinople, and even to make moves towards an alliance.[2]

While most writers have been aware, from Hakluyt, that there was a regular English trade with the Levant in the early sixteenth century, only Susan A. Skilliter appears to have considered whether this involved interaction with Ottoman officials or traders, and she confines her remarks to the period after 1535. Moreover, the decline of this intercourse in the 1530s and its collapse in the 1550s allowed several scholars to interpret the revival of English commerce in the region in the 1570s and 1580s as an almost entirely new departure, fostered by changed economic circumstances and, it was sometimes stated, by radically different political and religious ideologies. If most writers have provided primarily economic rather than ideological explanations for the disappearance and reappearance of English merchants and shipping in the Levant,[3] many have also noted the English need for allies against Spain and some have hinted that England's rejection of Rome and its strictures on contact with the infidel and the more rational spirit of enquiry and interest in the classics inculcated by the Elizabethan Renaissance encouraged the English to boldly go where no English merchants, diplomats or travellers had gone before.[4] Contributing to these assumptions in some cases seems to be the suspicion that medieval Englishmen and women were fundamentally hostile to, and incurious of, the lands and peoples of the Levant, happy to rely on the stereotypical images of undifferentiated Saracens and Turks conveyed to them through such media as romances and mystery plays.[5]

---

[2] Vella, *Elizabethan-Ottoman Conspiracy*, passim.

[3] Davis, "England and the Mediterranean", p. 117; Lawrence Stone, "Elizabethan Overseas Trade", *Economic History Review*, n.s., 2 (1949), 30–58, at pp. 40, 43–4; Willan, "Some Aspects", passim; J. A. Williamson, *A Short History of British Expansion*, I, *The Old Colonial Empire*, 3rd ed. (London, 1965), p. 49; Fernand Braudel, *The Mediterranean and the Mediterranean World in the Age of Philip II*, trans. Siân Reynolds, 2 vols. (London, 1972), 1:614–15; Vella, "Elizabethan Merchant", pp. 198–99; idem, *Elizabethan-Ottoman Conspiracy*, p. 16; Scammell, *World Encompassed*, p. 463; Andrews, *Trade, Plunder and Settlement*, pp. 87–88.

[4] Chew, *Crescent and the Rose*, p. 104; Stone, "Elizabethan Overseas Trade", pp. 30, 32–33, 43–44; Vella, *Elizabethan-Ottoman Conspiracy*, passim; Scammell, *World Encompassed*, p. 494; Matar, *Islam in Britain*, p. 121; Rice, "Early English Travellers", pp. 206–14; Wood, *Levant Company*, p. 5.

[5] Hence, for example, Dorothée Metlitzki's contention that what Englishmen knew or imagined about the Saracens remained essentially unchanged between c. 1300 and the Renaissance. Similarly, Samuel Chew's study of Renaissance drama led him to the conclusion that even then "no clear-cut distinction was made between Turks and Moors or 'Saracens', in the popular mind". Dorothée Metlitzki, *The Matter of Araby in Medieval England* (London, 1977), p. 120; Chew, *Crescent and the Rose*, pp. 104, 145. On this point see also Rana Kabbani, *Europe's Myths of Orient: Devise and Rule* (Basingstoke, 1986), pp. 15–22. The incurious nature of English pilgrims is remarked upon in Rice, "Early English Travellers", pp. 206–14, and Chew, *Crescent and the Rose*, pp. 59–60.

More recent scholarship, which often stresses the continuities between misconceived and negative medieval and Renaissance images of the infidel,[6] hardly serves to rehabilitate the medieval English mind, while the countervailing insistence of some scholars that even in the fifteenth century there was some admiration for the Turks and less readiness to lump all Muslims together as Saracens has largely been drawn from work on Italian sources rather than English.[7] In emphasizing, quite rightly, the lack of geographical or strategic focus in fourteenth- and much fifteenth-century crusading, the work of crusade historians has also contributed to the general sense that Latin and, perhaps especially, English impressions of the Turks were for a long time imprecise and unfocused. Nor have studies of the English contribution to the crusading movement had a great deal to say either about pre-1547 attitudes to the Ottomans or about non-crusading contacts with them.[8]

It is not the purpose of this paper to seek to challenge all the impressions provided in these various treatments, but it will be contended that from at least the mid-fifteenth century English contacts with the Turks were more varied, imaginative and discerning than has hitherto been supposed.

Outside the sphere of crusading, there has been little effort to search for either physical or ideological contacts between the English and the Osmanli Turks, rather than with the Levant or with "Saracens", before Elizabeth's reign. A recent study of contacts between England and Turkey is entitled simply "Four Centuries of Turco-British relations", and is introduced by the statement that "Britain's [*sic*] diplomatic relations with Turkey began in January 1583" with the posting to Istanbul as resident ambassador of William Harborne.[9] Some of those who have noticed earlier English visits to the Ottoman state have also made bold pronouncements about their pioneering nature. Nabil Matar, for instance, has recently asserted that the first recorded "Briton" to visit the empire was Anthony Jenkinson in 1553.[10] This, however, is to ignore the claims of an English knight of Malta, Richard Shelley, who

---

6 Kabbani, *Europe's Myths of Orient*, pp. 5–6, 14–22; Daniel J. Vitkus, "Early Modern Orientalism: Representations of Islam in Sixteenth- and Seventeenth-Century Europe" in *Western Views of Islam in Medieval and Early Modern Europe*, ed. David R. Blanks and Michael Frassetto (Basingstoke, 1999), pp. 207–30.

7 See, for example, the articles by Gloria Allaire and Nancy Bisaha in *Western Views of Islam*, ed. Blanks and Frassetto, pp. 173–206.

8 A partial exception is Robert Schwoebel, *The Shadow of the Crescent: The Renaissance Image of the Turk (1453–1517)* (Nieuwkoop, 1967), pp. 11–12, 48, 134–39, 184–86. For contributions with a particular relevance to English anti-Turkish crusading activity see Charles L. Tipton, "The English at Nicopolis", *Speculum* 33 (1962), 529–40; Maurice Keen, "Chaucer's Knight, the English Aristocracy and the Crusade" in *English Court Culture in the Later Middle Ages*, ed. V. J. Scattergood and J. Sherborne (London, 1983), reprinted in Maurice Keen, *Nobles, Knights and Men-at-arms* (London, 1996), pp. 101–19; Christopher Tyerman, *England and the Crusades, 1095–1588* (Chicago, 1988); A. T. Luttrell, "English Levantine Crusaders: 1363–1367", *Renaissance Studies* 2 (1988), 143–53; idem, "Chaucer's Knight and the Mediterranean", *Library of Mediterranean History* 1 (1994), 127–60.

9 William Hale, "Introduction: The Historical Background", in *Four Centuries of Turco-British Relations* (Beverley, 1984), ed. William Hale and Ali İhsan Bağiș, p. 1.

10 Matar, *Islam in Britain*, p. 5.

visited the Ottoman court in 1539, before his profession into the order, although he did so in company with the Venetian ambassador rather than as an emissary of Henry VIII. Shelley himself believed that he was the first Englishman to see Constantinople since 1453.[11] Susan Skilliter has been more cautious, suggesting that English persons may have visited the empire under French protection between the 1530s and 1570s, and that the remarkable trading concessions granted to Jenkinson in 1553/4 may not have been entirely unprecedented.[12] Equally carefully, Fernand Braudel simply noted the appearance of English merchants in Constantinople in 1544 without making any claims for the novelty of such contacts.[13] Nevertheless, neither considered the possibility that English travellers might have visited Ottoman territories in the fourteenth or fifteenth centuries.

It is easy to see why early modernists have generally concluded that English contacts with the Turks before the 1570s were without any great significance. Although Henry VII was a signatory to the truce agreed between European states and the Ottomans in 1502,[14] there are no letters from English monarchs to the sultan dating from before Elizabeth's reign and nor do medievalists' notices of English trade or pilgrimage in the Levant before 1558 pay much more attention to contacts with the Turks than to note a fear of Turkish piracy. This is understandable, as the ports most used by English travellers in the eastern Mediterranean in the late fifteenth and early sixteenth centuries were still in Venetian or Genoese hands. The English, it might thereby be assumed, had neither the occasion nor the necessity to deal with Ottoman officialdom at any level. Although it might be objected that English merchants in the eastern Mediterranean and especially Aegean would certainly have encountered Turkish merchants in ports like Chios and Rhodes, they clearly dealt predominantly with and through Italians. Nevertheless, at least some English merchants are known to have traded directly with the Ottomans, and if the pioneering nature of their endeavours has not been as trumpeted as it might have been by medievalists, nor has it been entirely overlooked.

It is now more than fifty years since Charles Singer discussed Nicholas Waring's 1505 visit to Asia Minor in the *Sovereign*, and his subsequent excommunication for buying alum from the Turks, but few recent scholars appear to have noticed this episode.[15] Moreover, Hakluyt's brief account of the activities of the small fleet of

---

[11] *The History of Parliament: the House of Commons 1509–1558*, ed. S. T. Bindoff, 3 vols. (London, 1982), 3:308–10.

[12] Skilliter, *Harborne*, pp. 5–9.

[13] Braudel, *Mediterranean*, 1:614.

[14] Dorothy M. Vaughan, *Europe and the Turk: A Pattern of Alliances* (Liverpool, 1954), pp. 92–93.

[15] Charles Singer, *The Earliest Chemical Industry: An Essay in the Historical Relations of Economics and Technology illustrated from the Alum Trade* (London, 1948), pp. 158–59. I am grateful to Dr Helen Nicholson for alerting me to this work. See also Alwyn A. Ruddock, *Italian Merchants and Shipping in Southampton 1270–1600* (Southampton, 1951), p. 221; D. S. Chambers, "English representation at the court of Rome in the early Tudor period", unpublished D. Phil thesis, Oxford, 1962, p. 168.

London merchantmen operating in the eastern Mediterranean between 1511 and 1534 mentions that they sometimes made landfall at Tripoli and Beirut and had traffic with Jews, Turks and other "foreigners", an observation which has passed almost without comment.[16] In fact, English sea captains appear to have penetrated Levantine waters by the late 1460s, shortly after they had begun to establish themselves as regular callers in Sicily, Pisa and Naples.[17] They were doubtless encouraged to do so by factors such as Henry VI's willingness to reward foreign merchants who brought him exotica purchased in Turkey,[18] by the pioneering voyages of Robert Sturmy in the 1440s and 1450s, and by Edward IV's well known interest in and support for mercantile ventures.[19] In June 1468 it was reported in Venice that two English ships loaded with spices and merchandise had been seized by the French on their way home from the Levant, only to then fall into the hands of the Castilians.[20] This episode did little to deter further expeditions, and by 1490–91 enough English vessels were trading in Crete for English merchants to find it worthwhile to protest to Henry VII at a tax imposed by the Venetians on foreign ships buying malmsey there, although the Venetians claimed in response that "but few" English ships and subjects came into those seas.[21]

Having reached Sicily or southern Italy, other English merchants took passage for the East on foreign shipping. In 1469 a vessel belonging to Andrea de Napoli with at least one English merchant,[22] William Cooper, on board, was attacked off

---

[16] R. Hakluyt, *The Principal Navigations, Voyages, Traffiques & Discoveries of the English Nation*, 2nd ed., 12 vols. (London, 1598–1600, repr. Glasgow, 1903–5), 5:62–64. Although Skilliter remarks on this, her discussion of the arrangements under which the English might have been allowed to trade in Ottoman ports does not extend to the period before 1535. By implication, however, and by analogy with the voyage of the *Bark Aucher* in 1551, it seems likely that when necessary, safe-conducts were procured on behalf of English traders by the Genoese or Venetians. Skilliter, *Harborne*, pp. 5, 9.

[17] Braudel, *Mediterranean*, 1:612–13; Ruddock, *Italian Merchants and Shipping*, pp. 208–9; M. E. Mallett, "Anglo-Florentine Commercial Relations, 1465–1491", *Economic History Review*, 2nd series, 15 (1962), 250–65.

[18] In 1443 Henry granted Nicholas "Jone", a Bolognese merchant domiciled in England and married to an Englishwoman, the office of the brokerage of exchanges and securities of carracks and other vessels coming to England. Jone had earlier brought him three camels and an ostrich from Turkey. *Calendar of Patent Rolls, Richard II–Henry VII* [hereafter cited as *CPR*], 23 vols. (London, 1895–1916), *1441–6*, p. 166. Schwoebel, *Shadow of the Crescent*, p. 134, wrongly assumed that "Jone" was an Englishman.

[19] E. M. Carus-Wilson, "The Overseas Trade of Bristol", in *Studies in English Trade in the Fifteenth Century*, ed. Eileen Power and M. M. Postan (London, 1933), pp. 225–29; C. L. Scofield, *The Life and Reign of Edward IV*, 2 vols. (London, 1923), 2:404–28; Charles Ross, *Edward IV* (London, 1974), pp. 362–63, 368–70.

[20] *Calendar of State Papers and Manuscripts, Relating to English Affairs, Existing in the Archives and Collections of Venice and in Other Libraries of Northern Italy* [hereafter cited as *CSPV*], vol. 1, *1202–1509* (London, 1864), no. 414.

[21] *CSPV*, nos. 544, 609; Ruddock, *Italian Merchants and Shipping*, pp. 221–23. The English presence in Crete before 1500 is also noticed by, among others, Wood, *Levant Company*, p. 2; Ramsay, *English Overseas Trade*, p. 36; Braudel, *Mediterranean*, 1:613; Williamson, *Old Colonial Empire*, pp. 43–44; Scammell, *World Encompassed*, p. 460.

[22] Another merchant, Zuan Bruzexe, complained of the seizure in London. It has been suggested that his name as given may be a rendering of "John Bridges", but this remains unproven. *CSPV*, no. 422.

Chios by the Venetian captain-general, Niccolò da Canale, and Cooper's goods, to the value of over 2000 ducats, seized. Most significantly from the point of view of English contacts with the Ottomans, de Napoli's ship was returning from Constantinople.[23] Here then was an English trader, admittedly not travelling on a vessel of his own nation, who was bold enough to venture into the very heart of the Ottoman empire, and in doing so had fallen foul not of the "chief enemy of the Christian name", Mehmed II, but of the Venetians. Had Venice not been at war with the Turks, de Napoli's vessel might not have been stopped, and evidence for Cooper's remarkable voyage might never have surfaced, a fact which should warn us against assuming that he was unique. Moreover, neither Edward IV's reaction to Cooper's plight, which was to confiscate the goods of Venetians in England, nor the blithe disregard demonstrated by Henry VII and his judges for papal prohibitions on trading in Turkish alum, indicates any aversion on the part of the English authorities to intercourse with the Ottomans.[24] The *Sovereign*, the vessel which visited Asia Minor in 1505, was in fact owned by Henry VII while Henry VIII, if at times proclaiming his enthusiasm for crusading and support for the Latin East, also demonstrated a cynical appreciation of the realities of Levantine politics and took a personal interest in Turkish textiles, music and even law.[25] As Norman Housley has shown, moreover, the Tudor regime's rhetorical animosity towards the Turk might easily be mapped onto the French, who at times were claimed to pose a more immediate threat to Christendom.[26] When they appeared in court pageants, indeed, "Turks" were not treated with anything like the hostility directed at Henry's more immediate political rivals and their subjects.[27]

Nor were merchants the only English persons in the Levant in the fifteenth and sixteenth centuries. Although numbers had probably diminished somewhat since the mid-fourteenth century, and did so again after c. 1460, English pilgrims continued to make the journey to Jerusalem until the very eve of the break with Rome. Judging by surviving accounts of their journeys, they were admittedly mostly rather unadventurous and incurious travellers, even by comparison with their fourteenth-century predecessors. Certainly none are known to have undertaken grand tours of the region along the lines of those conducted by continental adventurers or spies such as Ghillibert de Lannoy, Bertrandon de la Broquière or Pero Tafur.[28]

---

[23] *CSPV*, nos. 422, 424–25, 429–30, 436, 441.

[24] *CSPV*, nos. 425, 429, 441, 509.

[25] Alwyn Ruddock, "London Capitalists and the Decline of Southampton in the Early Tudor Period", *Economic History Review*, n.s., 2 (1949), 141; Vaughan, *Europe and the Turk*, p. 27.

[26] Norman Housley, *Religious Warfare in Europe, 1400–1536* (Oxford, 2002), pp. 142–43. See also *Letters and Papers Foreign and Domestic of the Reign of Henry VIII* [hereafter cited as *LP Henry VIII*], 22 vols. in 37 parts (London, 1864–1929), no. 4009.

[27] Sydney Anglo, *Spectacle, Pageantry and Early Tudor Policy*, 2nd ed. (Oxford, 1997), pp. 134–35.

[28] G. de Lannoy, *Œuvres*, ed. C. Potvin (Louvain, 1878); B. de la Broquière, *Le Voyage d'Outremer de Bertrandon de la Broquière*, ed. C. Schefer (Paris, 1892); P. Tafur, *Pero Tafur. Travels and*

Like most other European pilgrim writers, the English were generally content to take the Venetian "package tour", and to borrow their travel advice and descriptions of the holy places from previous authors, their purpose being rather to enumerate the spiritual benefits of their journey than to discuss the curiosities of foreign lands.[29] Yet if their expressed perceptions of the Holy Land were conventional, their accounts of their journeys to and from Jerusalem sometimes incorporated more personal material and do at least provide some mention of contact with the Turks prior to 1570, even if this occurred in unpromising circumstances. In 1458, for example, the fullest writer among the fifteenth-century pilgrims, William Wey, who visited the Holy Sepulchre twice, recounted seeing various forms of exemplary punishment being meted out to Turks who had been captured by the knights of St John in response to an Ottoman raid on Rhodes.[30]

Rather more common was an expressed fear of Turkish capture at sea or of shipwreck on the Turkish coast. The chaplain of the courtier Sir Richard Guildford, who visited the Holy Land in 1506, endured a difficult return passage to Venice through the equinoctial gales, during one of which, he reported, the crew were afraid of being driven "into the handes of (the) Infideles and extreme enemyes of our Cristen fayth" dwelling on the Adriatic, while both on the outward and return journeys Turkish vessels were reported to be lying in wait for Christian shipping.[31] This author also held to the common belief that the country of Troy in Asia Minor was the Turk's "rightful inheritance", but that "he" had lately usurped a great many other countries.[32] He was followed in this, as in much else, by the Norfolk chaplain, Richard Torkington, who visited the Holy Sepulchre in 1517.[33] Torkington demonstrated a more pronounced awareness of the Turks than Guildford's chaplain, noting that the pilgrim galleys dared not approach Rhodes "for fer of the Turkes", whose sultan took "greet Displesur" with anyone who visited this home of "hys mortall enimes" and that the Holy Land had recently passed into the hands of the Ottomans. Torkington was relatively careful to describe the officials of the sultan whom his party encountered in the Holy Land as Turks rather than Saracens, although he repeated much of the earlier writer's description of his treatment at the

---

Adventures, ed. and trans. Malcolm Letts (London, 1926). An English translation of Lannoy's account of his travels can be found in G. de Lannoy, "A survey of Egypt and Syria, undertaken in the year 1422, by Sir Gilbert de Lannoy, Knight", trans. J. Webb, *Archaeologia* 20 (1821), 281–444, and translations of Broquière's in *Early Travels in Palestine*, ed. T. Wright (London, 1848), pp. 283–382 and E. Hoade, *Western Pilgrims to the Holy Land* (Jerusalem, 1952).

29 Rice, "English Travellers", p. 206; Tyerman, *England and the Crusades*, p. 310.

30 W. Wey, *Itineraries* (Roxburghe Club, 1857), p. 78. Wey also noted the Hospitallers' celebrations on hearing of the slaughter of large numbers of Turks by Vlad the Impaler in the same year. Ibid, p. 101.

31 *The Pylgrymage of Sir Richard Guylforde to the Holy Land*, ed. H. Ellis, Camden Society, Original Series 51 (London, 1851), pp. 68, 11, 61.

32 Ibid., pp. 12–13.

33 *Ye Oldest Diarie of Englysshe Travell*, ed. W. J. Loftie (London, 1884), p. 19. Some examples of Torkington's plagiarism from Guildford's account, which had been printed in 1511, are listed in Tyerman, *England and the Crusades*, pp. 310–11.

hands of the Mamluks almost verbatim when complaining of the Ottoman officials who now held sway.[34] Yet he had at least formed a clear, if jaundiced, impression of "that hell broude" from personal observation as well as from the reports of writers and sailors.[35]

If the extant pilgrim narratives seem to strengthen the assumption that the English were not much interested in the Turks save as potential captors they do not encompass the whole of English experience in the region. Other evidence indicates that some English pilgrims were more adventurous than those who put quill to paper. A few, such as two unnamed English pilgrims encountered by Felix Fabri in 1480, travelled to Sinai, while rather more combined a visit to the Holy Sepulchre with some form of crusading activity. The Welsh knight Sir Hugh John, or Johnys, had by 1452 secured letters from the pope, the Byzantine emperor and the king of Cyprus testifying that he had visited Jerusalem and performed military service by land and sea in "the parts of Turkey, Greece and Troy".[36] Henry Lord Fitzhugh dispatched military supplies to Bodrum and perhaps served with the knights of St John in 1409,[37] while a number of less illustrious volunteers or mercenaries from England and Ireland also served in the order's galleys or performed garrison duty at Bodrum in Anatolia or on Rhodes itself.[38] Some made themselves useful enough to hold important positions: William Radcliff was appointed bailiff of Cos and Narangia in March 1454, and Stephen Ward was serving as the master of the arsenal on Rhodes in 1456.[39] One Englishman, John Wykes, was even sent on the order's business to the sultan of Egypt in 1458. He reached Alexandria, but was robbed by the Genoese when they captured the Catalan vessel he was on.[40] He may have been

---

34 *Ye Oldest Diarie*, ed. Loftie, pp. 21–22, 23, 25, 55. While apparently as callous and extortionate as their Mamluk predecessors, the Ottoman sultan's officials at least dealt with the pilgrims of 1517 without excessive delay. Cf. *Pylgrymage of Sir Richard Guylforde*, ed. Ellis, pp. 15–16, 56; *Ye Oldest Diarie*, ed. Loftie, pp. 23, 55.

35 *Ye Oldest Diarie*, ed. Loftie, p. 22.

36 *Calendar of Entries in the Papal Registers relating to Great Britain and Ireland. Papal Letters 1198–1513* [hereafter cited as *CPL*], 19 vols. in 20 (London and Dublin, 1893–1998), 9:519; *Foedera, conventiones, litterae, et cujuscunque generis, acta publica inter reges angliae, et alios quosvis imperatores, reges, pontifices, principes, vel communitates, ab ineunte saeculo duodecimo, viz. ab anno 1101 ad nostra usque tempora*, ed. Thomas Rymer, 3rd ed., 10 vols. (London, 1739–45; repr. Farnborough, 1967), 5/2:40–41; *CPR 1447–52*, p. 562. His career is discussed in W. R. B. Robinson, "Sir Hugh Johnys: a Fifteenth-Century Welsh Knight", *Morgannwg* 14 (1970), 5–34.

37 Dr Luttrell has questioned whether Fitzhugh actually travelled to the eastern Mediterranean as well as sending armaments to Bodrum. Anthony T. Luttrell, "English Contributions to the Hospitaller Castle at Bodrum in Turkey, 1407–1437", *MO, 2*, pp. 166–67. But cf. J. Hughes, *Pastors and Visionaries: Religion and Secular Life in Late Medieval Yorkshire* (Woodbridge, 1988), p. 22

38 Zacharias N. Tsirpanlis, *Anekdota eggrapha gia te Rodo kai te Noties Sporades apo to archeio ton Ionniton Ippoton* (unpublished documents concerning Rhodes and the south-eastern Aegean Islands from the Archives of the Order of St John) [in Greek] (Rhodes, 1995), no. 259; Valletta, National Library of Malta, Archives of the Knights [hereafter cited as NLM], Cod. 79, fol. 11v; 366, fol. 119v; 367, fols. 118v, 201v; 382, fol. 138r–v; 387, fol. 202r. I have used the modern foliation.

39 NLM, Cod. 364, fol. 175r; 366, fol. 174v.

40 NLM, Cod. 367, fol. 215v.

accompanied by William Brereton, who, having served the order at Bodrum and travelled to Alexandria and Cairo, was granted a safe conduct to return home in the same October.[41]

The near coincidence of Wykes' mission with Robert Sturmy's trading expedition to the Levant is perhaps suggestive of Hospitaller collusion in the latter's attempt to open up the eastern Mediterranean to English trade. Other fifteenth-century Englishmen served in crusading expeditions dispatched from Italy or Burgundy, or saw military service with the Byzantines or Hungarians.[42] Although it is probable that few travelled within the Ottoman empire, both occasional crusaders and those serving with the Hospitallers must sometimes have encountered Turks in both mercantile and military contexts. Robert Champlayn, a "knight croyse" granted royal letters in his favour in 1488, secured testimonials from Pius II, Paul II, and Matthias Corvinus that he had fought the Turk "many times" on the Hungarian frontier, but that they had wounded him, taken him prisoner and ransomed him for 1500 ducats, which had ruined him.[43] Rather luckier was Robert Gay, who having served seven years in Bodrum in pursuance of a vow to fight the Turks, but having found none who were willing to take him on, was granted a safe conduct to return home in 1474.[44]

Such interactions still leave us without much evidence of official or diplomatic contacts or of English travel within the Osmanli state. But there are indications that English rulers and travellers had contemplated making contact with the Ottoman court as early as the first half of the fifteenth century. English crusaders had been involved in war against the Turks, if not at first the Ottoman emirate, for still longer. A number of English knights had assisted in the building of the castle of Smyrna after its capture in 1344 and the first significant crusading expedition mounted against the Ottomans, the Lampsakos campaign of 1359, had included an English contingent. English troops had also fought with Amadeo of Savoy in 1366–67, while in 1368 John, lord Mowbray, was killed fighting the "Turks" and buried at Pera.[45]

Moreover, if fourteenth-century crusading activity in general lacked focus, from at least the 1370s there was an increased awareness in the West of the special threat posed by the Ottomans[46] and after the Anglo-French truce arranged in 1389 this bore ill-fated fruit in the Nicopolis campaign of 1396. Encouraged by Philippe de Mézières, Richard II's government had been involved to a significant degree in the planning of this expedition and had, it is often claimed, dispatched an English

[41] NLM, Cod. 367, fol. 201v.

[42] Schwoebel, *Shadow of the Crescent*, p. 136; Tyerman, *England and the Crusades*, pp. 302–23; Steven Runciman, *The Fall of Constantinople 1453* (Cambridge, 1965), p. 84.

[43] *CPR 1485–94*, p. 188.

[44] NLM, Cod. 382, fol. 138r–v.

[45] These and other early examples in Luttrell, "Chaucer's Knight", pp. 140–41, 143.

[46] Anthony T. Luttrell, "Latin Responses to Ottoman Expansion before 1389", *The Ottoman Emirate (1300–1389)*, ed. Elizabeth Zachariadou (Rethymnon, 1993), p. 126.

contingent with it.[47] Even if this was not the case, the king's half-brother, John Holland, earl of Huntingdon, travelled to Hungary in 1394 as a prelude to crusading against the Turks, and the household knights John Clanvow and William Neville visited Constantinople and died at Pera in 1391.[48]

Until at least the 1440s successive Lancastrian governments, too, thought seriously about organizing a crusade. When still earl of Derby, Henry IV had "reysed" in Prussia and visited Venice, Rhodes, and Cyprus on his way to Jerusalem.[49] The experience appears to have reinforced a dynastic fascination with crusading which only began to dissipate with the renewal of the French war in 1449.[50] At least in the case of Henry IV, this enthusiasm comprehended an attempt to contact Muslim dynasties in the Near and Middle East. While still a young man he had had to be dissuaded by his father from accompanying Marshal Boucicaut into Turkey,[51] and in 1403 Henry sent out letters to be carried by the bishop of Sultaniyeh, John of Padua, to Timur and his third son as well as to the rulers of Constantinople, Trebizond, Cyprus, Abkhasia, and Georgia.[52]

These contacts should be seen in the context of the excitement generated by Timur's victory over the Turks at the battle of Ankara and do not seem to have had any sequel, but both Henry IV and his successors remained interested in a crusade either to recover the Holy Land or against the Turks. In 1421–22, Henry V and Philip the Good of Burgundy sponsored the Burgundian nobleman Ghillibert de Lannoy's tour of the Balkans, Black Sea and eastern Mediterranean. Posing as a pilgrim, Lannoy wrote a detailed report on the military resources and defences of the Mamluk sultanate.[53] Ten years later, while the Anglo-Burgundian compact still held, another subject of Philip the Good, Bertrandon de la Broquière, travelled overland across Anatolia before presenting his memoirs to the duke.[54]

Several magnates and courtiers undertook pilgrimages to the Holy Land during the Lancastrian ascendancy, of whom some doubled as envoys to Cyprus and

---

47 On the issue of English participation see Charles L. Tipton, "The English at Nicopolis", passim; J. J. N. Palmer, *England, France and Christendom, 1377–99* (London, 1972); Luttrell, "Chaucer's Knight and the Mediterranean", p. 143 n. 61.

48 Tyerman, *England and the Crusades*, pp. 263–65; S. Düll, Anthony T. Luttrell and Maurice Keen, "Faithful unto Death: the Tomb Slab of Sir William Neville and Sir John Clanvow, Constantinople 1391", *Antiquaries Journal* 71 (1993), 174–90.

49 *Expeditions to Prussia and the Holy Land made by Henry Earl of Derby*, ed. Lucy Toulmin Smith, Camden Society, n.s. 52 (London, 1894).

50 This was embodied most clearly in J. Capgrave, *Liber de illustribus Henricis*, ed. F. Hingeston, RS 7 (London, 1858).

51 Lannoy, "Survey", trans. Webb, p. 284. This was presumably in 1388, when Boucicaut spent several months at the court of Murad I under a safe conduct obtained in Constantinople: *Le Livre des Fais du bon Messire Jehan le Maingre, dit Bouciquaut*, ed. Denis Lalande (Geneva, 1985), pp. 61–62.

52 H. Ellis, *Original Letters Illustrative of English History*, 2nd Series, vol. 1 (repr. London, 1969), pp. 54–58.

53 Lannoy, *Œuvres*; idem, "Survey", passim; J. H. Wylie, *History of England under Henry the Fourth*, 4 vols. (London, 1884–98), 1:316.

54 Broquière, *Voyage d'Outremer*, passim.

Rhodes, and some carried supplies for the Hospitallers.[55] These travellers included the earl of Warwick in 1408, the earl of Salisbury in c. 1411, lord Botreaux in 1413, cardinal Beaufort in 1417, the two lords Scrope in 1435, lords Willoughby and de la Warre in 1440, lord Scales in 1448 and the earl of Worcester in 1458.[56] The English tower at Bodrum, festooned in the 1430s with the arms of those leading Lancastrians who had presumably contributed to its construction, provides powerful testimony of continued English interest in the region.[57]

It is not certainly known whether any of these travellers were expected to report on what they saw in the eastern Mediterranean and still less whether any of them visited the Ottoman court, but it would certainly have made sense for any English government contemplating a crusade to have been provided with detailed information on the Turks and their rulers. A guide written for a prospective English traveller to the Levant and appended to the Cotton Manuscripts in the British Library provides an indication that at least one such envisaged presenting himself to the sultan.[58] From internal evidence this document is probably datable to between 1422 and 1451,[59] and the advice contained therein appears to have been directed at a traveller of high status. It is possible that this was a specific person, perhaps one of the emissaries-cum-pilgrims mentioned above, but possible too that this was generic advice to any traveller of means, as the addressee was presented with a number of possible routes by which he or she, after visiting the Holy Sepulchre, might make for a variety of locations.[60] Unlike other pilgrim guides and accounts in English, which list the indulgences to be acquired on the usual route to Jerusalem in detail, the tone of the Cotton guide is markedly unreligious and even "adventurous", appealing

---

55 Leading English visitors to Rhodes, Cyprus and Jerusalem during the reign of Richard II are noticed in Luttrell, "Chaucer's Knight and the Mediterranean", pp. 131–32, 145, 151.

56 *Pageant of the Birth, Life and Death of Richard Beauchamp Earl of Warwick 1389–1439*, ed. H. A. Dillon (London, 1914); *CSPV*, p. 46; *Calendar of Close Rolls, Richard II–Henry VII* [hereafter cited as *CCR*], 24 vols. (London, 1914–63), *1405–9*, p. 318; *Foedera*, 4/2:56; 5/1:14, 35, 167, 186; *Calendar of Papal Letters*, 7:6, 439–40; 11:580; Wey, *Itineraries*, p. 77. Willoughby and de la Warre did not reach the Holy Land in 1440, being captured and held to ransom in Germany during their journey. Willoughby redeemed his vow, but de la Warre set off again in 1446/7. T. Bekyngton, *Official Correspondence*, ed. G. Williams, 2 vols., RS 56 (London, 1872), 1:93; *CPL*, 9:84; *Foedera*, 5/1:175.

57 For the arms and the circumstances in which they were placed on the tower see Luttrell, "English Contributions", pp. 168–72.

58 London, British Library, MS Cotton Appendix VIII, fols. 108v–12v. This work follows a copy of Lydgate's *Life of Our Lady* addressed to a fellow monk at Bury, Edmund Fansi (ibid, fols. 2–108r), but is in a different hand. A competent transcription, but without commentary, can be found in "Rathschläge für eine Orientreise", ed. C. Horstmann, *Englische Studien* 8 (1893), 277–84.

59 The document makes reference to an independent Constantinople and to the Hospitaller castle of Bodrum, the construction of which began in 1407 or 1408. It is possible that it also refers to Murad II, Ottoman sultan between 1422 and 1451. See below, n. 65. Lydgate's *Life* was written at the behest of Henry V of England, probably in 1421–22, and the Cotton Appendix MS includes a note that Lydgate was a *sexagenarius* in 1440. *A Critical Edition of John Lydgate's Life of Our Lady*, ed. Joseph A. Lauritis, Ralph A. Klinefelter and Vernon F. Gallagher (Louvain, 1961), pp. 4–8, 44; BL Cotton Appendix VIII, fol. 1r.

60 BL Cotton Appendix VIII, fols. 111r–12r; "Rathschläge", 282–83.

rather to the curiosity than to the piety of the traveller, who was advised that he would encounter "many marvailles", such as the "mountayne that brenneth euere" on the "island" of Etna, during his travels.[61]

The recipient was evidently, or was expected to be, wealthy, a person "of estate", and intending to travel with servitors: he was warned that neither he "nor none othere of youres" should buy too many things "of hye pris for drede of suche aspies as be in meny places ... to Venyse-ward", and there are various other mentions of his "own men", who, among other things, were to fetch him fresh water at every landfall after they had set sail.[62] Once he reached Venice, he was advised to take passage with the galleys that sailed to Alexandria in September, for whether he intended to visit Egypt or Jerusalem the pilgrim galleys which sailed in March were hot, smelly, cramped and consequently best avoided. There, too, he would be able to hire an interpreter with knowledge of "Lumbard, Greke, Sarasyne and Turkesse".[63] After his initial landfall he was to proceed to Beirut, from where he might journey to Damascus and, it was implied, stay there with the Venetians. There was then the possibility of travel to the north-east to the Black Sea coast, a way "full of smale lordships and suspeccione" which the author did not advise to those who were not well disguised, adept in languages and accompanied by merchants or pilgrims, preferably by prior arrangement with the Venetian authorities. If the traveller was to go to Antioch and turn west he might reach Constantinople overland, but only "with grete trauaill and peyne". It was better, therefore, for him to "spede you to Rodes-ward, wher is good aire and felishipe of Ingeland" and counsel could be taken on the possibilities of travel to Turkey, Tartary, Russia, Vlachia, more or less Greece, Albania, Barbary or Spain.[64]

Admittedly this array of possible destinations hardly suggests that the traveller was exercising a formal commission or embassy, or indeed had any definite plans at all, but travel to the Turkish court was at least admitted as a possibility. The "grete lord" of the Turks, or "Amaratte", meaning either Murad (II) or perhaps simply "the emir",[65] could best be approached overland from Bodrum whether he was at Brusa, Ankara or any other "riall place" of his. Alternatively, the traveller could visit Constantinople and ask the Genoese of Pera to procure his admittance to the Turkish court.[66]

Not only does this document suggest that fifteenth-century Englishmen were more adventurous than the surviving accounts of their travels suggest, and that they were at least willing to contemplate visiting the courts of Muslim rulers, it also

---

61 BL Cotton Appendix VIII, fol. 112r, 112v; "Rathschläge", 283, 284.

62 BL Cotton Appendix VIII, fols. 108v, 110r; "Rathschläge", 277–78, 280.

63 BL Cotton Appendix VIII, fol. 109v; "Rathschläge", 279.

64 BL Cotton Appendix VIII, fol. 111r–v; "Rathschläge", 282.

65 For this reading of Froissart's references to *l'Amorath/Amorath* see Luttrell, "Latin Responses", p. 133. However, the Hospitaller chancery called the Ottoman ruler, Murad II, "Amaratum Bey" in 1439. Here, Amaratum appears to designate 'Murad'. NLM, Cod. 353, fol. 195r.

66 "Rathschläge", 282–83.

indicates that some among them had a detailed knowledge of the trade routes and major cities of the Near and Middle East. It seems probable that the author of the guide was either a frequent traveller to the region or, more likely still, someone who had resided there, a Franciscan or a Hospitaller. Given the specific attention the author drew to Rhodes as a place of counsel and fellowship and his neglect of the Franciscan convent on Mount Sion, it seems likely that he was a member of or well acquainted with the order of St John.

The existence of a community of English Hospitallers on Rhodes between 1309 and 1522 has not been much considered by those who have examined English pilgrimage or trade in the region. But pilgrim accounts make it clear that those English persons passing through the island were well catered and cared for, and a few documents in the order's archives suggest that the English merchants active in the eastern Mediterranean in late fifteenth and early sixteenth centuries were not averse to putting in at Rhodes, where they could both trade and receive advice about the movements of the Turkish fleet.[67] As is well known, the order possessed informants in the cities and ports of the Ottoman and Mamluk states who would warn it whenever significant naval operations were being planned by either power. The order's galleys and coastguard, which respectively patrolled and kept watch over the Dodecanese, could also usually be relied upon to produce up-to-date information about the movements of corsairs in the south-eastern Aegean and the officer in charge of the coastguard was an English Hospitaller, the Turcopolier.[68] Moreover, as suggested by the Cotton guide, the order had regular diplomatic contact with the Turks, and might be able to arrange passage or negotiate safe conducts for travellers who wished to have dealings with them.[69]

Although they were often employed on diplomatic business in the West, Levantine diplomacy was not the strong suit of the English brethren of the Hospital. The negotiators sent to Greek, Turkish and Mamluk rulers tended to be French and especially Italian speakers who could understand the mercantile lingua franca of the eastern Mediterranean. Often they also travelled with Greeks or Jews resident in Rhodes, the majority of the order's treaties with the Turks being set down in Greek and/or Italian.[70] But there were some English brethren who conducted diplomatic

---

67 NLM, Cod. 389, fol. 162r; 402, fol. 175r–v; 404, fol. 234v.

68 Jürgen Sarnowsky, *Macht und Herrschaft im Johanniterorden des 15. Jahrhunderts: Verfassung und Verwaitung der Johanniter auf Rhodos (1421–1522)* (Münster, 2001), pp. 287–88.

69 For diplomatic contacts after 1480 see Nicolas Vatin, *L'Ordre de Saint-Jean-de-Jérusalem, l'Empire ottoman et la Méditerranée orientale entre les deux sièges de Rhodes (1480–1522)* (Paris, 1994), passim. I have not consulted Z. N. Tsirpanlis, "Friendly Relations of the Knights of Rhodes with the Turks in the Fifteenth Century" [in Greek], *Byzantinische Forschungen* 3 (1968), 191–209.

70 E.g. Z. N. Tsirpanlis, *Rhodes and the South-East Aegean Islands under the Knights of St John (14th–16th cc): Collected Studies* [in Greek] (Rhodes, 1991), pp. 46–63. Nicolas Vatin has noted that as a result of their naval depradations, Turkish hostility to both the Hospitallers and the inhabitants of Rhodes increased to such a degree in the early sixteenth century that the order was sometimes represented in the empire by Jews unaccompanied by Christians. Vatin, *L'Ordre*, pp. 288–89, 332.

business in the region and who probably understood Italian and perhaps also Greek. The most frequently employed was Peter Holt, Turcopolier between 1396 and 1415, who was sent to Constantinople or the Morea on several occasions and helped to arrange the Byzantine emperor Manuel II's visit to England in 1400.[71]

In addition, many English Hospitallers must have had dealings, on various levels, with Ottoman subjects, encountering Turkish merchants on Rhodes, Turkish soldiers and villagers in the area of Bodrum, and Turkish sailors and pirates on the Aegean. As the march of Bodrum was by no means in a permanent state of war, those who held its captaincy, or served as the captain's deputy – including at least six Englishmen between 1408/9 and 1522 – must sometimes have negotiated, presumably through interpreters, with local Ottoman officials.

On occasion Ottoman diplomatic delegations, often representing individual sanjakbeys rather than the sultan himself, also visited Rhodes, where they would treat with representatives appointed by the Hospital's master and council. While these rarely included Englishmen, in 1504 the recently appointed prior of England, Thomas Docwra, was among those appointed to treat with the representative of Bajezid II's son, Korkud, who was demanding the return of his servant, Kemal Beg, recently captured by a knight of the order.[72]

The arrival of the fugitive Ottoman prince Jem Sultan in Rhodes in 1482 provided the occasion for more sustained contact. Two senior English Hospitallers, John Weston and John Kendal, helped to arrange the refugee's arrival, and shortly afterwards Kendal was among those appointed to negotiate a treaty with Bayezid's ambassador.[73] The terms of this arrangement were so acceptable to both sides that, with the exception of the pension provided by the sultan for Jem's safe keeping, they survived the latter's death and were even renewed following the Veneto-Turkish war of 1499–1503, into which the order was, rather reluctantly, drawn. Kendal's long diplomatic experience, his residence in Rome as the order's procurator there, and his previous acquaintance with Jem conspired to ensure that he was appointed the captain and prefect of his guard in 1488, shortly before his transfer into papal hands.[74] The appointment suggests that both the order and the prince himself trusted Kendal to keep his charge safely, securely and in the style to which he had become accustomed during his years of comfortable captivity. Whether they were right to do so, however, remains open to some question, for in 1496 Kendal was accused, admittedly rather implausibly, of having procured the murder of a Turk of Jem's

---

[71] For Holt's career in the East see Charles L. Tipton, "Peter Holt, Turcopolier of Rhodes and Prior of Ireland", *Annales de l'Ordre souverain de Malte* 22 (1964), 82–85; *Monumenta Peloponnesiaca: Documents for the History of the Peloponnese in the 14th and 15th centuries*, ed. J. Chrysostomides (Camberley, 1995), nos. 274–79, 283, 289.

[72] NLM, Cod. 80, fols. 81v–83r; Vatin, *L'Ordre*, p. 281.

[73] NLM, Cod. 76, fols. 109v, 125r–26r.

[74] NLM, Cod. 389, fols. 209v–10r.

household some years earlier in order to establish the credentials of a poisoner he wished to employ to eliminate Henry VII.[75]

Although admirably vigorous, the physical and symbolic interactions and perhaps even discourses between Englishmen and Turks in the summer and autumn of 1522 were of a notably uncompromising and undiplomatic nature, but after the Turks had breached the walls of Rhodes town in several places and the order had practically run out of ammunition, the master of the Hospital, Philippe Villiers de l'Isle Adam, agreed to discuss the surrender of the island and sent hostages to the Turkish camp. Among them was an English conventual knight, Nicholas Roberts, who was thus enabled to view sultan Suleiman and his entourage at close quarters. Roberts was impressed by the dignity and composure of the sultan, the sumptuousness of his pavilion and the appearance of his guards, and found the experience sufficiently memorable to describe it in the account of the siege he sent to the earl of Surrey. As was fitting for a professional military man, he also reported the names of the Turkish commanders and gave figures for the size of the Turkish host which, while probably exaggerated, at least agreed with both most Latin and some Turkish estimates.[76] Although damage to the manuscript has resulted in the loss of a word or two at the end of each line of text, what remains provides what may be the first recorded English impression of an Ottoman ruler, and therefore seems worth quoting *in extenso*:[77]

> I was on of those that the lord master [of the/owr] Religione sent to the gret turk for p[leges at] such time as the pact was made be*tween the Turks* and him the gret Turk ys of the age of … yers he ys uere wise discret and muc[h] … bothe in his wordes and allso in his … being of his age I was in his court*e* … at such time as we were browght firs*t to* mak our reuerence unto him we fou[nd him in] a red pavilion standing between too … lions mervelous ryche and sumptu … setting in a chayr and no creatur with … pavelione which chayr was of g … work of fin gold his gard stonding *near* his pavelion to the nomber of xxij … they be called sulakys thes nomber … contenually abowt his parson, he h*a* … nomber of xl thowsand of them they *wer on* ther hedes a long white cape, and *on the* tope of the cape a white ostrage … which gevith a gret show … [fol. 40v] *Ar*mye was divided in fowre parts, the capitaines

[75] F. Madden, "Documents Relating to Perkin Warbeck", *Archaelogia* 27 (1838), 153–210, at p. 173. Kendal's supposed plots against the king are discussed in Ian Arthurson, *The Perkin Warbeck Conspiracy* (Stroud, 1994), pp. 60, 76–77, 90–91, 98, 100, 103, 110–11, 135–37.

[76] Contemporary estimates, including Roberts', of the size of the Ottoman army are summarized in Kenneth M. Setton, *The Papacy and the Levant (1204–1571)*, 4 vols. (Philadelphia, 1976–84), 3:205 and n. 24. From 1453 or earlier, the total forces available to the Ottomans were often given as 200,000 in western sources. Schwoebel, *Shadow of the Crescent*, pp. 4, 6, 74, 195.

[77] London, British Library, MS Cotton Otho C. ix, fols. 39r–41r, at fol. 40r–v. A transcription of those portions of the letter relating to the siege of Rhodes, including Roberts' interview with Suleiman, is provided in Whitworth Porter, *The Knights of Malta*, 2nd ed. (London, 1883), pp. 711–13, at p. 712, who copied it from Taaffe. Taaffe supplied several words which are probably his interpolations rather than readings from the manuscript, the margins of which were damaged by fire in 1731. I have put these in italics. In addition I have placed some suggested interpolations of my own in square brackets.

> … war called as folowith. The principall capita*ine i*s called pero bashaw[78] second mustafa bashaw,[79] *t*he third hakmak bashaw,[80] the fowrth the … bigalarby of anatalya[81] they be the iiij govern*ours* under the gret turk euery one of them had fifte thowsand men under his Baner, and they lay at iiij severall places in the town.

The letters sent home by English Hospitallers based in Malta in the 1530s also have the character of military dispatches rather than of exercises in sensationalist scaremongering or proto-orientalist meditations on the exotic.[82] In 1532, for example, brother Clement West reported that he had a copy of a letter "off defyans" in which the sultan had supposedly threatened the pope, but that he had seen a similar production twenty years before and thus took it to be a forgery.[83]

Varied though their contacts were, none of these men appear to have visited the Ottoman state in any official capacity. In general, English Hospitallers appear to have been considered competent to deal with the Turks at a diplomatic level only in the company of brethren of other *langues* and on conventual or friendly territory. There is one striking exception, however. In late September 1453, four months after the fall of Constantinople to Mehmed II, the turcopolier and preceptor of Dinmore, William Dawney, was elected the order's orator to the sultan.[84]

The tenseness of the atmosphere in which Dawney was appointed hardly needs to be stressed. Despite its long-standing encirclement, the fall of Constantinople was greeted with widespread shock and consternation even in western Europe but its capture was felt still more keenly by those powers and populations within reach of the Turks, including the Hospitallers and their subjects. In its aftermath all able-bodied military brethren resident in the West were summoned to Rhodes, the order's fortifications were inspected and provisioned, and the pope was petitioned successfully to prolong the Jubilee indulgence of 1450 in the Hospital's favour.[85] In such circumstances it is clear that the master and council would only have entrusted a person of the highest capabilities with this mission. The impression of trust is strengthened by the fact that the order promised to accept whatever expenses he incurred in his legation against his accounts, perhaps an indication that substantial bribery of Ottoman officials and even the sultan was envisaged.

---

78 Pir Mehmed Pasha, the grand vizier.

79 Mustafa Pasha, the second vizier.

80 ?Ahmed Pasha, the third vizier and beylerbey of Rumelia.

81 Qasim Pasha, beylerbey of Anatolia.

82 *LP Henry VIII*, 5, no. 1626; 7, nos. 326, 1100, 1345–46; 8, no. 1155; 9, nos. 910, 920; 12/1, nos. 347, 1144, 1190; 12/2, nos. 129, 132, 355, 524, 792–93, 1258; 13/1, nos. 230, 1358, 1397–98; 13/2, nos. 87, 103, 162, 965–66; 14/2, nos. 404–5.

83 *LP Henry VIII*, 5, no. 1069.

84 Tsirpanlis, *Anecdota*, doc. 321 (pp. 739–40): NLM, Cod. 364, fol. 117v [116v].

85 Tsirpanlis, *Anecdota*, docs. 308–9A (pp. 707–15); *CPL*, 10:261–65; *Foedera*, 5/2:53, 57. R. Valentini, "L'Egeo dopo la caduta di Costantinopoli nelle relazioni dei Gran Maestri di Rodi", *Bullettino dell'Istituto Storico Italiano per il Medio Evo e Archivio Muratoriano* 51 (1936), 137–68, at pp. 139–42, 160–62.

Dawney, a Yorkshireman of knightly family who had been a preceptor since 1439, had been recommended to the order by Henry VI in 1440 and held a number of important conventual appointments in the 1440s and 1450s.[86] He had been elected turcopolier in 1449 and served as captain of Bodrum in 1448–49, visitor of Cos in 1452 and as a procurator of the common treasury from c. 1449 to c. 1456.[87] Between them, these posts would have involved him in dealings with the Greek inhabitants of the Dodecanese and the Anatolian Turks which might have equipped him for his appointment as ambassador in 1453.

Unfortunately, both the course and the result of Dawney's mission are unclear. It is possible that he did not set out or was not allowed to see the sultan, as the Byzantine chronicler Ducas reported that the order did not send an embassy until 1455, when its refusal to pay tribute prompted military action by Mehmed.[88] But a letter sent by the master of the order to the prior of Auvergne on 20 January 1454 indicates that Ottoman emissaries had already appeared demanding tribute, and been refused.[89] It seems perfectly feasible that Dawney had visited the sultan in the previous October and, having been unable to secure the renewal of the truce arranged between sultan and order in 1450, had at least managed to arrange for a reciprocal embassy to visit Rhodes. His mission, if indeed it took place, was thus not an unqualified success, but given that Mehmed was demanding tribute from all his Christian neighbours on the back of his success in taking Constantinople, it is difficult to see how it could have been.

The level and frequency of English contacts with the Ottomans before the 1550s were hardly spectacular, and were certainly not conducted on any kind of routine footing. Yet from the mid-fourteenth century there was an increasing amount of interaction between English crusaders, pilgrims, traders and Hospitallers and the inhabitants of Anatolia and Rumelia. If the reports of nervous, ill-informed and incurious pilgrims reinforced the common perception that Turks were cruel and hostile to Christianity, they at least demonstrate that by the early sixteenth century their authors were aware that the Turks were a separate people to the "Saracens", while those who had more sustained contact with the Ottomans were less uncomfortable with dealing with them, and more knowledgeable about their capabilities and customs. To a few enterprising fifteenth- and early sixteenth-century merchants, the Ottoman lands represented a potential source of profit, while

---

[86] *The Visitations of Yorkshire in the Years 1563 and 1564, made by William Flowers, Esquire, Norroy King of Arms*, ed. Charles Best Norcliffe, Harleian Society Publications 16 (London, 1881), p. 94; NLM, Cod. 354, fol. 200r; Bekynton, *Official Correspondence*, ed. Williams, 1:87.

[87] NLM, Cod. 361, fols. 237v–38r, 295r; Cod. 363, fols. 241v–42r, 242v–43r, 260r; Cod. 364, fol. 129r–v; Cod. 366, fol. 142r. Tsirpanlis, *Anecdota*, docs. 273–74, 277; Sarnowsky, *Macht und Herrschaft*, pp. 656, 673.

[88] Franz Babinger, *Mehmed the Conqueror and His Time*, trans. Ralph Manheim and ed. William C. Hickman (Princeton, 1978), pp. 129–30.

[89] Text in Valentini, "L'Egeo", pp. 161–62. Valentini was unaware of Dawney's appointment as orator.

individual Hospitallers might see the Turks as professional adversaries worthy of respect, and convey this impression in their letters home, a fact which suggests that their correspondents there were more eager for instruction than for sensation.

Despite their exchanges with popes and other rulers, which laid great stress on the defence of Christendom against the common enemy, successive English monarchs permitted and even encouraged their subjects to breach papal prohibitions on trade with the Ottomans, and Henry VIII, for all the appearance of "Turks" in his pageantry as emblems of the exotic, appears to have devoured information about them avidly. To what extent rulers drew on the experience of those of their subjects who confronted or contacted the Turk when deciding such policies is unclear, but the long tradition of dispatching officers of state and household servants to the eastern Mediterranean on combined pilgrimages and diplomatic business, as well as the frequent presence of the prior of St John at court and in council, suggests that they would have been able to inform themselves adequately, if not always accurately, about Turkish affairs.

English informants who had first-hand experience of the Turks may have been few and far between, but whether pilgrims, merchants or Hospitallers, they were often well connected, and they could recall encounters and impressions that were not merely formed during the course of military action. In consulting persons such as William Dawney, William Cooper or Nicholas Roberts, kings and courtiers might even hear accounts of the sultan or his capital. The knowledge travellers could impart may have been swamped by exaggeration, speculation and traditional prejudice by the time it made its way into popular drama, but it existed nonetheless, indicating that some of the English were neither as ignorant of nor as ideologically blinkered when considering the Turks as might be suggested by their popular entertainments.

REPORTS ON RECENT EXCAVATIONS

La forteresse médiévale de Safed: Données récentes de l'archéologie

Hervé Barbé et Emanuel Damati

Israel Antiquities Authority

Un programme de fouille archéologique, de conservation et de restauration des vestiges de la partie sud de la forteresse médiévale de Safed, financé par le ministère du tourisme israélien, est en cours depuis l'automne 2001. Si les terrassements préliminaires ont été réalisés globalement sur le tiers sud du site, la première campagne de fouille a ensuite porté sur le secteur sud-ouest (Fig. 1). Ces investigations ont permis de reconnaître des vestiges de salles intra-muros et du rempart interne de l'époque franque, lui-même flanqué d'un complexe de tour-porte avec rampe d'accès attribuable à une campagne de construction mamelouke. La question de la "grosse tour" ou donjon nous semble également pouvoir être réinterprétée.[1]

Deux sections du rempart interne ont été dégagées sans toutefois présenter de relations architecturales directes entre-elles. La première, un mur rectiligne de 2 m d'épaisseur mis au jour sur un linéaire de 25 m, correspond à la courtine ouest. Cinq archères à niches y sont aménagées (Fig. 2). La seconde section, un mur courbe de 3.20 m d'épaisseur, bien conservé en élévation sur un linéaire de 6m, correspond à la courtine sud. Deux marques de tâcherons sont présentes sur ces parements et les restes de deux archères à niches sont visibles dans son volume. Dans toute la partie sud du site, les parements ont été systématiquement récupérés et seuls subsistent les restes de son massif de maçonnerie. Légèrement en retrait de son parement interne, cette section de rempart est doublée par second mur, présentant une même courbure. L'espace intermédiaire atteste l'existence d'un couloir (S9). Ce type d'aménagement, appelé "gaine de circulation", en relation avec des archères à niches, plaide pour une attribution au XIIIe siècle. Si des exemples précurseurs de ce modèle sont connus pour la fin du XIIe siècle – comme dans la section de courtine du Caire construite par Saladin[2] – l'association de la gaine de circulation et de l'archère à niche connaît un développement, voir une systématisation au XIIIe

---

[1] Pour plus de détail, voir Hervé Barbé et Emanuel Damati, "Le château de Safed: sources historiques, problématique et premiers résultats des recherches". Article à paraître dans *La fortification au temps des croisades*, actes du colloque de Parthenay, 2002.

[2] Keppel A. C. Creswell, "Archeological Researches at the Citadel of Cairo", *Bulletin de l'Institut français d'archéologie orientale*, 23 (1924), 89–167.

siècle, tant en Orient qu'en Europe.[3] Enfin, l'épaisseur même du mur de courtine, qui correspondrait à 1.5 cannes chypriotes, renvoie au texte décrivant la construction du XIIIe siècle.[4]

Dans l'espace compris entre les deux sections de courtines, la partie supérieure d'une salle voûtée sur croisées d'ogives a été mise au jour (S8). Ce volume, compte tenu de sa situation, pourrait tout à fait correspondre au vestige d'une porte de la construction franque du XIIIe siècle. Le profil des nervures est par ailleurs identique à celles de la porte est du rempart de Césarée, érigé par Louis IX en 1251.

A l'intérieur du rempart, plusieurs pièces ont été en partie dégagées. L'ensemble le plus complet et le plus intéressant est constitué par une pièce quadrangulaire couverte à l'origine par une voûte d'ogive (S12). En témoignent, à chaque angle de la pièce, et dans des états de conservations différents, les retombées des nervures s'appuyant sur des consoles. L'exemple le mieux conservé, dans l'angle sud-ouest, présente des nervures à chanfrein reposant sur un culot décoré d'une fleur de lys surmontée d'un décor foliacé. L'allure générale n'est pas sans évoquer l'architecture des salles du XIIIe siècle du château templier de Tortose.[5] Les travaux de dégagement de la salle située immédiatement à l'est de celle-ci (S15) ont permis de mettre au jour une tête sculptée d'époque franque (Fig. 3).[6]

Les vestiges qui se développent sur le flanc ouest du rempart interne ne sont pas encore tous précisément datés (S5). Toutefois, la position des archères à niches systématiquement dotées d'un seuil plongeant, assurant la défense de la base des courtines, interdit un fonctionnement synchrone de l'ensemble. Le complexe de tour-porte (S1) et sa rampe d'accès (S4), dont l'aménagement a nécessité le percement d'une porte dans l'élévation de la courtine sud d'époque franque (S2), est en revanche attribuable à une campagne de construction mamelouke (Fig. 4). Un fragment de linteau découvert dans les couches de démolition de la porte de la rampe, sculpté d'un lion (Fig. 5), en attribuerait l'exécution au sultan Baybars.[7] La base d'une grosse tour a été presque intégralement dégagée dans la partie sommitale du site. La comparaison de son architecture avec les vestiges déjà interprétés et les

---

[3] Pierre Héliot, "Un organe peu connu de la fortification médiévale: la gaine", *Gladius* 10 (1972), 45–67.

[4] Robert Burchard Constantijn Huygens, *De constructione castri Saphet. Construction et fonctions d'un château fort franc en Terre Sainte*, Verhandelingen, Koninklijke Nederlandse Akademie van Wetenschappen, Afdeling Letterkunde 111 (Amsterdam, 1981).

[5] Camille Enlart, *Les monuments des croisés dans le royaume de Jérusalem. Architecture religieuse et civile*, Bibliothèque Archéologique et Historique 8 (Paris, 1927), 2e album, pl. 176–83.

[6] Hervé Barbé, "Recherches archéologiques sur la forteresse de Safed en Israël: découverte récente d'une tête sculptée d'époque franque ". Article à paraître dans *Bulletin Monumental* 161: 3 (2003).

[7] Parmi les nombreuses découvertes de ce symbole lapidaire nous mentionnerons, pour l'environnement proche, celles de Qal'at Namrud -al Subayba [Moshé Hartal, *The Al-Subayba (Nimrod) fortress, towers 11 and 9*, IAA Reports 11 (Jérusalem, 2001)], de la porte des Lions ou de St.Etienne à Jérusalem [Keppel A. C. Creswell, *The works of the sultan Bibars Al-Bunduqdari in Egypt* (1926)] ou encore du pont de Lydda [Charles Clermont-Ganneau, "Note d'épigraphie et d'histoire arabe. Le pont de Lydda construit par le Sultan Beibars", *Journal Asiatique* 5 (1887) and "Note d'épigraphie et d'histoire arabe. Le pont de Lydda", *Journal Asiatique* 6 (1888)].

renseignements fournis par les auteurs contemporains nous permettent également d'attribuer sa construction à l'occupation mamelouk de la fin du XIIIe siècle.[8] De nombreux vestiges, et plus particulièrement la tour-porte et sa rampe ont subit des dégradations attribuables à un tremblement de terre, sans doute celui de 1303.[9]

Concernant les techniques de construction, la présence de joints ruban caractérise presque systématiquement les appareils francs. Cette technique, dont la fonction consiste à cacher les irrégularités des vrais joints, est identifiée dans la phase ayyubide de la citadelle de Damas, réalisée vers 1210,[10] dans les maçonneries des constructions teutoniques de Qal'at Jiddin datées des années 1220–30[11] ou encore dans l'enceinte de Césarée déjà évoquée, érigée en 1251. Les constructions franques attestent la sélection de matériaux de meilleure qualité que ceux employés par les constructeurs mamelouks. Les veines de silex et les dégradations identifiables sur les constructions mameloukes sont visibles dans différentes coupes du rocher sur le site même et dans son environnement immédiat. Une étude pétrographique devra être menée pour déterminer les sites de carrière utilisés par les Francs. Concernant les ouvrages fortifiés, le module moyen des pierres de parement des constructions mameloukes est le double de celui des appareils francs.[12] Alors que les fortifications franques sont toujours à parement lisse, les ajouts mamelouks présentent régulièrement, mais pas exclusivement, un bossage peu développé, se dégageant légèrement de la ciselure d'encadrement.

La première partie de ce programme de fouille et de mise en valeur du site a déjà permis de dégager des vestiges importants de la grande forteresse franque du XIIIe siècle, en cohérence avec les sources médiévales et plus particulièrement le texte attribué au pèlerin français Benoît d'Alignan. Par contre, aucun vestige du XIIe siècle n'a encore été reconnu. Les campagnes futures devront chercher à identifier les occupations précoces tout en précisant le plan de la forteresse qui aurait constitué, pour Paul Deschamps, le chef-d'œuvre de l'art militaire du XIIIe siècle en Orient[13] (Deschamps, 1939).

---

[8] Bernard Lewis, "Traduction du manuscrit arabe d'Al-Ottmani daté de 1372, cote n°4525, bibliothèque de l'université d'Istanbul", *Bulletin of the School of Oriental and African Studies* 15 (1953), 477–88.

[9] D. Amiran and E. Arieh, "Earthquakes in Israel and Adjacent Areas. Macroseismic Observations since 100 B.C.E.", *Israel Exploration Journal* 44 (1994), 260–305.

[10] Jean-Claude Bessac, "Problématique et méthodologie archéologique de la construction de la citadelle de Damas", *Bulletin des études orientales* 53 (2002).

[11] Denys Pringle, Andrew Petersen, Martin Dow et Caroline Singer, "Qal`at Jiddin: a castle of the Crusader and Ottoman periods in Galilee", *Levant* 26 (1994), 135–66.

[12] Dimensions moyennes des pierres de parement des constructions franques: L.0.46m, h.0.29m, mamelouks: L.0.90m, h.0.59m (moyennes comparées des murs des deux sections de courtines, de la tour-porte et de la grosse tour, les calculs étant effectués sur un groupement de 10 pierres de parement reparties sur 3 assises).

[13] Paul Deschamps, *Les châteaux des Croisés en Terre Sainte 2. La défense du Royaume de Jérusalem. Etude historique, géographique et monumentale*, Bibliothèque Archéologique et Historique 34 (Paris, 1939).

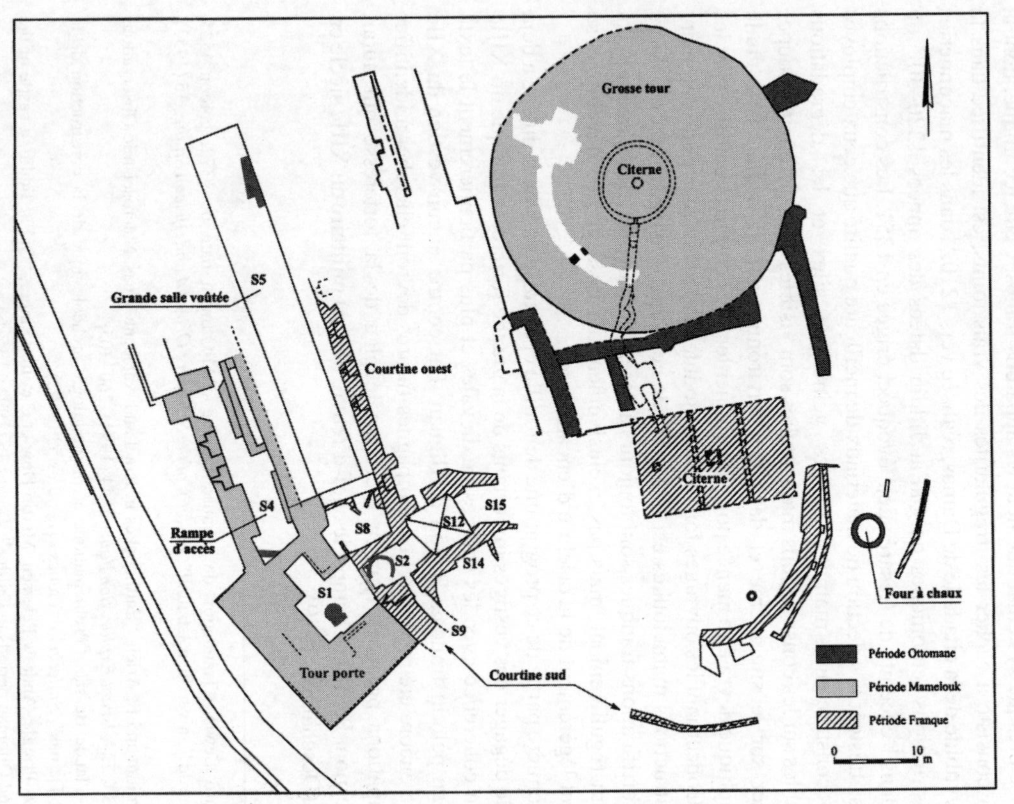

Fig. 1 **Plan schématique des vestiges dégagés dans le tiers sud de la forteresse de Safed** (Relevés de terrain: Vadim Essman et Slava Pirsky; Mise au net des plans: Nathalia Zak)

Fig. 2 **Le mur de courtine ouest et les archères à niche** (Crédit photographique IAA: Tsila Sagiv)

Fig. 3 La tête sculptée d’époque franque (Crédit photographique IAA: Clara Amit)

Fig. 4 Vue de la rampe d'accès et de la tour-porte au second plan (Crédit photographique IAA: Tsila Sagiv)

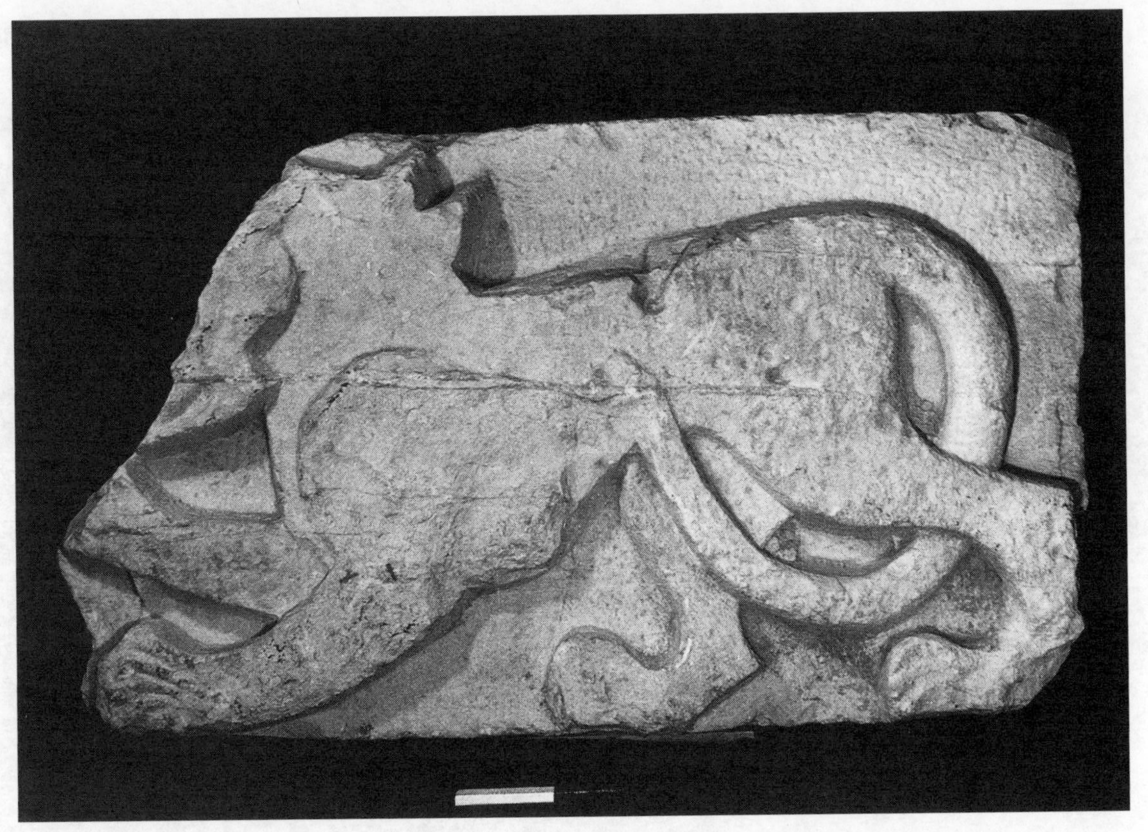

Fig. 5 Fragment de linteau sculpté d'un lion (Crédit photographique IAA: Tsila Sagiv)

The Crusader Castle of Tiberias

Yosef Stepansky

Israel Antiquities Authority

Salvage excavations during the months of May–September 2003 in Tiberias, Israel, have recently revealed monumental and excellently preserved remains of the twelfth-century crusader castle of Tiberias, located on the town's Sea of Galilee shorefront. The main discovery is a 3.5 m wide and 7 m long section of a fortification wall, most probably the northern wall of the citadel, embodying a 3 m wide gateway. A part of the northern façade of the wall, composed of large basalt ashlars and Roman-period architectural elements in secondary use, has so far been exposed intact to a height of 4 m, more than 5 m below current ground level without, as yet, reaching its foundations. A water filled moat connected to the lake probably existed in front of the wall, protecting the citadel on its northern side (as was found in the past on its southern side).

The exposed original parts of the gateway structure include a flagstone two-stepped floor, stone ashlar-constructed gateposts preserved to a height of 1 m, and grooves of the door jambs and of a portcullis (iron grille) – a typical crusader architectural trait. Other typical crusader traits include marginal drafting and diagonal serrated dressing of some of the stones, secondary use of column drums, a mason's "V" mark on the face of one of the stones found in the earthen fill of the excavation, and some imported Frankish pottery shards.

A unique feature is a large section of a magnificently ornamented Roman-period limestone lintel, most likely originating from an ancient synagogue in Tiberias, which was secondarily incorporated into the western gatepost, providing the gateway with an artistic grand appearance (Figs. 1 and 2); other parts of the lintel were discovered discarded within the earthen fill of the moat outside the confines of the gate. Parallels to the lintel may be found at some ancient Galilean synagogues, while an exact duplicate of it exists at Capernaum, decorating the eastern entranceway to the prayer hall of the synagogue.

It seems that after a relatively short time in use, the gateway was blocked up. This is evidenced by the erection of two stone walls, constructed with protruding mortar-filled fugues in a style common in the twelfth and thirteenth centuries, placed along the gateway's span. Eventually the gateway and remains of the fortress were filled in with dirt and debris, used only as nether-foundations for structures of the Jewish quarter of Tiberias erected during the Ottoman period. For hundreds of years the location and former grandeur of the crusader "Sea Fortress" of Tiberias was forgotten, until its recent re-exposure.

As we know from historical sources, Saladin's July 1187 siege of Tiberias – the capital of the principality of Galilee of the Latin kingdom of Jerusalem – preceded

Fig. 1 The castle gate with ornamented Roman lintel secondarily incorporated into the western gatepost (from the northeast) (Photograph courtesy IAA)

Fig. 2 The gate floor and western gatepost, May 2003 (from the east) (Photograph courtesy IAA)

the great and decisive battle of Hattin on 4 July of that year. For many years the crusader castle of Tiberias, conquered without battle by Saladin in the wake of his victory at Hattin, was sought outside the town limits. However, in the 1980s, owing to innovative historical research and archaeological soundings, it was proposed by Razi and Braun[1] that the castle should be located on the shorefront, within the Crusader town limits. The recent discovery, of course, greatly strengthens this conviction. Adding to the results of the earlier archaeological soundings, it may

[1] Z. Razi and E. Braun, "The Lost Crusader Castle of Tiberias", in *Horns*, pp. 216–27.

now be cautiously proposed that the castle was approximately 70 × 50 m in size, although much more work is needed for a detailed outline of its plan. In any case, the discovery opens the way for further research on this most interesting facet of Tiberias's long and rich history.

The excavations were carried out under the auspices of The Israel Antiquities Authority and sponsored by The Israel Government Tourist Corporation. As a result of the discovery, the gateway will be incorporated into the masterplan of this area as a tourist attraction.

Short Notes

The Church of St John in Acre

Eliezer Stern
Israel Antiquities Authority

In 1995 a trial excavation was conducted in the courtyard of the Ottoman Serai. Part of a floor composed of marble tiles in different colours, three fallen marble columns and two marble capitals were uncovered. One of the capitals, covered by a coloured fresco, was in the Corinthian style; the second, also with a coloured fresco, bears a Maltese cross painted in red on a black background. In addition, many stained-glass window fragments in various colours were found strewn on the floor. These elements apparently comprise parts of the nave of the church of St John.

Another excavation was carried out in the Serai in 2003. Two trenches were excavated in the western part of the building. The trenches exposed features associated with the principal west door of the church, among which was a threshold stone of black granite, 4 m wide, with two hewn door sockets. Bases of the pilasters that supported the ribs of a cross-vault were unearthed in two corners of the room.

Two additional trenches, excavated in the eastern part of the Serai, uncovered remains of a chancel screen. The northern face of the screen was exposed to a length of 4 m and a height of 0.60 m. The screen was carved in relief on slabs of hard *nari* limestone within a carved defining border. The slabs were positioned in a row, one adjacent to the other.

Remains of the church floor were found in all the excavated areas. The floor was composed of marble and glazed tiles in a variety of colours. Few of the tiles were found in their original setting, most having been robbed, leaving only their negative impressions in the floor make-up.

Acre: Northern Sea Promenade

Ayelet Tatcher
Israel Antiquities Authority

In June 2003 a sounding was conducted on the western sea shore of Acre, north of the Old City, prior to the construction of the promenade. The excavated areas were located beside and within the *kurkar* ridge, which rises 3 m above sea level in this area. Archaeological remains consisting of crusader ceramics were found.

A part of the *kurkar* cliff that had collapsed was found to have been repaired by the application of a patch of stones held by mortar. In addition, a 0.6 m-wide channel was found cut into the western edge of the *kurkar* ridge, forming a scarp. Beneath the scarp to below sea level, thirteenth-century pottery was found, including a proto-maiolica bowl, cooking pots and jugs.

In the area within the *kurkar* ridge a ditch was excavated. It contained thirteenth-century pottery as well.

This finding supports Frankel's proposal[1] that one should locate here the north-western corner of the crusader city wall enclosing Montmusard.

Latrun

Adrian Boas
Haifa University

In August 2003 clearance work and a surface survey were carried out at the site of the Templar castle Toron des Chevaliers (Latrun), near the Tel-Aviv–Jerusalem highway. The Israel Antiquities Authority with the support of the Armoured Corps Association organized the project, which was directed by Rafael Lewis, advised by Adrian Boas. It took place over a period of three weeks, employing about 65 workers. Clearance of the accumulated surface debris and vegetation exposed parts of the castle which had long been hidden from view and certain elements which were not previously recorded.

This castle has never been excavated, with the exception of limited investigations carried out within the grounds of the Trappist monastery to the north of the site by M. Louhivuori (for the university of Karlsruhe, Germany) in 1995. However, a number of surveys have been carried out in the past. The plans of an unpublished survey by D. Bellamy are located in the Palestine Exploration Fund offices in London. M. Ben Dov's survey was published in Hebrew in 1974.[2] D. Pringle carried out the survey for the British School of Archaeology in Jerusalem in 1989 (with a plan drawn by M. Pease).[3] Z. Greenhut's survey was conducted for an internal publication of the Israel Antiquities Authority in 2001. These examinations provided detailed plans of the site and the present survey aimed at clarifying certain discrepancies in these plans and providing new information.

The castle, which is located on an ancient tell, appears to consist of three main elements: a tower keep, a rectangular enclosure and an outer ward consisting of curtain walls, vaults and towers. The castle chapel is believed to have been located on the eastern side of the inner ward and a group of remarkably fine Romanesque capitals, found at the site in the early twentieth century and now in Istanbul, probably originated in it.

Discoveries made by the present survey include all four faces of the inner ward with its steep external talus (on the north this wall was exposed for almost its entire

---

1 Rafael Frankel, "The North-Western Corner of Crusader Acre", *IEJ* 37 (1987), pp. 256–61.

2 "The Fortress of Latrun", *Qadmoniot* 7.3–4:117–20.

3 Denys Pringle, *Secular Buildings in the Crusader Kingdom of Jerusalem* (Cambridge, 1997), pp. 64–5; *The Churches of the Crusader Kingdom of Jerusalem* 2 (Cambridge, 1998), pp. 5–9; "Templar Castles between Jaffa and Jerusalem", *MO* 2:89–109.

length). A portal in the barrel-vaulted hall on the northern side of this ward, which did not appear in the plans published by Bellamy and Pringle, was exposed and other elements in the southern groin-vaulted range were defined. Several architectural elements scattered around the site were photographed and measured, and masons' marks were recorded. Through the generous aid of Boaz Peleg and Ehud Heffer aerial photographs were taken of the site after the clearance was completed.

A paper describing these finds and discussing the history and architecture of the castle is being prepared and it is hoped that the present work will aid in providing funding for badly needed restoration and conservation work and for the future excavation of this important site.

REVIEWS

The Crusades, ed. Thomas F. Madden (Blackwell Essential Readings in History) Oxford: Blackwell, 2002. Pp. viii, 276. ISBN 0 631 23022 X (hardback); 0 631 23023 8 (paperback).

The inclusion of a volume on the crusades into the Blackwell Essential Readings in History series is to be welcomed wholeheartedly. The format, consisting of twelve articles previously published elsewhere with a general introduction and a short headnote to each of the articles, makes it a perfect tool for teaching beginners' courses on the crusades and introducing students to the present state of crusade scholarship. Thomas F. Madden's general introduction is lucid, sketching the developments of crusade historiography not only with regard to the history of scholarship but also in the light of the changing image of the crusades in the collective memory of the Western world. He justifies his choice of articles in terms of their decisive contribution to the modern scholarly views about the crusades, which he explains again masterfully in the headnotes preceding each article. There is no doubt that the chosen pieces are of outstanding quality and thus deserve their place in this distinguished selection.

The book is divided into three sections: Part I entitled "What Were the Crusades?" includes the following articles: H. E. J. Cowdrey, "Pope Urban II's Preaching of the First Crusade", Jonathan Riley-Smith, "Crusading as an Act of Love", R. A. Fletcher, "Reconquest and Crusade in Spain, c. 1050–1150", Norman Housley, "Crusades Against Christians: Their Origins and Early Development, c. 1000–1216", and Christopher J. Tyerman, "Were There Any Crusades in the Twelfth Century?"; Part II entitled "Who Were the Crusaders?" includes: Giles Constable, "Medieval Charters as a Source for the History of the Crusades", Jonathan Riley-Smith, "Early Crusaders to the East and the Cost of Crusading, 1095–1130", Marcus Bull, "The Roots of Lay Enthusiasm for the First Crusade", and John France, "Patronage and the Appeal of the First Crusade"; Part III entitled "Impact of the Crusades on the East" including: Sir Steven Runciman, "Byzantium and the Crusades", Nikita Elisséeff, "The Reaction of the Syrian Muslims after the Foundation of the First Latin Kingdom of Jerusalem", and Benjamin Z. Kedar, "The Subjected Muslims of the Frankish Levant".

As with any selection of articles meant to reflect the state of research in one particular scholarly field, the choice is a difficult one and must reflect the editor's own preferences. It would be easy to take issue and argue why this or that article might be replaced by another equally deserving one. In terms of subject matter, Madden's choice certainly is a conservative one, concentrating on traditional themes of crusade scholarship with an emphasis on the crusades to the Holy Land, the twelfth century and the impact of the crusades on the Levant. While the crusades against Muslims in Spain and against Christians in Europe get their due, there is little or nothing on other topics which take crusades studies out of their traditional confines, such as for example the crusades of the later Middle Ages, the Baltic crusades, or the role of women, to mention just a few areas which have attracted a fair amount of scholarly attention recently. *The Crusades* will thus prove to be very useful for teaching what we know best about the crusades but it does not necessarily help in guiding students towards some of the most exciting new paths of crusade history.

CHRISTOPH T. MAIER
UNIVERSITÄT ZÜRICH

Crusade and Conversion on the Baltic Frontier 1150–1500, ed. Alan V. Murray. Aldershot: Ashgate, 2002. Pp. xxv, 300. ISBN 0 7546 0325 3.

Crusade and Conversion grew out of papers and discussions of several sessions at the International Medieval Congress in Leeds in 1998 and 2000 organized by Kurt Villads Jensen, one of the leading historians of the Baltic crusades. Alan V. Murray took it upon himself to put together and edit this volume in the highly professional manner which has in the past established him as an outstanding facilitator – to use an awkwardly fashionable but fitting term – of crusade studies. The resulting collection of articles is a highly satisfactory contribution to an area of crusade studies, which has, with the exception of the history of the Teutonic Order, been neglected in the past. The volume, as well as the study of the Baltic crusades, profits from the engagement of scholars from throughout the Baltic region, Europe and the United States. They not only represent as many as eight different nationalities but also bring to the task a welcome variety of scholarly approaches and historiographical traditions. Inevitably in an area of scholarship which has been under-researched for a considerable time, the contributions lack the coherence afforded by a more solid scholarly tradition but they aptly reflect the vibrancy the study of the Baltic crusade has been gaining in the wake of the independence of the Baltic states after the fall the Soviet Union.

The volume is introduced by Kurt Villads Jensen ("Introduction", pp. xvii–xxv) and divided into four parts: Part I entitled "Theory and Practice of the Baltic Crusade" with contributions by Tiina Kala ("The Incorporation of the Northern Baltic Lands into the Western Christian World", pp. 3–20), Axel Ehlers ("The Crusade of the Teutonic Knights against Lithuania Reconsidered", pp. 21–44), and William Urban ("The Frontier Thesis and the Baltic Crusade", pp. 45–71); Part II entitled "The Crusading Countries of Northern Europe" with contributions by Carsten Selch Jensen ("Urban Life and the Crusades in Northern Germany and the Baltic Lands in the Early Thirteenth Century", pp. 75–94), Torben K. Nielsen ("The Missionary man: Archbishop Anders Sunesen and the Baltic Crusade, 1206–21", pp. 95–117), and Thomas Lindkvist, "Crusades and Crusading Ideology in the Political History of Sweden, 1140–1500", pp. 119–30); Part III entitled "The Target

Countries" with contributions by John H. Lind ("Consequences of the Baltic Crusades in Target Areas: The Case of Karelia", pp. 133–50), Anti Selart ("Confessional Conflict and Political Co-operation: Livonia and Russia in the Thirteenth Century", pp. 151–76), Evgeniya L. Nazarova ("The Crusades against Votians and Izhorians in the Thirteenth Century", pp. 177–95), Rasa Mazeika ("When Crusader and Pagan Agree: Conversion as a Point of Honour in the Baptism of king Mindaugas of Lithuania [c. 1240–63]", pp. 197–214), and Juhan Kreem ("The Teutonic Order as a Secular Ruler in Livonia: The Privileges and Oath of Reval", pp. 215–32); Part IV entitled "Literature and Historiography of the Baltic Crusades" with contributions by Alan V. Murray ("The Structure, Genre and Intended Audience of the *Livonian Rhymed Chronicle*", pp. 235–51); Vera I. Matuzova ("Mental Frontiers: Prussians as Seen by Peter von Dusburg", pp. 253–59), and Mary Fischer ("Biblical Heroes and the Uses of Literature: The Teutonic Order in the Late Thirteenth and Early Fourteenth Centuries", pp. 261–75). To round off this collection of essays there is a bibliography of publications about the Baltic crusades in English since 1945 compiled by Alan V. Murray, which will be particularly useful to those teaching the subject at an English-speaking university. There also are a couple of rough maps, tables of chronology and placename equivalents in various Baltic languages as well as an extensive index.

Particularly interesting in this array of essays are those which are concerned with the basic foundations of historical interpretation of the Baltic crusades either in terms of conceptual approaches or the appraisal of the available sources. William Urban puts to the test the very concept of the "frontier" as a interpretive tool in the context of the Christian colonization of the Baltic. In a somewhat laboured discussion of the origins of the frontier theory in the historiography of the US, he makes the important point that the concept of "frontier" is in itself not as clear-cut as it is often presumed and that it is likely to create its own myths when used without circumspection. At the same time, however, Urban extols the uses of the idea of the "frontier" for the interpretation of the expansion of medieval Europe in general and the Christian Baltic in particular, if it is updated and re-worked within the strict parameters of modern scholarship. Rasa Mazeika's essay on the episode of Mindaugas's conversion makes imaginative use of anthropological models of the practice of gift giving and the importance of notions of honour for explaining the relationship between the Lithuanian king and his Christian suitors. Given the scarcity and bias of the available sources, this type of approach, which is based on theory but takes full account of the particular character of the medieval texts, turns out to be most successful in uncovering the dynamics governing the cross-cultural exchanges which so dominate the history of the Baltic in medieval times. Both Alan Murray and Mary Fischer are concerned with the literary culture of the Teutonic Order which provided the main historical narratives for the Baltic crusades. In an attempt to analyse the intended audience of the *Livonian Rhymed Chronicle* Murray convincingly argues that the work "combined the function of documentary history of and for the Teutonic Order with that of an appeal to the crusading potential of

Germany as essential to the survival of Christian Livonia" (p. 250). This ties in with Fischer's argument claiming that the literary production of the Teutonic Order in the late thirteenth and early fourteenth centuries was first and foremost geared towards "the fostering of the Order's self-image and the justification of its crusades in Prussia and the Baltic" (p. 275).

Most contributions in *Crusade and Conversion* are of an exploratory rather than a synthetic character. The volume marks a point of departure and should serve well towards encouraging students to discuss the history of the Baltic crusades from new angles and showing scholars ways of mapping out bold plans of new research. It certainly has the potential to do both successfully.

CHRISTOPH T. MAIER
UNIVERSITÄT ZÜRICH

Alan Forey, *The Fall of the Templars in the Crown of Aragon*. Aldershot: Ashgate, 2001. Pp. xiii + 279. ISBN 0 7546 0519 1.

In November, 1307, with the Templars in France under arrest and the leaders having made public confessions, Clement V tried to wrest control of the proceedings from the French Crown; in the bull *Pastoralis preeminentie* he ordered the detention of the Templars in all the other countries in which they had members and property. Thus began a series of trials, interconnected in the sense that those conducting them were obliged to respond both to papal orders and to the course of events in France, but separate in that each trial displayed unique characteristics deriving from specific local circumstances. In recent years interest in these trials has grown considerably, not only because they are relevant to the histories of the countries concerned, but also because of the light they throw on the events in France. Comparison between countries with different legal systems, ruled by men of often sharply contrasting personalities and conceptions of government, undoubtedly gives such work a significance much wider than the restricted frame of reference which studies of the trials themselves might imply at first sight. This wider picture is now emerging much more clearly, as can be seen in the work of Anne Gilmour-Bryson on Cyprus, Fulvio Bramato on Italy and, still in course, Helen Nicholson on England.

Among English historians Alan Forey has an unrivalled knowledge of the Templar material in Aragonese archives and here he deploys that knowledge to great effect. In particular, by combining the excellent collection of published documents in vol. 2 of Heinrich Finke's *Papsttum und Untergang des Templerordens* with unpublished material from Barcelona and Madrid, he has established a more detailed, nuanced and accurate account of the trial in the *Corona de Aragón* than has hitherto been available either in Spain or elsewhere. Within the careful chronological structure which underpins the book, some extraordinary details emerge. In 1316, for example, during the protracted negotiations over the disposal of Templar lands, James II told his representatives to adopt the startling reserve position that, if his other proposals failed, the lands could be handed over to the Teutonic Knights. As the Teutonic Order had no property in Aragon this seems to have been aimed at avoiding the creation of an over-mighty Order in James's kingdoms, but it is nevertheless an incredible idea in view of the past and contemporary record of conflict between the Teutonic Knights and other secular and ecclesiastical rulers. Apparently, even rulers as shrewd as this one were prone to flights of fancy. Necessarily, the account of the negotiations over the property occupies a large section of the book, but individual Templars are not neglected. There are some fascinating vignettes. Thus, in bizarre betrayals of the original Templar aims, in 1316 a sergeant called Jaime de Mas began a career of piracy, robbing merchants at sea, while in the 1320s Guillermo de Castellbisbal, a knight who had remained a steadfast Christian during thirteen years of Muslim captivity and who had been freed through the efforts of James II, took to highway robbery and kidnapping for ransom.

However, in many ways this is as much a book about James II as it is about the Templars. Faced with an Order forewarned by the French arrests, in possession of castles far more formidable than any rural French preceptories, and made up of personnel with a higher proportion of fighting men than anywhere else except Cyprus, it is not surprising to find that the king was unable to follow the course urged on him by Philip the Fair. Indeed, it is clear from Forey's account that James had no desire to do so and that some of the inconsistencies and delays which occurred arose not from incompetence or greed but from his own lack of belief in the validity of the accusations. His actions during and after the trial confirm this view. He tried hard to ameliorate the material conditions of Templar captivity, to avoid using torture for as long as possible and to provide the Templars with decent pensions once the Order was dissolved. The one disappointment of the book therefore is that there is relatively little here about the king's personality and policies on the wider stage, which must be relevant to our understanding of his conduct during the trial. It is perhaps ironic that historians have expended so much effort trying to understand the strange personality of Philip IV, not the least in order to explain why he attacked the Templars, when more could be said about James's view of his role as monarch, especially as revealed in his prolific letter-writing. Only in the brief concluding section is this really tackled where there is a strong challenge to David Abulafia's description of James as "perhaps the wiliest of the thirteenth-century Aragonese rulers". Judged in the light of the trial documents, Forey offers a view closer to Thomas Bisson's description of him as "a man of piety, prudence, and perseverance". It may be, however, that James was a good deal more self-interested than either Forey or Bisson allow.

The evidence presented here demonstrates clearly that neither the king nor most of the leading ecclesiastics and nobles of his lands regarded the Order as either guilty of the accusations made by Philip IV's lawyers or, indeed, as having fallen into the state of general decline recently suggested by Jonathan Riley-Smith.

Despite past disputes and a falling number of donors, the Aragonese still believed that the Order was performing important functions. Dr Forey's final conclusion is surely correct: "The religious life of the Templars in Aragon deteriorated not because of internal decay within the Order during the decades before the trial but because of the circumstances created by those who accused and destroyed the Temple."

MALCOLM BARBER
UNIVERSITY OF READING (UK)

Helen Nicholson, *The Knights Hospitaller*. Woodbridge: The Boydell Press, 2001. Pp. xii, 180. ISBN 0 85115 845 5.

Anglo-Saxon universities cultivate an established tradition of fine textbooks which serve both as lucid introductions for students and as works of reference for advanced scholars. Outside the English-speaking world such textbooks are sometimes imitated, recently for the Teutonic Order by Hartmut Boockmann (*Der Deutsche Orden: Zwölf Kapitel aus seiner Geschichte,* 4th ed., 1994, repr. 1999). Books on the Templars abound, of course, Malcolm Barber's *The New Knighthood* (1994, repr. 1998) and Alain Demurger's (*Vie et mort de l'ordre du Temple*, 3rd ed., 1993) being probably the best choices. The Hospitallers, the third great military-religious order, have not been studied with the same enthusiasm, although they had a much longer history than the Templars and were much more wide-spread than the Teutonic Knights. Only a small part of Hospitaller history relates to England. Nevertheless, Nicholson's textbook has to compete with the short but masterly survey by Jonathan Riley-Smith, *Hospitallers: The History of the Order of St John* (1999). Whereas Riley-Smith wrote his amply illustrated work for a general public, Helen Nicholson's book will be useful for teaching. It has a fair number of illustrations (9 colour, 12 black-and-white, 4 maps, 1 family tree), a considerable number of footnotes, a long bibliography (pp. 147–67) and an invaluable index of persons, places and subjects (pp. 168–80).

Her seven chapters are arranged according to the history of the Order: (1) the origins of the Hospital of St John in Jerusalem, (2) the wars in the Latin East and on the European frontiers to 1291, (3) the Hospitallers on Rhodes 1306–1522, (6) the Order on Malta 1530–1798, and (7) the developments from 1798 to the present day. The two remaining chapters concern (4) organization and religious life, and (5) the priories and commanderies in Europe, which provided men and money for the headquarters in Jerusalem, Acre, Cyprus, Rhodes, and Malta. For a quick orientation this table of contents is detailed enough but the index supplies many well-chosen cross-references, which are extremely helpful for finding individual sections concerning, for example, care for the sick and hospitals, warfare, estate management, economic activities and even sugar production. Intelligent users will soon find out that clothing is treated under symbolism with a cross-reference from iconography. Since the Hospitallers were considered religious, and even knights or sergeants within the order had religious obligations, it may be surprising that liturgy, divine service, hours, feasts, fasting and related subjects are missing. This reveals a deficit in recent research, which Cristina Dondi and others are currently trying to rectify.

For a number of problems one would like to have had more footnotes, for example, on the pottery from the Hospitaller compound at Acre, on the Cypriot sugar mills, on the Canadian and Caribbean purchases by Maltese grand-masters. In an age of electronic bibliographies it should be possible to save the space for this by giving just the essentials (author, title, year, no sub-title, no place, no series-title). Controversial questions such as militarization, holy war, the role of the nobility, political influence, discipline and reforms are treated with great circumspection. There are many excellent paragraphs, for instance, on the situation in the Holy Land during the twelfth century, which is important for understanding why the Hospitallers gradually resorted to arms; on the conquest of Rhodes, which saved them after the loss of Acre in 1291, whilst the Templars were doomed; or on Hospitaller involvement in late fourteenth-century Morea. Many particular points were obviously discussed with specialists, Alan Forey, Anthony Luttrell and others are duly mentioned in the preface. Inevitably, there are some details which are probably oversimplified (p. 139: abolition of the bailiwick of Brandenburg in 1811) or doubtful (p. 77: in the first half of the fourteenth century the treasurer customarily being a German). Some important places and persons are missing: Prague and Strakonice in Bohemia, Eagle in England, the German prior Georg Schilling von Cannstatt, who served Charles V and was created prince of the Empire in 1547. Some outstanding non-English publications should not be withheld from readers, for example, Walter Gerd Rödel, *Das Großpriorat Deutschland*, 1972; Benoît Beaucage, *Visites générales Saint-Gilles*, 1982. But these are minor criticisms. On the whole, Helen Nicholson's textbook can be recommended not only to scholars but also to the general public. All those interested in the history of the crusades must be grateful to have so succinct, so reliable and so readable a summary of current scholarly work on the Hospitallers. Helen Nicholson has clearly filled a gap. Future research and public discussion on Christian warfare against the Muslims and similar enemies will certainly profit from the fact that now all three great military religious orders can be studied with the help of up-to-date textbooks.

KARL BORCHARDT
UNIVERSITÄT WÜRZBURG

Helen Nicholson, *The Knights Templar: A New History*. Stroud: Sutton Publishing, 2001. Pp. xviii, 278. ISBN 0 7509 2517 5.

It may be the general interest in allegedly "secret" societies combined with the story of this order's rather dramatic downfall which accounts for the great number of publications on the Templars, the oldest medieval religious military order. Many of these publications are products of their authors' imagination and wishful thinking, driven by the actually unattainable desire to link the Templars to the Freemasons or to the Grail legend. Fortunately, and to set the record straight, several fairly recent scholarly monographs have been devoted to the Templars, most notably Alain Demurger's *Vie et mort de l'ordre du Temple* (1985; revised 1989 and 1993) and Malcolm Barber's *The New Knighthood: A History of the Order of the Temple* (1994). Helen Nicholson's new book, *The Knights Templar: A New History*, now adds a skilful synthesis of recent scholarship to the rapidly growing field of research on the Templars. Nicholson, a Senior Lecturer in History at Cardiff University, has been a widely regarded contributor to the scholarship on the medieval religious military orders since the publication of her *Templars, Hospitallers, and Teutonic Knights: Images of the Military Orders, 1128–1291* (1993). In the past decade, she has edited the proceedings of the second quadrennial international conference on the military orders (*Welfare and Warfare*; 1997), translated the *Itinerarium Peregrinorum et Gesta Regis Ricardi* (1997), presented a popular survey on *The Knights Hospitaller* (2001) as well as an in-depth study of the military orders in medieval epic and romance (*Love, War, and the Grail;* 2001), and published a number of articles, with those on women in the crusades and military orders being of particular interest.

Following an introduction which is noteworthy for its succinct survey of the sources available for the study of the Templars, the nine chapters of Nicholson's *The Knights Templar* address the origins of the order in the early twelfth century, the Templars' activities in the crusader states of the Latin East, their considerable involvement in the Iberian Peninsula and Eastern Europe, the order's organization and government, its religious life, the Templars' service at the courts of European kings, their commercial activities, the trial, and the Templar myth. Thus, the book is not a chronological but a thematic treatment of the order's history, and it shows the Templars' involvement on all frontiers of medieval Latin Christendom. Considering Nicholson's previous research, it comes as no surprise that criticism directed at the Templars by contemporaries receives a masterful treatment in this new book as well. Nicholson makes it quite clear that the downfall of the Templars was not predictable. She successfully demonstrates how the order's early poverty, due to society's only slowly emerging support for this "new knighthood", led to the Templars' concern for resources and emphasis on stewardship, which the order's contemporaries, once donations started to flow more freely, eventually interpreted as "greed". However, while the Templars' ambiguous reputation did make them susceptible to constant criticism, this criticism actually became weaker in the second half of the thirteenth century. Nicholson shows that, in the thirteenth and fourteenth centuries, accusations levelled at religious orders, including charges of heresy, were, in fact, rather common, and that the Templars were only singled out by King Philip IV of France and his advisors when they had become particularly vulnerable after the fall of Acre in 1291. Since the Templars had been so prominent in the defence of the Holy Land, the loss of the crusader states left them, at least for the time being, without a meaningful task to perform, but with considerable wealth to administer. Thus, the book's chapter on the trial of the Templars offers a fascinating tour d'horizon of the many factors that contributed to the downfall of the order, culminating in the author's provocative but comprehensible claim that the destruction of the order's central convent in Cyprus by King Henry II in 1310 rendered the ongoing trial in France "irrelevant" as, in the future, the order would have been unable to function without its "centre of operations" (p. 237).

Next to *The Oxford Illustrated History of the Crusades* (ed. Jonathan Riley-Smith; 1995), Nicholson's *The Knights Templar* is probably the most superbly illustrated volume currently available in the field of crusade and military orders history. Over 150 plates of high quality, including magnificent pictures by Albatross Photography Ltd. (Israel) and excellent reproductions of manuscripts and seals from various European libraries and archives, heighten the reading and viewing pleasure. Among the maps and figures, some readers will find the side-by-side synopsis of the "monastic day" according to the Rule of Saint Benedict and the "Templars' day" according to the Rule of the Templars especially useful (pp. 138–39). With regard to its documentation style in the form of endnotes which, for the most part, guide the reader to a wide selection of scholarly works discussing specific points raised in the text, Nicholson's *The Knights Templar* is comparable to Demurger's *Vie et mort*, albeit naturally more up to date. It is also noteworthy that translations of a number of primary sources, particularly excerpts from chronicles and charters, are inserted throughout the text of the book, allowing the reader a direct glimpse at how contemporaries viewed the Templars. As Helen Nicholson is quick to point out, *The Knights Templar* is not only based on her research, but also on her teaching of the upper-division undergraduate course on the military orders at Cardiff University (p. xvii). The author of this review has used *The Knights Templar* as an additional text in his senior research seminar on the crusades and the Latin East where students have commented favourably on the book's high didactic value and readability. Thus, it is safe to say that, while "aimed at a general readership" (p. xviii), *The Knights Templar* will be welcomed by students, crusade historians, medievalists, and enthusiasts alike.

JOCHEN BURGTORF
CALIFORNIA STATE UNIVERSITY, FULLERTON

La Orden del Santo Sepulcro. III jornadas de estudio, ed. Centro de Estudios Sobre la Orden del Santo Sepulcro. Zaragoza: Tipo Linea S.A., 2000. Pp. 417. ISBN 84 8324 090 4.

In recent years, interest in the non-military orders of the crusader states has been growing. This is particularly true for the Order of the Holy Sepulchre, on which a number of monographs and conference proceedings have been published within the last decade. One of the areas where investigation into the Order of the Holy Sepulchre's history has recently been most vigorous has been Spain. A *Centro de Estudios sobre la Orden del Santo Sepulcro* was founded in 1991 with financial support from the Equestrian Order of the Holy Sepulchre and the Spanish Canonesses of the Holy Sepulchre. Under its auspices, *jornadas de estudio sobre la orden del Santo Sepulcro* have been organized periodically in Aragón (Spain). The proceedings of the third and hitherto last of these congresses follows the path laid down by its predecessors, first, by grouping the contributions under the three headings *historia*, *arte* and *espiritualidad*, and second (more importantly), by printing contributions by canonesses, members of the Equestrian Order of the Holy Sepulchre and by "professional historians" side by side. As each of these groups tends to approach the order's history with clearly defined heuristic aims, contradictions are bound to arise. The editors of the proceedings have not tried to even out the different points of view but have instead – perhaps wisely – opted for publishing contributions by all three groups jointly, inconsistent as the various approaches might be. Consequently, one finds highly specialized articles, some of which present important new archival findings, next to rather general overviews; contributions with a strong personal touch are combined with pointed statements about the past, present and future of the Equestrian Order of the Holy Sepulchre.

Not many articles of this volume refer directly to the crusades or the Latin East, with two exceptions: the concise overview of the kingdom and the patriarchate of Jerusalem from 1100 to 1130 by Luis García Guijarro (pp. 23–43), and the attempt by Emilio Quintanilla Martínez to maintain that the Dome of the Rock served as a model for some Spanish rotundae (pp. 331–39). Most contributions are centred on the sixteenth to twentieth centuries, by which time the order had become a largely regional institution and the crusader states no longer existed. Thus, the majority of the art-historical articles (pp. 221–318) are case studies of single churches, largely in Aragón. The section on spirituality (pp. 321–407) appears to be equally disengaged from the history of the Latin East, for it centres on the present day canonesses and their spiritual foundations. In one way, however, both sections are connected to the crusade period: these and most other contributions confirm the central role that the Holy Land – the Order of the Holy Sepulchre's place of origin – continued to play long after Jerusalem was lost to the Christians and the international Order of the Holy Sepulchre was abolished. The order's iconography and spirituality remained intimately connected to the Holy City.

Among the historical articles, some present general summaries of earlier historiography. José González Ayala, for example, introduces the volume with a short synopsis of his own path-breaking book of 1970 (pp. 11–21), and Isabel Carretero Gimeno lists the houses of canonesses in Spain (pp. 165–76). Other pieces reflect the wish to associate as many institutions as possible with the Order of the Holy Sepulchre or to establish a particularly long history for certain houses. In one such article, Philip L. Daniel presents a survey of the churches dedicated to the Holy Sepulchre in England (pp. 43–55). While one can only agree with his scepticism toward unsupported attribution of rotundae to the Templars or the Order of the Holy Sepulchre, his intent to extend the list of Holy Sepulchre houses presented by Nikolaus von der Decken during the second *jornadas de estudio* in 1995 lacks consistency by relying too often on "local folk memory" or other vague sources. Modesto Pedro Bescós Torres (pp. 139–53) goes much further: he does not produce any sound reason whatsoever for declaring the Holy Sepulchre church of Barbastro to have been a house of the order. Adrián Arcaz Pozo's article on the filiations in Galicia (pp. 177–88) is a good survey of the province's structure, but he is too uncritical in accepting the list of Galician houses named in Honorius II's bull *Habitantes in domo* of 1128 as a reflection of the order's true structure, although in reality many of the listed churches were never incorporated.

Some contributions should be singled out because they present new thoughts and findings based on a careful reading of the sources. A series of such articles deals with aspects of the history, architecture and art of particular Aragonese houses in the modern era. These include the works by Maria Concepción García Albares on the visitations and statutes of San Nicolás in Zaragoza during the sixteenth and seventeenth centuries (p. 77–87); José Ramón Villanueva Herrero's description of the effects the Napoleonic wars in Zaragoza in general and on San Nicolás in particular (pp. 89–102 and 103–17); the survey by Emilio Quintanilla Martínez and Wifredo Rincón García of the Zaragozan priors and the works of art or restorations they commissioned (pp. 119–38); and finally, Andrés Álvarez Gracia's and Amelia López-Yarto Elizalde's works on the ceramics and reliquaries of the Aragonese houses (pp. 253–62 and 273–85 respectively).

Other contributions are centred on the Middle Ages and consequently concern (if only indirectly) the crusades and the Latin East. Gloria López de la Plaza lists 108 documents from the fourteenth to seventeenth centuries, now housed in the Archivo Histórico Nacional in Madrid, that pertain to the house of San Nicolás in Zaragoza (pp. 57–76). Concepción de la Fuente Cobos's well-documented case study of the Aragonese commandery at Nuévalos (pp. 155–63) is particularly important, for it presents a summary of edited as well as unpublished material on the house's history. Carlos Barquero Goñi offers a series of new references on the abolition of the Order of the Holy Sepulchre in Castile which he compares to the situation in Aragón (pp. 189–97). It remains unclear, however, exactly why King Ferdinand of Aragon effectively defended the order's independence in his realm, contrary to the king of Castile's policy. Katharina Pieper draws on largely ignored documents in order to convincingly re-date the third phase of the impressive mudejar church at Tobed (pp. 287–91). And finally, Gabriel Llompart provides editions of four previously unknown thirteenth- and fourteenth-century charters on the history of the poorly documented Holy Sepulchre filiation of Mallorca (pp. 311–18). Thus, in spite of the inconsistencies among the articles assembled in this volume, one must congratulate the editors for having succeeded in publishing, for the third time in less than a decade, a collection that once again reflects the ample heuristic and methodological possibilities the Order of the Holy Sepulchre offers to historians, art historians and theologians alike.

NIKOLAS JASPERT
UNIVERSITÄT ERLANGEN-NÜRNBERG

Geoffrey Regan, *First Crusader: Byzantium's Holy Wars.* Stroud: Sutton Publishing Limited, 2001. Pp. vii, 280 pp. ISBN 0 75909 2026 2.

Regan's "First Crusader" is the Emperor Herakleios (610–641), who at the eleventh hour saved the Roman empire from conquest by the Persians. Key to his victory, Regan argues, was the concept of Holy War, which united and inspired Roman resistance. Less than five years later, however, all his gains were swept away by the armies of Islam, also inspired by a concept of holy war. In both cultures warfare continued to have a religious dimension through the following centuries, but in the Roman world (or Byzantium as its more convenient to call it) this was more ambiguous, and when Byzantine armies went on the offensive in the tenth century Regan believes that the appeal to Christianity was more a political device than an inspiring motive. Herakleios, the emperor who sacked the great Sasanian fire temple at Takht-i Sulaiman, was a crusader; Nikephoros Phokas and John Tzimiskes, warriors who did not try to recapture Jerusalem, were only "ersatz crusaders", imitations of the real thing.

Regan is certainly right to insist on the relevance of the earlier history of holy war to our understanding of post-1095 crusades. So much of the culture of the Middle Ages has its roots in late antiquity, and the crusades are no exception. Would-be crusaders need to know about Constantine and Theodosios, Herakleios and Muhammad, Nikephoros Phokas and Sayf al-Dawla. Unfortunately Regan is only patchily aware of scholarship over the last quarter century that has transformed our understanding of the period, and has not always paid attention to the works he does cite. Informed editing, and another six months research could have made a big difference. As it stands this is an unreliable book more likely to confuse than help.

MARK WHITTOW
ST PETER'S COLLEGE, OXFORD

The Synodicum Nicosiense and other Documents of the Latin Church of Cyprus, 1196–1373, selected and trans. by Christopher Schabel (Texts and Studies in the History of Cyprus 39). Nicosia: Cyprus Research Centre, 2001. Pp. 393. ISBN 9963 0 8073 1.

Il faut saluer d'abord la poursuite de l'effort du Centre de Recherches de Chypre pour publier les sources de l'histoire de Chypre. Il s'agit ici de textes concernant l'Eglise latine de Chypre aux XIIIe et XIVe siècles et qui font suite à l'édition du cartulaire de l'église Sainte-Sophie de Nicosie due au même auteur, associé à N. Coureas, parue dans la même série en 1997 (*The Cartulary of the Cathedral of Holy Wisdom of Nicosia* [Cyprus Research Centre, Texts and Studies in the History of Cyprus 25]). C. Schabel offre maintenant l'édition accompagnée d'une traduction en anglais d'un autre monument de l'histoire ecclésiastique chypriote à l'époque franque, le *Synodicum Nicosiense*, auquel l'auteur a ajouté en seconde partie la traduction d'un certain nombre de documents concernant notamment les relations entre Grecs et Latins, tirés soit du cartulaire de Sainte-Sophie, soit des lettres pontificales.

Le *Synodicum Nicosiense* appelé également *Constitutiones Nicosienses* est un ensemble de textes, sans ordre chronologique strict, réglant la vie de l'église de Chypre, rappelant la position de l'église romaine sur la place à réserver au clergé grec et sur les questions de morale et de doctrine. Il s'ouvre par un règlement de l'archevêque Hugues de Fagiano concernant la morale du clergé et des laïcs de 1252, mais les textes les plus anciens sont le fait du légat pontifical Eudes de Châteauroux, qui accompagnait la croisade de Louis IX, et datent de 1249. Cette compilation, selon un précédent article de C. Schabel ("Elias de Nabinaux, Archbishop of Nicosia, and the Intellectual History of Later Medieval Cyprus", *Cahiers de l'Institut du Moyen Age grec et latin*, 68 [1998], 35–52), est due à l'archevêque Elias de Nabinaux et date d'environ 1340; il s'y ajoute quelques textes de l'archevêque Philippe de 1353–54. Dans l'introduction de présentation des documents, Schabel est en mesure d'attribuer à l'archevêque Ranulph (1278–85) un ensemble de textes, le groupe marqué B, concernant l'église grecque et les sacrements, qui jusqu'alors avaient été attribués à un archevêque Raphael inconnu par ailleurs, qui peut donc être éliminé de la liste des archevêques latins de Nicosie.

Le texte du *Synodicum Nicosiense* était connu grâce notamment à l'édition de Mansi (*Sacrorum conciliorum nova et amplissima collectio*, vol. 26 [Venise, 1784], cols. 311–382 pour le Synodicum), la plus courante. Le manuscrit original a disparu; C. Schabel a repris le texte de la première édition, celle de Philippe Labbé et Gabriel Cossart (dans *Sacrosancta concilia ad regiam editionem exacta*, vol. 11, part. II [Paris, 1671], cols. 2376–2441), ajoutant en apparat critique les variantes des autres éditions. Le texte latin est clairement présenté sur la page de gauche, divisé en paragraphes, avec les insertions tirées de législations antérieures bien distinctes, ce qui rend son utilisation aisée. La traduction anglaise, sur la page de droite, respecte la même disposition. Les notes ont été réduites au minimum, indiquant seulement les variantes et les références aux textes bibliques ou à d'autres textes législatifs. L'ouvrage est de présentation agréable et de maniement aisé, grâce notamment à son index.

L'ouvrage s'ouvre par une bibliographie des travaux cités, suivi d'une introduction présentant les sources de l'histoire ecclésiastique de Chypre à l'époque franque, la composition du *Synodicum Nicosiense*, et justifiant la sélection des 61 textes traduits dans la seconde partie. Ces derniers sont les textes essentiels de l'histoire ecclésiastique de Chypre pendant les deux premiers siècles du gouvernement des Lusignan, comme les chartes de fondation de l'église latine de Célestin III (1196–97), les décrets de Pierre Capuano, que C. Schabel date de 1204 et non de 1223 comme il était généralement admis, des accords de Limassol (1220) et de Famagouste (1222), de plusieurs bulles pontificales dont la fameuse *Bulla Cypria*, et des documents concernant certaines affaires (visite apostolique de la cathédrale de Lefkara, élection de l'évêque de Solea, emprisonnement des évêques grecs, troubles au monastère de Saint-Georges des Manganes), à l'origine de textes contenus dans le *Synodicum*.

Une importante introduction historique est destinée à mettre en valeur les documents en suivant uniquement le fil directeur des relations entre Eglise latine et Eglise grecque: elle commence par une étude historiographique critique du sujet, de la confusion fréquente entre hérétique et schismatique, suivi d'un essai de 32 pages sur "l'église séculière latine de Chypre et les Grecs de 1196 à 1373", reprenant et mettant dans leur contexte les textes édités dans le volume. L'auteur suit de près l'action propre de chacun des archevêques et des légats, la politique pontificale vis-à-vis de l'Eglise grecque, et note que malgré des divergences doctrinales notamment concernant les azymes, les prélats grecs ont usé de la possibilité d'appel à Rome en cas de conflit avec l'église latine locale. Il est peut-être dommage que seul l'aspect des relations entre les deux Eglises ait été analysé en détail, et de plus séparé de l'ensemble du contexte politique de l'île.

En somme, ce livre, s'il ne présente pas de textes nouveaux, rectifie un certain nombre d'appréciations et de points de chronologie et rend facilement accessibles les principales sources concernant l'établissement et les premiers temps de l'église latine de Chypre ainsi que ses relations avec l'église grecque.

CATHERINE OTTEN
UNIVERSITÉ DE STRASBOURG

I Templari, la guerra e la santità, ed. Simonetta Cerrini. Rimini: Il Cerchio Iniziative Editoriali, 2000. Pp. 167. ISBN 88 86583 73 7 (paperback).

In July 1995 the abbey of Colomba di Chiaravalle, near Piacenza, hosted a one day conference on the knights of the Temple, as part of the celebrations for the 9th centenary of the Council of Piacenza – Clermont. Five years later, Simonetta Cerrini, well-known scholar of the rule of the Temple and organizer of the event, edited the proceedings of the conference, which constitute this collection of essays.

After a short introduction by the editor (pp. 5–8), Franco Cardini ("I cristiani, la guerra e la santità", pp. 9–17) surveys the complex relations between war and sanctity in the Christian world, showing how, within the framework of the evolving concept of *iustum bellum* ("just war"), the members of the new religious chivalric orders introduced a novelty that struck – not always positively – the contemporary observers. Simonetta Cerrini ("I templari: una vita da *fratres*, ma una regola anti-ascetica; una vita da cavalieri, ma una regola anti-eroica", pp. 19–48) explains the development of the rule of the Templars as an original re-interpretation of the Benedictine rule. Alain Demurger ("Gli ordini religioso-militari e la guerra tra il XII e il XIII secolo", pp. 49–68) examines the contribution of the military orders (Templars, Hospitallers, Teutonic Knights) to the war in the crusader states, stressing their innovations in castle building and in fighting techniques. Fulvio Bramato ("La 'guerra' e la 'santità' nelle *domus* templari italiane delle origini. Note ed appunti a margine di alcune fonti narrative", pp. 69–83) uses three narrative Latin texts (*Historia Mediolanensis* by Landolfo di San Paolo, *Vita S. Bernardi* by Geoffroi d'Auxerre, *Historia translationis sancti Nicolai Peregrini*) to clarify the political behaviour of the Templar community in twelfth-century Italy. In her long essay ("Manoscritti liturgici dei templari e degli ospitalieri: le nuove prospettive aperte dal sacramentario templare di Modena (Biblioteca capitolare O. II. 13)", pp. 85–131), Cristina Dondi carefully describes a *Sacramentarium* (end twelfth/beginning thirteenth centuries) used by the Templars of Modena; the evidence offered by this and other manuscripts points to a centrifugal trend in the liturgical domain, which fits with the relative independence from the central authority enjoyed by the European Templar communities. Finally, Anthony Luttrell ("Templari e ospitalieri: alcuni confronti", pp. 133–52) compares the two most prominent military orders and suggests that their differences could account for the diverging destinies of the Temple and the Hospital. The book is closed by a bibliographical survey by Simonetta Cerrini ("L'ordine del Tempio. Aggiornamento bibliografico", pp. 153–63), which covers the 1980s and 1990s.

LAURA MINERVINI
UNIVERSITÀ DI NAPOLI FEDERICO II

SOCIETY FOR THE STUDY OF THE CRUSADES AND THE LATIN EAST

BULLETIN No. 24, 2004

Editorial

Last year's resignation of our treasurer had some consequences for the present Bulletin. The reason for this was that the treasurer not only keeps the accounts and the official records with the members' addresses but that he also collects the information for the Bulletin. So this time the Bulletin editor has tried to contact the members directly, and he wishes to apologise for all confusions, troubles or delays that this procedure may have caused. We all hope that the Society will be able to find a new treasurer as soon as possible who will then settle all questions concerning membership fees and subscriptions.

Our journal entitled *Crusades* is now well established. It allows the Society to publish articles and texts; encourages research in neglected subfields; invites a number of authors to deal with a specific problem within a comparative framework; initiates and reports on joint programmes; and offers reviews of books and articles. Editors: Benjamin Z. Kedar and Jonathan Riley-Smith; associate editors: Helen Nicholson and Michael Evans; review editor: Christoph Maier.

Colleagues may submit papers for consideration to either of the editors, Professor Benjamin Z. Kedar and Professor Jonathan S. C. Riley-Smith. A copy of the most recent *Speculum* style sheet may be obtained either from one of the two editors or online at: http://freespace.virgin.net/nigel.nicholson/SSCLE/sscleguidelines.htm

The journal includes a section of book reviews. In order to facilitate the review editor's work, could members please tell their publishers about the new journal and ask them to send copies to: **Dr Christoph T. Maier, Review editor, *Crusades*, Sommergasse 20, CH-4056 Basel, Switzerland**. Please note that *Crusades* reviews books concerned with any aspect(s) of the history of the crusades and the crusade movement, the military orders and the Latin settlements in the Eastern Mediterranean, but not books which fall outside this range.

The cost of the journal to individual members is £20, $30 or €33; the cost to institutions and non-members is £65, $95 or €105. Cheques should be made payable to SSCLE.

Members may opt to receive the Bulletin alone at the current membership price (single £11, $15 or €17; student £6, $9 or €10; joint £15, $23 or €25). The new treasurer will take over the records and try to answer all questions concerning the membership fees in due time. Those members who do not subscibe to the journal will receive the Bulletin from the Bulletin editor to whom the publisher of *Crusades* sends the copies.

Although the Society does not have a formal website, there are two websites in existence set up by previous treasurers, Michael Markowski and Helen Nicholson:

http://people.westminstercollege.edu/faculty/mmarkowski/mmpage.html
http://freespace.virgin.net/nigel.nicholson/SSCLE

These contain information about how to join the Society and attempt to answer various questions about the crusades commonly asked by members of the public. There are also links to conferences and publications that may be of interest.

Karl Borchardt

Message from the President

Dear Member,

Our Society will be very busy in the next years. As you know, we are organizing the Conference in Istanbul from 25 to 30 August 2004. The main theme will deal with the Fourth Crusade, but every member can present a paper on every matter relating to the Crusades and the Latin East.

Then, in July 2005, we shall have a special session at the Conference of the International Commission of Historical Sciences in Sydney. The theme will be "Latins and Oriental Christians in the Crusader States", under Beni Kedar's and my responsibility. You can send your proposal to us from now on.

As you know, our periodical "Crusades" is a real success. The editorial board is accepting typescripts for publication in number 4, next year, so you are cordially invited to send a paper to the board.

I hope to see most of you at our great meeting in Istanbul, prepared with the collaboration of Nevra Necipoglu, professor of Byzantine History at the Bosphorus University. Sophia Menache, our secretary, will send you all the information requested in due course.

Michel Balard

Contents

List of abbreviations

20BS: XXe Congrès International des Études Byzantines, Paris, 19–25 August 2001.

CLE-Seminar: The Crusades and the Latin East Seminar, Institute of Historical Research and Emmanuel College, Cambridge or London.

EI: The Encyclopedia of Islam.

Els Catalans a la Mediterrània oriental a l'edat mitjana, Jornadas Cientifiques de l'Institut d'Estudis Catalans, Secciò Històrico-arqueològica, Barcelona, 16 i 17 de novembre de 2000, ed. Maria Teresa Ferrer i Mallol, Sèrie jornadas cientifiques 11 (Barcelona: Institut d'Estudis Catalans, 2003).

EncycCru: Encyclopedia of the Crusades, ed. Alan V. Murray (ABC-Clio, 2004).

Experience I and II: The Experience of Crusading, vol. 1: Western Approaches, ed. Norman Housley and Marcus Bull; vol. 2: Defining the Crusader Kingdom, ed. Peter Edbury and Jonathan Phillips (Cambridge: UP, 2003), 307pp., xvi+311pp.

Gesta: Dei Gesta per Francos, Crusade Studies in Honour of Jean Richard, ed. Michel Balard, Benjamin Z. Kedar and Jonathan Riley-Smith (Aldershot: Ashgate, 2001), 434pp.

HES: International colloquium on the History of Egypt and Syria in the Fatimid, Ayyubid and Mamluk Eras, Katholieke Universiteit Leuven.

IMC: International Medieval Congress, Kalamazoo or Leeds.

International Mobility: International Mobility in the Military Orders (Twelfth to Fifteenth Centuries), Selected Papers of the IMC, Leeds 8–9 July 2002, ed. Helen J. Nicholson and Jochen Burgtorf (Cardiff: Univ. of Wales Press).

MO3: The Military Orders, vol. 3: Their History and Heritage, ed. William G. Zajac (Aldershot: Ashgate, forthcoming).

Mosaics: Studies in Honor of Arthur H. S. Megaw, ed. J. Herrin, M. Mullett and Catherine Otten-Froux, Annual of the British School at Athens, Supplementary volume 8 (London, 2001).

OM XII: Ordines Militares – Colloquia Torunensia Historica XII, Die Ritterorden in der europäischen Wirtschaft des Mittelalters, ed. Roman Czaja and Jürgen Sarnowsky (Toruń, 2003), 214pp.; OM XIII: Selbstbild und Selbstverständnis der geistlichen Ritterorden, Self-Image and Self-Perception of the Military Orders, Toruń, 26–28 September 2003.

Porphyrogenita: Essays on the History and Literature of Byzantium and the Latin East in Honour of Julian Chrysostomides, ed. Charalambos Dendrinos, Eirene Harvalia-Crook, Jonathan Harris and Judith Herrin (Aldershot: Ashgate, 2003).

Runciman-Conference: Terceras Jornadas Internacionales: Medio siglo de estudios sobre las Cruzadas y las Órdenes Militares, 1951–2001, A Tribute to Sir Steven Runciman, Universidad de Zaragoza y Ayuntamiento de Teruel, Teruel (Aragon), 19–25 July 2001, ed. Luis García-Guijarro Ramos (Madrid: Castelló d'Impressió SL).

ZDPV: Zeitschrift des Deutschen Palästina-Vereins.

1. Recent publications

AHN, Sang-Joon, Besitz und Wirtschaft der Johanniterkommende "St. Johann und Cordula" in Köln (unter besonderer Berücksichtigung der Wirtschaftsführung in dem Johanniterdorf Lövenich), in: OM XII 71–88.

AIRALDI, Gabriella, Memoria e memorie di un cavaliere: Caffaro di Genova, in: Crusades 2 (2003), 25–39.

ANDREA, Alfred J., Encyclopedia of the Crusades (Westport/Connecticut: Greenwood Press, 2003), xxiii, 356pp.; with John C. Moore, A Question of Character: Two Views on Innocent III and the Fourth Crusade, in: Innocenzo III: Urbs et Orbis, Atti del Congresso internazionale Roma 9–15 settembre 1998, ed. Andrea Sommerlechner, vol. 1 (Roma, 2003), 525–585.

ASLANOV, Cyril, Languages in Contact in the Latin East: Acre and Cyprus, in: Crusades 1 (2002), 155–181.

BALARD, Michel, Veneziani e Genovesi nel mondo egeo del Trecento, in: Bisanzio, Venezia e il mondo franco-greco (XIII–XV secolo), ed. Chryssa Maltezou and Peter Schreiner (Venezia, 2002), 189–202; Genova e il Levante (secc. XI–XII), in: Comuni e memoria storica: alle origini del comune di Genova, Atti del Convegno di studi, Genova 24–26 settembre 2001 (Genova, 2002), 527–549; Venise et Chypre à la fin du XIIIe et au début du XIVe siècle, in: Kyprus – Benetia, Koines Historikes Tyches, Atene, 1–3 marzo 2001, ed. Chryssa Maltezou (Venezia, 2002), 45–58; La route de la foi: les chemins de la croisade, in: La Corse, carrefour des routes de Méditerranée, ed. Michel Vergé-Franceschi and Antoine-Marie Graziani (Ajaccio, 2003), 15–27; Les Catalans dans l'Outre-Mer génois aux XIIIe–XIVe siècles, in: Els Catalans 103–111; Costantinopoli e le città pontiche all'apogeo del Medioevo, in: Le città del Mediterraneo all'apogeo dello sviluppo medievale: aspetti economici e sociali, ed. Giovanni Cherubini, XVIII Convegno internazionale di studi (Pistoia, 2003), 1–18; Pisa e il mondo bizantino, in: Pisa e il Mediterraneo, ed. Marco Tangheroni (Milano, 2003), 228–233; A Christian Mediterranean, 1000–1500, in: The Mediterranean in History, ed. David Abulafia (London, 2003), 183–217; L'expansion occidentale (XIe–XVe siècles): Formes et conséquences, Introduction, in: L'expansion occidentale (XIe–XVe siècles): Formes et conséquences, Actes du XXXIIIe Congrès de la Société des Historiens Médiévistes de l'Enseignement Supérieur (Paris, 2003), 11–22; ed., Dictionnaire de la France médiévale (Paris: Hachette, 2003).

BALLETTO, Laura, Fonti notarili inedite su Caffa e sul Mar Nero tra XIV e XV secolo, in: Il Mar Nero, IV (1999/2000 [published 2003]), 161–177; Tra Andros veneziana e Chio dei Genovesi nel Quattrocento, in: Thesaurismata 31 (2001 [published 2003]), 89–105; L'isola di Chio nei traffici commerciali tra Occidente e Vicino Oriente nel XV secolo, in: Miscellanea 2002, Collana di Studi Valbormidesi, ed. Giannino Balbis, 5 (Millesimo, 2002), 17–37; Tra Cipro, Venezia e Genova nel XV secolo, in: Atti del Simposio internazionale Kyprus – Benetia, Koines Historikes Tyches, Atene, 1–3 marzo 2001, ed. Chryssa Maltezou, Istituto Ellenico di Studi Bizantini e Postbizantini di Venezia – Ambasciata di Cipro, Casa di Cipro – Biblioteca Gennadios, Scuola Americana di Studi Classici, Convegni 6 (Venezia, 2002), 85–106; Religione e potere politico negli insediamenti genovesi del Vicino Oriente, in: Studi in memoria di Giorgio Costamagna, ed. Dino Puncuh (Genova: Società Ligure di Storia Patria, 2003), 107–116; Fra Genovesi e Catalani nel Vicino Oriente nel secolo XV, in: Els Catalans 167–190.

BELLOMO, Elena, A servizio di Dio e del Santo Sepolcro: Caffaro e l'Oriente latino (Padova: Medioevo Europeo, Studi, 2002), 263pp.; Tra Bizantini e Normanni: i Genovesi in Oltremare agli esordi del XII secolo, in: Miscellanea in memoria di Giorgio Costamagna, ed. Dino Puncuh, Atti della Società Ligure di Storia Patria n.s. 43/I,1 (2003), 143–166; Italian translation of Translatio sancti Marci, in: Cronache, ed. Giorgio Fedalto and Luigi Andrea Berto, Corpus Scriptorum Ecclesiae Aquileiensis 12/2, Concili e cronache 2 (Aquileia, 2003), 468–485.

BEREND, Nora, Défense de la Chrétienté et naissance d'une identité: Hongrie, Pologne et péninsule Ibérique au Moyen Âge, in: Annales: Histoire, Sciences Sociales 58/5 (2003),

1009–1027; ed. with David Abulafia, Medieval Frontiers: Concepts and Practices (Aldershot: Ashgate, 2002).

BISAHA, Nancy, Pope Pius II's Letter to Sultan Mehmed II: a reexamination, in: Crusades 1 (2002), 183–200.

BOMBI, Barbara, I procuratori dell'Ordine Teutonico tra il XIII e XIV secolo: studi sopra un inedito rotolo pergamenaceo del Geheimes Staatsarchiv PK di Berlino, in: Römische Historische Mitteilungen 44 (2002), 193–297; Un inedito *memoriale* dell'Archivio dei procuratori dell'Ordine Teutonico del principio del XIV secolo, in: Quellen und Forschungen aus italienischen Archiven und Bibliotheken 82 (2002), 47–121; Gli archivi dei procuratori dell'Ordine Teutonico: Considerazioni intorno a due documenti inediti dell'inizio del XIV secolo, in: La memoria dei chiostri, Prima Giornata di Studi Medievali, Labratorio di storia monastica dell'Italia settentrionale, Castiglione delle Stiviere – Mantova 11–13 ottobre 2001, ed. Giancarlo Andenna and Renata Salvarani (Brescia, 2002), 257–267; Due inediti rotoli pergamenacei: L'Ordine Teutonico e la sua organizzazione archivistica al principio del XIV secolo, in: Scrineum 1 (2003) http://dobc.unipv.it/scrineum

BONNEAUD, Pierre, Le rôle politique des ordres militaires dans la Couronne d'Aragon pendant l'Interrègne de 1410 à 1412 à travers les 'Anales' de Zurita, in: Aragón e la Edad Media XIV–XV (Zaragoza, 1999), 119–141; Diferencias y conflictos entre Alfonso el Magnanimo, el Maestre de Rodas y los Hospitalarios Catalanes (1426–1436), in: Las Órdenes militares en la Península Ibérica, vol. 1: Edad Media, ed. Ricardo Izquierdo Benito and Francisco Ruiz Gómez (Cuenca, 2000).

BORCHARDT, Karl, Wirtschaft und Ordensreform im späten Mittelalter: Das Beispiel der Johanniter in Straßburg (mit Ausblick auf Breslau), in: OM XII 35–53; Soll-Zahlen zum Personalstand der deutschen Johanniter vom Jahre 1367, in: Revue Mabillon 75 (2003), 83–113.

CHĘĆ, Adam, Der Ordenshof in Klein-Montau: Die Ergebnisse der archäologischen Ausgrabungen im Jahr 2001, in: OM XII 183–195.

CIPOLLONE, Giulio, Foi et religions, proximitè et distance: les possibles chemins pour la paix, in: Les religions et la culture de la paix, Congresso organizzato dall'Università Ezzitouna (Tunis, 16–18 aprile 2001), Ettanouir 5 (2002/03), 1–39; La violenza nelle religioni, in: Le religioni di fronte al problema della violenza, Atti del Congresso 'Le religioni di fronte al problema della violenza' (Assisi, 22–26 agosto 2002), ed. Ignazio Sanna e Paola De Simone (Roma, 2003), 12–40; Europa e Islam: Il confronto sui valori, in: Rivista di Studi Politici Internazionali 70 (2003), 179–202.

CLAVERIE, Pierre-Vincent, De l'entourage royal à l'entourage pontifical: l'exemple méconnu de l'archêveque Gilles de Tyr (†1266), in: 'A l'ombre du pouvoir': Les entourages princiers au Moyen Âge, ed. Alain Marchandisse and Jean-Louis Kupper (Genève: Librairie Droz, 2003), 55–76; Vers un réexamen de la condition des Juifs sous les lois de Majorque, in: Perpignan: L'Histoire des Juifs dans la ville (XIIe–XXe siècles) (Perpignan: Agence Canibals, 2003), 91–98.

COUREAS, Nicholas, The Foundation Rules of Medieval Cypriot Monasteries: Makhairas and St. Neophytos (Nicosia: Cyprus Research Centre, 2002); Cyprus and Ragusa (Dubrovnik) 1280–1450, in: Mediterranean Historical Review (December 2002); Commercial Relations between Cyprus and Chios 1300–1480, in: Epetirida tou Kentrou Epistimonikon Erevnon 29 (Nicosia, 2003); The Role of the Templars and the Hospitallers in the Movement of Commodities Involving Cyprus 1291–1312, in: Experience II; The Greek-Rite Monastery of the Holy Saviour of Lingua Maris in Sicily 1334–1415, in: Porphyrogenita; The Genesis and

Development of Cyprus' Modern Latin Community after 1571 [in Greek], in: Epeteris tes Kypriakes Hetaireias Historikon Spoudon (Nicosia, 2003).

CRAWFORD, Paul, The Templar of Tyre: Part III of the Deeds of the Cypriots, Crusade Texts in Translation 6 (Aldershot: Ashgate, 2003); The Military Orders in Italy, in: Medieval Italy: An Encyclopedia, ed. Christopher Kleinhenz and John W. Barker (Routledge, 2003).

DEMIRKENT, Işin, Edessa in the Middle Ages, in: Edessa, the Gate to Civilization (Istanbul: YKV, 2002), 47–67; Recueil des Historiens des Croisades, II. Historiens grecs, in: Belleten LXV 244 (Ankara: Türk Tarih Kurumu, 2002), 921–958.

DICKSON, Gary, Innocent III and the Children's Crusade, in: Innocenzo III: Urbs et Orbis, Atti del Congresso internazionale Roma 9–15 settembre 1998, ed. Andrea Sommerlechner, vol. 1 (Roma 2003), 586–597.

DOSTOURIAN, Ara, Armenia and the Crusades: The Chronicle of Matthew of Edessa, Translated from the Original Armenian with Commentary and Introduction (Lanham Univ. Press of America, 1993).

DYGO, Marian, Die Wirtschaftstätigkeit des Deutschen Ordens in Preußen im 14.–15. Jahrhundert, in: OM XII 147–161.

EDBURY, Peter, ed., John of Ibelin, Le Livre des Assises (Leiden: Brill, 2003), x+854pp.; ed. with Jonathan Phillips, Experience II; Reading John of Jaffa, in: ibid. 135–157; Fiefs and Vassals in the Kingdom of Jerusalem: from the Twelfth Century to the Thirteenth, in: Crusades 1 (2002 [2003]), 49–62.

EDGINGTON, Susan B., Romance and Reality in the Sources for the Sieges of Antioch, 1097–8, in: Porphyrogenita 33–46; The First Crusade in Post-War Fiction, in: Experience I 255–280; 'Crusades', 'Richard I', in: The Reader's Guide to British History, ed. David M. Loades (Fitzroy-Dearborn, 2003), 323–324, 1118–1119; The First Crusade (New York: Rosen, 2004), 64pp. [schoolbook].

van EICKELS, Klaus, Wein, Zölle, Kredite: Wirtschaftliche Struktur, Verwaltungsaufgaben und Funktion der Deutschordensballei Koblenz für den Hochmeister, in: OM XII 129–146.

ELLENBLUM, Ronnie, Frontier Activities: the Transformation of a Muslim Sacred Site into the Frankish Castle of Vadum Iacob, in: Crusades 2 (2003), 83–97.

FAVREAU-LILIE, Marie-Luise, Frömmigkeit und Geschäft: Die vielen Motive der Kreuzfahrer, in: Welt und Umwelt der Bibel, Heft 3 / 2003 (Stuttgart, 2003), 15–17; Palästinareisen im späten Mittelalter: Die Bedeutung Venedigs als Einschiffungshafen, in: Berliner Wissenschaftliche Gesellschaft, Jahrbuch 2002, ed. Bernd Soesemann (Berlin, 2003), 137–162; Welf IV. und der Kreuzzug von 1101, in: Welf IV., Schlüsselfigur einer Wendezeit: Regionale und europäische Perspektiven, ed. Dieter Bauer and Matthias Becher (Frankfurt/Main, 2004), 420–447.

FLORI, Jean, Ricardo Cuor di Lione, Il re cavaliere (Torino: Einaudi, 2002); Ricardo corazon de Leon (Barcelona: Edhasa, 2002) [tr. of Richard Cœur de Lion (Paris, 1999)]; A propos de la première croisade: naissance et affirmation de l'idée de guerre sainte dans l'Occident chrétien (XIe s.), in: Imaginaires de guerre: L'histoire entre mythe et réalité, Textes réunis par Laurence van Ypersele, Transversalité 3 (Louvain, 2003), 31–43; De la paix de Dieu à la croisade? Un réexamen, in: Crusades 2 (2003), 1–23; Ambroise, propagateur de l'idéologie Plantagenêt?, in: Culture politique des Plantagenêts (1154–1224), Actes di Colloque tenu à Poitiers du 2 au 5 mai 2002, ed. Martin Aurell (Poitiers, 2003), 173–187; La guerra santa: la formazione dell'idea di crociata nell'Occidente cristiano (Bologna: Il mulino, 2003) [tr. of La guerre sainte (Paris, 2001)]; Le crociate (Bologna: Il mulino, 2003).

FOREY, Alan, The Charitable Activities of the Templars, in: Viator 34 (2003), 109–141.

GERTWAGEN, Ruthy, The Venetian Colonies in the Ionian Sea and the Aegean in the Venetian Defensive Policy in the Fifteenth Century, in: Journal of Mediterranean Studies 12/2 (2002), 351–384.

GILLINGHAM, John, Two Yorkshire Historians Compared: Roger of Howden and William of Newburgh, in: Haskins Society Journal 12 (2002 [2003]), 15–37 [inter alia their treatment of an enthusiastic crusader, Roger de Mowbray].

GRABOIS, Aryeh, Terre sainte et Orient latin vus par Willebrand d'Oldenbourg, in: Gesta 261–268.

GUTH, Klaus, Religionsgespräche im Mittelalter: Peter Abaelards *Dialogus*, in: Freiburger Zeitschrift für Philosophie und Theologie 50 (2003), 136–149.

HARRIS, Jonathan, Byzantium and the Crusades (London: Hambledon & London, 2003); ed. with others, Porphyrogenita; Edward II, Andronicus II, and Giles d'Argenteim: an Unnoticed Episode in Anglo-Byzantine Relations, in: ibid. 77–84; Laonikos Chalkokondyles and the Rise of the Ottoman Empire, in: Byzantine and Modern Greek Studies 27 (2003), 153–170.

HESSE, Christian, ed. with Beat Immenhauser, Oliver Landolt and Barbara Studer, Personen der Geschichte, Geschichte der Personen: Studien zur Kreuzzugs-, Sozial- und Bildungsgeschichte, Festschrift für Rainer Christoph Schwinges zum 60. Geburtstag (Basel: Schwabe, 2003), xvi+500pp.

HOLMES, Catherine, ed. with Janet Waring, Education, Literacy and Manuscript Transmission in Byzantium and Beyond (Leiden, 2002); Byzantium's Eastern Frontier in the Tenth and Eleventh Centuries, in: Medieval Frontiers: Concepts and Practices, ed. David Abulafia and Nora Berend (Aldershot: Ashgate, 2002); The Rhetorical Structures of John Skylitzes: Synopsis Historion, in: Rhetoric in Byzantium, ed. Elizabeth Jeffreys (Aldershot: Ashgate, 2003); Basil II (A.D. 976–1025), in: De Imperatoribus Romanis, ed. Michael di Maio and Lynda Garland, Online Encyclopedia of Roman Emperors.

HOUBEN, Hubert, Die Wirtschaftsführung der Niederlassungen des Deutschen Ordens in Süditalien und auf Sizilien, in: OM XII 89–106.

HOUSLEY, Norman, ed. with Marcus Bull, Experience I; Costing the Crusade: Budgeting for Crusading Activity in the Fourteenth Century, in: ibid. 45–59; One Man and his Wars: the Depiction of Warfare by Marshal Boucicaut's Biographer, in: Journal of Medieval History 29 (2003), 27–40.

HUNYADI, Zsolt, *Milites Christi* in the Medieval Kingdom of Hungary: a Historiographical Overview, in: Chronica 3 (2003), 50–57.

IRWIN, Robert, Mamluk Literature, in: Mamluk Studies Review 7/1 (2003), 1–29; Orientalism and the Early Development of Crusading Studies, in: Experience II 214–230; Al-Maqrizi and Ibn Khaldun: Historians of the Unseen, in: Mamluk Studies Review 7/2 (2003), 217–230; Rural Feuding and Mamluk Faction Fighting in Medieval Egypt and Syria, in: Texts, Documents and Artefacts in Honour of D. S. Richards, ed. Chase F. Robinson (Leiden: Brill, 2003), 251–264; Gunpowder and Firearms in the Mamluk Kingdom Reconsidered, in: The Mamluks in Egyptian and Syrian Politics and Society, ed. Michael Winter and Amalia Levanoni (Leiden: Brill, 2003), 117–139; The Alhambra (Profile, 2004).

JACOBY, David, Il ruolo di Acri nel pellegrinaggio a Gerusalemme, in: Il cammino di Gerusalemme, Atti del II Convegno internazionale di studio, Bari – Brindisi – Trani, 18–22 maggio 1999, ed. Maria Stella Calò Mariani, Rotte mediterranee della cultura 2 (Bari: Mario Adda Editore, 2002), 31–50; Benjamin of Tudela in Byzantium, in: Crush Porta / Zlatyia

Vrata: Essays presented to Ihor Ševčenko on his Eightieth Birthday, ed. Peter Schreiner and Olga Strakhov, Palaeoslavica 10/1 (Cambridge/Mass., 2002), 180–185; Thessalonique de la domination de Byzance à celle de Venise: Continuité, adaptation ou rupture?, in: Mélanges Gilbert Dagron, Traxaux et Mémoires 14 (Paris, 2002), 303–318; Greeks in the Maritime Trade of Cyprus around the Mid-Fourteenth Century, in: Kyprus – Benetia: Koines Historikes Tyches, Atti del simposio internazionale Atene 1–3 marzo 2001, ed. Chryssa Maltezou (Venezia, 2002), 59–83; New Evidence on the Greek Peasantry in Latin Romania, in: Porphyrogenita 239–252; New Venetian Evidence on Crusader Acre, in: Experience II 240–256; Byzantine Traders in Mamluk Egypt, in: Byzantium, State and Society, In Memory of Nikos Oikonomides, ed. Anna Avramea, Angelike Laiou, Evangelos Chrysos (Athens: The National Research Foundation, 2003), 249–268; L'état catalan en Grèce: société et institutions politiques, in: Els Catalans 79–101; L'apogeo di Acri nel medioevo, secc. XII–XIII, in: Le città del Mediterraneo all'apogeo dello sviluppo medievale: aspetti economici e sociali, ed. Giovanni Cherubini, XVIII Convegno internazionale di studi (Pistoia, 2003), 487–519.

JAN, Libor, Die wirtschaftliche Tätigkeit der Johanniter in Böhmen in der vorhussitischen Epoche, in: OM XII 55–69.

JASPERT, Nikolas, Die Kreuzzüge (Darmstadt, 2003), 180pp.; Bilder Jerusalems und ihre Vermittlung im späteren Mittelalter, in: Pilgerwege: Zur Geschichte und Spiritualität des Reisen, ed. Hans Ruh and Klaus Nagorni (Bad Herrenalb, 2003), 101–133; Karolingische Legitimation und Karlsverehrung in Katalonien, in: Jakobus und Karl der Große: Von Einhards Karlsvita zum Pseudo-Turpin, ed. Klaus Herbers, Jakobus-Studien 14 (Tübingen, 2003), 121-159; Historiografía y legitimación carolingia: El monasterio de Ripoll, el Pseudo-Turpín y los condes de Barcelona, in: El Pseudo-Turpín: Lazo entre el culto jacobeo y el culto de Carlomagno, Actas del VI Congreso internacional de estudios jacobeos (Santiago de Compostela, 2003), 297–315.

JENSEN, Janus Møller, *Sclavorum Expugnator*: Conquest, Crusade and Danish Royal Ideology in the Twelfth Century, in: Crusades 2 (2003), 55–81; *Peregrinatio sive expeditio*: Why the First Crusade was not a Pilgrimage, in: Al-Masâq 15 (2003), 119–137.

JORDAN, William Chester, Isabelle of France and Religious Devotion at the Court of Louis IX, in: Capetian Women, ed. Kathleen Nolan (New York – Houndsmill/U.K.: Palgrave Macmillan, 2003), 209–223; 'Excommunication by Christian Authority', 'French Law, Jews in', 'Louis IX', 'Philip II', in: Medieval Jewish Civilization: An Encyclopedia, ed. Norman Roth (New York – London: Routledge, 2003), 245, 273–275, 414–415, 497–498.

JOSSERAND, Philippe, Entre Orient et Occident: l'ordre du Temple dans le contexte castillan du règne d'Alphonse X, in: Alcanate: Revista de Estudios Alfonsíes 2 (2000/01), 131–150; Un corps d'armée spécialisé au service de la Reconquête: les ordres militaires dans le royaume de Castille, in: Bulletin de la Société Archéologique et Historique de Nantes et de Loire-Atlantique 137 (2002), 193–214; Enjeux de pouvoir et traitement historiographique: les ordres militaires dans la chronique royale castillane (XIIIe–XIVe siècles), in: Cahiers de linguistique et de civilisation hispaniques médiévales 25 (2002), 183–193; L'ordre de Santiago en France au Moyen Âge, in: Saint Jacques et la France, ed. Adeline Rucquoi (Paris, 2003), 451–468; Croisade et reconquête dans le royaume de Castille au XIIe siècle: élements de réflexion, in: L'expansion occidentale (XIe–XVe siècles): Formes et conséquences, Actes du XXXIIIe Congrès de la Société des Historiens Médiévistes de l'Enseignement Supérieur (Paris, 2003), 75–85; À l'épreuve d'une logique nationale: le prieuré castillan de l'Hôpital et Rhodes au XIVe siècle, in: Revue Mabillon 75 (2003), 115–138.

JÓŹWIAK, Slawomir, Provinz und Zentrum: Die finanzielle Unterstützung der Zentralbehörden in Marienburg durch die kujawischen Besitzungen des Deutschen Ordens bis 1410, in: OM XII 161–167.

KIESEWETTER, Andreas, Ricerche costituzionali e documenti per la signoria ed il ducato di Atene sotto i de la Roche e Gualteri V di Brienne (1204–1311), in: *Βυζάντιο, Βενετία και ελληνοφραγκικός κόσμος (13ος–15ος αιώνας): Πρακτικά του διεθνούς Συνεδρίου που οργανώθηκε με την ευκαιρία της εκατονταετηρίδας από τη γέννηση του* Raymond-Joseph Loenertz o.p. (*Βενετία*, 1–2 *δεκεμβρίου* 2000), ed. Chryssa Maltezou and Peter Schreiner (Venezia, 2002), 289–347; Bonifacio VIII e gli Angioini, in: Bonifacio VIII, Atti del XXXIX Convegno storico internazionale del Centro italiano di studi sul basso medioevo – Accademia Tudertina (Todi, 13–16 October 2002) (Spoleto, 2003), 171–214; Markgraf Theodoros Palaiologos von Montferrat (1306–1338), seine *Enseignements* und Byzanz, in: Medioevo greco 3 (2003), 121–180; La ristampa del «Diplomatari de l'Orient català» di Antoni Rubió i Lluch: Alcune osservazioni, in: Arxiu de textos catalans antics 22 (2003), 553–560.

KOLIA-DERMITZAKI, Athina, *Iter Hierosolymitanum – Ἐς Παλαιστίνην πορεία*: The Crusading Movement as a European Movement, in: The Idea of European Community in History, Conference Proceedings (Athens, 2003), 73–90.

KOOL, Robert, Coins at Vadum Jacob: New Evidence on the Circulation of Money in the Latin Kingdom of Jerusalem during the Second Half of the Twelfth Century, in: Crusades 1 (2002), 73–88.

LEV, Yaakov, Aspects of the Egyptian Society in the Fatimid Period, in: Egypt and Syria in the Fatimid, Ayyubid and Mamluk Eras, ed. Urbain Vermeulen and J. Van Steenbergen (Leuven, 2001), 1–31; The Cadi and the Urban Society: The Case Study of Medieval Egypt, 9th–12th Centuries, in: Towns and Material Culture in the Medieval Middle East, ed. idem (Leiden: Brill, 2002), 103–119; Ismaili and Fatimid History: A Review Article, in: Jerusalem Studies in Arabic and Islam 27 (2002), 583–587.

LIGATO, Giuseppe, La prima crociata nel mosaico di S. Colombano a Bobbio: ideologia e iconografia di una celebrazione, in: Archivum Bobiense 23 (2001), 243–264, 24 (2002), 343–410; I francescani, le reliquie e la predicazione della crociata, in: Frate Francescano: Rivista di cultura francescana 67 (2001), 99–124; Gerberto e il suo appello in favore di Gerusalemme, in: Gerberto da abate di Bobbio a papa dell'anno 1000, Atti del Congresso internazionale Bobbio 28–30 settembre 2000 (Bobbio, 2001), 127–172; La basilica del Santo Sepolcro, centro politico del regno crociato di Gerusalemme, in: Notiziario dell'Ordine Equestre del Santo Sepolcro di Gerusalemme, Luogotenenza per l'Italia settentrionale 18 (gennaio 2001), 8–13; San Bernardo e il 'De laude novae militiae', in: Fondazione «Abbazia Sancte Marie de Morimundo» 8 (2001), 133–142; Renaud de Chatillon, croisé fanatique, in: La Terre Sainte (mars–avril 2002), 100–102; Etienne de Blois, croisé repenti, in: ibid. 106–108; La croisade du marquis Conrad de Montferrat, in: ibid. (juillet–août 2002), 209–212; Riccardo Cuor di Leone, in: La Terra Santa (luglio–agosto 2002), 40–46 = Richard Cœur de Lion, in: La Terre Sainte (septembre–octobre 2003), 267–271; Il regno di Napoli e la situazione politica nel XIV secolo, in: Io notaio Nicola de Martoni: Il pellegrinaggio ai Luoghi Santi da Carniola a Gerusalemme, 1394–1395, ed. with Michele Piccirillo and Franco Cardini (Gerusalemme, 2003), 211–218; Le vicende della crociata lombarda: Gerusalemme o 'regnum Babilonicum'?, in: Deus non voluit: I lombardi alla prima crociata: dal mito alla ricostruzione della realtà, in: Atti del Convegno Milano 10–11 dicembre 1999, ed. Giancarlo Andenna and Renata Salvarani (Milano, 2003).

LOUD, Graham, The Kingdom of Sicily and the Kingdom of England, 1066–1266, in: History 88 (2003), 540–567; The Monastic Economy in the Principality of Salerno during the Eleventh and Twelfth centuries, in: Papers of the British School at Rome 71 (2003), 141–179.

LUCHITSKAYA, Svetlana, Les idôles musulmanes: images et réalités, in: Das europäische Mittelalter im Spannungsbogen des Vergleichs, ed. Michael Borgolte (Berlin, 2001), 283–298; L'idée de la conversion dans les chroniques de la Première croisade, in: Cahiers de civilisation médiévale 45 (2002), 39–53; The Quotations from the Bible in the Crusade Chronicles, in: Odysseus: Man in History 16 (Moscow, 2003), 65–73 [in Russian].

LUTTRELL, Anthony, The Town of Rhodes, 1306–1356 (Rhodes: City of Rhodes Office for the Medieval Town, 2003), xxiv+304pp.; The Contribution to Rhodes of the Hospitaller Priory of Venice, 1410–1415, in: *Βυζάντιο, Βενετία και ελληνοψραγκικός κόσμος (13ος–15ος αιώνας): Πρακτικά του διεθνούς Συνεδρίου που οϱλανώθηκε με την ευκαιϱία της εκατονταετηϱίδας από τη γέννηση του* Raymond-Joseph Loenertz o.p. (*Βενετία*, 1–2 *δεκεμϱίου* 2000), ed. Chryssa Maltezou and Peter Schreiner (Venezia, 2002), 65–78; The Hospitaller Commandery of the Morea, 1366, in: Porphyrogenita 291–300; The Hospitallers in Twelfth-Century Constantinople, in: Experience I 225–232; Hospitaller Birgu, 1530–1536, in: Crusades 2 (2003), 121–150; The Island of Rhodes and the Hospitallers of Catalunya in the Fourteenth Century, in: Els Catalans 155–165; The Hospitallers' Early Statutes, in: Revue Mabillon 75 (2003), 9–22.

MADDEN, Thomas F., Enrico Dandolo and the Rise of Venice (Baltimore: Johns Hopkins UP, 2003); The Crusades, in: Encyclopaedia Britannica (Chicago: Britannica Press, 2003).

MAIER, Christoph T., The *Bible moralisée* and the Crusades, in: Experience I 209–222; Crusades, in: New Catholic Encyclopedia 4 (Detroit, 2003), 405–415.

MARVIN, Laurence, 'Giralda de Laurac', 'Alice de Montmorency', in: Amazons to Fighter Pilots: A Biographical Dictionary of Military Women, ed. Reina Pennington (Greenwood Press, 2003).

MAYER, Hans Eberhard, Zwei unedierte Texte aus den Kreuzfahrerstaaten, in: Archiv für Diplomatik 47/48 (2001/02), 91–103; Das Turiner Lazariter-Chartular, in: Quellen und Forschungen aus italienischen Archiven und Bibliotheken 82 (2002), 663–676; Ein vergessenes Kreuzfahrertestament und die Affaire de Bouillon, in: Geschichtsbilder: Festschrift für Michael Salewski zum 65. Geburtstag = Historische Mitteilungen der Ranke Gesellschaft Beiheft 47 (2003), 19–24.

MESERVE, Margaret, Patronage and Propaganda at the First Paris Press: Guillaume Fichet and the First Edition of Bessarion's 'Orations against the Turks', in: Papers of the Bibliographical Society of America 97 (2003); From Samarkand to Scythia: Reinventions of Asia in Renaissance Geography and Political Thought, in: Pius II, 'El piu expeditivo pontefece', Selected Studies on Aeneas Silvius Piccolomini (1405–1464), ed. Arie Johan Vanderjagt and Zweder R. W. M. von Martels, Brill's Studies in Intellectual History 117 (Leiden: Brill, 2003); ed. with Marcello Simonetta, Pius II, 'Commentaries' (Cambridge/Mass.: The Tatti Renaissance Library / Harvard UP, 2003).

MILITZER, Klaus, Die Einbindung des Deutschen Ordens in das europäische Finanzsystem, in: OM XII 7–17.

MITCHELL, Piers D., Pre-Columbian Treponemal Disease from 14th Century AD Safed, Israel, and the Implications for the Medieval Eastern Mediterranean, in: American Journal of Physical Anthropolgy 121 (2003), 117–124.

MOL, Johannes A., Frisian Fighters and the Crusade, in: Crusades 1 (2002), 89–110; Wirtschaftsführung der Ritterorden in den friesischen Ländern, in: OM XII 107–128.

NICHOLSON, Helen, Serving King and Crusade: The Military Orders in Royal Service in Ireland, 1220–1400, in: Experience I 233–252; Medieval Warfare: Theory and Practice of War in Europe, 300–1500 (Basingstoke – New York: Palgrave Macmillan, 2003), xx+231pp.; The Hospitallers and the 'Peasants'' Revolt of 1381 Revisited, in: St. John Historical Society Proceedings (2001), 43–55.

NICOLAOU-KONNARI, Angel, Strategies of Distinction: The Construction of the Ethnic Name *Griffon* and the Western Perception of the Greeks (Twelfth – Fourteenth Centuries), in: Byzantinistica: Rivista di Studi Bizantini e Slavi II/4 (2002), 181–196; ed. with Michalis Pieris, Leontios Makhairas, Chronicle of Cyprus, Parallel Diplomatic Edition of the three Manuscripts (Nicosia: Cyprus Research Centre, 2003) [in Greek].

NICOLLE, David, Warriors and Weapons around the Time of the Crusades, Variorum Collected Studies Series (Aldershot: Ashgate, 2002); Medieval Siege Weapons (2): Byzantium, the Islamic World & India AD 476–1562, Osprey New Vanguard 16 (Oxford, 2002); The Siege of the Cave de Sueth, in: Battlefields Review 21 (October 2002), 55–60; Armes et Armures Islamiques, in: Chevaux et cavaliers arabes dans les arts d'Orient et d'Occident, exhibition catalogue, ed. Eric Delpont (Paris, 2002), 95–99; Two Swords from the Foundation of Gibraltar, in: Gladius 22 (2002), 147–200; Historical Atlas of the Islamic World (Ludlow: Thalamus, 2003); The First Crusade 1096–99, Osprey Campaign 132 (Oxford, 2003); with David Lindholm, Medieval Scandinavian Armies (1) 1100–1300 and (2) 1300–1500, Osprey MAA 396 and 399 (Oxford, 2003).

NIELEN, Marie-Adélaïde, Lignages d'Outremer: Introduction, notes et édition critique, Documents relatifs à l'Histoire des Croisades 18, Académie des Inscriptions et des Belles-Lettres (Paris: De Boccard, 2003); Sceaux et usages de sceaux: images de la Champagne médiévale, in: Catalogue de l'exposition, ed. Jean-Luc Chassel (Paris: Somogy éditions d'art, 2003) [chapters on crusaders from Champagne, Joinville].

OTTEN, Catherine, Notes sur quelques monuments de Famagouste à la fin du Moyen Âge, in: Mosaics 145–154; Les investissements financiers des Chypriotes en Italie, in: Kyprus – Benetia, Koines Historikes Tyches, Atti del simposio internazionale Atene 1–3 marzo 2001, ed. Chryssa Maltezou (Venezia, 2002), 107–134; Chypre, un des centres du commerce catalan en Orient, in: Els Catalans 129–153.

PAHLITZSCH, Johannes, Die Bedeutung Jerusalems für Königtum und Kirche in Georgien zur Zeit der Kreuzzüge im Vergleich zu Armenien, in: L'idea di Gerusalemme nella spiritualità cristiana del medioevo, Atti del Convegno internazionale in collaborazione con l'Istituto della Görres-Gesellschaft di Gerusalemme, Gerusalemme, Notre Dame of Jerusalem Center, 31 agosto–6 settembre 1999, Pontificio Comitato di Scienze Storiche, Atti e documenti 12 (Città del Vaticano, 2003), 104–131.

PALÁGYI, Tivadar, Regards croisés sur l'épopée française et le *destān* turc, in: Crusades 2 (2003), 41–54.

PHILLIPS, Jonathan, Odo of Deuil's *De profectione Ludovici VII in orientem* as a source for the Second Crusade, in: Experience I 80–95; ed. with Peter Edbury, Experience II; with Peter Edbury, Jonathan Riley-Smith and the Latin East – An Appreciation, ibid. 1–8; The Fourth Crusade and the Sack of Constantinople (Jonathan Cape / Viking Penguin, 2004), 360pp.

POWELL, James M., The Deeds of Pope Innocent III, Translated with an Introduction and Notes (Washington/D.C.: Catholic Univ. of America Press, 2004); Innocent III and Alexius III: A Crusade Plan that Failed, in: Experience I 96–102; Innocent III: The Making of an Image, in: Innocenzo III: Urbs et Orbis, Atti del Congresso internazionale Roma 9–15 September 1998, ed. Andreas Sommerlechner, vol. 2 (Roma, 2003), 1363–1373.

PRINGLE, R. Denys, Churches and Settlement in Crusader Palestine, in: Experience II 161–178 + fig. 7; with Andrew Petersen, Gazetteer of Medieval and Ottoman Buildings in Palestine, Part II, CBRL 2003: Newsletter of the Council for British Research in the Levant (2003), 18.

REYNOLDS, Susan, Fiefs and Vassals in the Kingdom of Jerusalem: a View from the West, in: Crusades 1 (2002), 29–48.

RICHARD, Jean, Latino-Ierusalemskoe Korolevstvo, trad. A. Y. Karatchinskij, pref. Svetlana V. Bliznuk (Sankt Petersburg: Evrazya, 2002), 448pp. [translation of Le royaume latin de Jérusalem, 1953]; De Jean-Baptiste Mailly à Joseph-François Michaud: un moment de l'historiographie des croisades (1774–1841), in: Crusades 1 (2002), 1–12; La relation de pèlerinage à Jérusalem, instrument de dévotion, in: L'idea di Gerusalemme nella spiritualità cristiana del medioevo, Atti del Convegno internazionale, 1999 (Città del Vaticano, 2003), 20–28; The Adventure of John Gale, Knight of Tyre, in: Experience II 189–195; Pouvoir royal et patriarcat au temps de la Cinquième Croisade, à propos du rapport du patriarche Raoul, in: Crusades 2 (2002), 109–119.

RIST, Rebecca, Papal Policy and the Albigensian Crusades: Continutiy or Change?, in: Crusades 2 (2003), 99–108.

RILEY-SMITH, Jonathan, Casualties and the Number of Knights on the First Crusade, in: Crusades 1 (2002), 13–28; Islam and the Crusades in History and Imagination, 8 November 1898 – 11 September 2001, in: Crusades 2 (2003), 151–167.

RYAN, James D., Conversion or the Crown of Martyrdom: Conflicting Goals for Fourteenth-Century Missionaries in Central Asia?, in: Medieval Cultures in Contact, ed. Richard Gyug (Fordham UP, 2003), 19–38; Missionary Saints of the High Middle Ages: Martyrdom, Popular Veneration and Canonization, in: Catholic Historical Review 90 (2004), 1–28.

SARNOWSKY, Jürgen, ed. with Roman Czaja, OM XII; Handel und Geldwirtschaft der Johanniter auf Rhodos, in: ibid. 19–34.

SAVVIDES, Alexios, The Alans of Caucasus and their Migration in Late Antiquity and the Middle Ages (Athens: Goulandre-Horn Foundation, 2003), 149pp. [in Greek]; In the Roots of Ottoman Historiography: Historiographers and Chroniclers of the 16th–18th Centuries (Athens: Enalios, 2003), 94pp. [in Greek]; Introduction to Byzantine History, A.D. 284–1461, Greek transl. A. Kondyles (Thessalonika: A Stamoules / Herodotos, 2003), 322pp.; History of Byzantium, vol. 3: The Later Byzantine Empire and Medieval Hellenism, A.D. 1025–1461 (Athens: Patakes, 2004), 278pp. [in Greek]; Byzantium – Medieval World – Islam, 3rd ed. with additions (Athens: Papazeses, 2004), 337pp. [in Greek]; Tzannoi – Djanik – Djanit – Tzanichitai: The Problem of the Survival of a Caucasian People in the Byzantine Pontos of the Grand Komnenoi, in: Archeion Pontou 49 (Athens, 2002 [2003]), 129–148 [in Greek]; Suleyman Shah of Rum, Byzantium, Cilician Armenia and Georgia, A.D. 1197–1204, in: Byzantion 73 (Brussels, 2003), 96–111; Notes on the Ghazi Warriors of the Muslim Faith in the Middle Ages, in: Journal of Oriental and African Studies 11 (Athens, 2000/02 [2003]), 211–214; The Mediterranean State of Cilician or Lesser Armenia (Armenian Cilicia) in the Later Middle Ages among Byzantines, Crusaders and Islam, in: Corpus 50 (Athens, 2003), 72–81 [in Greek]; The Byzantines vis-a-vis the Peoples of the Eastern and Balkan Worlds, in: The Byzantine State and Society: New Trends of Research (Athens: Herodotos / Hellenic National Research Foundation, 2003), 125–155 [in Greek]; The Chronicle of the Turkish Sultans: a 16th Century Greek Source on the Early Centuries of Ottoman Conquests, in: Historika Themata 23 (2003), 62–69 [in Greek].

SCHUSTER, Beate, The Strange Pilgrimage of Odo of Deuil, in: Medieval Concepts of Past:

Ritual, Memory, Historiography, ed. Gerd Althoff, Johannes Fried and Patrick Geary (Cambridge/Mass., 2002), 253–278; Raimond d'Aguilers – un chantre de l'hérésie avant l'heure?, in: Heresis 36/37 (2002), 161–183.

SHAGRIR, Iris, Naming Patterns in the Latin Kingdom of Jerusalem, Proposographica et Genealogica (Oxford, 2003).

SHEPARD, Jonathan, The 'Muddy Road' of Odo Arpin: from Bourges to La Charité-sur-Loire, in: Experience II 11–28.

STEFANIDOU, Alexandra, Lighting and Lampburnishing of the Monastery of Theologos of Patmos during Byzantine and Post-Byzantine Period, in: Byzantios Domos 13 (2002/03), 143–161; The Generation Trees of the Catholic Archdiocese's Archive of Santorin, in: Eoa and Esperia 5 (2001/03), 9–18.

TALMON-HELLER, Daniella, *The Cited Tales of the Wondrous Doings of the Shaykhs of the Holy Land by Ḍiyā' al-Dīn Abū 'Abd Allāh Muammad b. 'Abd al-Wāḥid al-Maqdisī (569/1173–643/1245)*: Text, Translation and Commentary, in: Crusades 1 (2002), 111–154.

TANDECKI, Janusz, Der Deutsche Orden und das städtische Handwerk in Preußen, in: OM XII 169–181.

TESSERA, Miriam Rita, *"Prudentes homines ... qui sensus habebant magis exercitatos"*: a Preliminary Enquiry into William of Tyre's Vocabulary of Power, in: Crusades 1 (2002), 63–71.

TOLAN, John Victor, Saracens: Islam in the Medieval European Imagination (New York: Columbia UP, 2002); French transl.: Les Sarrasins: l'Islam dans l'imagination européenne au moyen âge (Paris: Aubier, 2003); Using the Middle Ages to Construct Spanish Identity: *Reconquista*, *repoblación*, and *convivencia* in nineteenth- and twentieth-century Spanish historiography, in: Historiogrpahical Approaches to Medieval Colonization of East Central Europe: A Comparative Analysis against the Background of Other European Inter-Ethnic Colonization Processes in the Middle Ages (Boulder: Eastern European Monographs and New York: Columbia UP, 2002), 329–347; Saracen Philosophers Secretly Deride Islam, in: Medieval Encounters: Jewish, Christian and Muslim Culture in Confluence and Dialogue 8 (2002), 185–208; *Veneratio Sarracenorum*: dévotion commune entre musulmans et chrétiens selon Burchard de Strasbourg, amassadeur de Frédéric Barberousse auprès de Saladin (v.1175), in: Chrétiens et musulmans en méditerranée médiévale (VIIIe–XIIIe siècle): échanges et contacts, ed. Nathalie Prouteau and Philippe Sénac (Poitiers: Centre d'Études Supérieures de Civilisation Médiévale, 2003), 185–195.

URBAN, William, The Teutonic Order: A Military History (London: Greenhill, 2003).

von WARTBURG MAIER, Marie-Louise, Bowls and Birds: Some Middle Byzantine Glazed Bowls from Swiss Private Collections, in: Mosaics 115–129; Types of Imported Tableware at Kouklia in the Ottoman Period: A Preliminary Survey, in: Report of the Department of Antiquities Cyprus (2001), 360–389; Venice and Cyprus: The Archaeology of Cultural and Economic Relations, in: Bisanzio, Venezia e il mondo franco-greco (XIII–XV secolo), ed. Chryssa Maltezou and Peter Schreiner (Venezia, 2002), 503–559; Venetian Buildings in Cyprus: Impact and Feed Back, in: Kyprus – Venetia, Koines Historikes Tyches, ed. Chryssa Maltezou (Venezia, 2002), 27–43; Cypriot Contacts with East and West as Reflected in Medieval Glazed Pottery from the Paphos Region, in: Actes VIIe Congrès international sur la Céramique Médiévale en Méditerranées, Thessaloniki, 11–16 Octobre 1999, ed. Charalampos Bakirtzis (Athens, 2003), 153–166; Vestigia Leonis: Art and Architecture in Cyprus under Venetian Rule, in: Cyprus, Jewel in the Crown of Venice, Exhibition

Catalogue, 15 October – 15 November 2003, A. G. Leventis Foundation (Nicosia, 2003), 57–73.

WILLIAMS, Ann, "Boys will be Boys": The Problem of the Novitiate in the Order of St. John in the Late Sixteenth and Early Seventeenth Centuries, in: Melitensium Amor: Festschrift in Honour of Dun Gwann Azzopardi, ed. Toni Cortis, Thomas Freller and Lino Bugeja (Malta, 2002), 179–184.

van WINTER, Johanna Maria, Hospitalitas – Gastverzorging of ziekenzorg?, in: Hospitalitas en de aanwezigheit van leken in de middeleeuwse premonstratenzer kloosters, Werkgroep Norbertijner Geschiedenis in de Nederlanden, Bijdragen van de contactdag 12 (Averbode, 2002), 7–12.

2. Recently completed theses

BOMBI, Barbara, Innocent III and the *predicatio* to the Heathen in Northern Europe: Mission and Crusade 1198–1216, Università Cattolica del Sacro Cuore, Milano, 1 March 2001, supervised by Petro Zerbi and Annamaria Ambrosioni.

HUNYADI, Zsolt, Hospitallers in the Medieval Kingdom of Hungary, c.1150–1387, Dept. of Medieval Studies, Central European Univ., Budapest, supervised by József Laszlovszky.

PETERSEN, Andrew, The Towns of Palestine under Muslim Rule: An Archaeological Perspective, PhD, Cardiff Univ. 2002, supervised by Denys Pringle.

3. Papers read by members of the Society and others

ANDREA, Alfred J., 1204 Seen from 2004: Teaching the Fourth Crusade, at: American Historical Association Annual Meeting, 10 January 2004; Innocent III and the Greek Church, 1198–1216, at: The Fourth Crusade and its Consequences, Athens, March 2004.

ARNOLD, Udo, Die Sicht des Deutschen Ordens im 16.–18. Jahrhundert auf seine Anfänge, at: OM XIII, Toruń, 26–28 September 2003.

BALARD, Michel, Gli aspetti tecnici del commercio italiano e di quello dell'Europa occidentale, at: IX° Convegno internazionale di studi 'L'Italia alla fine del Medioevo: i caratteri originali nel quadro europeo', San Miniato, 10–12 October 2002 (in press); Carlo I° d'Angiò e lo spazio mediterraneo, at: XV Giornate normano-sveve, Bari, October 2002 (in press); Constantinople dans la Première moitié du XVe siècle d'après les récits de voyages et les témoins du siège de 1453, at: 9th Scientific Forum on Greece 'Constantinople: 550 Years since the Fall', Granada, 4–6 December 2003.

BALLETTO, Laura, Hommes et marchandises entre Gênes et la Corse au XVe siècle, at: 128° Congrès des Sociétés Historiques: Relations, échanges et coopération en Mediterranée, Bastia (Corsica), 14–21 April 2003; L'impresa di Filippo Doria contro Tripoli (1355), at: La Libia nella storia del Mediterraneo, Roma, 10–12 May 2003; Brevi note su Caffa genovese nel XIV secolo, at: 8th International symposium 'Bulgaria Pontica Medii Aevi', Nessebar, 11–12 September 2003; Echi genovesi della conquista turca di Costantinopoli, at: La conquête de Constantinople: l'événement, sa portée et ses échos (1453–2003), Tunis, 11–13 December 2003.

BELLOMO, Elena, La Translatio sancti Nicolai come fonte per la storia dei Veneziani nell'Oriente latino, at: Seminar for post-doctoral fellows, Univ. of Padova, Dept. of History, 27 January 2004; La nuova cavalleria di Cristo: realtà e mito dell'ordine templare, at: La cavalleria nel Medioevo e nel Rinascimento, Istituto Studi Umanistici F. Petrarca, Istituto Lombardo-Accademia di Scienza e Lettere, Milano, 2 March 2004.

Bird, Jessalynn, Heretics or allies? Oliver of Paderborn and James of Vitry on Eastern Christians, at: IMC Kalamazoo 2003; Crusade and conversion after the Fourth Lateran Council (1215): Oliver of Paderborn's and James of Vitry's missions to Muslims reconsidered, at: Illinois Medieval Association Annual Meeting, February 2004.

Bombi, Barbara, Gli archivi centrali dell'Ordine Teutonic all'inizio del XIV secolo, at: Deutsches Historisches Institut, Roma, 16 January 2002; French attitudes towards Denmark: archbishop Eskil of Lund and his exile in Clairvaux, at: IMC Leeds 8–11 July 2002; Andreas Sapiti, un procuratore Trecentesco, fra la curia avignonese, Firenze e l'Inghilterra, at: Circolo medievistico romano, Roma, 22 October 2002; Approbation of papal supplications in the early fourteenth century, at: IMC Leeds 14–17 July 2003; The *Dialogus miraculorum* of Caesarius of Heisterbach as a source for the Livonian Crusade, at: Signs, Wonders, Miracles: Representations of Divine Power in the Life of the Church, The Ecclesiastical History Society Colloquium, Exeter, 23–26 July 2003; Il registro di Andrea Sapiti, un procuratore di curia nei primi decenni del XIV secolo, at: Papauté, offices et charges publiques (XIVe–XVIIe siècle) III: une culture exacerbè de l'ècrit, Paris, 25–26 September 2003; L'Ordine Teutonico nell'Italia centrale, at: L'Ordine Teutonico nel Mediterraneo, Torre Alemanna – Cerignola – Mesagne – Lecce, 16–18 October 2003.

Borchardt, Karl, Leitbilder und Ziele von Ordensreformen bei den Johannitern in Mitteleuropa während des 14. Jahrhunderts, at: OM XIII, Toruń, 26–28 September 2003; Die deutschen Johanniter im 13./14. Jahrhundert zwischen Ministerialität und Meliorat, Ritteradel und Patriziat, at: Städtische Gesellschaft und Kirche im Spätmittelalter, Johann-Gutenberg-Universität Mainz and Deutsches Historisches Institut in Rom, Schloß Dhaun / Germany, 27 February 2004; Die deutschen Johanniter in der Reformationszeit, at: Die Ritterorden in der Reformationszeit, Utrecht, 30 September–3 October 2004.

Bronstein, Judith, The perception of members of military orders as crusaders, at: OM XIII, Toruń, 26–28 September 2003.

Burgtorf, Jochen, The military orders in the crusader principality of Antioch, at: Brediusstichting Antioch-Conference, Kasteel Hernen, Netherlands, 30 May 2003; Das Selbstverständnis von Templern und Johannitern im Spiegel von Briefen und Urkunden (12. und 13. Jahrhundert), at: OM XIII, Toruń, 26–28 September 2003.

Bysted, Ane, The formation of the theology of the crusade indulgences: the spirit of the spiritual privilege, at: IMC Leeds 14–17 July 2003.

Cipollone, Giulio, Culture et cultures entre foi et religions: une lecture historique, at: Civilisation et/ou Civilisations, Colloque organisé par l'Université Ezzitouna, Tunis, 14–16 April 2002; En Sicile: les chrétiens 'pires que les sarrasins': aspects de la politique papale, at: Relations, échanges et coopération en Méditerranée, 128° Congrès des Sociétés historiques et scientifiques, Bastia (Corsica), 14–21 April 2003; In the language of Innocent III: the good to the one side, the bad to the other: the Venetians *satellites sathanae*, at: IMC Kalamazoo 6–9 May 2004; In the language of Innocent III: Christians worse than Saracens, Jews, and pagans: the case of the Venetians, at: SSCLE-conference, Istanbul 25–29 August 2004; Fe y religión: la *oblocutio conscientiae* de Juan de Matha, at: Entre Cristiandad e Islam, Granada 18–21 November 2004.

Claverie, Pierre-Vincent, Notes sur la mort de saint Louis et les finalités de sa croisade, at: 12th HES, 12–14 May 2003.

Coureas, Nicholas, Commercial relations between Cyprus and Mamluk Egypt and Syria, with special reference to Nicosia and Famagusta, in the 15th and 16th centuries, at: 12th HES,

12–14 May 2003; The Copts in Cyprus during the 15th and 16th centuries, in: 13th HES, May 2004.

CRAWFORD, Paul, Were the Templars unimaginative? Attempts to recover the Holy Land, 1300–1302, at: IMC Kalamazoo, 2 May 2002.

CZAJA, Roman, Das Selbstverständnis der geistlichen Ritterorden im Mittelalter: Bilanz und Forschungsperspektiven, at: OM XIII, Toruń, 26–28 September 2003.

DEMIRKENT, Işin, The guild in Byzantium, at: Istanbul Oniversitesi Tarih Semineri, 8 May 2002; A Byzantine commander of Turkish origin in the 11th century, at: 14th Uluslurarasi Turk Tarih Kongresi, Ankara, 9–13 September 2002.

DICKSON, Gary, Massacre of the innocents? Sacral violence and the paradox of the children's crusade, at: Children under Fire: Childhood and War, Cotsen Children's Library, Princeton Univ., 9–11 October 2003.

DOUROU-ELIOPOULOU, Mary, Angevins and Lusignans in the eastern Mediterranean in the second half of the 13th centuy, at: 5th Meeting of the Byzantinologues of Greece and Cyprus, Corfu, 3–5 October 2003; The Aragonese, Venetians and Angevins on the eve of the fall of Constantinople, at: 9th Scientific Forum on Greece 'Constantinople: 550 Years since the Fall', Granada, 4–6 December 2003.

EDBURY, Peter, The suppression of the Templars in Cyprus, 1307–1312, at: Univ. of Nicosia, April 2003, and at: St John Historical Society, St John's Gate, London, October 2003; The siege of Acre during the Third Crusade, 1189–91, at: Historic Acre as a Living City, Akko, Israel, 13 July 2003.

EDGINGTON, Susan B., Advice for old people going on crusade, at: St John's Historical Society, 25 April 2003; Antioch: medieval city of culture, at: Brediusstichting Antioch-Conference, Kasteel Hernen, Netherlands, 30 May 2003; Antioch as a cultural centre at the time of the crusades, at: CLE-Seminar London, 20 October 2003.

EHLERS, Axel, John Malkaw of Prussia: preacher, commander, renegade, c.1400, at: IMC Leeds July 2002.

FAVREAU-LILIE, Marie-Luise, Das Bild des Vierten Kreuzzugs in der 'unbeteiligten' westlichen Geschichtsschreibung, at: Der Vierte Kreuzzug und die Eroberung von Konstantinopel 1204, Internationales Kolloquium, Insel Andros, Kaireos-Bibiliothek, 27–30 May 2004.

FOLDA, Jaroslav, Empty spaces in medieval images: icon painting and spiritual reality, at: Claremont Graduate Univ., California, 22 February 2003; Scriptoria and workshops, scribes and painters in crusader Acre during the later 13th century, at: Historic Acre as a Living City, Akko, Israel, 13 July 2003.

FOREY, Alan, How the Aragonese Templars viewed themselves in the late 13th and early 14th centuries, at: OM XIII, Toruń, 26–28 September 2003.

FRIEDMAN, Yvonne, Peace processes between Muslims and Franks in the Latin East, at: Institute of Historical Research, London, 2 February 2002; Miracle, meaning and narrative in the Latin East, at: Signs, Wonders, Miracles, CIHEC and The Ecclesiastical History Society, Univ. of Exeter, 2003; Itineraria in the Mamluk period, at: Travellers and Pilgrims, Tel-Hai College, 2 January 2003; Concepts of leadership in the Latin kingdom of Jerusalem, at: Leadership in History, Bar-Ilan Univ., December 2003.

GERTWAGEN, Ruthi, Naval warfare along the Levantine coastline in the Crusader Period, at: Conference on the Crusades, Haifa Univ., December 2003.

GUTH, Klaus, Pilgerfahrt, Wallfahrt, Pilgerreise in Vergangenheit und Gegenwart, at: DAM, Univ. Augsburg, November 2003.

HARRIS, Jonathan, What was really important about 1054?, at: Colloquium on the Schism of 1054, Exeter College, Oxford, November 2003; Fortune and Virtue in Laonikos Chalkokondyles's Account of the Fall of Constantinople, at: 9th Scientific Forum on Greece 'Constantinople: 550 Years since the Fall', Granada, 4–6 December 2003.

HECKMANN, Dieter, Vom 'eraftigen' zum 'erwirdigen': Die Selbstdarstellung des Deutschen Ordens im Spiegel der Anreden und Titulaturen (13.–16. Jh.), at: OM XIII, Toruń, 26–28 September 2003.

HOCH, Martin, Die Schlacht von Hattin und der Zusammenbruch des Kreuzfahrerkönigreiches Jerusalem (1187), at: Technische Universität Darmstadt, Germany, 21 May 2003.

HOUBEN, Hubert, Eine Quelle zum Selbstverständnis des Deutschen Ordens im 14. Jahrhundert: der Codex Vat. Ottobon. lat. 528, at: OM XIII, Toruń, 26–28 September 2003.

HUNYADI, Zsolt, Hospitallers in Hungary and Croatia, at: 6th International Congress of the Mediterranean Studies Association, The Mediterranean and Central Europe, Budapest, 28–31 May 2003; (Self)Representation: Hospitaller Seals in the Hungarian-Slavonian Priory up to c.1400, at: OM XIII, Toruń, 26–28 September 2003.

IRWIN, Robert, How Circassian Were the Circassian Mamluks?, at: Circassian Mamluks, Royal Asiatic Society, December 2003.

JENSEN, Janus Møller, Denmark and the crusade in the 16th century, at: IMC Kalamazoo 2003; Post-reformation idea of crusade: a Danish penitential crusader from the 1590s, at: IMC Leeds 2003; Fra Korstog til Religionskrig? Korstogstanken i Skandinavien 1400–1600, at: Clio-Mars Seminar, The Norwegian Armed Forces Museum, Oslo, 6–7 November 2003.

KIESEWETTER, Andreas, Il governo centrale del Regno, at: Le eredità normanno-sveve nell'età angioina: Persistenze e mutamenti nel Mezzogiorno, Quindicesime Giornate normanno-sveve, Bari, 22–25 October 2002; La consistenza territoriale del Principato di Taranto tra l'età sveva e quella angioina, at: Il recupero di una identità storica attraverso le fonti d'archivio, Taranto, 12 April 2003; L'Ordine Teutonico in Grecia e Armenia, at: L'Ordine Teutonico nel Mediterraneo, Convegno internazionale di studio, Torre Alemanna (Cerignola) – Mesagne – Lecce, 16–19 October 2003.

KREEM, Juhan, Einige Bemerkungen über die Siegel der Gebietiger des Deutschen Ordens in Livland, at: OM XIII, Toruń, 26–28 September 2003.

KWIATKOWSKI, Stefan, Der Deutsche Orden in Preußen: Auf der Suche nach den moralischen Grundlagen, at: OM XIII, Toruń, 26–28 September 2003.

LIGATO, Giuseppe, Il primo insediamento francescano in Terra Santa, at: La Custodia francescana di Terra Santa, architettura e diritto delle origini, Pontifio Ateneo 'Antonianum', 23–26 February 2004; Bonifacio VIII, la Terra Santa e la crociata, at: Bonifacio VIII: ideologia e azione politica, Istituto Storico Italiano per il Medio Evo, 26–28 April 2004.

MADDEN, Thomas F., The enduring myths of the Fourth Crusade, at: American Historical Association, 2004.

MENACHE, Sophia, A clash of expectations: self-image versus the image of the Knights Templar in medieval narrative sources, at: OM XIII, Toruń, 26–28 September 2003.

MESERVE, Margaret, From Magi to Mahdi: Renaissance concepts of Persian kingship, at: Annual Meeting of the Renaissance Society of America, Toronto, April 2003; The news from Negroponte: printed debates on the Turkish problem and the Renaissance origins of the newsbook, at: Seminar on the History of the Material Text, Univ. of Pennsylvania, December 2003.

MITCHELL, Piers D., Caesarea Maritima: challenges in the palaeopathological study of a major ancient Mediterranean city, at: Conference of the British Association for Osteoarchaeology, Southampton Univ., August 2003; Torture in the crusades, at: 33rd Medieval Workshop 'Noble Ideals and Bloody Realities: Warfare in the Middle Ages 378–1492', Univ. of British Colombia, Vancouver, November 2003; The archaeology of disease in the crusader period, at: The Venerable Order of St. John, London, November 2003.

NICHOLSON, Helen, The motivations of the Hospitallers and Templars in their involvement in the Fourth Crusade and its aftermath, at: Malta Study Center, St John's Univ., Minnesota, 6 May 2003 and IMC Kalamazoo, 11 May 2003; Saints venerated in the military orders, at: OM XIII, Toruń, 26–28 September 2003; The beliefs of the Templars (1120–1312), at: Meeting of the Saunière Society, London, 4 October 2003; 'La roine preude femme et bonne dame': Queen Sybil of Jerusalem (1186–1190) in history and legend, 1186–1300, at: Haskins Society Conference, Cornell Univ., Ithaca NY, 2 November 2003; Love in a hot climate: gender relations in *Florent et Octavien*, at: IMC Leeds, July 2004.

NICOLAOU-KONNARI, Angel, Identity in the diaspora: works and days of Pietro (before 1570(?)–after 1645) and Giorgio de Nores (1619–1638), at: Identités croisées en un milieu méditerranéen: le cas de Cypre, Univ. de Rouen, 11–13 March 2004.

NICOLLE, David, Two medieval Islamic arms caches, at: Arms & Armour Society, Tower of London, 7 August 2003; Byzantine, Western European, Islamic and Central Asian influence in the field of arms and armour from the 7th to the 14th century AD, at: Islamic Crosspolinations Colloquium, Cambridge Univ., 24 January 2004.

PHILLIPS, Jonathan, The legacy of the First Crusade and the origins of the Second Crusade, at: Univ. of York, November 2003, and Cardiff Univ. Centre for Crusade Studies, March 2004.

PIANA, Mathias, Knotensäulen [Temple Mount examples and their relations to the West], at: Landauer Staufertagung, Univ. of Landau, Germany, 27–29 June 2003.

POSPIESZNY, Kazimierz, Die Architektur des Deutschordenshauses in Preußen als Ausdruck- und Herstellungsmittel der Ordensmission und Herrscherpolitik, at: OM XIII, Toruń, 26–28 September 2003.

PRICE, Jennifer Ann, The vow to crusade in the 12th century, at: CLE-Seminar, Cambridge, 26 May 2003.

RICHARD, Jean, Le système défensif des états francs: programme et évolution, at: La fortification au temps des croisades, Parthenay 2002; Les missions au nord de la Mer Noire, at: Il codice cumanico e il suo mondo, Venezia, 2002.

RYAN, James D., Missionaries, crusaders, and martyrs in early thirteenth century Spain, at: IMC Kalamazoo, May 2004.

SARNOWSKY, Jürgen, Ritterorden als Landesherren: Münzen und Siegel als Selbstzeugnisse, at: OM XIII, Toruń, 26–28 September 2003.

SAVVIDES, Alexios, On the terms Latinokratia and Frankokratia in Greek lands after 1204, at: 24th Panhellenic Historical Congress, Thessalonika, May 2003; Seven important Muslim historiographical sources of the later Middle Ages (14th–15th centuries) on the relations between the Oriental world and the Byzantine Pontos of the Grand Komnenoi, at: 1st International Congress of Oriental and African Studies 'Arab and Islamic World: History, Civilization, Relations with Hellenism', Lampe Elis, Greece, September 2003.

SCHWINGES, Rainer Christoph, Vom Einfluß der Kreuzzüge auf europäische Kulturen, at:

Ernst-Moritz-Arndt-Universität Greifswald, Germany, 30 June 2003, and at: Ruprecht-Karls-Universität Heidelberg, 11 December 2003.

STARNAWSKA, Maria, Das Bild der Kreuzherren-Hospitaliterorden (die Chorherren des Heiligen Grabes, die Kreuzherren mit dem roten Stern) in den polnischen Ländern während der frühen Neuzeit, at: OM XIII, Toruń, 26–28 September 2003.

TESSERA, Miriam Rita, Memorie d'Oriente: traslazioni di reliquie da Oltremare nell'Italia del XIII secolo, Il caso del braccio di s. Filippo, in: La Palestina nella coscienza dell'Occidente dal secolo XIII al secolo XVI, at: 8th Seminario di studi, Montaione (Firenze), 2–4 July 2003.

WENTA, Jaroslaw, Der Deutschordenspriester Peter von Dusburg und sein Bemühen um die geistige Bildung der Laienbrüder, at: OM XIII, Toruń, 26–28 September 2003.

van WINTER, Johanna Maria, Sugar, spice of the crusades, at: Ethnological Food Research Conference, Dubrovnik, 27 September–3 October 2004.

4. Forthcoming publications

ANDREA, Alfred J., Innocent III, the Fourth Crusade, and the End of Time, in: The Fourth Crusade and its Consequences (Athens, March 2004).

BALLETTO, Laura, Nuclei familiari da Genova a Chio nel Quattrocento, in: Due popoli – una storia, Studi di storia ellenica (Atene); Commerci e rotte commerciali nel Mediterraneo orientale alla metá del Quattrocento: l'importanza dell'isola di Chio, in: Money and Markets in the Palaeologian Era, Atti del Convegno, Chalkis June 1998 (Atene); Il Mar Nero nei notai genovesi: panoramica generale, stato degli studi, progetti di pubblicazione, in: The Black Sea Region in the Middle Ages (Historical Faculty Moscow State University); Uomini e merci dalla Krämerthal sulla via del mare, in: Atti del'Accademia Ligure di Scienze e Lettere (Genova); Tra Genova e Chio nel tempo di Cristoforo Colombo, in: Mélanges Michel Balard (Paris); La Storia Medievale, in: Storia della Facoltà di Lettere dell'Università di Genova (Genova).

BELLOMO, Elena, Cronache genovesi di crociata (secoli XII–XIII): Caffaro, Ystoria captionis Almarie et Tortuose and De Liberatione civitatum Orientis liber; Regni Ierosolymitani brevis hystoria, Medioevo Europeo 4 (Padova: CLEUP, summer 2004); Mobility of Templar Brothers and High Dignitaries: The case of North-Western Italy, in: International Mobility; The First Crusade and the Latin East seen from the Adriatic: Venice and the Translatio sancti Nicolai, in: Early Medieval Adriatic, monographic essay of Early Medieval Europe, ed. T. Skinner; The Templar Order in North-Western Italy: a General Picture (1142–1312), in: MO3.

BENNETT, Matthew, Amphibious Operations from the Norman Conquest to the Egyptian Crusades c.1050–c.1250, in: Amphibious Warfare 1000–1700, ed. M. Fissel and D. Trim (Leiden: Brill, 2004).

BEREND, Jessalynn, The 'Historia Orientalis' of Jacques de Vitry: Visual and Written Commentaries as Evidence of a Text's Audience, Reception and Utilization, in: Essays in Medieval Studies: Proceedings of the Illionois Medieval Association (2004); The Victorines, Peter the Chanter's Circle and the Crusade: Two Unpublished Crusading Appeals in Paris, Bibliothèque Nationale, MS Latin 14470, in: Medieval Sermon Studies (2004).

BOMBI, Barbara, ed. with M. P. Alberzoni, Giacomo di Vitry, La quinta Crociata, ed. Marietti 1820 (Milano, 2004); L'Ordine Teutonico nell'Italia centrale, in: L'Ordine Teutonico nel Mediterraneo, ed. Hubert Houben (Lecce, 2004); Innocent III and the *praedicatio* to Heathens in Livonia (1198–1204), in: Medieval History Writing and Crusading Ideology, ed.

Kurt Villads Jensen and T. Lehtonen, Finnish Historical Society (2004); Innocent III and the Origin of the Sword Brethren, in: MO3.

BONNEAUD, Pierre, Le prieuré de Catalogne, le couvent de Rhodes et la couronne d'Aragon (Conservatoire Larzac Templier et Hospitalier, March 2004); Catalan Hospitallers in Rhodes in the first half of the 15th century, in: International Mobility.

BORCHARDT, Karl, articles for EncycCru.

BURGTORF, Jochen, ed. with Helen Nicholson, International Mobility.

BYSTED, Ane, Danske korstog: Krig og mission i Østersøen [Danish Crusades: War and Mission in the Baltic], ed. John H. Lind, Carsten Selch Jensen, Kurt Villads Jensen and Ane L. Bysted.

CLAVERIE, Pierre-Vincent, L'ambassade au Caire de Philippe Mainebeuf (1291), in: Egypt and Syria in the Fatimid, Ayyubid and Mamluk Eras 4, Proceedings of the 9th, 10th and 11th HES, ed. Urbain Vermeulen (Louvain: Peters, 2004); Les «mauvais chrétiens» dans l'Orient des croisades, in: ibid.; La perception des musulmanes dans l'œuvre d'Héthoum de Korykos, in: ibid.

COUREAS, Nicholas, Controlled Contacts: The Papacy, the Latin Church of Cyprus and Mamluk Egypt, in: Egypt and Syria in the Fatimid, Ayyubid and Mamluk Eras 4, Proceedings of the 9th, 10th and 11th HES, ed. Urbain Vermeulen (Louvain: Peters, 2004); The Role of Cyprus in Provisioning the Latin Churches of the Holy Land in the 13th and Early 14th Centuries, in: ibid.; with G. Grivaud and Christopher Schabel, The Capital of the Sweet Land of Cyprus: Frankish and Venetian Nicosia, in: A History of Nicosia, ed. Demetrios Michaelides (Nicosia, 2004); Commercial Relations between Cyprus and Euboea 1300–1362, in: Symmeikta tou Ethnikon Idrymatos Erevnon (Athens, 2003); Genoese Merchants Resident in Nicosia in 1297, ed. Geo Pistarino (2004); Cyprus as a Place of Settlement and Refuge 1191–1373, in: Kypriakai Spoudai (Nicosia, 2001 [2003/04]); Commercial Relations between Cyprus, Pera and Caffa 1300–1450, in: Epeterida tou Kentrou Epistimonikon Erevnon 30 (Nicosia, 2004).

CRAWFORD, Paul, The Trial of the Templars and the University of Paris, in: MO3; articles for EncycCru and for New Westminster Dictionary of Church History, ed. Christopher Ocker (Westminster: John Knox Press, 2004).

DEMEL, Bernhard, Der Deutsche Orden im Spiegel seiner Besitzungen und Beziehungen in Europa (2004) [collected studies and essays].

DICKSON, Gary, Crusades as Metaphor, in: Encyclopaedia Britannica, text & electronic format.

DOUROU-ELIOPOULOU, Mary, The Fourth Crusade: Preparation and Deviation, Anniversary volume for 1204 (National Hellenic Research Foundation, 2003).

ECHEVARRÍA ARSUAGA, Ana, The Queen and the Master: Catalina of Lancaster and the Military Orders, in: Partners in Politics: Queens and Kings in Late Medieval and Early Modern Spain, ed. T. Earenfight (London – New York: Ashgate, 2004); The Mendicant Use of Crusades in Fifteenth-Century Literature, in: The Crusades: Other Experiences, Alternate Perspectives (2004).

EDBURY, Peter, Ramla: The Crusader Town and Lordship (1099–1268), in: Ramla project, ed. Denys Pringle; British Historiography on the Crusades and Military Orders: from Barker and Smail to Contemporary Historians, in: Runciman-Conference; Women and the Customs of the High Court of Jerusalem according to John of Ibelin, in: a festschrift; The Suppression of the Templars in Cyprus, 1307–1312, in: St John Historical Society Proceedings; Society and Ethnicity: The Franks, in: A Collaborative History of Cyprus under Latin Rule, ed. Angel Nicolaou-Konnari and Christopher Schabel; articles for EncycCru.

EDGINGTON, Susan B., Medicine and surgery in the Livre des Assises de la Cour des Bourgeois de Jerusalem, in: Al-Masâq 18 (2005); The Crusaders Write Home: The Experience of the First Crusade as Described in Participants' Letters, in: Segundas Jornadas Internacionales sobre la Primera Cruzada, ed. Luis García-Guijarro Ramos (Zaragoza, 2004); Crusader Chronicles: Revisions and Additions to the Nineteenth-Century Texts, in: Runciman-Conference; articles for EncycCru.

EHLERS, Axel, articles for EncycCru; The Use of Indulgences by the Teutonic Order in the Middle Ages, in: MO3; John Malkaw of Prussia: A Case of Individual Mobility within the Teutonic Order c.1400, in: International Mobility; Die Ablaßpraxis des Deutschen Ordens im Mittelalter (2004/05) [book].

EKDAHL, Sven, articles for EncycCru; Crusades and Colonialism in the Baltic, in: The Palgrave Guide to the Crusades, ed. Helen J. Nicholson; Soldtruppen des Deutschen Ordens im Krieg gegen Polen 1409, in: Wyprawa wojenna, ed. Tadeusz Poklewski-Koziełł and Witold Świętosławski, Acta Archaeologica Lodziensia (Łódz: Instytut Archeologii i Etnologii Polskiej Akademii Nauk, Oddział w Łodzi); Christianisierung – Siedlung – Litauerreise: Die Christianisierung Litauens als Dilemma des Deutschen Ordens, in: Christianisierung Litauens im mitteleurpäischen Kontext, ed. Romualdas Budrys and Vydas Dolinskas (Vilnius: Lithuanian Art Museum, 2004); The Battle of Tannenberg – Grunwald – Žalgiris (1410) as Reflected in Monuments of the Twentieth Century, in: MO3.

FAVREAU-LILIE, Marie-Luise, Die italienischen Seerepubliken und ihre Interessen: Die Rolle der Stadtrepubliken Venedig, Pisa, Genua (Amalfi) für die Geschichte der Kreuzzüge, in: Die Kreuzfahrer – Europas Begegnung mit dem Orient, Essayband zur Ausstellung im Bischöflichen Dom- und Diözesanmuseum Mainz, 2. April–31. Juli 2004 (Mainz, 2004); 'Geroldo di Losanna (Valenza), Patriarca di Gerusalemme', 'Gerusalemme, Patriarcato Latino', in: Enciclopedia Federiciana, ed. Girolamo Arnaldi, Arnold Esch, Cosimo Damiano Fonseca, Alberto Várvaro, Ortensio Zecchino, 2 vols. (Roma, 2004); L'Ordine Teutonico in Terra Santa, in: L'Ordine Teutonico nel Mediterraneo, Atti del Convegno internazionale organizato del Centro di Studi sulla Storia dell'Ordine Teutonico nel Mediterraneo, Torre Alemanna (Cerignola) in collaborazione con il Comune die Cerignola, il Comune di Mesagne, il Dipartimento dei Beni delle Arti e della Storia dell'Università degli Studi di Lecce, 16–18 ottobre 2003, ed. Hubert Houben (2004); 1099: Die Eroberung Jerusalems, in: Höhepunkte des Mittelalters, ed. Georg Scheibelreiter (Darmstadt, 2004); articles for EncycCru.

FLORI, Jean, Aliénor d'Aquitaine, reine et femme insoumise (Paris: Payot, 2004) [March 2004]; Jérusalem terrestre, céleste et spirituelle: trois facteurs de sacralisation de la première croisade, in: Segundas Jornadas Internacionales sobre la Primera Cruzada, Huesca 7–11 set. 1999, ed. Luis García-Guijarro Ramos; Croisade et chevalerie (1950–2000), in: Runciman-Conference.

FOLDA, Jaroslav, Before Louis IX: Crusader Art in Acre, 1194–1244, in: France and the Holy Land: Frankish Culture at the End of the Crusades (Baltimore: Johns Hopkins, March 2004); articles for the exhibition catalogue Faith and Power: Byzantine Art, 1261–1577 (New York: Metropolitan Museum of Art, March 2004); The Figural Arts in Crusader Syria and Palestine, 1187–1291: Some New Realities, in: Dumbarton Oaks Papers 58 (2004); East meets West: The Art and Architecture of the Crusader States [a bibliographical essay], in: A Companion to Medieval Art, ed. C. Rudolph (Oxford: Blackwell, 2004).

FOREY, Alan, The Templar James of Carrigans: Illuminator and Deserter, in: MO3; The Siege of Lisbon and the Second Crusade, in: Portuguese Studies; Templar Knights and Sergeants in the *Corona de Aragón* at the Turn of the Thirteenth and Fourteenth Centuries, in: Proceedings of the IV Encontro sobre Ordens Militares.

FRIEDMAN, Yvonne, The Responsibility of the Community toward its Members, in: Holy People, Jewish and Christian Perspectives, ed. J. Schwartz and M. Porthuis (Leiden: Brill); Miracle, Meaning and Narrative in the Latin East, in: Studies in Church History 41; Leadership in the Latin Kingdom of Jerusalem, in: Bar-Ilan Studies in History 5.

GERTWAGEN, Ruthi, Does Naval Activity – Military and Commercial – Need Artificial Ports? The Case of Venetian Harbours and Ports in the Ionian and Aegean till 1500, in: Graeco-Arabica 9/10 (2004); Harbour and Port Facilities along the Sea Lanes to the Holy Land (12th–13th Centuries), in: How They Made War in the Crusader Period, ed. John Pryor (Brookfield: Ashgate, 2004); Characteristics of Mediterranean Sea Going Ships of the 13th–15th Centuries EC, in: Splendour of the Medieval Mediterranean Art, Culture, Politics, Navigation and Commerce in the Mediterranean Maritime Cities (13th–15th Centuries) [exhibition catalogue Barcelona 2004]; The Medieval Palestinian Shore of Israel – A Coastline without Ports, in: Mediterranée [special issue].

GRABOIS, Aryeh, Image and Reality of the Holy Land in the Descriptions of the Fourteenth-Century European Pilgrims, in: Proceedings of Pilgrimage Conference, Cork; La description de l'Egypte au XIVe siècle par les pèlerins et les voyageurs occidentaux, in: Moyen Âge; The First Crusade and the Jews, in: Proceedings of the 32d Annual Conference of C.E.M.E.R.S.

HARRIS, Jonathan, The Later Crusades, in: Crusades: The Illustrated History, ed. Thomas Madden (London: Duncan Baird); articles for EncycCru.

HOCH, Martin, articles for EncycCru.

HOLMES, Catherine, Basil II and the Government of Empire (Oxford Univ. Press).

HOUSLEY, Norman, Giovanni da Capistrano and the Crusade of 1456, in: Crusading in the Fifteenth Century: Message and Impact, ed. idem (Palgrave, 2004/05); Crusading Indulgences, 1417–1517, in: Indulgences in Late-Medieval Europe, ed. Robert Swanson (Leiden: Brill, 2004).

HUNYADI, Zsolt, Hospitaller Officials of Foreign Origin in the Hungarian-Slavonian Priory: Thirteenth to Fourteenth Centuries, in: International Mobility; Hospitaller Commanderies in the Kingdom of Hungary (c.1150–c.1330), in: MO3.

HUYGENS, Robert B.C., The Fall of Acre, a critical edition of the Excidium Aconis and Magister Thadeus of Naples, with contributions by Alan Forey and David Nicolle (2004).

JASPERT, Nikolas, "Wo die Füsse einst standen" – Jerusalemsehnsucht und andere Motivationen mittelalterlicher Kreuzfahrer (article for a catalogue); Ein Polymythos: Die Kreuzzüge, in: Mythen in der Geschichte, ed. Helmut Altrichter, Klaus Herbers and Helmut Neuhaus (Freiburg im Breisgau, 2004); articles for EncycCru.

JENSEN, Janus Møller, Denmark and the Holy War: A Redefinition of a Traditional Pattern of Conflict, 1147–1169, in: Scandinavia and Europe 800–1350: Contact, Conflict, and Coexistence, ed. Jonathan Adams and Katherine Holman (Turnhout, 2004), 221–238; Vejen til Jerusalem: Danmark og Pilgrimsvejen til Jerusalem i det 12. århundrede, En Islandsk Vejviser, in: Ett annat 1100-tal, ed. Peter Carelli and Lars Hermanson (Gothenburg, 2004), 282–335 [with English summary].

JOSSERAND, Philippe, Par-delà l'an mil: le discours des origines dans l'ordre de Santiago au Moyen Âge, in: Guerre, idéologie et pouvoirs dans l'Espagne de l'an mil, ed. Th. Deswarte and Philippe Sénac; Les ordres militaires dans la chronique castillane à l'époque de Rodrigo Jiménez de Rada, in: Rodrigue Jiménez de Rada: Castille, première moitié du XIIIe siècle, Histoire, historiographie, ed. G. Martin; D'un couvent à l'autre: l'abbaye de Morimond et les ordres militaires hispaniques de filiation cistercienne au Moyen Âge, in: L'abbaye de Morimond: Histoire et rayonnement, ed. G. Viard et M. Parisse; Las órdenes militares y el mar en el contexto de la batalla del Estrecho, in: Terceras Jornadas Rubicenses, ed. O. Brito González; Une raison d'être en repli? Critiques et contestation des ordres militaires en Castille aux XIIIe et XIVe siècle, in: IV Encontro sobre Ordens Militares: As ordens militares e da cavaleria na construço do mundo ocidental, ed. I. C. Ferreira Fernandes; with Carlos de Ayala Martínez, La actitud de los freiles de las órdenes militares ante el problema de la muerte en Castilla (siglos XIII–XIV), in: Dejar los muertos enterrar a los muertos: El difunto entre el aquí y el más alla en Francia y en España (siglos XI–XV), ed. I. Bango Torviso and X. Dectot; La charge de défendre la frontière: les châteaux des ordres militaires dans la Cordillère Bétique aux XIIIe et XIVe siècles, in: II Congreso de Castellología Peninsular, ed. A. Ruibal Rodríguez.

Kolia-Dermitzaki, Athina, The Image of the Bulgarians in the Byzantine Sources of the 11th and 12th Centuries, in: Byzantium and Bulgaria (1085–1185) (Athens).

Lev, Yaakov, The Use of Infantry in Muslim Armies During the Crusades, in: How They Made War in the Age of the Crusades, ed. John H. Pryor (Brookfield: Ashgate, 2004).

Ligato, Giuseppe, Sibilla regina crociata (Milano: Jaca, spring 2004); La croce in catene: prigioneri e ostaggi nelle guerre di Saladino (1169–1193) (Spoleto: Centro Italiano di Studi sull'Alto Medioevo, spring 2004); Reliquie di Terra Santa nei cartigli della chiesa di S. Maria in Aracoeli sul Campidoglio, in: Frate Francescano (2004).

Loud, Graham, The History of the Normans by Amatus of Montecassino, tr. Prescott Dunbar, notes and introduction (Boydell & Brewer).

Luchitskaya, Svetlana, Ad succurrendum: Wie starben die Jerusalemer Könige?, in: Im Kreis der Seinen: Das Individuum und die Gruppe im Westen und Osten Europas im Mittelalter, ed. Otto Gerhard Oexle (Göttingen).

Madden, Thomas F., ed., Crusades: The Illustrated History (London: Duncan Baird, 2004); Food and the Fourth Crusades: a New Approach to the 'Diversion Question', in: How They Made War in the Age of the Crusades, ed. John H. Pryor (Brookfield: Ashgate, 2004).

Maier, Christoph T., The Roles of Women in the Crusade Movement: a Survey, in: Journal of Medieval History 30 (2004); Die Rolle der Frauen in der Kreuzzugsbewegung, in: a festschrift (2004).

Menache, Sophia, *Regnum*, *Studium*, and *Sacerdotium* in the Early Angevin Period: the University of Paris, in: Univ. of Minnesota Proceedings; The Catholic Church in the Middle Ages: Ideology and Politics, 4 vols. (Open Univ., 2003) [in Hebrew].

Meserve, Margaret, Renaissance Humanists and the Crusade, in: The Crusade in the Fifteenth Century: Message and Impact, ed. Norman Housley (Palgrave Macmillan, 2004).

Mitchell, Piers D., Medicine in the Crusades: Military Medicine and the Medieval Cyrurgicus (Cambridge: UP); The Palaeopatholgy of Skulls Recovered from a Medieval Cave Cemetery at Safed, Israel, in: Levant; with J. Huntley and E. Sterns, Bioarchaeological Analysis of the 13th Century Latrines of the Crusader Hospital of St. John at Acre, Israel, at: MO3; 'Disease', 'War Injuries', articles for EncycCru; The Infirmaries of the Order of the Temple in the Frankish States of the Medieval Eastern Mediterranean, in: The Medieval Hospital and Medical Practice: Bridging the Evidence, ed. B. Bowers (Aldershot: Ashgate); Evidence for Elective Surgery in the Frankish States on the Near East in the Crusader Period

(12th–13th Centuries), in: Wissen zwischen Brücken und Brüchen: Der Umgang mit Krankheit und Gesundheit in kulturellen Kontexten von der Spätantike bis zur Reformation, ed. Kay Peter Jankrift and Florian Steger (Köln: Böhlau).

MOLIN, Kristian, entries for EncycCru; Castles Belonging to the Teutonic Knights in Cilician Armenia: A Reappraisal, in: MO3.

de NÈVE, Michael, Templer- und Johanniterkomturei Tempelhof (Berlin), I. Mittelalter bis Reformation, in: Brandenburgisches Klosterbuch, ed. Heinz-Dieter Heimann [article].

NICOLLE, David, The Technology of War and the Craft of Arms 1050–1350 AD, in: Die Kreuzzüge, exhibition catalogue, Dommuseum Mainz, 2 April–30 July 2004; Crusader Castles (1): The Holy Land 12th Century, Osprey Fortress series (2004); Poitiers 1356, Osprey Campaign series (2004); Saladin and the Art of War in the late 12th century Islamic Middle East, in: Holy War, Papers of the Manorial Society Conference, Pembroke College, Oxford 2002; articles for EncycCru and EI^2; A Medieval Islamic Arms Cache, in: Papers of the 7th International Congress on Graeco-Oriental and African Studies, Cairo Univ. 1999, in: Graeco-Arabica; The Early Trebuchet, Documentary and Archaeological Evidence, in: Papers of the Colloque international de Castellologie 'La Fortification au Temps des Croisades', Parthenay, September 2002; Appendix on the terminology of military equipment, in: Excidium Aconis, ed. Robert B. C. Huygens.

NIELEN, Marie-Adélaïde, Nouvelles preuves de l'histoire des vicomtes de Tripoli: tentative de reconstitution de la généalogie de la famille Visconte, in: Le comté de Tripoli: état multiculturel et multi-confessionnel, Univ. du Saint-Esprit de Kaslik, 2–3 december 2002; Richard Cœur de Lion à la Croisade, in: Actes du colloque Richard Cœur de Lion, roi d'Angleterre, duc de Normandie, Caen, Archives départementales du Calvados, 6–8 april 1999; entries for EncycCru; De la Champagne aux royaumes d'Orient: sceaux et armoiries des comtes de Brienne, in: Mélanges offerts à Michel Balard.

NOBLE, Peter, critical edition and translation of Robert de Clari, La Conquête de Constantinople.

OTTEN, Catherine, Famagouste génoise, in: Lacrimae Cypriae, ed. B. Imhaus; Les Occidentaux dans les villes de province de l'empire byzantine: le cas de Chypre, in: 20BS; Un notaire vénitien à Famagouste au XIVe siècle: les actes de Simeone, prêtre de San Giacomo dell'Orio, in: Thesaurismata.

PAHLITZSCH, Johannes, with Christian Müller, Baybars I and the Georgians – in the Light of Two New Arabic Documents from the Archive of the Greek Orthodox Patriarchate of Jerusalem, in: Arabica 50 (2003); Georgians and Greeks in Jerusalem from the End of the 11th to the Early 14th Century, in: East and West in the Crusader States: Context – Contacts – Confrontations III, ed. Krijnie N. Ciggaar and Hermann Teule; Ärzte ohne Grenzen: Melkitische, jüdische und samaritanische Ärzte in Ägypten und Syrien zur Zeit der Kreuzzüge, in: Wissen zwischen Brücken und Brüchen: Der Umgang mit Krankheit und Gesundheit in kulturellen Kontexten von der Spätantike bis zur Reformation, ed. Kay Peter Jankrift and Florian Steger (Köln: Böhlau); The Transformation of Latin Religious Institutions into Islamic Endowments by Saladin in Jerusalem, in: Governing the Holy City: The Interaction of Social Groups in Medieval Jerusalem, ed. together with Lorenz Korn; Griechisch-Syrisch-Arabisch: Zum Verhältnis von Liturgie- und Umgangssprache bei den Melkiten Palästinas im Mittelalter, in: Language of Religion – Language of the People: Judaism, Medieval Christianity and Islam, ed. Michael Richter and David Wasserstein.

PIANA, Mathias, The castle of Toron / Qal'at Tibnīn Project: Preliminary Report, in: Bulletin d'Archéologie et d'Architecture Libanaises 2004/05.

POWELL, James M., Crusading in the 13th Century, in: The Illustrated History of the Crusades, ed. Thomas F. Madden.

PRINGLE, R. Denys, Il castello di Belmonte e la proprietà della Terra di Emmaus nel regno crociato di Gerusalemme, in: Apollo: Bolletino dei Musei provinciali del Salernitano; A Lesser Known Byzantine and Medieval Church on the Mount of Olives, in: Two Millennia of Christianity in Jerusalem: The Third International Conference on Christian Heritage, June 28, 29, 30, Year 2000, ed. K. Hintlian, Swedish Christian Study Centre, Jerusalem, 2004; The Castles of Ayla (al-'Aqaba) in the Crusader, Ayyubid and Mamluk Periods, in: Egypt and Syria in the Fatimid, Ayyubid and Mamluk Eras, vol. 4, ed. Urbain Vermeulen and J. Van Steenbergen, Orientalia Lovaniensia Analecta (Leuven: Peters, 2004); Arqueología, Cruzadas y Órdenes militares en Outremer, 1951–2001, in: Medio siglo de estudios sobre las Cruzadas y las Órdenes militares, 1951–2001, ed. Luis García-Guijarro Ramos (Madrid: Castelló d'Impressió SL, 2004); entries for EncycCru; The Red Tower, in: The New Encyclopedia of Archaeological Excavations in the Holy Land, vol. 5, ed. E. Stern (Jerusalem: Israel Exploration Society); Suba (Zova, Belmont Castle), in: ibid.; Castle Chapels in the Frankish East, in: La Fortification au Temps des Croisades, ed. J. Mesqui and N. Faucherre (Rennes: Presses Universitaires).

PURKIS, William J., Stigmata on the First Crusade, in: Signs, Wonders, Miracles: Representations of Divine Power in the Life of the Church, ed. K. Cooper and J. Gregory, Studies in Church History 41 (Woodbridge, 2004).

RODRÍGUEZ GARCÍA, Jose Manuel, El asalto naval alfonsí a la fortaleza africana (1240–1280): Estrategia e historia, in: Revista de Historia Naval (2004); Consideraciones geostratégicas de índole naval ante la <fortaleza> africana, in: El reinado de Alfonso X de Castilla y León, Actas V Jornadas internacionales de estudios de Frontera, Fortalezas y Redes castrales (Jaén, 2004).

RYAN, James D., The Choir Stalls of Toledo and the Crusade to Capture Granada, in: Les Arts profanes du Moyen Âge (2004); China, in: First Supplement to the Dictionary of the Middle Ages, ed. William C. Jordan (Charles Scribner's Sons, 2004).

SAVVIDES, Alexios, Essays on Ottoman History, 2nd ed. (Athens: Papazeses, 2004) [in Greek]; The Foundation of the Mongol Empire, A.D. 1206–1294 (Athens: Iolcos, 2004) [in Greek]; George Maniakes – Conquest and Undermining in 11th-Century Byzantium, A.D. 1030–1043 (Athens: Periplous, 2004); Notes on Byzantine-Norman Relations in the Period Prior to the Norman Invasions (till A.D. 1081), in: The Ancient World, Festschrift for John Fossey.

SCHUSTER, Beate, Die Stimme des falschen Paupers: Der Kreuzugsbericht des Raimund von Aguilers und die Armenfrage, in: Armut im Mittelalter, ed. Otto Gerhard Oexle (Sigmaringen, 2004).

SCHWINGES, Rainer Christoph, Regionale Identität und Begegnung der Kulturen in Stadt und 'Kreuzfahrer-Königreich' Jerusalem, in: a festschrift (2004); Wider Heiden, Teufel und Dämonen: Mission im Mittelalter, in: Engel, Teufel und Dämonen: Einblicke in die Geisteswelt des Mittelalters, ed. Hubert Herkommer and idem (Basel: Schwabe, 2004).

SHAGRIR, Iris, The Anthroponymic Patterns of Frankish Settlers in the Mediterranean: The Franks of the Holy Land and the Normans of Southern Italy, in: La Puglia tra Gerusalemme e Santiago di Compostela, Atti del III Convegno Internazionale di Studio, ed. M. S. Calò Mariani; The Naming Patterns of the Inhabitants of Frankish Acre, in: Crusades 3 (2004).

SHEPARD, Jonathan, How St. James the Persian's Head Came to Cormery: a Relic Collection in the Era of the First Crusade, in: Festschrift für Günter Prinzing (Harassowitz, 2004);

"Manners maketh Romans?": Young Barbarians at the Imperial Court, in: a volume for Steven Runciman (Cambridge).

STEFANIDOU, Alexandra, The Medieval Fortifications of the Countryside in Rhodes, based on J. Hedenborg's Manuscript and its Illustrations (1854) as well as Other Travellers' Impressions of the 19th Century, in: Proceedings of the 24th Panhellenic History Conference, Thessaloniki 30 May – 1 June 2003.

TOLAN, John Victor, ed. with François Clément and Malika Pondevie, L'Inconnu au turban dans l'album de famille: Réflexions sur l'apport de la culture arabe à la construction de la culture européenne (Paris: L'Harmattan, 2004).

URBAN, William, The Livonian Crusade, 2nd, enlarged ed. (Chicago: Lithuanian Research and Studies Center, 2003); a Lithuanian transl. of Tannenberg and After.

WILLIAMS, Ann, "Sad Stories of the Death of Kings": Last Illnesses and Funerary Rites of the Grand Masters of the Order of St. John from Aubusson to the Cottoner, in: MO3; Servants of the Sick: The Convent of the Order of St. John in Rhodes and Malta, 1421–1631.

5. Work in progress

BALARD, Michel, The Latins in the Near East [book].

BARTOS, Sebastian, Gender and Power in the Latin East: the Perception of Female Authority in the Chronicle of William of Tyre [book].

BEREND, Nora, Christianization and state-formation in Northern and Central Europa c.950–c.1200 (a collaborative project including historians, art historians and archaeologists).

BIRD, Jessalynn, An Annotated Translation of the 'Historia Occidentalis' of Jacques de Vitry; Women and the Crusades (London Books); Christian Society and the Crusades, 1198–1274 (a sourcebook in collaboration with Edward Peters and James Powell).

BOMBI, Barbara, Edition of the inedited cartulary of the Teutonic Knights house of Beuggen, Switzerland.

BORCHARDT, Karl, Die Johanniter in den ältesten Supplikenregistern der römischen Kurie des 14. Jahrhunderts, for a festschrift [article].

CIPOLLONE, Giulio, Retrospettiva culturale di tolleranza nella documentazione tra Papato e Islam nel Medioevo [book].

COLE, Penny J., a critical edition of Humbert of Romans, De predicatione crucis.

COUREAS, Nicholas, The Latin Church in Cyprus 1313–1378 (Ashgate); The Chronicle of George Boustronios: a New English Translation (Cyprus Research Centre and Greece and Cyprus Research Centre, Univ. of Albany); The Life of Peter Thomas by Philippe de Mézières: a Translation into English (Cyprus Research Centre).

CRAWFORD, Paul, a journal article on the involvement of the University of Paris in the trial of the Templars; a course reader on crusade historiography and on Just War theory; a book on the Templars and Hospitallers.

DEMIRKENT, Işin, Antakya Haçlı Devleti Tarihi (The History of the Principality of Antioch); Son Dönem Bizans İmparatorluğu Bibliyografyasi 1261–1453 (The Bibliography of the Last Period of Byzantium).

DICKSON, Gary, The Children's Crusade [book].

EDBURY, Peter, a critical edition of Philip of Novara, 'Livre de forme de plait'; research into the Old French translation of William of Tyre.

EDGINGTON, Susan B., ed. and tr. Albert of Aachen, Historia Iherosolimitana (Oxford Medieval Texts); Crusader Medicine [book]; a comparative edition of Guido da Vigevano, Regimen sanitatis.

FLORI, Jean, Islam et fin des temps: la perception de l'islam dans l'eschatologie chrétienne de l'Occident médiéval (2005).

FOLDA, Jaroslav, Crusader Art in the Holy Land (Cambridge UP, 2004).

FOREY, Alan, Desertions and Transfers from Military Orders (12th to Early 14th Centuries); The Papacy and the Spanish Reconquest; Marriage and Sexual Relations between Western Christians and Outsiders in the Crusading Period.

GERTWAGEN, Ruthi, Venice and the Defense of its Maritime Empire in the 14th and 15th Centuries [book]; Ports and Harbours in the Medieval Eastern Mediterranean to the 15th Century [book].

HARRIS, Jonathan, ed., Palgrave Guide to Byzantine History (Basingstoke: Palgrave Macmillan); Byzantium's Alliance with Saladin, 1185–1192.

HOCH, Martin, Saladin, in: Kriegsherren der Weltgeschichte: Von Xerxes bis Nixon, ed. Stig Förster et al. (München: Beck).

HOUSLEY, Norman, Contesting the Crusades (Blackwell, 2006).

IRWIN, Robert, A history of orientalism; ed. vol. 4 The New Cambridge History of Islam: Islamic Cultures and Societies to 1800; studies on Sufism; article on futuwwa; Muslim militias in late medieval Syria; Petrarch and Averroes.

JENSEN, Janus Møller, Denmark and the Crusade, 1400–1600 [article]; The Forgotten Periphery and the Forgotten Crusades: Greenland and the Crusade, 1400–1536 [article].

JOSSERAND, Philippe, Les ordres militaires et la construction de la légitimité royale en Castille du XIIe au XIVe siècle.

KOLIA-DERMITZAKI, Athina, The self-image of the Byzantines (10th to 12th centuries); The role played by the Normans in the mutual alienation of Byzantines and Latins; The siege of Constantinple (1204) and the transfer of movable and cultural goods to the West; The 'tyrant of Sicily': Byzantine political theory and the Normans; Byzantine attitudes towards the Latins in religious matters as reflected in non-ecclesiastical texts (11th to 13th centuries); The Montferrat family and Byzantium.

LUCHITSKAYA, Svetlana, Muslim-Christian Polemics on the Images [book].

MADDEN, Thomas F., A general history of Venice.

MAIER, Christoph T., with Nicole Bériou, Les sermons de la croisade Albigeoise de 1226 (Les Classiques de l'histoire de France au Moyen Âge); Crusades against Christians (Hambledon & London).

MARVIN, Laurence, Military History of the Albigensian Crusade, 1209–1218.

MITCHELL, Piers D., Palaeopathology of the Crusader Period Cemeteries from Caesarea Maritima, a Major Fortified City of the Eastern Mediterranean [article]; with Y. Naggar and Ronnie Ellenblum, Weapon Injuries in the Slaughtered 12th Century Crusader Garrison of Vadum Iacob Castle, Israel [article].

MOLIN, Kristian, research on and translation of the Old French version of the 'Chronicle of Morea'.

de NÈVE, Michael, Der 'Kreuzzug' Kaiser Friedrichs II. als historiographisches Problem; Der Fall von Akkon – vom Ende des Bistums (1261) bis zum Untergang der Stadt (1291); Der Templerprozeß im Vergleich mit den Ritterordensprozessen des 14. und 15. Jahrhunderts;

Von der *renovatio urbis* zur *reformatio orbis* – Nikolaus V. und der Kreuzzugsgedanke zwischen dem Anno Santo und dem Fall von Konstantinopel.

NICHOLSON, Helen, ed. with Jochen Burgtorf, International Mobility; Documents Relating to the Trial of the Templars in the British Isles: Transcription and Translation [to be completed with a 2003/04 British Academy / Leverhulme Trust Senior Research Fellowship]; The 'Sisters' House at Slebech: an analysis of the archaeological and documentary evidence [article]; ed. with Anthony Luttrell, Hospitaller Women in the Middle Ages (Ashgate); The Hospitallers in the British Isles in the 14th Century [articles]; ed., The Palgrave Guide to the Crusades.

NICOLLE, David, Carolingian Cavalryman, Osprey Warrior series; Crusade Castles (2): The Holy Land 13th Century, Osprey Fortress series; Crusader Castles (3): The Aegean, Osprey Fortress series; Warfare in the Crusader World, Crusader World series (London: Hambledon); Saracen Citadels, Osprey Fortress series; a large cache of 12th-early 14th century Islamic arms, armour, horseharness and other military equipment; the relief carvings of zodiac figures on the 12th–13th century ruined Tigris bridge at Ain Diwar, Syria, with special attention to a representation of a fully armed horseman.

NOBLE, Peter, 1204 – the Crusade without Epic Heroes.

OTTEN, Catherine, Publication of sources concerning Cyprus, 13th–14th centuries.

PHILLIPS, Jonathan, The Second Crusade: Expanding the Frontiers of Christianity (Yale, 2006); Armenia and the Second Crusade [article].

POWELL, James M., Civic Culture in Communal Italy in the 13th Century; with Edward M. Peters and Jessalyn Bird, rev. ed. of Christian Society and the Crusades (Univ. of Pennsylvania Press); Innocent III and Secular Law [article]; The Misericorida of Bergamo and the Frescoes in the Aula Diocesana: a Chapter in Communal History [article].

PRINGLE, R. Denys, The Churches of the Crusader Kingdom of Jerusalem: A Corpus, vol. 3: The Cities of Jerusalem, Acre and Tyre; ed., History and Archaeology of the City of Rama (c.715–1917); with J. De Meulemeester, The Mamluk Castle of al-'Aqaba and its Predecessors, Monograph series of the Division du Patrimoine, Ministère de la Région Wallonne.

RICHARD, Jean, Bullaire de Chypre (14 sec.); The discovery of the Mongols from the Latin East: the origins of the Franco-Mongol alliance, 1145–1262.

RYAN, James D., John of Montecorvino (1247–1328): Medieval Missionary and First Archbishop of Beijing [book].

STEFANIDOU, Alexandra, The Tower (Goulas) of Saint Nicholas (of Oia) in Santorin based on the 16th and 17th Century as well as Descriptions by Travellers; Byzantine and Post-Byzantine Churches of Patmos.

TESSERA, Miriam Rita, Papato, chiesa e regno latino di Gerusalemme nel XII secolo, 1099–1187 [book]; Monachus of Caesarea's The Expugnata Accone liber tetrastichus, critical edition, Italian translation and commentary with Marc Petoletti; Amalric I's Dream and the True Cross Sent to Clairvaux Abbey [article].

TOLAN, John Victor, The Friar and the Sultan: Francis of Assisi's Mission to al-Malik al-Kâmil of Egypt in Western Art and Historiography (2005) [book].

von WARTBURG MAIER, Marie-Louise, Final reports on the excavations at medieval Kouklia (Palaiopaphos, Cyprus) in the series 'Ausgrabungen in Alt-Paphos auf Cypern'; studies on find material, primarily medieval pottery, from excavations in Kouklia, Paphos and Nikosia on Cyprus.

WILLIAMS, Ann, The Hospital of the Order of St. John in Malta, 1530–1798.

6. Theses in progress

BYSTED, Ane, In Merit as well as in Reward: Indulgences, Spiritual Merit and the Theology of the Crusades c.1095–1216, Univ. of Southern Denmark at Odense.

CLAVERIE, Pierre-Vincent, The Order of the Temple in the Holy Land and Cyprus in the Thirteenth Century, Univ. Paris I Panthéon-Sorbonne, supervised by Michel Balard.

HODGSON, Natasha, Perceptions of Women in Crusade Narratives, Univ. of Hull, supervised by Jonathan Phillips.

JENSEN, Janus Møller, Crusade in Scandinavia during the Renaissance, Reformation and the Early Modern State, 1450–1650, PhD, Univ. of Southern Denmark.

JINKS, Alison, Philip Augustus and the Crusades, Royal Holloway Univ. of London, supervised by Jonathan Phillips.

KAFFA, Elena, The Orthodox Church in Cyprus during the Frankish Period, Univ. of Wales, supervised by Peter W. Edbury.

MAIOR, Balazs, The Medieval Settlement Pattern on the Syrian Littoral, 11th–13th Centuries, PhD, Cardiff Univ., supervised by Denys Pringle.

de NÈVE, Michael, Jakob von Vitry (1160/70–1240), Freie Universität Berlin.

PETRE, James, Crusader Castles of Cyprus: The Fortification of Cyprus under the Lusignans, 1191–1489, MPhil, Cardiff Univ., supervised by Denys Pringle.

PHILLIPS, Simon, The Role of the Prior of St. John in Late Medieval England, 1300–1540, King Alfred's College Univ. of Southampton, supervised by M. A. Hicks.

PRICE, Jennifer Ann, The Vow to Crusade: Origins and Development, Dept. of History, Univ. of Washington.

PURKIS, William J., Crusade and Pilgrimage Spirituality, c.1095–c.1187, PhD in History, Univ. of Cambridge, supervised by Jonathan Riley-Smith.

SCHUSTER, Beate, The Crusade Chronicle of Raymond of Aguilers between Testimony and Fiction, Habilitationsschrift, Univ. of Göttingen.

THOMPSON, Jennifer, Death and Burial in the Latin East: A Study of the Crusader Cemetery at 'Atlit, Israel, PhD, Cardiff Univ., supervised by Denys Pringle.

WAGNER, Thomas, Krankheiten und Krankenversorgung zur Zeit der Kreuzzüge: Epidemien, Verwundetenpflege, historische Krankheitsbilder, Univ. Würzburg.

7. Fieldwork planned or undertaken recently

ANDREA, Alfred J., travelled to Halberstadt Cathedral, February 2004, to catalogue and photograph Constantinopolitan relics brought back to Halberstadt by Bishop Conrad von Krosigk in 1205.

BALARD, Michel, Spices in the Middle Ages [book].

CLAVERIE, Pierre-Vincent, research on the bishop Nivelon of Quierzy and his participation to the Fourth Crusade under the auspices of the Istituto Veneto di Scienze, Lettere ed Arti.

MITCHELL, Piers D., visited medieval excavations at Caesarea, Vadum Iacob, Le Petit Gerin and Caymont in December 2003 to obtain samples for his interdisciplinary project studying crusader and Frankish diet.

NICOLLE, David, studied late Mamluk, late 15th – very early 16th century, military artefacts and military costume excavated in the Citadel of Damascus by a French archaeological mission headed by Sophie Berthier, for inclusion in an eventual publication of the find by the French Institute of Near Eastern Studies.

PIANA, Mathias, survey and excavation of the Castle of Toron in Southern Lebanon.

PRINGLE, R. Denys, November–December 2003, third season of survey and excavation on the castle of al-'Aqaba (Jordan), postponed from January 2003, in collaboration with Dr Johnny De Meulemeester (Division du Patrimoine du Ministère de la Région Wallonne) and Mrs Sawsan al-Fakhri (Department of Antiquities of Jordan).

8. News of interest to members

a) Conferences and seminars

2004 May 6–9 IMC Kalamazoo, 'The Fourth Crusade and the Conquest of Constantinople, 1204–2004'; 'Preaching, Conversion, and the Crusades'; 'Crusades and Crusaders'. Contact Thomas Madden, Dept. of History, Saint Louis Univ., 3800 Lindell Bvld., St. Louis MO 63108, U.S.A.

2004 July 12–15 IMC Leeds, 'Clash of Civilisations'. Contact: Axel E. W. Mueller or Claire Clarke, International Medieval Institute, Parkinson 1.03, Univ. of Leeds, Leeds LS2 9JT, England, U.K., www.leeds.ac.uk/imi/imc/imc.htm On behalf of the SSCLE Matthew Bennett, Susan Edgington and Sarah Lambert organize sessions 504, 604, 704 (July 13) entitled 'Languages of Love and Hate' devoted to papers analysing relationships between Christians, Muslims, Jews and 'Other', chiefly through the interpretation of vernacular texts.

2004 August 25–29 Istanbul, 6th Conference of the SSCLE on the general topic '1204, a Turning Point in the Relations between Eastern and Western Christians?', organized by Michel Balard, Sophia Menache and Nevra Necipoglu; contact: menache@research.haifa.ac.il. See provisional programme below.

2004 September 29–October 3 Utrecht, 'The Military Orders and the Reformation'; contact: Johannes A. Mol, Fryske Akademÿ, Leeuwarden/Leiden, zeemol@oprit.rug.nl

2004 November 18–21 Granada, Entre Cristiandad e Islam.

2005 May IMC Kalamazoo: Members who would like to give a paper in the SSCLE-sponsored sessions should send abstract proposals by September 15, 2004, to Thomas F. Madden, Dept. of History, Saint Louis Univ., 3800 Lindell Blvd., St. Louis, MO 63108, U.S.A. or via email to <maddentf@slu.edu>.

2005 May: Regards croisés sur la guerre sainte dans le monde latin du XIe au XIIIe siècle, conference and seminar at the Casa de Velázquez, Madrid, organized by Philippe Josserand in collaboration with Daniel Baloup.

2005 July Sydney, International Congress of Historical Sciences, two-days session organized by Michel Balard and Benjamin Z. Kedar on 'The Oriental Christians in the Latin States'; call for papers and contact: balard@univ-paris1.fr

2005 July 15–19, IV Medieval Chronicles Conference, Univ. of Reading, offers for papers on any aspect of chronicles welcome or requests to be added to mailing list lfsnoble@ reading.ac.uk

2005 September 8–11, London: The Fourth Military Orders Conference will take place at St. John's Gate, Clerkenwell. The provisional title is "The Military Orders by Land and on Sea", which, as usual, means that twenty-minute papers on any military order history, preferably but not necessarily in English, will be welcomed. The registration fee will be £90 (£70 for postgraduate students). Registration forms will be sent on application to The Museum of the Order of St. John, St. John's Gate, Clerkenwell, London EC1M 4DA. e-mail: museum@mhq.sja.org.uk

SOCIETY FOR THE STUDY OF THE CRUSADES AND THE LATIN EAST

Provisional Programme for the Sixth SSCLE Conference, Istanbul 25–30 August 2004

Wednesday, 25 August 2004

Optional tour: Highlights of Istanbul **(9.00–17 hrs)**

Bogazici University
Early Afternoon: Registration and distribution of Conference dossiers

18.30 – Plenary Session
Chair: Nevra Necipoglu (Bogazici University)

Presidential Address: Michel Balard (Sorbonne)
Opening Lecture:
Thomas Madden (Saint Louis University), "1204 and Historical Memory"

20.00: Welcome Banquet hosted by the president of Bogazici University

Thursday, 26 August

9.30–11.00

[a] The Fourth Crusade
Chair: John France

Jonathan Riley Smith (Emmanuel College, Cambridge), "An Alternative Approach to the Fourth Crusade"
Aryeh Grabois (University of Haifa), "The Fourth Crusade and the Holy Land"
Lucie Kuhse (University of Hamburg), "The Conquest of Constantinople: A Question of Honour?"

[b] The Military Orders: The Templars
Chair: Malcolm Barber

Elena Bellomo (Università Cattolica del Sacro Cuore), "Barotius, Crusader and Templar Master of Lombardy and Italy"
Ignacio de la Torre (UNED), "The Templars as Papal Bankers"
Paul Crawford (Alma College), "Templars and Masters: A Second Look at the Involvement of the University of Paris in the Trial of the Templars"

[c] Crusader Archaeology
Chair: Benjamin Kedar

Mathias Piana (University of Augsburg, Germany), "The Crusader Castle of Toron: First Results of its Investigation"

Adrian J. Boaz (University of Haifa), "Crusader and Armenian Castles: Architectural Interchange and Adaptation"

Kate Raphael (Hebrew University of Jerusalem), "Arrows and Catapult Stones: Hard Evidence from the Siege of Arsuf (1265) and Acre (1291)"

Coffee Break

11.30–13.00

[a] Different Perspectives of the Fourth Crusade
Chair: Susan Edgington

S.I. Luchitskaya (Institute of General History, Moscow), "Russian Medieval Perceptions of the Fourth Crusade"

Christer Carlsson (Stockholm), "1204 – The Time of the Fourth Crusade from a Northern Perspective"

Aphrodite Papayianni (University of London), "The Byzantines' Views on the Events of 1204: 1204–1453"

[b] The Ideal of Knighthood and the Military Orders
Chair: Jonathan Riley Smith

Malcolm Barber (University of Reading), "The Reputation of Gerard of Ridefort"

Sophia Menache (University of Haifa), "Don Alonso of Aragon, Master of Calatrava"

Zsolt Hunyadi (University of Szeged), "Hospitallers, Templars, and Teutonic Knights in the Medieval Kingdom of Hungary"

[c] Military History
Chair: Matthew Bennett

Piers Mitchell (Imperial College, London), "Weapon Injuries Sustained by the Frankish Garrison during the Siege of Vadum Iacob Castle"

Reuven Amitai (Hebrew University of Jerusalem), "Slowly but Surely: Mamluk Siege Methods against the Franks"

B. Vasiliki A. Simpson, "The Fires of the Fourth Crusade: A Memoir of the Architectural Loss"

14.30–16.00

[a] Economic Aspects of the Fourth Crusade
Chair: David Jacoby

Merav Mack (Hebrew University of Jerusalem), "Commercial Aspects of the Fourth Crusade"

Kelly Linardou (Birmingham University) and Titos Papanastorakis (Aegean University), "Politics of Looting and the Formation of Symbolic Identities: The Choice of Venetians and Franks and the Distribution of Constantinopolitan Booty after the Conquest of 1204"

Robert D. Leonard (NCIS), "The Effects of the Fourth Crusade on European Gold Coinage"

[b] The Second Crusade
Chair: Aryeh Grabois

William J. Purkis (Emmanuel College, Cambridge), "Bernard of Clairvaux and the Preaching of the Second Crusade"

G.A. Loud (University of Leeds), "The Failure of the Second Crusade: A Reconsideration"

Jonathan Phillips (Royal Holloway University of London), "Armenia and the Second Crusade"

[c] The Crusades, Before and After
Chair: Yvonne Friedman

Tracy Smith (Berkeley), "The Crusades: A Cultural Anthropological Study"

Charles R. Bowlus (University of Arkansas), "The Origins of Byzantine-Latin Animosities in East-Central Europe"

Janus Möller Jensen (University of Southern Denmark), "The Forgotten Periphery and the Forgotten Crusades: Greenland and the Crusades, 1400–1536"

Coffee Break

16.30-18.00

[a] The Conquest and Sack of Constantinople, 1204
Chair: Thomas Madden

John H. Pryor (University of Sidney), "The Chain of the Golden Horn"

David Perry (University of Minnesota), "The *Translatio Symonensis* and the Seven Thieves: A Venetian Fourth Crusade *furta sacra* Narrative and the Looting of Constantinople"

Michael Angold (University of Edinburgh), "The Debate over the Sack of Constantinople, 1204"

[b] The Papacy and the Crusades
Chair: Jonathan Phillips

Theresa M. Vann (Hill Monastic Manuscript Library), "Eleventh- and Twelfth-Century Vocabulary of Holy War in the Mediterranean"

John France (Swansea University), "The Papacy and its Byzantine Strategy"

Ane Bysted (University of Southern Denmark), "Crusade Indulgences in Twelfh- Century Theology: The Spirit of the Spiritual Privilege"

[c] The Crusader Kingdom of Jerusalem
Chair: Michel Balard

Benjamin Kedar (Hebrew University of Jerusalem), "Enhancing Holy Places in the Kingdom of Jerusalem: The Diverging Fortunes of Hebron and Sebaste"

Sylvia Schein (University of Haifa), "The Twelfth-Century Communication Network between the Kingdom of Jerusalem and Byzantium"

Ronnie Ellenblum (Hebrew University of Jerusalem), "Crusader History and Plate Tecotincs: Vadum Iacob and the Earthquakes of 1202 and 1759"

Friday, 27 August

9.30–11.00

[a] Innocent III and the Fourth Crusade
Chair: Brenda Bolton

Jonathan Harris (Royal Holloway University of London), "Collusion with the Infidel as a Pretext for Military Action against Byzantium"

Jennifer A. Price (University of Washington), "Legatine Power and the Crusade Vow: Innocent III, Peter Capuano, and the Conquest of Constantinople"

Giulio Cipollone (Pontifical Gregorian University), "In the Language of Innocent III: Christians are worse than Saracens, Jews and Pagans: the Case of the Venetians"

[b] *Jihad*, Military Orders, and Crusades in Spain
Chair: Theresa Vann (Monastic Hill Library)

Cristina de la Puente (CSIC, Madrid), "*Jihad* and *Reconquista* in al-Andalus"

Simon F. Barton (University of Exeter), "The Nobility and the Iberian Crusades"

Ana Echevarria (UNED, Madrid), "Muslim Vassals of the Military Orders and their Conversion"

[c] The Latin East
Chair: Gilles Grivaud

Jean Richard (Académie des inscriptions et belles-lettres), "Les Etats Latins du Levant face à la conquête de Constantinople"

Yvonne Friedman (Bar Ilan University), "Christian-Muslim Peace Endeavors and Conflict Resolution"

Ronnie Ellenblum (Hebrew University of Jerusalem), "'Crusader Cities', 'Muslim Cities', and the Post-Colonial Debate"

Coffee Break

11.30–13.00

[a] The Fourth Crusade: Different Perspectives
Chair: Jenny Horowitz

Monique Zerner (University of Nice), "Ceux qui refusèrent le détournement de la croisade vers Contantinople"

Philippe Gardette (Trinity College, Cambridge), "Jews and the Capture of Constantinople in 1204 and in 1453: A Parallel"

Marco Meschini (Università Cattolica del Sacro Cuore, Milano), "Les quatre croisades de 1204"

[b] Crusade Historiography
Chair: David Perry

Tivadar Palagyi (University of Budapest), "Images byzantines et persanes de Constantinople dans des texts épiques de Georges de Pisidie et de Firdousi"

Serban Marin (Istituto Romeno di cultura), "The Venetian Chronicles' Viewpoint regarding the Fourth Crusade: Between Justification and Glory"

Konstantinos A. Zafeiris (University of St. Andrews), "The *Synopsis Chronike* and its Selective Use of the Sources"

[c] The Art of War and the Conquest of Constantinople
Chair: Reuven Amitai

Birsel Kücüksipahioglu (Istanbul University), "The Western Plans to Capture Byzantium from the Beginnings of the Crusades to 1204"

Francesco dall'Aglio (Istituto Italiano per gli studi filosofici), "Brothers in Arms: The Art of War according to Balduin and Henry"

Matthew Bennett (Royal Military Academy, Sandhurst), "Why and How were the Fourth Crusaders Able to Capture Constantinople?"

Lunch Break

14.30–16.00

[a] The Fourth Crusade and the Byzantine World
Chair: John W. Barker

Alfred J. Andrea (University of Vermont), "'What we have here is a Failure to Communicate': Innocent III and Alexius III on the Eve of the Fourth Crusade"

Thomas F. Madden (Saint Louis University), "The Latin Empire's Fractured Foundation: The Rift between Boniface of Montferrat and Baldwin of Flanders"

Michael Lower (University of Minnesota), "Pope Gregory IX and the Latin Empire"

[b] Frankish Greece
Chair: Jean Richard

Gilles Grivaud (Université de Rouen), "La place du clergé mineur grec dans la société des Etats francs après 1204"

Diana Gililand Wright (New School University), "The Parlement of Ravenika"

David Jacoby (Hebrew University of Jerusalem), "Demography and Society in Latin Constantinople, 1204–1261"

[c] The Kingdom of Lesser Armenia and the Crusades
Chair: Sylvia Schein

Christopher MacEvitt (Dartmouth College), "Matthew of Edessa and the Problem of Tolerance in the Latin East"

Karl Borchardt (University of Würzburg), "'Good Heretics'?: Western Attitudes towards the Armenians in the Fourteenth Century"

Zara Pogossian (Central European University), "Crossing Cultures in the Text of the *Letter of Love and Concord:* an Armenian Apocryphal Source from the Period of the Fourth Crusade"

Coffee Break

16.30–18.00

[a] Historiography of the Fourth Crusade
Chair: Jonathan Harris

Alicia J. Simpson (King's College, London), "Before and After 1204: the Versions of Niketas Choniates' *Historia* and the Collapse of Byzantium"

Jenny Horowitz (University of Haifa), "'By overturning the Cross with the Cross they Bore Sewn on their Backs, the Latins rejected Christ': Niketas Choniates' Testimony as a Reflection of the Byzantine Stance towards the Franks"

Elizabeth Siberry (Independent Scholar), "The Fourth Crusade: some Later Perspectives"

[b] Commemorating the Crusades and Artistic Patronage
Chair: Nurith Kenaan Kedar

Christine Verzar (Ohio State University), "The Artistic Patronage of the Returning Crusader: The Arm of St. George and Ferrara Cathedral"

Montserrat Pages (Museu Nacional d'art, Catalunya), "Ripoll and Taull, Memory and Patronage after the Reconquista"

Nurith Kenaan-Kedar (Tel Aviv University), "Returning Crusades and the Mural Cycle of Saint-Chef (Dauphine)"

Hanna Taragan (Tel Aviv University), "Mamluk Patronage and Crusader Memories"

[c] Dynastic Politics and the Crusades
Chair: Ronnie Ellenblum

Torben K. Nielsen (Aalborg University), "War and Marriage: Cultural Encounters in the Baltic Crusades"

John W. Barker (University of Wisconsin-Madison), "Crusading and Matrimony in the Dynastic Policies of Montferrat and Savoy"

Jochen G. Schenk (Emmanuel College, Cambridge), "Templar Support and the Crusading Tradition of Noble French Families"

Saturday, 28 August

9.30–11.00

[a] Historiography of the Crusade
Chair: Boaz Adrian

Cyril Aslanov (Hebrew University of Jerusalem), "Villehardouin and Robert de Clari on the Conquest of Constantinople: The Rise of a New Historiography?"

Luis Garcia Guijarro (University of Zaragoza) and Manuel Rojas (University of Extremadura), "Crusader Historiography and Reconquista: A Spanish View of Existing Clichés"

Taef el-Azhari (Helwan University, Cairo), "The Muslim Perspectives of the Middle East during the Fourth Crusade"

[b] The First Crusade
Chair: G. A. Loud

Johanna Maria Van Winter (University of Utrecht), "The Origins of the Priest Godschalk the Crusader"

Koray Durak (Harvard), "Byzantine Imperial Discourse on the Crusaders in Anna Komnena's *Alexiad* as a Mechanism of Imperial Control"

Sini Kangas (University of Helsinki), "The Image of the Greeks in the Sources of the First Crusade"

[c] Rulers, Crusades, and the Military Orders
Chair: Alfred J. Andrea

J. T. Roche (University of St Andrews), “Conrad III and the Second Crusade, 1147–1148: Retreat from Dorylaeum?”

Peter S. Peleg (University of Haifa), “Frederick II and the Major Military Orders”

José Manuel Rodríguez García (University of Salamanca), “1269–1271: The Spanish and St. Louis’ Second Crusade”

Coffee Break

11.30–13.00

[a] The Fourth Crusade
Chair: Luis Garcia Guijarro

Ebru Altan (Istanbul University), “Anatolia after the Fourth Crusade”

Susan B. Edgington (Queen Mary, University of London), “A Female Physician on the Fourth Crusade? Laurette de Saint-Valery”

Jürgen Krüger (University of Karlsruhe), “Relics, Spoils, and Mosaics: St Marc in Venice and its Relation to the Churches of Constantinople and of the Holy Sepulchre in Jerusalem”

[b] Venice and the Crusades
Chair: Karl Borchardt

Pierre A. MacKKay (University of Washington), “Walking the Streets of Negropont”

Ruth Gertwagen (Oranim College, Israel), “Maritime Factors in the Formation of the so-called Venetian Maritime Empire and the Development of its ports System”

P. Racine (Université Marc Bloch, Strasbourg), “Venise et son arrière-pays continental à l’époque de la 4ème Croisade”

[c] Additional Session

Ioanna Christoforaki (Academy of Athens), “Circulating Images, Transmitting Ideas: The Cultural Economy of Crusader Cyprus”

14.30–16.00

Plenary Session
Chair: Benjamin Kedar
New and Old in the Research of the Fourth Crusade

Panel: David Jacoby, Jonathan Riley Smith, Michel Balard, Thomas Madden, and Alfred J. Andrea.

20.00
Farewell Banquet

Sunday, 29 August
Tour: Princes’ Island and Bosphorus Highlights

Monday, 30 August
Optional tour: Byzantine Highlights (**9.00–17.00**)

b) Other news

Paul Crawford reports that the library of the University of Wisconsin has scanned the entire six-volume 'History of the Crusades', ed. Kenneth Setton, and placed it on the web at <libtext.library.wisc.edu/HistCrusades/About.html>.

Martin Hoch reports the the exhibition "The Crusaders: Europe's Encounter with the Orient' originally co-scheduled for Mainz and Mannheim from April through July 2004 has been split up. The 'Bischöfliches Dom- und Diözesanmuseum' in Mainz will host the exhibition 'The Crusades' from 2 April through 30 July 2004; see <http://www.kath.de/bistum/mainz/dommuseum/kreuzfahrer/index engl.htm>. The 'Reiss-Engelhard-Museen' in Mannheim will host the exhibition 'Saladin and the Crusaders' from 15 October 2005 through 29 January 2006; see <http://www.mannheim.de/museen-archiv/reiss-engelhorn-museen/de/ausstellungen/2005.htm>.

Zsolt Hunyadi reports that there has been a workshop on the Fourth Crusade, Central European Univ., Budapest 26–28 February 2003.

David Nicolle reports that the Royal Institute for Arabian Horsemanship (Al Ma'had al-Maliki li'l-Furusiya al-'Arabiya) has been established at Madaba, Jordan. Based at an existing privately owned equestrian complex, and directed by Prince Talal Bin Muhammad and Mr. Said Huneidi, the Institute intends to revive the now extinct Arab and Islamic military equestrian heritage, with a special focus on medieval Arab-Islamic furusiya training and skills.

Marie-Adélaïde Nielen reports that there is an exhibition 'Sceaux et usages de sceaux: images de la Champagne médiévale', important for crusaders from Champagne such as Joinville, Brienne, Champlitte, Villehardouin, Châlons (Marne): Archives départementales, Reims (Marne): Palais du Tau, and Paris, May 2004 to September 2005.

Jonathan Phillips reports that from September 2004 the History Departments of Royal Holloway, Univ. of London and Queen Mary, Univ. of London, will jointly offer an MA in Crusader Studies. The course will include units on: The Crusade of Louis IX, Mongols and Mamluks; The Early Latin East, 1098–1144; Byzantium and the Crusader States and Recording the Crusades (Sources and Historiography). There is also a Research Skills seminar, and there are appropriate language component options as well. With the superb resources of the Institute of Historical Research, London and the British Library, this MA offers a highly stimulating course in its own right and will also act as an excellent preparation for doctoral research. For further details, contact j.p.phillips@rhul.ac.uk

9. Members' queries

Axel EHLERS would be grateful for any references to unpublished material touching on the military orders and their use of vow redemptions, especially of crusade vows.

Janus Møller JENSEN asks if anyone knows of a crusade preaching manual for the *minus doctis* from the pontificate of Martin V.

10. Officers of the Society

President: Professor Michel Balard. Honorary Vice-Presidents: Professor Jean Richard, Professor Jonathan Riley-Smith. Secretary: Professor Sophia Menache. Assistant Secretary: Professor Luis García-Guijarro Ramos. Editor of the Bulletin: Professor Karl Borchardt. Treasurer: Dr Ian Quelch.

Committee of the Society: Professor Antonio Carile (Bologna), Professor Robert Huygens (Leiden), Professor Hans Eberhard Mayer (Kiel).

11. Income and expenditure account for the Society

The accounts starting from 18 September 2002 will be established by the new treasurer.

12. List of members and their addresses

Shawn D. Abbott, 924 Greenbriar Road, Muncie IN 47304-3260, U.S.A.; sdbabbott@hotmail.com

Prof. Baudouin van den Abeele, Rue C. Wolles 3, B-1030 Bruxelles, BELGIUM; vandenabeele@mage.ucl.ac.be

Dr Anna Sapir Abulafia, Lucy Cavendish College, Cambridge CB3 0BU, ENGLAND, U.K.

Dr David S. H. Abulafia, Gonville and Caius College, Cambridge CB2 1TA, ENGLAND, U.K.

Gabriella Airaldi, Dipartimento di Scienze dell'antichità e del medioevo (DISAM), Università di Genova, Via Lomellini 8, I-16124 Genoa, ITALY; tel.: 0039-010-2465897 and 2099602, fax: 0039-010-2465810

Brian Allison Lewis, c/o Sabic, PO Box 5101, Riyadh 11422, SAUDI ARABIA

Prof. Reuven Amitai-Preiss, Dept. of Islamic and Middle Eastern Studies, Hebrew Univ., Jerusalem 91905, ISRAEL; amitai@h2.hum.huji.ac.il

Dr Monique Amouroux, 2, Avenue de Montchalette, Cassy, F-33138 Lanton, FRANCE

Prof. Alfred J. Andrea, 161 Austin Drive #3, Burlington VT 05401, U.S.A.; aandrea@uvm.edu

Dr Benjamin Arbel, School of History, Tel-Aviv Univ., Tel-Aviv 69978, ISRAEL; arbel@ccsg.tau.ac.il

Dr Marco Arosio, Università del Sacro Cuore, Milano, ITALY; marco_arosio@tin.it

Dr Thomas S. Asbridge, Dept. of History, Queen Mary and Westfield College, Univ. of London, Mile End Road, London E1 4NS, ENGLAND, U.K.; t_asbridge@qmul.ac.uk

Dr Hussein M. Attiya, 20 Ahmed Sidik Street, Sidi Gaber El-Shiek, Alexandria, EGYPT

Prof. Taef K. el-Azhari, 6/14 Zahraa El-Maadi, Second Sector, Cairo 11435, EGYPT; taef@tedata.net.eg

Dr Mohammed Aziz, PO Box 135513, Beirut, LEBANON

Dr Bernard S. Bachrach, Univ. of Minnesota, Dept. of History, 633 Social Sciences Building, Minneapolis MN 55455, U.S.A.

Dr Dan Bahat, PO Box 738, Mevasseret Zion 90805, ISRAEL; danbahat@yahoo.com

Prof. Michel Balard, 4, rue des Remparts, F-94370 Sucy-en-Brie, FRANCE, balard@univ-paris1.fr

Laura Balletto, Via Orsini 40/B, I-16146 Genoa, ITALY; lauraballettolettere@unige.it

Paul Walden Bamford, 2204 West Lake of the Isles Parkway, Minneapolis MN 55405-2426, U.S.A.

Prof. Malcolm Barber, Dept. of History, Univ. of Reading, PO Box 218, Whiteknights, Reading RG6 6AA, ENGLAND, U.K.; m.c.barber@reading.ac.uk

Prof. John W. Barker, Dept. of History, Univ. of Wisconsin, 3211 Humanities Building, Madison WI 53706, U.S.A.; jwbarker@facstaff.wisc.edu

Sebastian Bartos, 6762 4th Avenue, Brooklyn NY 11220, U.S.A.; sebartos@hotmail.com

The Rev. Fr. Robert L. BECERRA, Senior Associate Pastor, St Luke Catholic Church, 2892 South Congress Avenue, Palm Springs FL 33461-2170, U.S.A.; SinaiPantocrator@aol.com

Dr Bruce BEEBE, 1490 Mars Lakewood OH 44107, U.S.A.; lgbeebe@aol.com

Prof. George BEECH, Dept. of History, Western Michigan Univ., Kalamazoo MI 49008, U.S.A.; beech@wmich.edu

Elena BELLOMO, via dei Rospigliosi 1, I-20151 Milano, ITALY; elena.bellomo@libero.it

Jacob BEN-CNAAN, 52 Katz Street, Petakh-Tikva 49374, ISRAEL; ponar@zahav.net.il

Matthew BENNETT, 58 Mitchell Avenue, Hartley Wintney, Hampshire RG27 8HG, ENGLAND, U.K.; mattbennett@waitrose.com

Dr Nora BEREND, St Catharine's College, Cambridge CB2 1RL, ENGLAND, U.K.; nb213@cam.ac.uk

Jessalynn BIRD, 1514 Cortland Drive, Naperville IL 60565, U.S.A; jessalynn.bird@iname.com

Prof. Nancy BISAHA, Dept. of History, Vassar College, Maildrop 81, 124 Raymond Avenue, Poughkeepsie NY 12604, U.S.A.; nabisaha@vassar.edu

Prof. John R. E. BLIESE, Communication Studies Dept., Texas Tech Univ., Lubbock TX 79409, U.S.A.

Dr Adrian J. BOAS, Institute of Archaeology, Hebrew Univ. of Jerusalem, Jerusalem 91905, ISRAEL

Prof. Mark S. BOCIJA, Columbus State Community College, 550 E. Spring Street, Columbus OH 43216-1609, U.S.A.; mbocija@cscc.edu

Louis BOISSET, Université Saint-Joseph de Beyrouth, BP 166 778, Achrafieh, Beirut, LEBANON

Brenda M. BOLTON, 8 Watling Street, St Albans AL1 2PT, ENGLAND, U.K.; brenda@bolton.vianw.co.uk

Barbara BOMBI, via Leonardo da Vinci 26, I-27029 Vigevano (PV), ITALY; bbombi@libero.it

Pierre BONNEAUD, Carretera de Sant Vicenç 47, E-08394 Sant Vicenç de Montalt (Barcelona), SPAIN; pierrebonneaud@yahoo.es

Prof. Karl BORCHARDT, Wiesenstraße 18, D-91541 Rothenburg ob der Tauber, GERMANY; stadtarchiv@rothenburg.de

Prof. Charles R. BOWLUS, History Dept., Univ. of Arkansas, 8081 Mabelvale, Little Rock AR 72209-1099, U.S.A.; carolus22000@yahoo.com

Prof. Charles M. BRAND, 508 West Montgomery Avenue, Haverford PA 19041-1409, U.S.A.; cmbrand4@mac.com

Dr Michael BRETT, School of Oriental and African Studies, Univ. of London, Malet Street, London WC1E 7HP, ENGLAND, U.K.

Robert BRODIE, 61 St Saviours Wharf, 8 Shad Thames, London SE1 2YP, ENGLAND, U.K.; robert@dbrodie.demon.co.uk

Judith BRONSTEIN, Ilanot 29/2, Haifa 34324, ISRAEL; Judith_Bronstein@hotmail.com

Prof. Elizabeth A. R. BROWN, 160 West 86th Street PH4, New York NY 10024, U.S.A.; rsbrown160@aol.com

Prof. James A. BRUNDAGE, 1102 Sunset Drive, Lawrence KS 66044-4548, U.S.A.; jabrun@ku.edu

Dr Marcus G. BULL, Dept. of Historical Studies, Univ. of Bristol, 13–15 Woodland Road, Clifton, Bristol BS8 1TB, ENGLAND, U.K.; m.g.bull@bris.ac.uk

SSG Almyr L. BUMP, 7070 Austrian Pine Way #1, Portage MI 49204, U.S.A.; bump4@juno.com

Dr Jochen BURGTORF, California State Univ., Dept. of History, Fullerton CA 92834-6846, U.S.A.; jburgtorf@fullerton.edu

Olivier BURLOTTE, Appartment 79, Smolensky Boulvard 6–8, Moscow 119 034, RUSSIA, oburlotte@yahoo.com

Charles BURNETT, Warburg Institute, Woburn Square, London WC1H 0AB, ENGLAND, U.K.; ch-burne@sas.ac.uk

The Rev. Prof. Robert I. BURNS, History Dept., UCLA, Los Angeles CA 90095, U.S.A.; fax: (310) 338-3002

Dr Peter BURRIDGE, Harmer Mill, Millington, York YO4 2TX, ENGLAND, U.K.

Ane Lise BYSTED, Dept. of History, Univ. of Southern Denmark, Campusvej 55, DK-5230 Odense M, DENMARK; bysted@hist.sdu.dk

Dr J. P. CANNING, History Dept. Univ. College of North Wales, Bangor, Gwynedd, WALES, U.K.

Franco CARDINI, PO Box 2358, I-50123 Firenze Ferrovia, ITALY

Christer CARLSSON, Medieval Archaeologist, Litsbyvägen 66, 18746 Täby, SWEDEN

Alan Brady CARR, 2522 20th Street, Lubbock TX 79410, U.S.A.

Dr Annemarie Weyl CARR, Division of Art History, Southern Methodist Univ., PO Box 750356, Dallas TX 75275-0356, U.S.A.; acarr@mail.smu.edu

Marc CARRIER, 500 Alexandre-Dumas, Granby Quebec J2J 1B2, CANADA

Jennifer CASTEN, 875 Western Avenue, Apt. 3, Brattleboro VT 05301, U.S.A.; nulla@macol.net

Prof. Brian CATLOS, Univ. of California Santa Cruz, Stevenson Academic Center, 1156 High Street, Santa Cruz CA 95064, U.S.A.; bcatlos@ucsc.edu

Prof. Fred A. CAZEL Jr., 309 Gurleyville Road, Storrs Mansfield CT 06268-1439, U.S.A.

Dr Simonetta CERRINI[-ALLOISIO], Via Antonio Gramsci 109/32, I-15076 Ovada (Alessandria), ITALY; alloisiocerrini@inwind.it

Anton CHARLTON, 16 Muswell Hill, Muswell Hill, London NJ0 3TA, ENGLAND, U.K.

Dr Martin CHASIN, 1125 Church Hill Road, Fairfield CT 06432-1371, U.S.A.; mchasin@worldnet.att.net

Dr Katherine CHRISTENSEN, CPO 1756 Berea College, Berea KY 40404, U.S.A.; katherine_christensen@berea.edu

Dr Niall G. F. CHRISTIE, Dept. of Classical, Near Eastern and Religious Studies, The Univ. of British Columbia, BUCH C260-1866 Main Hall, Vancouver B.C. V6T 1Z1, CANADA; niall.christie@yahoo.com

Ioanna CHRISTOFORAKI, Aristotelous 26, Chalandri, Athens 15234, GREECE; joanna.christoforaki@archeology.oxford.ac.uk

Dr Juliana CHRYSOSTOMIDES, Dept. of History, Egham Hill, Egham, Surrey, ENGLAND, U.K.; j.chysostomides@rhul.ac.uk

Padre Giulio CIPOLLONE, B.S.S.T., Padri Trinitari, Piazza S. Maria alle Fornaci 30, I-00165 Roma, ITALY; cipolloneunigre6009@fastwebnet.it

Dr G. H. M. Claassens, Departement Literatuurwetenschap, Katholieke Universiteit Leuven, Blijde Inkomststraat 21, Postbus 33, B-3000 Leuven, BELGIUM

Pierre-Vincent Claverie, 9, rue du Bois-Rondel, F-35700 Rennes, FRANCE; pvclaverie@minitel.net

Dr Penny J. Cole, Trinity College, 6 Hoskin Avenue, Toronto, Ontario M5S 1HB, CANADA; pjcole@trinity.utoronto.ca

Prof. Eleanor A. Congdon, Youngstown State Univ., One University Plaza, Youngstown OH 44555, U.S.A.; eacongdon@ysu.edu

Prof. Giles Constable, 506 Quaker Road, Princeton NJ 08540, U.S.A.

Prof. Olivia Remie Constable, Dept. of History, Univ. of Notre Dame, Notre Dame, IN 46556-0368, U.S.A.; constable1@nd.edu

Prof. Robert F. Cook, French Language and General Linguistics Dept., Univ. of Virginia, 302 Cabell Hall, Charlottesville VA 22903, U.S.A.

Prof. Rebecca W. Corrie, Phillips Professor of Art, Bates College, Lewiston ME 04240, U.S.A.; rcorrie@bates.edu

Prof. Ricardo Luiz Silveira da Costa, Rua Joao Nunes Coelho 264 apto. 203, Ed. Tom Jobim – Bairro Mata da Praia – Vitória – Espíritó Santo (ES), CEP 29.065-490, BRAZIL; riccosta@npd.ufes.br or ricardo@ricardocosta.com

Dr Nicholas S. Coureas, PO Box 26619, Lykarittos, CY-1640 Nicosia, CYPRUS

The Rev. H. E. J. Cowdrey, 30 Oxford Road, Old Marston, Oxford 0X3 0PQ, ENGLAND, U.K.; fax (0) 1865 279090

Dr Paul Crawford, History Dept., Alma College, 614 West Superior Street, Alma MI 48801, U.S.A.; crawford@alma.edu

Prof. Larry S. Crist, 6609 Rolling Fork Drive, Nashville TN 37205, U.S.A.

B. Thomas Curtis, 36 Brockswood Lane, Welwyn Garden City, Herts. AL8 /BG, ENGLAND, U.K.; btcurtis@btinternet.com

Dana [Dennis-]Cushing, PO Box 9088, Waukegan IL 60079, U.S.A.; denniscushingdl@mfr.usmc.mil

Charles Dalli, Dept. of History, Faculty of Arts, Univ. of Malta, Msida MSD06, MALTA; cdalli@arts.um.edu.mt

Philip Louis Daniel, Archivist, Equestrian Order of the Holy Sepuchre of Jerusalem, 37 Somerset Road, Meadvale, Redhill, Surrey RH1 6LT, ENGLAND, U.K.; fax: 01737-240722

Dr Béatrice Dansette, 175, Boulevard Malesherbes, F-75017 Paris, FRANCE

Nicole Dawe, 21 New Road, Okehampton, Devon EX20 1JE, ENGLAND, U.K.; ndawe@hotmail.com

Julian Deahl, c/o E. J. Brill, PO Box 9000, NL-2300 PA Leiden, THE NETHERLANDS; deahl@brill.nl

Dr Bernhard Demel O.T., Leiter des Deutschordenszentralarchivs, Singerstraße 7, A-1010 Wien, AUSTRIA; tel. 513 70 14

Prof. Işin Demirkent, Head of Middle Ages History Dept., İstanbul Üniversitesi Edebiyat Fakültesi Tarih Bölümü, Beyazıt – İstanbul, TURKEY; address for all correspondence: Darıca, Tuzla Cad. 67 Kocaeli, TURKEY; fax: 212.6290312

John A. Dempsey, 218 Edgehill Road, Milton MA 02186-5310, U.S.A.; milton1@bu.edu

Prof. Alain DEMURGER, 5, rue de l'Abricotier, F-95000 Cergy, FRANCE; Alain.Demurger@wanadoo.fr

Prof. George T. DENNIS, Loyola Marymount Univ., PO Box 45041, Los Angeles CA 90045-0041, U.S.A.; nauarchos@aol.com

Prof. Lucy DER MANUELIAN, 10 Garfield Road, Belmont MA 02178-3309, U.S.A.; lucy.manuelian@tufts.edu

Americo DE SANTIS, 88 East Main Street, Box Number 141, Mendham NJ 07945, U.S.A.; ricodesantis@hotmail.com

Dr M. Gary DICKSON, History, School of History and Classics, Univ. of Edinburgh, Wm. Robertson Building, 50 George Square, Edinburgh EH8 9JY, SCOTLAND, U.K.; Gary.Dickson@ed.ac.uk

Prof. Richard DIVALL, 301 Arcadia, 228 The Avenue, Parkville, Victoria 3052, AUSTRALIA; naestro@spin.net.au

Dr Erica Cruikshank DODD, 4208 Wakefield Place, Victoria, B.C. V8N 6E5, CANADA

César DOMÍNGUEZ, Universidad de Santiago de Compostela, Facultad de Filologia, Avda. Castealo s/n, E-15704 Santiago (La Coruna), SPAIN

Cristina DONDI, 12 Battishill Street, London N1 1TE, ENGLAND, U.K.; cfd@bodley.ox.ac.uk

Ara DOSTOURIAN, Box 420, Harmony RI 02829, U.S.A.

Mary DOUROU-ELIOPOULOU, Kephallenias 24, Althea 36km.Sounion Ave., 19400 Attiki, GREECE; meliop@cc.uoa.gr

Dr Jean DUNBABIN, St Anne's College, Oxford OX2 6HS, ENGLAND, U.K.

Mark DUPUY, 119 South Sixth Avenue, Apartment A, Clarion PA 16214, U.S.A.; mdupuy@clarion.edu

John DURANT, 32 Maple Street, PO Box 373, West Newbury MA 01985, U.S.A.

Dr Valerie EADS, 308 West 97th Street, New York NY 10025, U.S.A.; pkve@earthlink.net

Prof. Richard EALES, School of History, Univ. of Kent, Canterbury CT2 7NX, ENGLAND, U.K.; rgel@ukc.ac.uk

Ana ECHEVARRÍA ARSUAGA, Facultad de Geografia e Historia, Departimento de Historia Medieval, C/ Senda del Rey, E-28040 Madrid, SPAIN; anaevjosem@wanadoo.es

Prof. Peter W. EDBURY, School of History and Archaeology, Cardiff Univ., PO Box 909, Cardiff CF10 3XU, WALES, U.K.; edbury@cardiff.ac.uk

Dr Susan B. EDGINGTON, 3 West Street, Huntingdon, Cambs PE29 1WT, ENGLAND, U.K.; s.b.edgington@btopenworld.com

Axel EHLERS, Berdingstraße 4a, D-30451 Hannover, GERMANY; aehlers1@gwdg.de

Prof. Sven EKDAHL, Sponholzstraße 38, D-12159 Berlin, GERMANY; Sven.Ekdahl@t-online.de

Dr Ronnie ELLENBLUM, 13 Reuven Street, Jerusalem 93510, ISRAEL; msronni@pluto.mscc.huji.ac.il

Prof. Kasper ELM, Koserstraße 20, D-14195 Berlin, GERMANY

Prof. Steven A. EPSTEIN, Dept. of History, Univ. of Kansas, Lawrence KS 66049-7590, U.S.A.; sae@ku.edu

Dr Helen C. EVANS, The Medieval Dept., The Metropolitan Museum of Art, 1000 Fifth Avenue, New York NY 10028, U.S.A.; helenevans@metmuseum.org

Michael EVANS, Flat 6, Marston Ferry Court, Oxford OX2 7XH, ENGLAND, U.K.; m_r_evans@hotmail.com

Prof. Theodore EVERGATES, 146 West Main Street, Westminster MD 21157, U.S.A.

John C. FARQUHARSON, 19 Long Croft Lane, Cheadle Hulme, Cheadle Cheshire SK8 6SE, ENGLAND, U.K.; johnfarquharson@easicom.com

Prof. Marie-Luise FAVREAU-LILIE, Kaiser-Friedrich-Straße 106, D-10585 Berlin, GERMANY; mlfavre@zedat.fu-berlin.de

Jack FERGUSSON, Dept. of Chemistry, Univ. of Canterbury, Christchurch, NEW ZEALAND; j.fergusson@chem.canterbury.ac.nz

P. J. FLAHERTY, 9 Oak Street, Braintree MA 02184, U.S.A.

Prof. Richard A. FLETCHER, Low Pasture House, Nunnington, York YO62 5XQ, ENGLAND, U.K.; richardfletcher@ukonline.co.uk

Prof. Jean FLORI, Docteur d'État des Lettres et Sciences Humaines, Directeur de Recherche au Centre d'Études Supérieures de Civilisation Médiévale de Poitiers, 69 rue Saint Cornély, F-56340 Carnac, FRANCE; flori.jean@wanadoo.fr

Prof. Jaroslav FOLDA, Dept. of Art, Univ. of North Carolina, Chapel Hill NC 27599-3405, U.S.A.; jfolda@email.unc.edu

Michelle FOLTZ, M.D., PMB 33, PO Box 1226, Columbus MT 59019, U.S.A.

Dr Alan FOREY, The Bell House, Church Lane, Kirtlington, Oxon. OX5 3HJ, ENGLAND, U.K.

Edith FORMAN, 38 Burnham Hill, Westport CT 06880, U.S.A.

Barbara FRALE, via A. Gramsci 17, I-01028 Orte (VT), ITALY; barbara-frale@libero.it

Dr John FRANCE, History Dept., Univ. of Wales, Swansea SA2 7PP, WALES, U.K.; j.france@swansea.ac.uk

Dr Peter FRANKOPAN, Worcester College, Oxford OX1 2HB, ENGLAND, U.K.; peter.frankopan@worcester.ox.ac.uk

Dr Yvonne FRIEDMAN, Dept. of History, Bar-Ilan Univ., Ramat-Gan 55900, ISRAEL; yfried@mail.biu.ac.il

Stuart FROST, 44 Ratumore Road Charlton, London SE7 7QW, ENGLAND, U.K.; stuartfrost@fsmail.net

R. FROUMIN, Neve Eitan, D. N. Beit Shean 10840, ISRAEL; froumin@yahoo.com

Michael and Neathery FULLER, 13530 Clayton Road, St Louis MO 63141, U.S.A.; mfuller@artsci.wustl.edu

Prof. Luis GARCÍA-GUIJARRO RAMOS, Professor titular de Historia Medieval, Facultad de Huesca, Plaza de la Universidad 3, E-22002 Huesca, SPAIN; luguijar@posta.unizar.es

Dr Christopher K. GARDNER, Univ. of Nebraska, Dept. of History ASH 287X, Omaha NE 68182, U.S.A.; cgardner@jhu.edu

Giles E. M. GASPER, Wolfson College, Linton Road, Oxford OX2 6UD, ENGLAND, U.K.; giles.gasper@wolfson.ox.ac.uk

F. Gregory GAUSE Jr., 207 Bayard Avenue, Rehoboth Beach DE 19971, U.S.A.; prgause@aol.com

Sabine GELDSETZER, M.A., Westheide 6, D-44892 Bochum, GERMANY; sabine.geldsetzer@ruhr-uni-bochum.de

Prof. Maria GEORGOPOULOU, Dept. of the History of Art, Yale Univ., PO Box 208272, New Haven CT 06520-8272, U.S.A.; maria.georgopoulou@yale.edu

Deborah GERISH, Dept. of Social Sciences Box 32, Emporia State Univ., 1200 Commercial, Emporia KS 66801, U.S.A.; dgerish@netscape.net

Dr Ruthi GERTWAGEN, 30 Ranas Street, PO Box 117, Qiryat Motzkin 26317, ISRAEL; ruger@macam98.ac.il

Prof. John B. GILLINGHAM, 49 Old Shoreham Road, Brighton, Sussex BN1 5DQ, ENGLAND, U.K.; jgilli49@aol.com

Prof. Anne GILMOUR-BRYSON, 1935 Westview Drive, North Vancouver, B.C. V7M 3B1, CANADA; annegb@telus.net

J. L. GILS, Gouden Leeuw 820, NL-1103 KS Amsterdam, THE NETHERLANDS

Prof. Dorothy F. GLASS, 11 Riverside Drive, Apartment 6-OW, New York NY 10023, U.S.A.; dglass1@att.net

Prof. Aryeh GRABOIS, History Dept., Univ. of Haifa, Mount Carmel, Haifa 31905, ISRAEL; fax 972-4-82499195

Michael GRAYER, 192 York Road, Shrewsbury, Shropshire SY1 3QH, ENGLAND, U.K.

Gilles GRIVAUD, 8 rue de Général de Miribel, F-69007 Lyon, FRANCE

The Rev. Joseph J. GROSS, Trinitarian History Studies, PO Box 42056, Baltimore MD 21284, U.S.A.; jjg62osst@aol.com

Prof. Klaus GUTH, Greiffenbergstraße 35, D-96052 Bamberg, GERMANY

Dr Mark E. HALL, 6826 Walso Avenue, El Cerrito CA 94530, U.S.A.; markhall@gol.com

Adina HAMILTON, 469 Albert Street, Brunswick West Victoria 3055, AUSTRALIA or History Dept., Univ. of Melbourne, Parkville Victoria 3052, AUSTRALIA

Prof. Bernard HAMILTON, 7 Lenton Avenue, The Park, Nottingham NG7 IDX, ENGLAND, U.K.

Peter HARITATOS Jr., 1500 North George Street, Rome NY 13440, U.S.A.

Jonathan HARRIS, Dept. of History, Royal Holloway, Univ. of London, Egham, Surrey TW20 0EX, ENGLAND, U.K.; jonathan.harris@rhul.ac.uk

Kathryn D. HARRIS, 6 Gallows Hill, Saffron Walden, Essex CB11 4DA, ENGLAND, U.K.

Dr Alan HARVEY, Dept. of Historical and Critical Studies, Univ. of Northumbria, Newcastle-upon-Tyne NE1 8ST, ENGLAND, U.K.; alan.harvey@unn.ac.uk

David HAY, 164 McCaul Street Apt. 1, Toronto, Ontario M5T 1WA, CANADA

Dr Bodo HECHELHAMMER, Erzbergerstraße 8, D-64823 Groß-Umstadt/Heubach, GERMANY; bodo.hechelhammer@t-online.de or Institut für Geschichte, Residenzschloß, D-64283 Darmstadt, GERMANY; bh@polihist.pg.tu-darmstadt.de

Prof. Thérèse de HEMPTINNE, Universiteit Gent, Faculteit van de Letteren, Vakgroep Middeleeuwse Geschiedenis, Blandijnberg 2, B-9000 Gent, BELGIUM

Michael HESLOP, 2, Boulevard J.-Dalcroze, CH-1204 Geneva, SWITZERLAND; michaelheslop@atlworld.com

Dr Paul HETHERINGTON, 15 Luttrell Avenue, London SW15 6PD, ENGLAND, U.K.; phetherington@ukonline.co.uk

Dr Avital HEYMAN, 12 Hertzel Street, Ness-Ziona 74084, ISRAEL; avital-h@internet-zahav.net

Prof. Rudolf HIESTAND, Brehmstraße 76, D-40239 Düsseldorf, GERMANY

Charles A. HILKEN, PO Box 4825, St Mary's College, Moraga CA 94575, U.S.A.; chilken@stmarys-ca.edu

Dr George HINTLIAN, Armenian Patriarchate, PO Box, Jerusalem 14001, ISRAEL

Dr Martin HOCH, Konrad-Adenauer-Stiftung, Rathausallee 12, D-53757 Sankt Augustin, GERMANY; Lobebaer@web.de

Dr Catherine HOLMES, University College, Oxford OX1 4BH, ENGLAND, U.K.; catherine.holmes@univ.ox.ac.uk

Prof. Peter M. HOLT, Dryden Spinney, Bletchington Road, Kirtlington, Kidlington, Oxon OX5 3HF, ENGLAND, U.K.

Prof. Hubert HOUBEN, Via Marugi 38, I-73100 Lecce, ITALY; houben@sesia.unile.it

Prof. Norman J. HOUSLEY, School of Historical Studies, The Univ. of Leicester, Leicester LE1 7RH, ENGLAND, U.K.; hou@le.ac.uk

Prof. Lucy-Anne HUNT, Dept. of History of Art and Design, Righton Building, Cavendish Street, Manchester M15 6BK, ENGLAND, U.K.; l.a.hunt@mmu.ac.uk

Zsolt HUNYADI, 27 Szekeres u., H-6725 Szeged, HUNGARY; hunyadiz@hist.u-szeged.hu

Prof. Robert B. C. HUYGENS, Witte Singel 28, NL-2311 BH Leiden, THE NETHERLANDS

Sheldon IBBOTSON, PO Box 258, Rimbey, Alberta T0C 2JO, CANADA; bronwen@telusplanet.net

Robert IRWIN, 39 Harleyford Road, London SE11 5AX, ENGLAND, U.K.; robert@robertirwin.demon.co.uk

Prof. Peter JACKSON, History Dept., Univ. of Keele, Keele, Staffs. ST5 5BG, ENGLAND, U.K.; hia08@keele.ac.uk

Martin JACOBOWITZ, The Towers of Windsor Park, 3005 Chapel Avenue – 11P, Cherry Hill NJ 08002, U.S.A.

Prof. David JACOBY, Dept. of History, The Hebrew Univ., Jerusalem 91905, ISRAEL; jacobgab@h2.hum.huji.ac.il

Dr Kay Peter JANKRIFT, Institut für Geschichte der Medizin der Robert Bosch Stiftung, Straußweg 17, D-70184 Stuttgart, GERMANY

Dr Nikolas JASPERT, Institut für Geschichte, Universität Erlangen-Nürnberg, Kochstraße 4, D-91056 Erlangen, GERMANY; nsjasper@phil.uni-erlangen.de

Prof. Carsten Selch JENSEN, Dept. of Church History, Univ. of Copenhagen, Købmagergade 46, POB 2164, DK-1150 Copenhagen K, DENMARK; csj@teol.ku.dk

Janus Møller JENSEN, Institute of History and Civilization, Univ. of Southern Denmark, DK-5230 Odense M, DENMARK; jamj@hist.sdu.dk

Prof. Kurt Villads JENSEN, Dept. of History, Odense Univ., Campusvej 55, DK-5230 Odense M, DENMARK; kurt.villads.jensen@humanities.dk

Prof. William Chester JORDAN, Dept. of History, Princeton Univ., Princeton NJ 08544, U.S.A.; wchester@princeton.edu

Philippe JOSSERAND, 1 rue Rubens, F-44000 Nantes, FRANCE; philippe.josserand@humana.univ-nantes.fr

Dr Andrew JOTISCHKY, Dept. of History, Univ. of Lancaster, Bailrigg, Lancaster LA1 4YG, ENGLAND, U.K.; a.jotischky@lancaster.ac.uk

Dr Margaret A. JUBB, Dept. of French, Taylor Building, Univ. of Aberdeen, Old Aberdeen, AB24 3UB, SCOTLAND, U.K.; m.jubb@abdn.ac.uk

Dr Fotini KARASSAVA-TSILINGIRI, Chrysostomou Smyrnis 14, N. Smyrni, Athens 17121, GREECE

Prof. Benjamin Z. KEDAR, Dept. of History, The Hebrew Univ., Jerusalem 91905, ISRAEL; fax (home): 972-3-9720802, bzkedar@h2.hum.huji.ac.il

Prof. Nurith KENAAN-KEDAR, Dept. of Art History, Tel-Aviv Univ., Tel-Aviv 69978, ISRAEL

Dr Hugh KENNEDY, Medieval History Dept., Univ. of St Andrews, St Andrews, Fife KY16 9AL, SCOTLAND, U.K.

Dr Andreas KIESEWETTER, Via La Sila 16/8, I-00135 Roma, ITALY; leonidas@ilink.it

Sharon KINOSHITA, Associate Professor of Literature, Univ. of California Santa Cruz, Santa Cruz CA 95064, U.S.A.

Dr Klaus-Peter KIRSTEIN, Lerchenstraße 60, D-45134 Essen, GERMANY; kirstein-musemeyer@t-online.de

Dr Michael A. KOEHLER, Hertogenlaan 14, B-1970 Wezembeek-Oppem, BELGIUM

Prof. Athina KOLIA-DERMITZAKI, Plateia Kalliga 3, Athens 11253, GREECE; akolia@arch.uoa.gr

Wolf KONRAD, 6240 Phillips Road, Mundaring 6073, West Australia, AUSTRALIA; wolf17.telstra.easymail.com.au

Prof. Barbara M. KREUTZ, 1411 Orchard Way, Rosemont PA 19010, U.S.A.

Prof. Jürgen KRÜGER, Edelsheimstraße 2, D-76131 Karlsruhe, GERMANY; juergen.krueger@geist-soz.uni-karlsruhe.de

Hans-Ulrich KÜHN, Silcherstraße 9/1, D-71254 Ditzingen-Schöckingen, GERMANY; hans-ulrich.kuehn@web.de

Sarah LAMBERT, 35 Cromer Road, London SW17 9JN, ENGLAND, U.K.; slambert@gold.ac.uk

The Rev. William LANE, Charterhouse, Godalming Surrey GU7 2DF, ENGLAND, U.K.; wjl@peperharow.freeserve.co.uk

Dr Robert A. LAURES, 1434 West Maplewood Court, Milwaukee WI 53221-4348, U.S.A.; dr001@voyager.net

Stephen LAY, c/o Dept. of History, Monash Univ., Melbourne, AUSTRALIA; stephen_lay@hotmail.com

Eric LEGG, PSC 98 Box 36, Apo AE 09830, U.S.A.; ericlegg@hotmail.com

Robert D. LEONARD Jr., 1065 Spruce Street, Winnetka IL 60093, U.S.A.; rlwinnetka@aol.com

Dr Antony LEOPOLD, 62 Grafton Road, Acton, London W3 6PD, ENGLAND, U.K.

Richard A. LESON, 2720 St Paul Street #2FF, Baltimore MD 21218, U.S.A.; ral2@jhunix.hef.jhu.edu

Dr Yaacov LEV, PO Box 167, Holon 58101, ISRAEL; yglev@actcom.net.il

Dr Christopher G. LIBERTINI, 27 Lombard Lane, Sudbury MA 01776, U.S.A.; clibertini@aol.com

Dr Giuseppe LIGATO, Viale San Gimignano 18, I-20146 Milano, ITALY

Prof. Ralph-Johannes LILIE, Kaiser-Friedrich-Straße 106, D-10585 Berlin, GERMANY; mlfavre@zedat.fu.berlin.de

Dr Ora LIMOR, The Open Univ., 16 Klausner Street, Tel Aviv 61392, ISRAEL; orali@openu.ac.il

Prof. John LIND, Dept. of History, Univ. of Odense, Campusvej 55, DK-5230 Odense M, DENMARK; john_lind@hist.ou.dk

Dr Simon D. LLOYD, Dept. of History, Univ. of Newcastle-upon-Tyne, Newcastle Upon Tyne NE1 7RU, ENGLAND, U.K.; s.d.lloyd@ncl.ac.uk

Prof. Peter W. LOCK, 9 Straylands Grove, Stockton Lane, York YO31 1EB, ENGLAND, U.K.; p.lock@venysj.ac.uk

Scott LONEY, 4153 Wendell Road, West Bloomfield MI 48323, U.S.A.; scottloney@ameritech.net

Prof. Graham A. LOUD, School of History, Univ. of Leeds, Leeds LS2 9JT, ENGLAND, U.K.; g.a.loud@leeds.ac.uk

Prof. Michael LOWER, Dept. of History, Univ. of Minnesota, 614 Social Sciences Building, 267 19th Avenue South, Minneapolis MN 55455, U.S.A.; mlower@umn.edu

Zoyd R. LUCE, 2441 Creekside Court, Hayward CA 94542, U.S.A.; zluce1@earthlink.net

Dr Svetlana LUCHITSKAYA, Institute of General History, Leninski pr. 89-346, Moscow 119313, RUSSIA; svetlana@mega.ru

Andrew John LUFF, Flat 3, The Hermitage, St Dunstans Road, Lower Feltham, Middlesex TW13 4HR, ENGLAND, U.K.; andrew@luffa.freeserve.co.uk

Dr Anthony LUTTRELL, 20 Richmond Place, Bath BA1 5PZ, ENGLAND, U.K.

Christopher MACEVITT, Dumbarton Oaks, 1703 32nd Street NW, Washington DC 20007, U.S.A.; macevitt@princeton.edu

Merav MACK, Lucy Cavendish College, Cambridge CB3 0BU, ENGLAD, U.K.

Dr Alan D. MACQUARRIE, 173 Queen Victoria Drive, Glasgow G14 7BP, SCOTLAND, U.K.

Thomas F. MADDEN, Dept. of History, Saint Louis Univ., 3800 Lindell Boulevard, PO Box 56907, St Louis MO 63156-0907, U.S.A.; maddentf@slu.edu

Ben MAHONEY, 19 Bond Street, Mount Waverly, Victoria 3149, AUSTRALIA

Dr Christoph T. MAIER, Sommergasse 20, CH-4056 Basel, SWITZERLAND; ctmaier@hist.unizh.ch

Chryssa MALTEZOU, Istituto Ellenico di Studi Bizantini e Postbizantini di Venezia, Castello 3412, I-30122 Venezia, ITALY; hellenic.inst.@gold.ghnet.it

Prof. Michael MARKOWSKI, Dept. of History, Westminster College, 1840 South 1300 East, Salt Lake City UT 84105, U.S.A.

Dr Christopher J. MARSHALL, 8 Courtyard Way, Cottenham, Cambridge CB4 8SF, ENGLAND, U.K.

Dr Carlos de Ayala MARTINEZ, Historia Medieval, Ciudad Universitaria de Cantoblanco, Ctra. De Colmenar, E-28049 Madrid, SPAIN

Prof. Laurence W. MARVIN, History Dept., Evans School of Humanities and Social Sciences, Berry College, Mount Berry GA 30149-5010, U.S.A.; lmarvin@berry.edu

Dr John F. A. MASON, Christ Church College, Oxford OX1 1DP, ENGLAND, U.K.

Kathleen MAXWELL, 4016 26th Street, San Francisco CA 94131, U.S.A.; kmaxwell@scu.edu

Prof. Hans Eberhard MAYER, Historisches Seminar der Universität Kiel, D-24098 Kiel, GERMANY

Robert Maynard, Cuba Villa, 146 Wick Road, Bristol BS4 4HQ, ENGLAND, U.K.; robian@btinternet.com

Andreas Mazarakis, Rizou 3, Athens 10434, GREECE; amazarakis@tee.gr

Prof. Rasa Mazeika, 48A Arcadian Circle, Toronto, Ontario M8W 4W2, CANADA

Arthur H. S. Megaw, 27 Perrins' Walk, London NW3 6TH, ENGLAND, U.K.

Prof. Sophia Menache, Dept. of History, Univ. of Haifa, Haifa 31905, ISRAEL; menache@research.haifa.ac.il

Marco Meschini, Via Fé 15, I-21100 Varese, ITALY; marco.meschini@libero.it

Margaret Meserve, Assistant Professor of History, Univ. of Notre Dame, 219 O'Shaughnessy Hall, Notre Dame IN 46556, U.S.A.; margaret.h.meserve.1@nd.edu

Prof. D. Michael Metcalf, Ashmolean Museum, Oxford OX1 2PH, ENGLAND, U.K.

Françoise Micheau, 8bis, rue du Buisson Saint-Louis, F-75011 Paris, FRANCE; fmicheau@univ-paris.fr

Prof. Klaus Militzer, Winckelmannstraße 32, D-50825 Köln, GERMANY; klaus.militzer@uni-koeln.de

Greg Miller, Financial Consultant, Private Client Group, Merrill Lynch, 200 North 4th Street, Burlington IA 52601, U.S.A.

Peter John Mills, 3 Huxley Road, Leyton, London E10 5QT, ENGLAND, U.K.; petermills@lireone.net

Prof. Laura Minervini, Dipartimento di Filologia Moderna, Università di Napoli Federico II, Via Porta Di Massa 1, I-80133 Napoli, ITALY; lrminer@unina.it

Dr Piers D. Mitchell, 84 Huntingdon Road, East Finchley, London N2 9DU, ENGLAND, U.K.; p.mitchell@clara.co.uk

PD Dr Hannes Möhring, Wilhelm-Bode-Straße 11, D-38104 Braunschweig, GERMANY

Dr Johannes A. Mol, Grote Dijlakker 29, NL-8701 KW Bolsward, THE NETHERLANDS; zeemol@oprit.rug.nl

Dr Kristian Molin, 38 Vessey Terrace, Newcastle-under-Lyme, Staffordshire ST5 1LS, ENGLAND, U.K.; kristian.molin@nulc.ac.uk

Lisa K. Monroe, 7417 Park Terrace Drive, Alexandria VA 22307, U.S.A.; nlmonroe@earthlink.net

Dauvergne C. Morgan, 235 Tooronga Road, Glen Iris, Melbourne, Victoria 3142, AUSTRALIA

Dr David O. Morgan, 302 Orchard Drive, Madison WI 53705, U.S.A.; domorgan@facstaff.wisc.edu

Jonathan C. Morgan, 19 Elia Street, Islington, London N1 8DE, ENGLAND, U.K.; jonathan.morgan@whb.co.uk

J. Diana Morgan, 64 Victoria Avenue, Swanage, Dorset BH19 1AR, ENGLAND, U.K.

Hiroki Moritake, Kami-Ono 371, Hiyoshi-mura, Kitauwa-gun, Ehime-ken 798-1503, JAPAN; jerus@hiroshima-u.ac.jp

The Rev. Prof. Colin Morris, 12 Bassett Crescent East, Southampton SO16 7PB, ENGLAND, U.K.; cm5@soton.ac.uk

Cécile Morrisson, 36, chemin Desvallières, F-92410 Ville d'Avray, FRANCE

Roger D. Mulhollen, Center for Study of Ancient Religious History, 13217 W. Serenade Circle, Sun City West AZ 85375-1707, U.S.A.; audrog@aol.com

Prof. M. E. MULLETT, Institute of Byzantine Studies, Queen's Univ. of Belfast, Belfast BT7 1NN, NORTHERN IRELAND, U.K.; n.mullett@aub.ac.uk

Dr Alan V. MURRAY, International Medieval Institute, Parkinson 103, The Univ. of Leeds, Leeds LS2 9JT, ENGLAND, U.K.; a.v.murray@leeds.ac.uk

Stephen R. A. MURRAY, Apartment 2419, 77 Huntley Street, Toronto, Ontario M4Y 2P3, CANADA; sramurray@hotmail.com

Claude MUTAFIAN, 216 rue Saint-Jacques, F-75005 Paris, FRANCE; claude.mutafian@wanadoo.fr

Alan NEILL, 13 Chesham Crescent, Belfast BT6 8GW, NORTHERN IRELAND, U.K.; neilla@rescueteam.com

Prof. Robert S. NELSON, Dept. of Art, Univ. of Chicago, 5540 South Greenwood Avenue, Chicago IL 60637, U.S.A.

Michael de NÈVE, Laubacher Straße 9, D-14197 Berlin, GERMANY or Freie Universität Berlin, FB Geschichts- und Kulturwissenschaften, Koserstraße 20, D-14195 Berlin, GERMANY; michaeldeneve@web.de

Dr Helen J. NICHOLSON, School of History and Archaeology, Cardiff Univ., PO Box 909, Cardiff CF10 3XU, WALES, U.K.; nicholsonhj@cardiff.ac.uk

Angel NICOLAOU-KONNARI, 10 Philiou Zannetou Street, 3021 Limassol, CYPRUS; an.konnaris@cytanet.com.cy

Dr David NICOLLE, 67 Maplewell Road, Woodhouse Eaves, Leics. LE12 8RG, ENGLAND, U.K.; david.nicolle@tesco.net

Mark John NICOVICH, 4497 Pershing Avenue #201, St Louis MO 63108, U.S.A.

Marie-Adelaïde NIELEN, 254, avenue Daumesnil, F-75012 Paris, FRANCE; marie-adelaide.nielen@culture.gouv.fr

Torben K. NIELSEN, History Dept., Aalborg Univ., Fibigerstraede 5, DK-9220 Aalborg, DENMARK; histkn@i4.avc.dk

Yoav NITZAN, 4 H'Adereth Street, Jerusalem 92343, ISRAEL; famnitzan@altavista.com

Prof. Peter S. NOBLE, Dept. of French Studies, SML, Univ. of Reading, Whiteknights, Reading RG6 6AA, ENGLAND, U.K.; p.s.noble@reading.ac.uk

Dr Gregory O'MALLEY, 23 Spencer View, Ellistown, Coalville, Leics LE67 1FW., ENGLAND, U.K.; OMalley_Greg_J@cat.com

Prof. Mahmoud Said OMRAN, History Dept., Faculty of Arts, Univ. of Alexandria, Alexandria, EGYPT; msomran@dataxprs.com.eg

Col. Erhard (Erik) OPSAHL, 5303 Dennis Drive, McFarland WI 53558, U.S.A.; epopsahlw@aol.com

Catherine OTTEN, 9, rue de Londres, F-67000 Strasbourg, FRANCE; otten@umb.u-strasbg.fr.

Robert OUSTERHOUT, School of Architecture, Univ. of Illinois, 611 Taft Drive, Champaign IL 61820-6921, U.S.A.; rgouster@unic.edu

Dr Johannes PAHLITZSCH, Parallelstraße 12, D-12209 Berlin, GERMANY; pahlitz@zedat.fu-berlin.de

Tivadar PALÁGYI, Tapolcsanyi u. 8, H-1022 Budapest, HUNGARY; tivadarp@hotmail.com

Dr Aphrodite PAPAYIANNI, 40 Inverness Terrace, London W2 3JB, ENGLAND, U.K.; aphroditepapayianni@hotmail.com

Dr Peter D. PARTNER, 17 Clausentum Road, Winchester, Hampshire, S023 9QE, ENGLAND, U.K.; pdp4@aol.com

Prof. Jacques PAVIOT, 21, rue de Vouillé, F-75015 Paris, FRANCE; Jacques.Paviot@wanadoo.fr or paviot@univ-paris12.fr

Peter Shlomo PELEG, 2 Mordhai Street, Kiryat Tivon 36023, ISRAEL; fax: 972 4 9931 122; ppeleg@netvision.net.il

Nicholas J. PERRY, PO Box 389, La Mesa NM 88044, U.S.A.; nicholasperry@earthlink.net

Theodore D. PETRO, 517 McAlpin Avenue, Cincinnati OH 45220, U.S.A.; petrod@email.uc.edu

Dr Jonathan P. PHILLIPS, Dept. of History, Royal Holloway Univ. of London, Egham, Surrey TW20 0EX, ENGLAND, U.K.; j.p.phillips@rhul.ac.uk

Simon D. PHILLIPS, 1 Turtle Close, Stubbington, Hampshire PO14 3JG, ENGLAND, U.K.; phillips_s_d@lycos.co.uk

Dr Mathias PIANA, Benzstraße 9, D-86420 Diedorf, GERMANY; mathias.piana@phil.uni-augsburg.de

Brenda POCHNA, 17 Berryhill, Eltham Park, London SE9 1QP, ENGLAND, U.K.

Dr John PORTEOUS, 52 Elgin Crescent, London W11, ENGLAND, U.K.

Prof. James M. POWELL, 5100 Highbridge Street, Apartment 18D, Fayetteville NY 13066, U.S.A.; mpowell@dreamscape.com

Jon POWELL, 711 SE 11th #43, Portland OR 97214, U.S.A.; jonp@pdx.edu

Dr Karen PRATT, French Dept., King's College London, Strand, London WC2R 2LS, ENGLAND, U.K.

Jennifer Ann PRICE, Dept. of History, Univ. of Washington, PO Box 353560, Seattle WA 98195-3560, U.S.A.; japrice@u.washington.edu

Prof. R. Denys PRINGLE, School of History and Archaeology, Cardiff Univ., PO Box 909, Cardiff CF10 3XU, WALES, U.K.; pringlerd@cardiff.ac.uk

Dragan PROKIC, M.A., Rubensallee 47, D-55127 Mainz, GERMANY; dp.symbulos@t-online.de

Prof. John H. PRYOR, History Dept., Univ. of Sydney, Sydney, N.S.W. 2006, AUSTRALIA

William J. PURKIS, 46 Fennec Close, Cherry Hinton, Cambridge CB1 9GG, ENGLAND, U.K.; william_purkis@hotmail.com

Ian D. QUELCH, 20 Copperfields, Fetcham, Surrey KT22 9PD, ENGLAND, U.K.; jo.quelch@virgin.net

Yevgeniy / Eugene RASSKAZOV, Worth Avenue Station, PO Box 3497, Palm Beach FL 33480-3497, U.S.A.; medievaleurope@apexmail.com

Prof. Geoffrey W. RICE, History Dept., Univ. of Canterbury, Private Bag 4800, Christchurch, NEW ZEALAND; g.rice@hist.canterbury.ac.nz

Prof. Jean RICHARD, 12, rue Pelletier de Chambure, F-21000 Dijon, FRANCE

Maurice RILEY Esq., PO Box 15819, Adliya, BAHRAIN, Arabian Gulf; mriley@batelco.com.bh

Prof. Jonathan S. C. RILEY-SMITH, The Downs, Croxton, St Neots, Cambridgeshire PE19 4SX, ENGLAND, U.K.; jsr22@cam.ac.uk

Rebecca RIST, 50 Roseford Road, Cambridge CB4 2HD, ENGLAND, U.K.; raw2@corn.ac.uk

The Rev. Leonard Stanley RIVETT, 47 Ryecroft Avenue, Woodthorpe, York YO24 2SD, ENGLAND, U.K.

Prof. Louise Buenger ROBBERT, 709 South Skinker Boulevard Apartment 701, St Louis MO 63105, U.S.A.; lrobbert@mindspring.com

Jason ROCHÉ, Seaview, Kings Highway, Largoward, Fife KY9 1HX, SCOTLAND, U.K.; sharon@showard1.fsnet.co.uk

José Manuel RODRÍGUEZ-GARCÍA, C/ San Ernesto 4.5° C, E-28002 Madrid, SPAIN; anaevjosem@wanadoo.es

Prof. Israel ROLL, Dept. of Classics, Tel-Aviv Univ., Ramat Aviv, Tel-Aviv 69978, ISRAEL; rolli@post.tau.ac.il

Dean Richard B. ROSE, 119 Grandview Place, San Antonio TX 78209, U.S.A.

Prof. Myriam ROSEN-AYALON, Institute of Asian and African Studies, The Hebrew Univ., Jerusalem 91905, ISRAEL

Dvora ROSHAL, PO Box 3558, Beer-Sheva 84135, ISRAEL; devorahr@afikim.co.il

Linda Ross, Dept. of History, Royal Holloway Univ. of London, Egham, Surrey TW20 0EX, ENGLAND, U.K.; linde@lross22.freeserve.co.uk

Prof. John ROSSER, Dept. of History, Boston College, Chestnut Hill MA 02467, U.S.A.; rosserj@bc.edu

Prof. Miri RUBIN, Dept. of History, Queen Mary, Univ. of London, Mile End Road, London E1 4NS, ENGLAND, U.K.; m.e.rubin@qmw.ac.uk

James RUEL, Ground Floor Flat, 63 Redland Road, Redland, Bristol B56 6AQ, England, U.K.; james-ruel@hotmail.com

Prof. Frederick H. RUSSELL, Dept. of History, Rutgers Univ., Newark NJ 07102, U.S.A.; frussell@andromeda.rutgers.edu

Prof. James D. RYAN, 100 West 94th Street, Apartment #26M, New York NY 10025, U.S.A.; james.d.ryan@verizon.net

Dr Andrew J. SARGENT, 33 Coborn Street, Bow, London E3 2AB, ENGLAND, U.K.; andrewsargent@newham.gov.uk

Prof. Jürgen SARNOWSKY, Historisches Seminar, Universität Hamburg, Von-Melle-Park 6, D-20146 Hamburg, GERMANY; juergen.sarnowsky@uni-hamburg.de

Christopher SAUNDERS OBE, Watery Hey, Spring Vale Road, Hayfield, Hig Peak SK22 2LD, ENGLAND, U.K.

Prof. Alexios G. C. SAVVIDES, Aegean Univ., Dept. of Mediterranean Studies, Rhodes, GREECE; or: 7 Tralleon Street, Nea Smyrne, Athens 17121, GREECE; savvides@rhodes.aegean.gr

Christopher SCHABEL, Dept. of History and Archaeology, Univ. of Cyprus, PO Box 20537, CY-1678 Nicosia, CYPRUS; schabel@ucy.ac.cy

Jochen SCHENK, Emmanuel College, Cambridge CB2 3AP, ENGLAND, U.K.; jgs29@cam.ac.uk

Prof. Paul Gerhard SCHMIDT, Seminar für lateinische Philologie des Mittelalters, Albert-Ludwigs-Universität Freiburg, Werderring 8, D-79085 Freiburg i. Br., GERMANY

Dr Beate SCHUSTER, 19, rue Vauban, F-67000 Strasbourg, FRANCE; beaschu@compuserve.com

Prof. Rainer C. SCHWINGES, Historisches Institut der Universität Bern, Unitobler – Länggass-Straße 49, CH-3000 Bern 9, SWITZERLAND

Kaare SEEBERG SIDSELRUD, Solbergliveien 87 B, NO-0683 Oslo, NORWAY; kaares@mail.hf.uio.no

Iris SHAGRIR, Dept. of History, The Open Univ., 16 Klausner Street, POB 39328, Tel Aviv 61392, ISRAEL; irissh@openu.ac.il

Prof. Maya SHATZMILLER, Dept. of History, The Univ. of Western Ontario, London, Ontario N6A 5C2, CANADA

Karl W. SHEA, Unit 6, 93 Avocca Street, Randwick 2031, New South Wales, AUSTRALIA; sangrail@bigpond.com

Dr Jonathan SHEPARD, 14 Hartley Court, Woodstock Road, Oxford OX2 7PF, ENGLAND, U.K.; nshepard@easynet.co.uk

Dr Elizabeth J. SIBERRY, 28 The Mall, Surbiton, Surrey KT6 4E9, ENGLAND, U.K.

Alicia SIMPSON, 8 Karaiskaki Street, Athens GR-18345, GREECE

Dr Gordon Andreas SINGER, PO Box 235, Greenbelt MD 20768-0235, U.S.A.; andysinger@att.net

Dr Corliss K. SLACK, Dept. of History #1103, Whitworth College, Spokane WA 99251, U.S.A.; cslack@whitworth.edu

Rima E. SMINE, 25541 Altamont Road, Los Altos Hills CA 94022, U.S.A.

Sheila R. SMITH, 111 Coleshill Road Chapelend, Nuneaton Warwickshire CV10 0PG, ENGLAND, U.K.

Simon SONNAK, PO Box 1206, Windsor 3181, Victoria, AUSTRALIA; heliade@bigpond.com.au

Arnold SPAER, PO Box 7530, Jerusalem 91079, ISRAEL; hui@spaersitton.co.il

Brent SPENCER, 3 9701 89 Street, Fort Saskatchewan, Alberta T8L IJ3, CANADA; ktcrusader@yahoo.com

Dr Alan M. STAHL, 11 Fairview Place, Ossining NY 10562, U.S.A.

Prof. Harvey STAHL, Dept. of the History of Art, Univ. of California, Berkeley CA 94720, U.S.A.; hstahl@socrates.berkeley.edu

Dr Alexandra STEFANIDOU, 35 Amerikis Street, Rhodos 85100, GREECE; aleste@otenet.gr

Eliezer and J. Edna STERN, Israel Antiquities Authority, PO Box 1094, Acre 24110, ISRAEL; fax: 04-9911682 or 9918074

Alan D. STEVENS, Campbell College, Dept. of History, Belmont Road, Belfast BT4 2ND, NORTHERN IRELAND, U.K.; alan.d.stevens@ntlworld.com

Paula STILES, Dept. of Medieval History, 71 South Street, Univ. of St Andrews, St Andrews, Scotland KY16 9AJ, SCOTLAND, U.K.; thesnowleopard@hotmail.com

Myra STRUCKMEYER, 29 Flemington Road, Chapel Hill NC 27517, U.S.A.; struckme@email.unc.edu

Shaul TAMIRI, Hachail-Halmoni #8, Rishon le Zion 75255, ISRAEL

Olivier TERLINDEN, Avenue des Ramiers 8, B-1950 Kraaïnem, BELGIUM; olivierterlinden@yahoo.com

Miriam Rita TESSERA, via Moncalvo 16, I-20146 Milano, ITALY; monachus_it@yahoo.it

Kenneth J. THOMSON, Edessa, 8 Salterfell Road, Scale Hall, Lancaster LA1 2PX, ENGLAND, U.K.; kenneth@thomsonk91.fsnet.co.uk

Prof. Peter THORAU, Historisches Institut, Universität des Saarlandes, Postfach 15 11 50, D-66041 Saarbrücken, GERMANY

Prof. Hirofumi TOKO, 605-3 Kogasaka, Machida, Tokyo 194-0014, JAPAN; ttokou@toyonet.toyo.ac.jp

Prof. John Victor TOLAN, Département d'Histoire, Université de Nantes, B.P. 81227, F-44312 Nantes, FRANCE, or: 2, rue de la Chevalerie, F-44300 Nantes, FRANCE; john.tolan@humana.univ-nantes.fr

Catherine B. TURNER, Flat 3, 1055 Christchurch Road, Boscombe East, Bournemouth BH7 6BE, ENGLAND, U.K.

Dr Judith M. UPTON-WARD, Flat 6, Haywood Court, Reading RG1 3QF, ENGLAND, U.K.; juptonward@btopenworld.com

Prof. William L. URBAN, Dept. of History, Monmouth College, 700 East Broadway, Monmouth IL 61462, U.S.A.; urban@monm.edu

Theresa M. VANN, Hill Monastic Manuscript Library, St John's Univ., Collegeville MN 56321, U.S.A.; www.hmml.org

Dr Marie-Louise von WARTBURG MAIER, Paphosprojekt der Universität Zürich, Rämistraße 71, CH-8006 Zürich, SWITZERLAND; paphos@hist.unizh.ch

Benjamin WEBER, 1, Residence du Parc, F-31520 Ramonville, FRANCE; benyi_tigrou@hotmail.com

Dr Daniel WEISS, History of Art Dept., Johns Hopkins Univ., 3400 North Charles Street, Baltimore MD 21218, U.S.A.; dweiss@jho.edu

Brett E. WHALEN, 119 Quillen Court, Stanford CA 94305, U.S.A.

Dr Mark WHITTOW, St Peter's College, Oxford OX1 2DL, ENGLAND, U.K.

Timothy WILKES, A. H. Baldwin & Sons Ltd., 11 Adelphi Terrace, London WC2N 6BJ, ENGLAND, U.K.; timwilkes@baldwin.sh

The Rev. Dr John D. WILKINSON, 7 Tenniel Close, London W2 3LE, ENGLAND, U.K.

Dr Ann WILLIAMS, 40 Greenwich South Street, London SE10 8UN, ENGLAND, U.K.; ann.williams@talk21.com

Prof. Steven James WILLIAMS, Dept. of History, New Mexico Highlands Univ., PO Box 9000, Las Vegas NM 87701, U.S.A.; stevenjameswilliams@yahoo.com

Gayle A. WILSON, PO Box 712, Diamond Springs CA 95619, U.S.A.; gayle@inforum.net

Peter van WINDEKENS, Kleine Ganzendries 38, B-3212 Pellenberg, BELGIUM

Prof. Johanna Maria van WINTER, Brigittenstraat 20, NL-3512 KM Utrecht, THE NETHERLANDS; j.m.vanwinter@let.uu.nl

Prof. Kenneth B. WOLF, Dept. of History, Pomona College, Pearsons Hall, 551 North College Avenue, Claremont CA 91711-6337, U.S.A.

Dr Noah WOLFSON, 13 Avuqa Street, Tel-Aviv 69086, ISRAEL; noah@meteo-tech.co.il

Peter WOODHEAD, Tarry Cottage, Church Lane, Daglingworth near Cirencester, Gloucestershire GL7 7AG, ENGLAND, U.K.

Dr John WREGLESWORTH, Fountain Cottage, 98 West Town Road, Backwell, North Somerset BS48 3BE, ENGLAND, U.K.; john@wreg.freeserve.co.uk

Prof. Shunji YATSUZUKA, 10-22 Matsumoto 2 chome, Otsu-shi, Shiga 520, JAPAN

William G. ZAJAC, 9 Station Terrace, Pen-y-rheal, Caerphilly CF83 2RH, WALES, U.K.

Prof. Ossama Zaki ZEID, 189 Abd al-Salam Aref Tharwat, Alexandria, EGYPT; ossama_zeid@hotmail.com

Prof. Monique ZERNER, Villa Stella, Chemin des Pins, F-06000 Nice, FRANCE; zernerm@unice.fr

Institutions subscribing to the SSCLE

Atatürk Kültür, Dil ve Tarih Yüsek Kumuru, Türk Tarih Kumuru, Baskanligi, TURKEY

Brepols Publishers, Steenweg op Tielen 68, B-2300 Turnhout, BELGIUM

Bibliothécaire Guy Cobolet, Le Bibliothécaire, École Française d'Athènes, 6, Didotou 10680 Athènes, GREECE

Centre de Recherches d'histoire et civilisation de Byzance et du Proche-Orient Chétien, Université de Paris 1, 17, rue de la Sorbonne, 75231 Paris Cedex, FRANCE

Centre for Byzantine, Ottoman and Modern Greek Studies, Univ. of Birmingham, Edgbaston, Birmingham B15 2TT, ENGLAND, U.K.

Couvent des Dominicains, École Biblique et Archéologique Français, 6 Nablus Road, Jerusalem 91190, ISRAEL

Deutsches Historisches Institut in Rom, Via Aurelia Antica 391, I-00165 Rome, ITALY

Deutschordenszentralarchiv (DOZA), Singerstraße 7, A-1010 Wien, AUSTRIA

Dumbarton Oaks Research Library, 1703 32nd Street North West, Washington D.C. 20007, U.S.A.

Germanisches Nationalmuseum, Bibliothek, Kornmarkt 1, D-90402 Nürnberg, GERMANY

History Department, Campbell College, Belfast BT4 2 ND, NORTHERN IRELAND, U.K.

The Jewish National and University Library, PO Box 34165, Jerusalem 91341, ISRAEL

The Library, The Priory of Scotland of the Most Venerable Order of St John, 21 St John Street, Edinburgh EH8 8DG, SCOTLAND, U.K.

The Stephen Chan Library, Institute of Fine Arts, New York Univ., 1 East 78th Street, New York NY 10021, U.S.A.

Metropolitan Museum of Art, Thomas J. Watson Library, Serials Dept., 5th Avenue at 82nd Street, New York NY 10028, U.S.A.

Museum and Library of the Order of St John, St John's Gate, Clerkenwell, London EC1M 4DA, ENGLAND, U.K.

Order of the Temple of Jerusalem, The Autonomous Priory of England, Affiliate Order of the Industrial Temple, 151 Glebe Road, Norwich, Norfolk NR2 3JH, ENGLAND, U.K.

Serials Department, 11717 Young Research Library, Univ. of California, Box 951575, Los Angeles CA 90095-1575, U.S.A.

Sourasky Library, Tel-Aviv Univ., Periodical Dept., PO Box 39038, Tel-Aviv, ISRAEL

Teutonic Order Bailiwick of Utrecht, Dr John J. Quarles van Ufford, Secretary of the Bailliwick, Springweg 25, NL-3511 VJ Utrecht, THE NETHERLANDS

The Warburg Institute, Univ. of London, Woburn Square, London WC1H 0AB, ENGLAND, U.K. [John PERKINS, Deputy Librarian, jperkins@a1.sas.ac.uk]

Eberhard-Karls-Universität Tübingen, Orientalisches Seminar, Münzgasse 30, D-72072 Tübingen, GERMANY

University of California Los Angeles Serials Dept. / YRL, 11717 Young Research Library, Box 951575, Los Angeles CA 90095-1575, U.S.A.

University of London Library, Periodicals Section, Senate House, Malet Street, London WC1E 7HU, ENGLAND, U.K.

University of North Carolina, Davis Library CB 3938, Periodicals and Serials Dept., Chapel Hill NC 27514-8890, U.S.A.

Universitätsbibliothek Tübingen, Wilhelmstraße 32, Postfach 26 20, D-72016 Tübingen, GERMANY

University of Reading, Graduate Centre for Medieval Studies, Whiteknights, PO Box 218, Reading, Berks. RG6 6AA, ENGLAND, U.K.

University of Washington, Libraries, Serials Division, PO Box 352900, Seattle WA 98195, U.S.A.

University of Western Ontario Library, Acquisitions Dept., Room M1, D. B. Weldon Library, London, Ontario N6A 3K7, CANADA

W. F. Albright Institute of Archaeological Research, 26 Salah ed-Din Street, PO Box 19096, Jerusalem 91190, ISRAEL

Guidelines for the Submission of Papers

The editors ask contributors to adhere to the following guidelines. Failure to do so will result in the article being returned to the author for amendment, or may result in its having to be excluded from the volume.

1. Submissions. Submissions should be made on 3.5 inch, high-density IBM compatible disks and in two typescripts, double-spaced with wide margins. Please send these to one of the editors. Remember to include your name and address on your paper.

2. Length. Normally, the maximum length of articles should not exceed 6,000 words, not including notes. The editors reserve the right to edit papers that exceed these limits.

3. Notes. Normally, notes should be REFERENCE ONLY and placed at the end of the paper. Number continuously.

4. Style sheet. Please use the most recent *Speculum* style sheet (currently *Speculum* 75 (2000), 547–52). This sets out the format to be used for notes. Failure to follow the *Speculum* format will result in accepted articles being returned to the author for amendment. In the main body of the paper you may adhere to either British or American spelling, but it must be consistent throughout the article.

5. Language. Papers will be published in English, French, German, Italian and Spanish.

6. Abbreviations. Please use the abbreviation list on p. vii–viii of this journal.

7. Diagrams and Maps should be referred to as figures and photographs as plates. Please keep illustrations to the essential minimum, since it will be possible to include only a limited number. All illustrations must be supplied by the contributor in camera-ready copy, and free from all copyright restrictions.

8. Italics. Words to be printed as italics should be italicised if possible. Failing this they should be underlined.

9. Capitals. Please take every care to ensure consistency in your use of capitals and lower case letters. Use initial capitals to distinguish the general from the specific (for example, “the count of Flanders” but “Count Philip of Flanders”).

Editors

Professor Benjamin Z. Kedar
The Institute for Advanced Studies
The Hebrew University of Jerusalem
Jerusalem 91904, Israel

Professor Jonathan S. C. Riley-Smith
Emmanuel College
Cambridge CB2 3AP
U.K.

SOCIETY FOR THE STUDY OF THE CRUSADES AND THE LATIN EAST MEMBERSHIP INFORMATION

The primary function of the Society for the Study of the Crusades and the Latin East is to enable members to learn about current work being done in the field of crusading history, and to contact members who share research interests through the information in the Society's Bulletin. There are currently 420 members of the SSCLE from 30 countries. The Society also organizes a major international conference every four years, as well as sections on crusading history at other conferences where appropriate.

The committee of the SSCLE consists of:
Prof. Michel Balard, *President*
Prof. Jean Richard and Prof. Jonathan Riley-Smith, *Honorary Vice-presidents*
Prof. Sofia Menache and Luis Garcìa-Guijarro Ramos, *Secretary and Assistant Secretary*
Dr Ian Quelch, *Treasurer*
Prof. Karl Borchardt, *Bulletin Editor.*

Current subscription fees are as follows:

- Membership and Bulletin of the Society: Single £11, $15 or €17;
- Student £6, $9 or €10;
- Joint membership £15, $23 or €25;
- Membership and the journal *Crusades*, including the Bulletin: £20, $30 or €33.